Planning Law and Procedure

Planning Law and Procedure

Eighth edition

A E Telling MA
of the Inner Temple and the
Midland and Oxford Circuit, Barrister

with a chapter on the role of the courts and the ombudsmen by

R M C Duxbury LLB
Barrister; Principal Lecturer in Law,
Nottingham Law School,
Nottingham Polytechnic

Butterworths
London, Dublin, Edinburgh
1990

United Kingdom	Butterworth & Co (Publishers) Ltd, 88 Kingsway, LONDON WC2B 6AB and 4 Hill Street, EDINBURGH EH2 3JZ
Australia	Butterworths Pty Ltd, SYDNEY, MELBOURNE, BRISBANE, ADELAIDE, PERTH, CANBERRA and HOBART
Canada	Butterworths Canada Ltd, TORONTO and VANCOUVER
Ireland	Butterworth (Ireland) Ltd, DUBLIN
Malaysia	Malayan Law Journal Sdn Bhd, KUALA LUMPUR
New Zealand	Butterworths of New Zealand Ltd, WELLINGTON and AUCKLAND
Puerto Rico	Equity de Puerto Rico, Inc, HATO REY
Singapore	Malayan Law Journal Pte Ltd, SINGAPORE
USA	Butterworth Legal Publishers, AUSTIN, Texas; BOSTON, Massachusetts; CLEARWATER, Florida (D & S Publishers); ORFORD, New Hampshire (Equity Publishing); ST PAUL, Minnesota; and SEATTLE, Washington

A CIP Catalogue record for this book is available from the British Library

ISBN 0 406 60876 8

Printed and bound in Great Britain by
Mackays of Chatham PLC, Chatham, Kent

Preface to eighth edition

The seventh edition of this book was published some four years ago. Much has happened since then. The statute law relating to town and country planning has been consolidated in three new enactments passed in 1990: the Town and Country Planning Act, the Planning (Listed Buildings and Conservation Areas) Act and the Planning (Hazardous Substances) Act.

Prior to that the Housing and Planning Act 1986 had given local planning authorities the power to make simplified planning zone schemes which will confer upon developers the right to carry out development within the limits of the scheme without having to apply for express permission; in effect a kind of local general development order. The Act of 1986 also made provision for controlling the storage or use of hazardous substances; when these provisions are brought into force the introduction of any such hazard will require specific consent under a code of procedure based on, but independent of, the procedure for obtaining planning permission.

Even more significant for the content of planning law is the subordinate legislation of the past four years. The Assessment of Environmental Effects Regulations, made in response to a European Community directive, are an important innovation; when applying for planning permission in a wide range of cases, the prospective developer will be required to submit his assessment of the likely environmental effects together with his proposals for remedying those effects. The new Use Classes Order made in 1987 has completely recast the schedule of use classes thus facilitating many changes of use without the need for planning permission. A new general development order made in 1988 has consolidated the provisions of the 1977 order and subsequent amendments and the special development orders relating to national parks, conservation areas and other sensitive areas.

There have also been some important changes in the procedure for planning appeals. New inquiries procedure rules now require the appellant (as well as the local planning authority) to submit a written statement of case well before the date of the hearing, and third parties proposing to adduce evidence must now send an advance copy of this evidence to the inspector; these and other changes are intended to facilitate and hopefully shorten proceedings at public inquiries. For the very large number of appeals now dealt with on the basis of written representations there are now, for the first time, regulations governing this form of procedure.

There has been a considerable amount of new case law. In *R v Westminster City Council, ex p Monahan*, concerning the Royal Opera House in Covent Garden, the Court of Appeal upheld the grant of planning permission for the development of adjoining land, contrary to the provisions of the development plan, as a means of raising the finance required for the reconstruction and modernisation of the opera house. The principle was subsequently applied in *Northumberland County Council v Secretary of State for the Environment* in more controversial circumstances. The judgments in a number of cases in the Court of Appeal and at first instance have indicated the proper scope of section 52 agreements and should help to lay to rest the long running controversy over the use and abuse of section 52.

The decision in *Cranford Hall Parking Ltd v Secretary of State for the Environment* gave judicial recognition to the 'presumption in favour of development' thus establishing it as a principle of law and not merely a matter of ministerial policy.

Several recent decisions on the validity of enforcement notices have indicated a willingness on the part of the courts to take a broad view of the Secretary of State's powers to amend enforcement notices and to disregard defects where no injustice would be caused.

There have also been important decisions relating to listed buildings and conservation. In *Debenhams v Westminster City Council* the House of Lords took a fairly strict view of what should be regarded as a curtilage of a listed building; the likely effect will be to reduce the number of buildings brought indirectly under listed building control through proximity to a building which has been specifically listed. The decision of the High Court in *Steinberg v Secretary of State for the Environment* has given prominence to the duty of planning authorities to give special attention to the need to enhance, as well as merely preserving, the character and appearance of conservation areas.

This edition makes two changes in the arrangement of chapters. The amount of new text on the various forms of planning permission led me to divide what was chapter 6 in previous editions into two: chapter 6 now deals with permitted development and a new chapter 7 with applications for express permission. I have also removed the section on listed buildings from the chapter dealing with special forms of control and placed it alongside conservation areas in a separate chapter.

I am much indebted to Mr R M C Duxbury, LLB, Barrister, Principal Lecturer in Law at Nottingham Polytechnic for revising the chapter on the role of the courts and the ombudsmen.

The text of this new edition, on the basis of the law as at the end of 1989, had already been submitted to my publishers when the Bills for the consolidating legislation were published. I am grateful to my publishers for enabling me to make the necessary revision to the text and for their efforts in publishing this edition with hardly any delay. Otherwise I have endeavoured to state the law as at the end of 1989.

Once again I must record my thanks to Mr Antony Shaw, MC, MA, Solicitor for his kindness in sharing with me the reading of the proofs.

A E Telling
Nottingham
1990

Preface to first edition

The comprehensive system of land use control introduced by the Town and Country Planning Act 1947 has now been in force for some fifteen years. The Act of 1947 and the subsequent amending Acts (now consolidated in the Act of 1962) together with the numerous orders and regulations have been the subject of a good many excellent works. Experience of lecturing and examining in planning law and procedure, however, has convinced me that there is scope for a more academic treatment of the subject, and this book is offered in the hope that it will be of value to students reading for degrees and professional qualifications requiring a knowledge of this subject.

I am indebted to Mr V W Taylor, LLM, Senior Lecturer in Law at the College of Estate Management for his helpful advice and criticisms; to Mr Keith Davies, MA, LLB, Barrister-at-Law, Lecturer in Law at the College of Estate Management for undertaking the laborious task of revising Part I of the book to take account of the passing of the Act of 1962 and other changes, and for reading the proofs; to many anonymous students whose questions have sometimes opened up new channels of thought; to my publishers for their patience and helpfulness; and finally to my wife who typed much of the manuscript.

I have endeavoured to state the law as at 10 July 1963 – the date on which the Town and Country Planning Act 1963 received the Royal Assent.

A E Telling
Nottingham
1963

Contents

Table of abbreviations

Act of 1947	Town and Country Planning Act 1947
Act of 1954	Town and Country Planning Act 1954
Act of 1962	Town and Country Planning Act 1962
Act of 1968	Town and Country Planning Act 1968
Act of 1971	Town and Country Planning Act 1971
Act of 1990	Town and Country Planning Act 1990
Listed Buildings Act	Planning (Listed Buildings and Conservation Areas) Act 1990
Hazardous Substances Act	Planning (Hazardous Substances) Act 1990
Minerals Act	Town and Country (Minerals) Act 1981
Advertisements Regulations	Town and Country Planning (Control of Advertisements) Regulations 1989, SI 1989 No. 670
Assessment of Environmental Effects Regulations	1988, SI 1988 No. 1199
Compensation Regulations	Town and Country Planning (Compensation and Certificates) Regulations 1974, SI 1974 No. 1242
Determination by Inspectors Rules	Town and Country Planning (Determination by Appointed Persons) (Inquiries Procedure) Rules 1988, SI 1988 No. 945)
Development Plans Regulations	Town and Country Planning (Development Plans) Regulations 1965, SI 1965 No. 1453
General Development Order / *GDO*	Town and Country Planning General Development Order 1988, SI 1988 No. 1813 amended by Town and Country Planning General Development (Amendment) Orders 1988, SI 1988 No. 2091 and 1989, SI 1989 Nos. 603 and 1590

General Regulations	Town and Country Planning (General) Regulations 1976, SI 1976 No. 1419
Inquiries Procedure Rules	Town and Country Planning (Inquiries Procedure) Rules 1988, SI 1988 No. 944
Listed Building Regulations	Town and Country Planning (Listed Buildings and Buildings in Conservation Areas) Regulations 1987, SI 1987 No. 349
Minerals Regulations	Town and Country Planning (Minerals) Regulations 1971, SI 1971 No. 756
Plans Regulations	Town and Country Planning (Structure and Local Plans) Regulations 1982, SI 1982 No. 555
Tree Preservation Regulations	Town and Country Planning (Tree Preservation Order) Regulations 1969, SI 1969 No. 17, amended by Town and Country Planning Tree Preservation Order (Amendment) Regulations 1981, SI 1981 No. 14 and 1988, SI 1988 No. 963
Use Classes Order	Town and Country Planning (Use Classes) Order 1987, SI 1987 No. 764
The Minister	The Minister of Town and Country Planning (from 1943 to Jan. 1951); the Minister of Local Government and Planning (from Jan. 1951 to Nov. 1951); the Minister of Housing and Local Government (from Nov. 1951 to 1970)
The Secretary of State	The Secretary of State for The Environment (in Wales the Secretary of State for Wales)
Franks Committee	The Committee on Administrative Tribunals and Inquiries 1957, Cmnd 218

Table of statutes

References in this Table to *Statutes* are to Halsbury's Statutes of England (Fourth Edition) showing the volume and page at which the annotated text of an Act may be found.

List of cases

PAGE

PAGE

W

Part One

Planning control

Chapter 1

Historical development of planning law

Introduction

The problems of town and country planning in Britain arise mainly from the profound revolution through which the country has passed in the last two hundred years. The most important feature of the revolution has been the enormous growth in the population, especially during the nineteenth century. In 1800 the population was about $10\frac{1}{2}$ million; by 1850 it had increased to nearly 21 million and by 1900 it had nearly doubled again to 37 million. Since then the rate of increase has been considerably less but even so the population has grown to over 50 million. Such an increase could not fail to alter the physical appearance of the country and to bring in its train a whole host of problems.

It is doubtful whether the country could have sustained so large a growth in the population but for the industrial revolution which changed Britain from a predominantly agricultural nation to an industrial one. The early industrial revolution was centred on the coalfields and on the wool and cotton towns of the north, and was assisted by the building first of canals and later of railways. The result was to concentrate the population in certain parts of the country, chiefly the north of England, the Midlands and South Wales. The industrial towns grew in size more dramatically even than the general population and people left the countryside to find work in the new factories. During the first half of the nineteenth century the number of people in the countryside increased since the growth in population was greater than the migration to the towns; but with the decline in agriculture after 1850 the population of the countryside declined absolutely.

Conditions in the new industrial towns were often appalling. Factories and houses sprang up side by side without any attempt at zoning; although it must be remembered that until the coming of the railways, most people had to live within walking distance of their work. Still worse, there was no attempt even to control standards of building construction and sanitation. Although the housing conditions of the skilled artisan and the miners were often better than is now realised, conditions generally were very bad.[1] The foul state of the houses encouraged the spread of disease and there were serious outbreaks of cholera and typhoid in the 1830s and 1840s. Local boards of health had been set up after the cholera epidemic of 1831–1833 but were allowed to lapse. In 1838 the Poor Law Commissioners published a report showing evidence obtained when they employed a number of doctors to inquire into the causes of death and destitution in London. They then commissioned the energetic public health reformer Edwin Chadwick to carry out a similar investigation over the whole country. The publication of the results of this in 1842 led to the appointment of a Royal Commission on the Health of Towns, which published its first report in 1844 (to a considerable extent the work of Chadwick) and its second report in 1845. These reports were followed in 1848 by two Acts of Parliament which, although very limited in scope and effect, are significant as laying the foundations of permanent statutory restrictions on the freedom of landowners to build as they pleased. The Public Health Act 1848, set up a General Board of Health with powers to create local boards on the petition of ten per cent of the inhabitants of a district and to enforce boards where the death rate was above 23 per 1000. The boards were given powers to ensure that both new and existing houses were provided with water and drainage: the building of new houses was not to be commenced until the board had been given notice of the position of privies and drains. The Nuisance Removal and Disease Prevention Act 1848 applied throughout the country and made it an offence to build a new house to drain into an open ditch. This Act was replaced in 1855 by the Nuisances Removal Act, which enabled the local authority to complain to the justices where any premises were in such a state as to be a nuisance or injurious to health. The justices' order could require the provision of sufficient privy accommodation, means of drainage and ventilation to make the house safe and habitable: and, if the house were unfit for habitation, could prohibit its use for that purpose. The Act of 1855 was extended by the Sanitary Act 1866, which inter alia enabled the local council or board of health to deal with houses lacking proper drainage by compelling their connection with a public sewer (if within 100 feet) or with a cesspool or some other place.

At the same time, the more enterprising municipalities were

1 For a general account of conditions in the towns, see for instance: *The Town Labourer* and *The Bleak Age* by J L and Barbara Hammond; and *An Economic History of Modern Britain* by J H Clapham, vol I.

obtaining extended powers by petitioning Parliament for local Acts. These local Acts were of special significance in that they paved the way for the great Public Health Act 1875. This consolidated the earlier public general Acts and gave national application to provisions previously found only in local Acts. Local authorities were given power not only to secure proper standards of drainage and closet accommodation, but also to make byelaws regulating the size of rooms, the space about the houses and the width of the street in front of them; provision was also made for the making up and sewering of unadopted streets at the expense of the frontages.

Builders were anxious to get as many houses as possible to the acre, and the byelaw minimum became accordingly the maximum and the minimum at once. The result was the sea of uniform rows of streets and houses which surrounds the centre of many of our industrial towns and whose dreary and unbroken regularity is too well known to require description. Nevertheless, byelaw control was an important step forward.

The powers of local government in the field of public health were supplemented by housing legislation beginning with the Artisans and Labourers' Dwellings Act 1868, which gave powers to deal with individual insanitary houses. This was followed in 1875 by powers to undertake slum clearance[2] and in 1890 by powers to build tenements and cottages for the housing of the working classes.[3]

This activity in the fields of public health and housing was followed by a sweeping reform of local government. Outside the boroughs, local government was entrusted to a patchwork of authorities often of an ad hoc character such as the local boards of health. These were replaced by the establishment of county councils in 1888, and urban and rural district councils in 1894.

Thus, by the end of the century, there existed an effective system of local government with substantial powers in the fields of public health and housing. It soon became apparent, however, that something more was necessary. The possibility of more satisfactory conditions of living and working was being demonstrated by the building of such places as Bournville and Port Sunlight by enlightened industrialists. About the same time, Ebenezer Howard wrote the famous book *Garden Cities of Tomorrow*, which may be taken as the starting point of the new towns movement, as well as the immediate inspiration for the first 'garden city' of Letchworth started in 1903.

2 Artisans and Labourers' Dwellings Improvement Acts 1875 and 1879.
3 Housing of the Working Classes Act 1890.

The development of regulatory planning

THE ACTS OF 1909 TO 1943

The first Planning Act was passed in 1909.[4] It authorised the preparation by local councils of planning schemes for any land 'which is in course of development or appears likely to be used for building purposes', ie suburban land. Such schemes were to be prepared with the object of ensuring 'that in future land in the vicinity of towns shall be developed in such a way as to secure proper sanitary conditions, amenity and convenience in connection with the laying out of the land itself and any neighbouring land'.

Thus to the search for good sanitary conditions, which had characterised the nineteenth century reforms, there were added the claims of amenity and convenience. The planning scheme was far more ambitious and flexible than the byelaw. Not only could it regulate the number of buildings on a site and the space about them, but it could provide both for the control of their appearance and the way in which they might be used. The scheme might also define zones in which only certain specific types of building use would be permitted, and it could list types of development which could not be undertaken without specific application to the local authority.

The preparation and approval of a scheme was necessarily a lengthy process, and an Act of 1919[5] introduced the concept of interim development control: that is during the period from the passing by the council of a resolution to prepare a scheme until the scheme became effective. Under interim control, a developer was not obliged to apply for permission but if his development conflicted with the scheme as ultimately approved he could not obtain compensation. On the other hand, if he obtained interim development consent, he was safeguarded.

The next major step forward was the Act of 1932[6] which enabled local authorities to prepare planning schemes for any land in England and Wales and not merely for surburban land as hitherto. The Act of 1932 was purely permissive, but it was supplemented in 1935 by the Restriction of Ribbon Development Act which made new building within 220 feet of classified roads, or roads made the subject of a resolution under the Act, subject to control. And in 1943 (when 73 per cent of the land in England and 36 per cent of the land in Wales had become subject to interim control under the Act of 1932) it was provided that all land in England and Wales should be deemed to be

---

4 Housing, Town Planning, &c. Act 1909.
5 Housing, Town Planning, &c. Act 1919.
6 Town and Country Planning Act 1932.

subject to interim control whether or not the local authority had passed a resolution to prepare a scheme.[7]

NEW PROBLEMS

The Acts of 1909 to 1943 had all been based on the concept of the planning scheme. Such schemes were undoubtedly useful in ensuring that new development conformed to certain standards of amenity and convenience and in controlling changes in the use of existing buildings. But new problems were coming into prominence and it soon became apparent that the planning scheme was unsuitable for dealing with these. The population continued to grow substantially although less dramatically than in the nineteenth century. The advent of road transport and a cheap supply of electric power was changing the face of the country. These influences resulted in a new growth in the size of towns and cities and of many places beyond their boundaries. Industry was no longer tied to the coalfields and railways, and between the two wars a major relocation of the nation's industrial power took place. Some of the older industrial areas went through a period of prolonged and at times severe depression which led to the appointment of Commissioners for Special Areas. The Commissioners, whilst emphasising that economic considerations must in the main determine the location of industry, drew attention to the dangers involved in the continued haphazard growth of the Metropolis and considered that much of the growth was not based on strictly economic factors.[8] The result was the appointment of the Royal Commission on the Distribution of the Industrial Population (the Barlow Commission).

The Barlow Report,[9] after lengthy examination of the advantages and disadvantages of the swollen state of the cities, came to the definite conclusion that:[10]

> the disadvantages in many, if not in most of the great industrial concentrations, alike on the strategical, the social, and the economic side, do constitute serious handicaps and even in some respects dangers to the nation's life and development, and we are of opinion that definite action should be taken by the Government towards remedying them.

The Report also commented on the serious loss of agricultural land which they said:[11]

7 Town and Country Planning (Interim Development) Act 1943.
8 Third Report of the Commissioners for Special Areas, 1936 (Cmd 5303).
9 Cmd 6153.
10 Cmd 6153, para 413.
11 Cmd 6153, paras 36 and 37.

since 1900 has been so rapid that it is stated to have covered with bricks and mortar an area equal in size to the counties of Buckingham and Bedford combined. Alike in urban extensions and in expropriation of land by Government Departments for military, Royal Air Force, or other national requirements, regard must be had to the agricultural needs of the country.

Nor is it merely the agricultural needs of the country that should be borne in mind. Providence has endowed Great Britain not only with wide tracts of fertile soil, but with mineral wealth in the form of tin, lead, iron-ore, and, above all, coal; with abundant supplies of water, hard and soft, corresponding to the various needs of industry; with rivers and harbours apt for transport and for both foreign and internal trade; and last, but by no means least, with amenities and recreational opportunities, with hills and dales, with forests, moors and headlands – precious possessions for fostering and enriching the nation's well-being and vitality.

Publication of the Barlow Report was followed by the appointment of a Committee on Land Utilisation in Rural Areas under the chairmanship of the late Lord Justice Scott.[12] Both the Barlow Report and the Scott Report urged that more effective action should be taken to control the siting of development and both pointed to the weaknesses of the Act of 1932. As the Barlow Report put it:[13]

> While present statutory town planning tends towards producing a more pleasant, healthier and more convenient local environment, it is not adapted to check the spread of great towns or agglomerations, nor, so long as their growth continues, to arrest the tendency to increasing central density and traffic congestion … Present town planning does not concern itself with the larger question of the general and national grouping of the population.

To remedy this situation both reports recommended the establishment of a central planning authority: the immediate extension of planning control to all parts of the country: and the formulation of a national plan for the location of industry and population.

The immediate results were the passing in 1943 of two Acts concerned with planning. The first provided for the appointment for the first time of a Minister 'charged with the duty of securing consistency and continuity in the framing and execution of a national policy with respect to the use and development of land throughout England and Wales'.[14] The other Act[15] extended, as already explained, interim control under the Act of 1932 to the whole country: legislation more suited to the control of land use generally, as distinct from local

12 Cmd 6378.
13 Cmd 6153, para 219.
14 Minister of Town and Country Planning Act 1943, s. 1.
15 Town and Country Planning (Interim Development) Act 1943.

amenity and environment, did not come until the passing of the Act of 1947.

Problems of redevelopment

THE ACT OF 1944

In the meantime another problem had come into prominence: the redevelopment of older built-up areas. Existing planning legislation was concerned only with the preparation of schemes for regulating the activities of developers. These developers would normally be private individuals and companies, though there was a certain amount of development by local and other public authorities which was equally subject to the regulatory control of the planning scheme. Although the scheme would indicate what was desirable, it could not compel development to take place.

The limits of the approach became obvious during the Second World War when a good deal of thought was given to the physical reconstruction of older cities and towns. Although the immediate stimulus to this new thinking came from the opportunities created by the bombing, people were soon thinking of bolder schemes of reconstruction. For this purpose something more than regulatory planning was wanted, namely, publicly organized schemes of redevelopment. Although town improvement schemes had been authorised in part by local Acts, local authorities had no general powers to carry out redevelopment schemes until 1944.

The Town and Country Planning Act of that year[16] gave local authorities power to designate for general reconstruction areas which had been heavily bombed, or had been badly laid out and whose development was now obsolete. These were known as 'declaratory areas' and the local authority could compulsorily purchase any land in a declaratory area and carry out their development either themselves or by disposing of their land to private developers for approved schemes.

16 Town and Country Planning Act 1944.

Chapter 2

Basis and objects of modern planning law

Planning legislation

The framework of the modern system of planning law was established with the passing of the Act of 1947. It repealed all previous legislation (with the exception of the Minister of Town and Country Planning Act 1943) and made a completely new start with effect from 1 July 1948.

In setting up the new system, Parliament was plainly guided to a large extent by the recommendations of the Barlow and Scott reports. For instance the Act of 1947 set up a powerful system of central administration. Although the Act did not create a 'central planning authority' as recommended by the reports, the Minister was given very strong powers which, taken with his general duties under the Act of 1943, enabled him to act to all intents and purposes as a central planning authority. The recommendations of the Barlow report about the location of population and industry were given effect by providing that applications for planning permission to build all but the smallest factories should require the support of the Board of Trade. Certain powers were also given to the Minister of Transport.

The Act of 1947 also strengthened local administration. Under the previous Acts, non-county boroughs and district councils as well as county boroughs were entrusted with the preparation of planning schemes. The Act of 1947 provided that the local planning authority should normally be the county council or county borough council, the former providing a larger and more realistic area for the preparation of development plans.

Each local planning authority was required under the Act of 1947 to carry out a survey of the whole of its area and to prepare a development plan based on the results of the survey; the development plan was to be reviewed every five years from the date of approval in the light of a fresh survey of the area. By requiring that development plans should be based on the results of a physical, social and economic survey of the area, the Act moved away from planning primarily in terms of amenity and convenience to planning on the basis of securing proper control over the use of land. The plans embodied both concepts of planning as described in the previous chapter – regulatory and positive. In the sphere of positive planning, the Act provided for areas of comprehensive development similar to the declaratory areas of the Act of 1944, but including areas which require total replanning for reasons other than extensive war damage.

With regard to regulatory planning, however, the development plan was materially different from the old planning scheme in that it did not confer any rights to develop. Henceforth, no development was to take place without planning permission; normally this would require an application to the local planning authority who would then decide whether to grant planning permission, with or without conditions, having regard to the provisions of the development plan and any other material considerations. There were additional powers of control in the case of buildings of architectural or historic interest, trees and outdoor advertisements.

The Act of 1947 also contained some complex provisions for dealing with the financial problems inherent in any comprehensive planning control. These will be discussed in more detail in a later chapter.[1] It will suffice to say here that normally no compensation was payable under the Act of 1947 where permission was either refused or granted subject to conditions. However, where land had become incapable of reasonably beneficial use, certain persons falling within a somewhat artificial definition of 'owner' might serve a purchase notice.

The following years were to see a number of amending Acts. The Acts of 1953 and 1954 radically altered the financial provisions of the Act of 1947. The Acts of 1959 and 1960 made some improvements in the system of planning control without disturbing the framework of physical planning established by the Act of 1947: the concept of the purchase notice was extended to cases of planning blight, provision was made for appeals to the courts on points of law, and the system of enforcement was strengthened.

The Act of 1947 and the subsequent amending legislation were repealed and consolidated in the Act of 1962. But it was not long before further changes were made. The Civic Amenities Act 1967 introduced the conservation area and strengthened the earlier provisions regarding trees and buildings of special architectural or historic interest.

In the meantime, the Minister had appointed a Planning Advisory Group to review the system of town and country planning and to see what changes were required to meet the needs of the next 20

1 See ch 19, below.

years and beyond. The Group reported in 1965 that the system of control was effective, but that control was based on plans which were out of date and technically inadequate. In 1948 it had been assumed that the population of Great Britain would become static round about 1953; this assumption had proved entirely false, and the more conservative estimates were suggesting an increase to over 70 million by the year 2000. Again, in 1948, no one forecast the enormous increase in the volume of motor traffic. In the light of these two trends, the Planning Advisory Group saw the need for a much more flexible type of development plan; they recommended that there should be broad structure plans which would require the approval of the Minister, and local plans which would not require ministerial approval. These, together with some other changes, were put into effect by the Act of 1968.

The Act of 1962 and subsequent legislation were then repealed and consolidated in the Act of 1971. This Act was in its turn amended by several Acts passed between 1972 and 1986. As a result, another consolidation took place in 1990; the existing legislation was consolidated in three separate Acts: the Town and Country Planning Act 1990, the Town and Country Planning (Listed Buildings and Construction Areas) Act 1990, and the Town and Country Planning (Hazardous Substances) Act 1990. Throughout this book the Town and Country Planning Act 1990 will be referred to as 'the Act of 1990'; the other Acts will be referred to as 'the Listed Buildings Act' and the 'Hazardous Substances Act'. These Acts are supplemented by the Planning (Consequential Provisions) Act 1990 which is mainly concerned with the repeal of the pre-1990 legislation and with consequential amendments to some other legislation.

OUTLINE OF THE CURRENT PLANNING ACTS

The current legislation continues the principle of a strong system of central administration, even though some detailed controls over the local planning authorities have been relaxed in recent years. The Secretary of State for the Environment (referred to in this book as 'the Secretary of State') has a very wide range of powers and duties which enable him to control the policies of the local planning authorities and also to initiate policies; indeed, it is his duty to secure consistency in planning policies.[2] The extent to which he actually initiates policy will depend partly on the state of public opinion as to

2 This derives from the Minister of Town and Country Planning Act 1943.

the desirability of forceful action by 'Whitehall'[3] and partly on the personality of the particular minister. Some aspects of planning policy – e g the moving of population and industry from London and the 'green belts' – owe much to a strong lead by ministers.

The Secretary of State for Transport and the Minister of Agriculture also have important functions under current planning legislation.[4]

Until 1974 the local planning authority was usually the county council or the county borough council. On 1 April 1974 a new system of local government was introduced. Outside Greater London, the whole country was divided into metropolitan counties and non-metro-politan counties each county having two tiers of local authorities concerned with town and county planning. Some planning functions – notably the preparation of the structure plans – became the responsibility of the county council as 'county planning authority', but many matters have been entrusted to the district councils.

Further radical changes came into effect on 1 April 1986; the Greater London Council and the metropolitan county councils have been abolished with the result that in Greater London and the metropolitan counties, all aspects of town and country planning are now entrusted to the Greater London borough councils and the metropolitan district councils. Elsewhere in England and throughout Wales, the two tier system continues as before.[5]

The new system of structure and local plans was introduced into different parts of the country at different times. When provision for the new system was first made by the Act of 1968, the Minister invited a number of authorities to prepare structure plans for certain specified areas. The first formal orders were made in 1972 to enable the authorities concerned to embark upon the statutory procedures for public participation and the submission of the plans to the Secretary of State. By 1974 all the authorities concerned (normally the county planning authorities) had been requested to prepare structure plans. All the original structure plans have been approved: indeed some have already been the subject of formal review. However, this does not mean the 1947-type plans are no longer of any importance; these older plans remain in force until repealed by the Secretary of State. In Greater London and the metropolitan counties further changes are under way. Structure and local plans are to be replaced by unitary development plans for each of the London boroughs and metropolitan districts.[6]

3 See the Report of the Royal Commission on London Government, para 352, for a comment on the desirability of *not* taking a strong lead in forming policy.
4 See ch 3, p. 31, below.
5 See ch 3, below.
6 See ch 4, pp. 68ff, below.

Structure plans are in the nature of policy documents concerned with the main planning problems of the area and the best way of dealing with these problems. The detailed solutions, including land allocations, will be found in the local plans. An important feature of the new system is the emphasis laid on the positive aspects of planning. In preparing the new plans, the local planning authorities are specifically required to consider measures for the improvement of the environment and the management of traffic; and they will be expected to identify action areas, that is, areas requiring comprehensive treatment in the comparatively near future by way of development, redevelopment or improvement or by a combination of these methods.

The structure and local plans will also be of importance in regulatory planning; in considering an application for planning permission, for instance, the local planning authority will need to consider the policies laid down in the structure plan and the more detailed provisions of any local plans in force in the locality concerned.[7]

The requirements as to planning permission are the king-pin of the whole system of regulatory planning. They depend on the definition of development in section 55 of the Act of 1990 – namely, the carrying out of building, engineering, mining or other operations or the making of any material change in the use of buildings or other land. This definition is not as simple as might appear[8] and has given rise to a large number of High Court actions as well as numerous appeals to the Secretary of State. Any person who is in doubt as to whether a proposed operation or change of use would constitute development may apply to the local planning authority for a determination and, if dissatisfied with that determination, may appeal to the Secretary of State; there is also a further right of appeal to the High Court.[9] There is now similar machinery for enabling interested persons to obtain a determination in some cases as to the established use rights of buildings or other land.[10]

Where planning permission is required it is sometimes granted by the Secretary of State by development order and there are a few cases in which planning permission is deemed to be granted. Otherwise application should be made to the local planning authority; if the applicant is aggrieved by their decision he may appeal to the Secretary

---

7 For development plans see ch 4, below.
8 This definition is discussed fully in ch 5, below.
9 See ch 5, below.
10 See ch 10, below.

of State whose decision is final except for an appeal to the High Court on points of law.[11]

Where planning permission is refused, persons entitled to a legal interest in the land may have a claim for compensation;[12] and where the land has become incapable of reasonably beneficial use, or the chances of selling it are adversely affected by planning proposals, certain categories of owner may serve a purchase notice.[13]

If development is carried out without planning permission or in breach of conditions attached to the permission, the local planning authority may issue an enforcement notice. There are certain rights of appeal to the Secretary of State but, once the notice takes effect, failure to comply with it is an offence punishable by fine; if the notice relates to the carrying out of building or other operations the planning authority have additional powers of enforcement.[14]

A grant of planning permission may be revoked or modified before it is acted upon,[15] and the local planning authority have certain powers to require the removal or alteration of existing buildings and uses.[16]

The importance of conserving and where possible of enhancing the physical environment is recognised by giving local planning authorities certain additional powers of control which are not dependent upon the definition of development. These relate to the preservation of trees and woodlands, the control of advertisements and the tidying up of waste land, the control of hazardous substances[17] and the preservation of buildings of special architectural and historic interest.[18] The local planning authority may also designate conservation areas in which special attention will be paid to conservation and improvement.[19]

Some new concepts have been introduced into planning law by recent legislation. The first of these is the 'urban development area' introduced by the Act of 1980; if the Secretary of State considers it to be in the national interest he may designate an urban development area and set up an urban development corporation to secure the regeneration of that area.[20]

---

11 See ch 18, below.
12 As to compensation for planning restrictions, see chs 20, 21, below.
13 See ch 12, below.
14 See ch 10, below.
15 See ch 9, below.
16 See ch 11, below.
17 See ch 13, below.
18 See ch 14, below.
19 See ch 14, below.
20 See p. 18, below.

The Act of 1980 also introduced the concept of 'enterprise zones'. The Secretary of State may designate enterprise zones within which developers will have considerable freedom to carry out industrial and commercial development without the necessity of applying for planning permission; firms operating within the area will also enjoy fiscal advantages such as relief from local authority rates.[1]

Subsequently, the Act of 1986 introduced the concept of 'simplified planning zones'. These extend to other areas the type of planning regime already established in the enterprise zones.[2]

Other planning legislation

The consolidating Acts passed in 1990 provide the main statutory framework for town and country planning in England and Wales. There are in addition some other Acts dealing with special problems associated with planning, notably the New Towns Act 1981 (re-enacting earlier legislation on new towns): the Town Development Act 1952; the National Parks and Access to the Countryside Act 1949; the Countryside Act 1968; and the Wildlife and Countryside Act 1981.

THE NEW TOWNS ACT

The genesis of the new towns movement is to be found in Ebenezer Howard's *Garden Cities*, published in 1899. It led to the formation of the Garden Cities Association[3] and two voluntary experiments in the building of garden cities at Letchworth and Welwyn. The importance of garden cities was recognised by the Acts of 1925 and 1932 which gave the Minister power to acquire land required for garden city development by compulsory purchase, although these powers were in fact never used. Fresh impetus to the movement was given by the Barlow and Scott reports[4] which drew attention to the importance of securing the decentralisation of urban areas without at the same time creating fresh suburban sprawl. Finally, it was recognised that the redevelopment of older towns, on account of war damage or for other reasons, would inevitably create an over-spill problem. In 1945 a

---

1 See p. 127, below.
2 See p. 127, below.
3 Later known as the Town and Country Planning Association.
4 See ch 1, pp. 7, 8, above.

government committee on new towns was appointed 'to consider the general questions of the establishment, development, organisation and administration that will arise in the promotion of new towns in the furtherance of a policy of planned decentralisation from congested urban areas; and in accordance therewith to suggest guiding principles on which such towns should be established as balanced communities for work and living.' In the first interim report[5] the committee came to the conclusion that the most effective agencies for the purpose would be state-appointed development corporations.

This recommendation was adopted and the New Towns Act 1946 was passed 'to provide for the creation of new towns by means of development corporations and for purposes connected therewith'.[6]

The initiative in establishing a new town is taken by the Secretary of State. If satisfied that it would be in the national interest that any area of land should be developed as a new town, he makes an order designating that area as the site of the proposed new town.

A development corporation will then be appointed,[7] the corporation will submit proposals to the Secretary of State for the development of the new town[8] and subject to the approval of the Secretary of State may compulsorily acquire any land in the designated area.[9] Such land may either be developed by the corporation itself, or sold or leased for private development.[10] The development of the new town will be financed partly by government loans and partly by grants under the Act of 1981 or under the Housing Acts.

When the development of the new town is complete, the development corporation will be wound up. The assets will be transferred to the Commission for New Towns set up 'for the purpose of taking over, with a view to its eventual disposal, holding, managing and turning to account the property previously vested in the development corporation for a new town'.[11]

Twenty three new towns were designated between 1946 and 1970; none have been designated since then.

5 Cmd 6759.
6 1946 Act.
7 1981 Act, s. 3.
8 Ibid, s. 7.
9 Ibid, s. 10.
10 Ibid, s. 17.
11 Ibid, s. 36 amended by the New Towns and Urban Development Corporations Act 1985.

THE TOWN DEVELOPMENT ACT 1952

This Act was passed 'to encourage town development in county districts for the relief of congestion or overpopulation elsewhere'.[12] It thus has the same fundamental purpose as the new towns legislation. But whereas the new towns legislation provides for the creation of new towns by state appointed corporations the Act of 1952 is directed rather to the extension of existing towns[13] by local authorities.

The scheme must be a substantial one and provide for the relief of congestion or overpopulation in an area outside the county in which the development is to be carried out.[14]

The district in which the development is to be carried out is known as the receiving district.[15] The council of the receiving district may compulsorily acquire land required for the development.[16] The Secretary of State will make substantial grants to the council to enable them to carry out the development[17] and he may also approve the making of grants by the 'exporting authority'.[18] It is usual in practice for the exporting authority and the council to work in close co-operation; for instance, the exporting authority may provide technical assistance for the development.

URBAN DEVELOPMENT AREAS

In recent years the emphasis has changed from the development of new towns to the regeneration of major areas of social and industrial decay. The Secretary of State is empowered to designate any area of land as an urban development area subject to the restriction in England that (a) it is in a metropolitan district or (b) it is in an inner London borough or partly in an inner London borough and partly in an adjoining outer London borough.[19] Designation is achieved by an order confirmed by both Houses of Parliament.[20]

The Secretary of State will establish an urban development corporation for each such area with the object of the regeneration of the area. That object is to be achieved in particular 'by bringing land

12 1952 Act.
13 The 1952 Act appears wide enough to permit the building of an entirely new town by local authorities, but this is not the primary purpose of the Act.
14 1952 Act, s. 2(1), as amended by the Local Government Act 1972, s. 185, Schs 18 and 20.
15 Ibid, s. 1.
16 1952 Acts, s. 6.
17 Ibid, s. 2(2).
18 Ibid, s. 4.
19 No such restriction applies in Wales.
20 1980 Act, s. 134.

and buildings into effective use, encouraging the development of existing and new industry and commerce, creating an attractive environment and ensuring that housing and social facilities are available to encourage people to live and work in the area.[1]

As with the new towns, the members of the development corporation will be appointed by the Secretary of State.[2] Government grants are available for the carrying out of the corporation's functions.[3]

Various local government functions may be transferred to the development corporation; these include housing, highways, sewerage.[4] As respects town and county planning the 1980 Act contains a number of very important provisions. In the first place, the development corporation may submit a specific development plan for the whole or part of the urban development area to the Secretary of State for his approval, after consulting the local planning authorities concerned, the Secretary of State may approve the plan with or without modifications.[5] The Secretary of State may then make a special development order granting planning permission for any development in accordance with the plan.[6] Secondly, the development corporation may by order of the Secretary of State be made the local planning authority for development control purposes under Part III of the Act of 1990; it may likewise be authorised to exercise functions relating to buildings of special architectural or historic interest, trees, control of advertisements and conservation areas.[7] Originally only two urban development areas were designated: Merseyside and the London Docklands, but several more have now been designated.

NATIONAL PARKS AND THE COUNTRYSIDE

There is now a considerable amount of legislation specifically designed to secure the preservation and enhancement of the natural beauty of the countryside and to promote public enjoyment of the countryside. This legislation now comprises the National Parks and Countryside Act 1949, the Countryside Act 1968, and the Wildlife and Countryside Act 1981.[8]

The Act of 1949 established a National Parks Commission, which

1 1980 Act, ss. 135, 136.
2 Ibid, Sch 26.
3 Ibid, Sch 31.
4 Ibid, ss. 153 to 159.
5 1980 Act, s. 147.
6 Ibid, s. 148. As to special development orders see ch 6, p. 126, below.
7 Ibid, s. 149.
8 As amended by the Wildlife and Countryside (Amendment) Act 1985.

in 1968 was re-named the Countryside Commission. It is concerned not only with national parks; it also has duties in connection with the preservation and enhancement of the beauty of the countryside and encouraging the provision of facilities for the enjoyment of the country-side. The achievement of these objectives is not left solely to the Commission: the legislation gives important powers and duties to local authorities.

We will consider some of the important features of the legislation: national parks, country parks, areas of outstanding natural beauty, nature reserves, access to open country and rights of way.

National parks The Commission may, by order submitted to and confirmed by the Secretary of State, designate an extensive tract of countryside as a national park, with a view to preserving and enhanc-ing the natural beauty of the area[9] and to promoting its enjoyment by the public. It must be an area which affords opportunities of open-air recreation[10] by reason of its character and its position in relation to centres of population.[11]

The responsibility for seeing that these objects are carried out rests on the local planning authorities rather than the Commission.[12] This will be done in three ways. First, there will be a strict control over development; some permitted development rights are reduced and others withdrawn entirely.[13] A national park will not be exclusively devoted to enjoyment by the public. The life of the area is to go on and the various authorities are to have due regard to the needs of agriculture and forestry.[14] Other land uses, such as mineral develop-ment, may be permitted in exceptional circumstances.[15] A national park will in fact be an area of special control in which amenity considerations will be predominant but not necessarily decisive.

Secondly, the local planning authority may provide various facilities for public enjoyment such as accommodation, meals and refreshment, camping sites and parking grounds; and they may compulsorily acquire land for these purposes.[16] They may also improve waterways for sailing, bathing or fishing.[17]

---

9 Including flora, fauna and geological and physiographical features: 1949 Act, s. 114(2), amended by Countryside Act 1968.
10 'Open air recreation' does not include organised games: 1949 Act, s. 114(1).
11 1949 Act, s. 5.
12 As to planning authorities in a national park, see ch 3, pp. 41, 42, below.
13 See ch 6, below.
14 1949 Act, s. 84.
15 See the Minister's statement on the Second Reading of the Bill: 463 H of C Official Report (5th series) col 1492.
16 1949 Act, s. 12.
17 Ibid, s. 13.

Thirdly, the Act provides for extended Government grants to encourage the local planning authorities to use their powers to preserve and enhance the natural beauty of the area. Thus an authority wishing to make an order under section 102 of the Act of 1990 for the removal of an authorised use[18] in a national park would get a special grant for the purpose.

There are now ten national parks in England and Wales covering a total of 13,600 square kilometres which is 9 per cent of the total land area of England and Wales.

Country parks The country parks differ radically in concept from the national parks. A national park is a very large area which is not wholly devoted to public enjoyment; the ordinary life of the area goes on, and the authorities have a special duty to have regard to the needs of agriculture and forestry. A country park will be a site to be laid out as a park or pleasure ground by the local authority.[19] Having defined the site of a country park, the local authority have power to purchase land, lay out the site, provide buildings and such facilities as refreshments, lavatories, car parks, fishing and sailing on waterways.[20]

Areas of outstanding natural beauty There will be many areas of outstanding natural beauty which are not suitable for designation as national parks either because they are too small or for some other reason. The Commission may designate such areas as areas of outstanding natural beauty. In addition, some areas may be so designated pending designation as national parks. The local planning authority will be able to do all such things as appear expedient for preserving and enhancing the natural beauty of the area and special grants will be available for the purpose, but there is no power to provide facilities for public enjoyment as in a national park.[1]

Nature reserves The local planning authority was given power in the Act of 1947 to define sites of nature reserves in the development plan but it was left to the Act of 1949 to give any real meaning to the concept of a nature reserve. The phrase is defined in the latter Act as land managed for either of the following purposes:[2]

(a) 'providing, under suitable conditions and control, special opportunities for the study of and research into, matters relating to the fauna and flora

18 See ch 11, below.
19 Countryside Act 1968, s. 7.
20 Ibid, ss. 8(1) and 9(3).
 1 1949 Act, ss. 87 and 88.
 2 1949 Act, s. 15.

of Great Britain and the physical conditions in which they live, and for the study of geological and physiographical features of special interest in the area'; or

(b) 'preserving flora, fauna or geological or physiographical features of special interest in the area.'

The establishment of a nature reserve will normally be undertaken by the Nature Conservancy Council[3] who may either enter into agreements with the landowners or compulsorily purchase the land.

Access to open country   This is defined as any area consisting 'wholly or predominantly of mountain, moor, heath, down, cliff or foreshore (including any bank, barrier, dune, beach, flat or other land adjacent to the foreshore)'. Local planning authorities are enabled to secure public access for the purpose of open-air recreation by entering into an access agreement with the owner of land, or by making an access order, or by compulsorily purchasing the land.[4]

Sites of special scientific interest   SSSIs are designated by the Nature Conservancy Council under section 28 of the Wildlife and Countryside Act 1981. By the end of 1989 over 4,000 sites, covering a total of over 8,700 square kilometres, had been designated in England and Wales. The Act of 1981 prohibits owners and occupiers of designated sites from carrying out potentially damaging operations for a period of four months unless the Council grants consent or enters into a management agreement with the owner or occupier; if an agreement is not reached, the Secretary of State may take steps to protect the site by a nature conservation order or a compulsory purchase order.

Rights of way   The Act of 1949 introduced provisions to promote public enjoyment of the countryside by means of public footpaths. These provisions, which apply throughout the whole of England and Wales and not merely to special areas such as national parks and open country, are now contained in the Highways Act 1980. Local authorities are empowered to enter into agreements with land-owners for the creation of new public paths[5] and in certain cases to make compulsory orders creating such paths.[6] Local authorities may also make diversion orders or stop up an existing path and replace it by a new path.[7] And, where the local authority consider that a public path

3 Nature Conservancy Council Act 1973.
4 1949 Act, s. 59.
5 Highways Act 1980, s. 25.
6 Ibid, s. 26.
7 Ibid, s. 119.

is no longer needed, they may make an extinguishment order without having to provide an alternative path.[8]

Current planning problems

What is the purpose of all this planning legislation? In chapter 1 an outline was given of the development of our planning problems from the industrial revolution to the end of the Second World War. Most of these problems still exist and indeed have been intensified by current trends. Some new problems have come into existence more recently.

The main planning issues at the beginning of the 1990s can be summarised as follows.

THE NATIONAL ECONOMY

Throughout the four decades since the passing of the Act of 1947, the national economy has been under strain. The promotion of exports has been a prime objective of governments. During the late 1970s and early 1980s the economy went through a period of severe depression; much of the country's manufacturing base has disappeared as a result of overseas competition and new technology. In spite of the recent improvement in the economy and a substantial fall in unemployment, reducing unemployment – 'creating jobs' in today's jargon – is still a matter of public concern. At the end of the decade, a new problem emerged – a huge deficit in the balance of payments.

Town and country planning cannot produce exports or create jobs; but, in the formulation of structure and local plans, industrial development and employment are very important issues. With these considerations in mind the Secretary of State has urged that plans be kept up-to-date:

> Structure and local plans have a central part to play in facilitating appropriate development. There may be potential for conflict between approved and adopted plans, perhaps evolved some years ago, and the present needs of industry. At a time when technology and other requirements of modern industry are changing rapidly, plans which are realistic, up-to-date and make adequate provision for current and likely future industrial development in the light of the circumstances prevailing in the area will minimise this conflict and will also be an important source of information for industry.[9]

8 Highways Act 1980, s. 118.
9 Circular 16/84, para 6.

The need to encourage industrial development and the creation of jobs are also matters to be taken into account in deciding individual planning applications. Sometimes these economic considerations prevail over other planning objectives.

> A company manufacturing steel castings sought permission to extend their factory to nearly twice the previous size. The local planning authority refused permission: the existing works constituted a serious injury to local amenities, and any extension would increase this injury; any reconstruction or extension should take place on the opposite side of the road on land which was likely to be zoned for industrial purposes.
>
> The Minister considered that the company's objections to the use of the alternative site were well founded. The factory was wrongly sited but its complete re-siting could only be considered as a long-term project which might become practicable at some future date. In the meantime, there was immediate need for expansion of the existing works to enable the company to meet their commitments and satisfy important export demands. The proposed developments would also benefit amenity by improving the appearance of the works. The Minister accordingly allowed the company's appeal.[10]

Recent circulars issued on behalf of the Secretary of State have laid strong emphasis on economic considerations.[11]

DISTRIBUTION OF POPULATION AND EMPLOYMENT

In 1940 the Barlow Report had commented on the over-concentration of population and industry in the large conurbations and on the tendency of industry to move from some of the older industrial areas to London and the South-East. The tendency of industry to move to certain favoured areas is just as strong today; much of the new 'High Tech' industrial development is concentrated in the south of England. There is also a heavy concentration of new office buildings in London and some large provincial cities. The result is serious congestion particularly in London. As a former Minister put it:

> At the root of almost all London's planning problems is the evil of congestion and its effects upon living and working conditions ... It is the enormous number of offices and office workers which constitutes the greatest single cause of congestion.[12]

One of the major problems of planning therefore is to restrain these tendencies and to try to steer new factories and offices to less crowded

10 Bulletin of Selected Appeal Decisions VIII/14.
11 See circulars 22/80 and 14/85.
12 Letter approving the County of London Development Plan, 1955.

areas. This is largely a problem of 'regulatory planning'; the development plans will indicate where land is available for new factories and offices and planning authorities may also lay down density standards for new buildings.

THE BOOM IN DEVELOPMENT

During the 1960s and early 1970s there was a considerable boom in development schemes. Its most outstanding feature was the unprecedented demand for new homes; the total population continued to increase; the number of separate householders increased even more rapidly because couples were married at an earlier age; and, with a comparatively high level of prosperity, the effective demand for better homes was greater than ever before.

Again more and more people were able to take holidays away from home with the result that there was a great demand for holiday facilities; much of this demand was channelled into caravan sites, the location of which produced special problems for planning authorities.

The economic recession of the later seventies and early eighties restrained effective demand and reduced the number of new development schemes. However, as the country climbed out of recession, there has been another boom in development. In addition to the demand for land for new homes and for holiday facilities, the growth of leisure activities generally will almost certainly increase pressure on the countryside.

Two statistics illustrate the strength of the present boom in development; the number of planning applications submitted to local planning authorities increased by about 25 per cent from 1987 to 1989, and the number of appeals lodged with the Department of the Environment doubled in the period from 1983 to 1989.[13]

THE OUTWARD SPREAD OF TOWNS: GREEN BELTS

With a high level of building activity, there is a natural tendency for many towns to spread outwards into the surrounding countryside. The outward spread has many disadvantages; those who live in the inner areas are further removed from the countryside; those who find homes further out have a long journey – often in crowded public transport – to their work; and in some cases towns may merge to form an almost continuous urban agglomeration. One very important method of checking the unrestrained sprawl of the towns is the

13 JPL Occasional Paper No 16, p. 1.

establishment of green belts. Since 1955 local planning authorities have been urged formally to designate green belts initially by means of sketch plans and ultimately by incorporation in the development plans. The green belts are now seen as serving five purposes: checking the unrestrained sprawl of large built-up areas; safeguarding the surrounding countryside from further encroachment; preventing neighbouring towns from merging into each other; preserving the special character of historic towns; and to assist in urban regeneration. They are also seen as having a positive role in providing access to the countryside for the urban population, both for active outdoor sports and for passive recreation.[14]

By January 1988 the green belts approved through structure plans covered 14 per cent of England,[15] but in many cases it is still necessary to define the precise boundaries of the green belts in local plans.

The establishment of green belts may assist in urban regeneration by encouraging investment in the improvement and re-development of older built-up areas. But there will almost certainly be increased demand for building land beyond the green belts and difficult decisions to be made about the location of new developments; a recent example was the controversy over a proposed 'new town' at Foxley Wood.

AGRICULTURE AND THE COUNTRYSIDE

Two of the most important aims of planning over the years have been the need in the interests of food production to safeguard good agricultural land and also to preserve the countryside for its own sake. Building in the open country away from existing settlements or from areas allocated for development in development plans has therefore been strictly controlled.

These remain important aims, but with some change of emphasis. As explained in a Planning Policy Guidance Note:[16]

> However, at a time of surpluses in agricultural production, it no longer makes sense to retain as much land as possible in agricultural use, though the need for an efficient and flexible agricultural industry remains as important as ever. The need now is to foster the diversification of the rural economy so as to open up wider and more varied employment opportunities, and to balance that need against protection of the environment without giving agricultural production a special priority.[17]

14 Planning Policy Guidance Note No 2, paras 4, 5.
15 Ibid, para 3.
16 Planning Policy Guidance Note No 7, para 8.
17 See ibid, paras 18, 19.

The changes in agriculture are likely to result in the need to find acceptable alternative uses for redundant buildings.

URBAN RENEWAL AND RECONSTRUCTION

The problems of urban renewal and reconstruction are difficult and urgent. At the centre and within the inner suburban ring of many large towns there are now large areas of obsolescent buildings and badly laid out development. In some of the older conurbations there are vast areas of industrial dereliction. In twilight areas of a predominantly residential character some remedial action can be taken by local authorities under the Housing Acts either by way of clearance schemes or by the designation of housing action areas and general improvement areas; but even these types of action often create problems of overspill of population and the need to relocate badly sited industry.

Large scale redevelopment is also needed to cope with the problem of the motor vehicle. Professor Buchanan has described the traffic problem as one of the most extraordinary facing modern society.

> It arises directly out of man's own ingenuity and growing affluence – his invention of a go-anywhere, self-powered machine for transport and personal locomotion, and his growing ability and inclination to invest in it. It is an extraordinary problem because nothing less is involved than a threat to the whole familiar physical forms of towns.[18]

A quarter of a century later the problems of traffic congestion are as great, if not greater, than ever.

There is thus scope and need for a great deal of comprehensive redevelopment, but this presents formidable problems of finance, administration and land ownership. To quote the Buchanan Report again:

> Local authorities can undertake it, provided they own the land, either themselves or by letting off the land on building leases. But this is almost certain to require compulsory acquisition on a big scale, with vast financial outlay bringing no returns in the early stages. Private developers can undertake it provided they can overcome the difficulties presented by multiplicity of ownership. These difficulties are acute. Moreover, as matters stand at present, private enterprise is, naturally enough, interested only in the profitable rebuilding of commercial and business centres and finds little inducement to tackle the enormous 'twilight areas' of obsolescent 'byelaw housing' of which there is so much in our towns.

18 *Traffic in Towns*, published by HMSO (1963). An abbreviated edition was published by Penguin Books in 1964.

Notwithstanding Professor Buchanan's pessimism, private enterprise is becoming involved in the provision of new homes in twilight
areas; in some towns and cities, local authorities and private builders
have entered into partnership arrangements. But the problem remains
formidable – a fact recognised by the provision in the Act of 1980 for
the establishment of urban development corporations for some major
areas of urban dereliction.

MINERAL DEPOSITS

Mineral deposits are a precious national asset. Coal is regaining some
of its former importance, and other minerals – notably ironstone and
sand and gravel – are of increasing importance. Since minerals must
be worked where they are found, it must be one of the objects of town
and country planning to see that valuable deposits are not sterilised by
premature building or other forms of development. Mineral working
(whether surface or underground) is a form of development for the
purposes of the Act of 1990 and is thus subject to the ordinary processes
of planning control: these are supplemented by the Mineral Workings
Act 1951, the Town and Country Planning (Minerals) Act 1981 and
by special regulations.[19]

TRAFFIC AND ACCESS PROBLEMS

In deciding upon the location of new development it is important to
consider the effect on traffic and access to roads. Certain types of
building – offices, hotels, and places of public entertainment – obviously attract traffic and create problems of parking and access. Or,
to take a rather different example, the siting of a new housing development may depend upon the adequacy of public transport facilities.

PRESERVATION AND ENHANCEMENT OF AMENITY

One of the objects of planning control is to preserve and where possible
to improve the pleasant appearance of streets and buildings and of
the countryside. There are several aspects of this problem. First, to
see that new buildings are of good design; thus planning permission
may be refused for a building which is ugly or of poor design or which
would be unsuitable in its surroundings.[20] Or conditions may be

19 See ch 15, below.
20 Selected Planning Appeals, vol III.

imposed requiring the use of certain materials; for instance, requiring a new house in the Cotswolds to be built of stone. Secondly, permission may be refused for development which would be 'unneighbourly', such as development which would give rise to noise, smoke, smell or dirt, or which would interfere with the day-lighting of adjoining buildings, or which would obtrude upon the privacy of neighbouring residents. Noise, smoke, smell and other interference with the comfortable enjoyment of land may constitute a nuisance at common law or may be regulated under such legislation as the Control of Pollution Act 1974, or the Clean Air Act 1956. Planning permission does not override common law rights or statutory restrictions and so in some cases it may be reasonable to permit development in the knowledge that neighbouring residents or landowners are adequately protected. But in other cases, the planning authority may consider that common law rights or other statutes do not afford sufficient protection and may accordingly refuse permission or impose conditions. The growing public concern about 'green issues' may well lead local planning authorities to deal with the problem of pollution when dealing with applications for planning permission; indeed new legislation in the shape of the Environmental Assessment Regulations will require this approach in a significant number of cases.[1]

Thirdly, it may be necessary to give permission for development even though it involves some loss of amenity; mineral workings are an example. In such cases conditions may be imposed in order to minimise the interference with amenity.

The preservation and enhancement of amenity is not entirely a matter of regulatory planning however. The designation of conservation areas gives the planning authority the opportunity to promote positive measures for improving the physical environment in conservation areas and the Act of 1990 makes provision for central government grants for such areas.[2]

PLANNING AND ECONOMIC COMPETITION

As mentioned earlier, planning has to take account of general economic needs, such as the promotion of exports or mineral supplies. It must also take account of local economic requirements, such as the need for shops or petrol stations. Where there is a conflict with other planning objectives – e g the preservation of amenity – the planning authority will have to decide whether the need outweighs the objec-

---

1 See ch 7, pp. 138 ff, below.
2 See ch 14, below.

tions. If there is an appeal, the appellant may have to satisfy the Secretary of State that the need exists.

Where there is no objection on other planning grounds, however, the question of need will not be relevant. For example, if a proposed petrol station would not be detrimental to amenity and the requirements of public safety, permission ought not to be refused on the ground that there is no need for another petrol station in the locality.[3] Planning control, it is submitted, should not be used merely to restrict competition.

There may, however, be circumstances in which the effects of competition are relevant to planning. For instance, a proposal for a hypermarket on the outskirts of a small town may threaten the viability of the town's traditional shopping centre; here the question is not the protection of individual businesses from competition, but the protection of the town centre.[4]

3 Circular 25/58.
4 The impact of large new shopping stores is discussed in Planning Policy Guidance Note No 6. And as to the question of preserving industrial uses important to the character, vitality and functions of a district, see *Great Portland Estates v City of Westminster* [1984] 3 All ER 744, [1984] 3 WLR 1035, discussed in ch 4, pp. 52, 53, below.

Chapter 3

Central and local administration

The administration of town and country planning in England and Wales is the responsibility mainly of the Secretary of State for the Environment and the local planning authorities. The Secretary of State exercises the functions in respect of town and country planning which were previously the responsibility of the Minister of Housing and Local Government and the Minister of Public Buildings and Works.[1] In Wales these functions are exercised by the Secretary of State for Wales.[2]

Some other ministers are also concerned with the administration of town and country planning. The Secretary of State for Transport has powers in connection with development affecting motorways and trunk roads.[3] The Minister of Agriculture is concerned with the contents of local plans as they affect agricultural land, and in certain cases he must be consulted before planning permission is granted for non-agricultural development not in accordance with a development plan.

1 The derivation of the Secretary of State's powers is as follows: The functions of the Minister of Town and Country Planning were transferred in January 1951 to a new Minister of Local Government and Planning; see the Transfer of Functions (Minister of Health and Minister of Local Government and Planning) (No 1) Order 1951 (SI 1951 No 142). In November 1951 the style and title of this Minister was changed to Minister of Housing and Local Government: see the Minister of Local Government and Planning (Change of Style and Title) Order 1951 (SI 1951 No 1900). All the functions of the Minister of Housing and Local Government, the Minister of Public Buildings and Works, and the Minister of Transport were transferred to the Secretary of State in 1970: see the Secretary of State for the Environment Order 1970 (SI 1970 No 1681). A separate Department of Transport was re-established in 1976: see the Secretary of State for Transport Order, 1976 SI No 1775.

2 In Wales and Monmouthshire most of the functions of the former Minister of Housing and Local Government were transferred to the Secretary of State for Wales in 1965 – see the Secretary of State for Wales Order 1965 (SI 1965 No 319). See also 1968 Act, s. 104(1).

3 The 1990 Act refers simply to the Secretary of State. This is because in constitutional theory there is one *office* of Secretary of State although in practice there are always several Secretaries of State each in charge of a separate department.

The Secretary of State

As the successor to the Minister of Town and Country Planning the Secretary of State for the Environment is charged by statute[4] with the duty of 'securing consistency and continuity in the framing and execution of a national policy with respect to the use and development of land throughout England and Wales'. It will be observed that his duty relates to the framing and execution of a national *policy:* he is not called upon to prepare a *plan* in the sense in which local planning authorities are required to do. Moreover, the Secretary of State has over the years laid down *policies* rather than a single policy statement. Thus, he has laid down policies with regard to the dispersal of population and industry from London and other urban centres, green belts, the preservation of agricultural land and so on.

In fact, the real authority of the Secretary of State derives from his specific powers and duties under the Town and Country Planning Acts and other planning legislation. The nature and extent of these duties may be illustrated by a few examples.

DUTIES OF THE SECRETARY OF STATE

(1) Making of regulations The law of town and country planning is to be found not only in various Acts of Parliament but also in orders and regulations made by the Secretary of State in the form of statutory instruments relevant to planning. Their importance can hardly be exaggerated. The Use Classes Order[5] for instance excludes certain changes of use from the definition of development and thus removes them altogether from planning control. By the General Development Order, the Secretary of State has given a general planning permission for a wide variety of development with the result that it is not necessary in these cases to apply for permission to the local planning authority.[6]

(2) Approval Some actions of the local planning authority require the approval of the Secretary of State. For example, structure plans do not become effective unless and until they are confirmed by the Secretary of State.[7] The same principle applies (with a few exceptions)

---

4 Minister of Town and Country Planning Act 1943, s. 1. This section was repealed by the Secretary of State for the Environment Order 1970 (SI 1970 No 1681), but that Order transferred the functions of the former Minister of Local Government (who had inherited the functions of the former Minister of Town and Country Planning) to the Secretary of State; it would appear therefore that the duty imposed by the 1943 Act, s. 1, still survives.
5 See ch. 5, pp. 89 ff, below.
6 See ch. 6, pp. 116 ff, below.
7 See ch 4, below.

to orders for the revocation or modification of planning permission,[8] and orders establishing areas of special control for outdoor advertisements.[9]

(3) Appeals Other actions of the local planning authority do not require the approval of the Secretary of State, but persons affected may have a right of appeal to him. The most important example is the right of appeal against a decision of the local planning authority refusing planning permission or granting it subject only to conditions. Although the Secretary of State decides each case on its merits and does not move from precedent to precedent as does a judge in a court of law, his decisions nevertheless form something like a body of 'case law' which is invaluable to local authorities and developers in that it shows what policy the Secretary of State is likely to adopt in future cases.

(4) Powers of direction In some cases the Secretary of State may give directions either of a general or a particular nature. An example of a general direction is the Development Plans Direction 1981[10] which lays down the procedure to be followed where the planning authority wish to grant planning permission for development which does not accord with the development plan. The Secretary of State may also issue a direction to a local planning authority with regard to a particular matter: he may for instance 'call in' an application for planning permission so that he may give a decision himself,[11] this may be done where the proposed development would conflict with the development plan or where the development is of especial public interest such as the application for the processing of atomic waste at Windscale.

(5) Default powers If the Secretary of State considers that a local planning authority have failed to fulfil some function under the Act of 1990, he may himself take action. He may, for instance, revoke a planning permission,[12] issue an enforcement notice in respect of a breach of planning control,[13] or make a tree preservation order.[14]

(6) Claims for compensation Claims for compensation under Part V of the Act of 1990 for refusal of planning permission or for conditions

8 See ch 9, below.
9 See ch 13, below.
10 This direction is printed as an appendix to circular 2/81.
11 The power to do this is conferred by the 1990 Act, s. 77.
12 Ibid, s. 100.
13 Ibid, s. 182.
14 Ibid, s. 202.

attached to a planning permission are dealt with by the Secretary of State.[15]

(7) Judicial determinations The whole machinery of planning control depends on the definition of 'development' in the 1990 Act.[16] Under section 64 of the Act of 1990 the Secretary of State may, on appeal from the local planning authority or (if he so decides) at first instance, be called upon to give a determination as to whether a proposed operation or change of use would constitute development and, if so, whether an application for planning permission is required.[17] Under section 195, he may be required to certify what is the established use of any land.[18] And, on an appeal against an enforcement notice in respect of a breach of planning control, he may have to decide whether the matters complained of in the notice constituted development.[19]

In addition to these statutory functions, the Secretary of State is able to shape planning policy through advice and information. Circulars are sent from time to time to local planning authorities on various aspects of planning control, and frequently contain statements of policy; these circulars are usually available to the public as well, so they are often of considerable assistance to landowners and their professional advisers in negotiations with the local planning authority and in conducting appeals to the Secretary of State. Where a circular contains a statement of the Secretary of State's policy on a particular matter, that statement is a 'material consideration' to be taken into account in deciding upon an application for planning permission: indeed, it has been stated to be binding upon the Secretary of State himself to the extent that, if he is seen to have departed from his policy without some good reason, his decision may be quashed by the court.[20] Information and advice are also conveyed through the Planning Policy Guidance Notes, and handbooks and other publications on such matters as the density of residential areas and the redevelopment of central areas of towns.

Obviously the Secretary of State cannot exercise all these functions personally. Most of the decisions are made on his behalf and given in his name by senior civil servants; and, in the case of many planning appeals, the decision may be given by the inspector who conducted the inquiry. Nevertheless, the Secretary of State is responsible for

15 See ch 20, below.
16 See ch 5, below.
17 See ch 5, below.
18 See ch 10, below.
19 1990, Act, s. 174. See ch 10, below.
20 *J A Pye (Oxford) Estates Ltd v West Oxfordshire District Council* [1982] JPL 577.

every decision, and (except perhaps for the judicial determinations mentioned above) answerable for it in Parliament.

NATURE OF THE SECRETARY OF STATE'S DECISION

The Secretary of State's decisions are of two kinds: policy decisions and judicial determinations.

Policy decisions The most important examples arise in connection with planning appeals and development plans. When considering an appeal against a refusal of planning permission or in deciding whether or not to confirm a development plan, the Secretary of State's concern is to achieve or uphold good standards of planning and to ensure that land is not used in a manner detrimental to the public interest. In other words, he is concerned with questions of policy rather than law. He must act within a legal framework – that is, he must not exceed the powers given him by the Planning Acts and he must observe the relevant statutory procedures – and, if he fails in either of these respects, the decision may be challenged in the courts. But the courts will not go into the question whether his decision represents good planning policy. Subject to his responsibility to Parliament, the Secretary of State is the final arbiter of what is good planning.

Before reaching the decision in any particular case, the Secretary of State usually has to give the parties concerned the opportunity of being heard by a person appointed for the purpose, usually an inspector from the Department of the Environment. The hearing by the inspector often takes the form of a public local inquiry at which the persons immediately affected – that is, the landowner (or developer) and the planning authority – will state their case and members of the public can make representations. The parties will often be represented by counsel or a solicitor, and will usually call witnesses on questions of fact or expert opinion. The hearing thus has some of the characteristics of a court of law. But the inspector is not a judge. Until recently, the duty of the inspector was limited to making a report to the Secretary of State presenting the facts (as they have emerged from the evidence at the inquiry or from his own inspection of the land in question) together with his own conclusions and recommendations. The Secretary of State is not obliged to accept the report but will reach his own decision.[1] The role of the inspector has been enhanced in recent years and in many cases he now gives the actual decision on behalf of the Secretary of State.

1 For a full account of the procedure at a public inquiry see ch 17, below.

Public inquiries of this kind have for many years formed part of the procedure for slum clearance schemes made under the Housing Acts and for compulsory purchase under a number of statutes. Recently, however, there has been much controversy as to their nature and purpose. In some quarters they have been regarded simply as part of the machinery by which Ministers collect information and opinion to enable them to make their decisions. This was described by the Franks Committee Report (1957) as the 'administrative' view.[2] The courts have held, in cases under the Housing Acts, that the rules of natural justice must apply to the conduct of the inquiry and that the Secretary of State must not receive information from one party to the inquiry behind the back of the other.[3] It has always been assumed that (except in relation to structure plans, for which there are special provisions)[4] the same principle applies to planning inquiries. But the courts have never questioned the right of Ministers to obtain information and opinion from other quarters, particularly from other government departments. The administrative school of thought considers it is both proper and reasonable for Ministers to obtain information in this way.

Diametrically opposed to the administrative view is what the Franks Committee called the 'judicial' view.[5] This regards a planning inquiry as a dispute between the local planning authority and the individual: the ensuing decision should be judicial in the sense that it should be based wholly and directly upon the evidence presented at the inquiry.

These two opposing views were considered by the Franks Committee, which came to the conclusion that neither provided a satisfactory analysis.[6]

> Our general conclusion is that these procedures cannot be classified as purely administrative or purely judicial. They are not purely administrative because of the provision for a special procedure preliminary to the decision – a feature not to be found in the ordinary course of administration – and because this procedure as we have shown, involves the testing of an issue, often partly in public. They are not on the other hand purely judicial, because the final decision cannot be reached by the application of rules and must allow the exercise of a wide discretion in the balancing of public and private interest. Neither view at its extreme is tenable, nor should either be emphasised at the expense of the other.
>
> If the administrative view is dominant the public inquiry cannot play its full part in the total process, and there is a danger that the rights and interests of the individual citizens affected will not be sufficiently protected.

---

2 Franks Committee Report, paras 262, 263.
3 The leading case is *Errington v Minister of Health* [1935] 1 KB 249.
4 1990 Act, s. 35(9). See ch 4, below.
5 Franks Committee Report, paras 262, 264.
6 Ibid, paras 272, 273, 274.

In these cases it is idle to argue that Parliament can be relied upon to protect the citizen, save exceptionally. We agree with the following views expressed in the pamphlet entitled *Rule of Law*. 'Whatever the theoretical validity of this argument, those of us who are Members of Parliament have no hesitation in saying that it bears little relation to reality. Parliament has neither the time nor the knowledge to supervise the Minister and call him to account for his administrative decisions.'

If the judicial view is dominant there is a danger that people will regard the person before whom they state their case as a kind of judge provisionally deciding the matter, subject to an appeal to the Minister. This view overlooks the true nature of the proceeding, the form of which is necessitated by the fact that the Minister himself, who is responsible to Parliament for the ultimate decision, cannot conduct the enquiry in person.

The Franks Committee endeavoured to find a reasonable balance between these two views by applying the tests of openness, fairness and impartiality to the current practice.[7] The application of these tests led to the conclusion that some reforms were necessary, and the Franks Committee recommended amongst other things that the case for the planning authority should be properly notified in advance and supported at the inquiry,[8] that the inspector's report should be available to the parties to the enquiry,[9] that the Minister should submit to the parties for their observations any factual evidence which he obtains after the inquiry, whatever the source, and that he should give the reasons for the decision.[10] These recommendations have largely been put into effect, partly by legislation[11] and partly by administrative action.

These changes undoubtedly bring current practice much nearer the judicial school of thought. It should not, however, be thought that they are detrimental to the interests of the administrative school. On the contrary, they should strengthen administration by ensuring that only tested and proven information is relied upon in reaching a decision; insistence upon the giving of reasons should also discourage ill-thought-out decisions.

Judicial determinations Examples of judicial determinations by the Secretary of State have been mentioned above.[12] They involve a decision on a point of law and he must not consider questions of good

7 Franks Committee Report, paras 276, 277.
8 Ibid, paras 280 ff.
9 Ibid, para 344.
10 Ibid, paras 347 ff.
11 Tribunals and Inquiries Act 1971, replacing the Tribunals and Inquiries Act 1958; Inquiries Procedure Rules 1974. See ch 17, below.
12 See this chapter, p. 34, above.

planning policy. Before making his decision he must give the parties involved an opportunity to be heard though often the parties agree to submit written representations instead.[13] The Secretary of State's decision may be the subject of an appeal to the High Court.[14]

THE SECRETARY OF STATE'S RESPONSIBILITY TO PARLIAMENT

The Secretary of State is responsible to Parliament for the manner in which he carries out his functions under the Planning Acts. Questions may be put to him at Question Time and debates held. Parliament has not the time to exercise any detailed supervision. It was also suggested in the pamphlet *Rule of Law*[15] that Parliament lacks the necessary knowledge, but this does not seem to be the case. There have from time to time been important and useful debates, particularly on broader topics such as the conduct of planning inquiries. The Minister's decisions in the 'Essex chalkpit' case and over Stansted airport were specifically debated. And it was as a result of questions in Parliament that the Minister decided to 'call in' the application in respect of the Monico café in Piccadilly Circus. Moreover, as an alternative to a formal parliamentary question, MPs often raise matters in correspondence with the Secretary of State.

There are, however, certain inherent difficulties about taking up individual cases with the Secretary of State. Four situations may arise:

(1) A planning application has been made to the local planning authority and awaits a formal decision. In this case, there is no particular difficulty. The matter can be freely debated in Parliament and the Secretary of State can 'call in' the application giving the parties an opportunity to be heard at a public inquiry.

(2) The local planning authority have refused permission, or granted it subject to conditions, and there is an appeal to the Secretary of State. Is it consistent with the principles laid down by the Franks Committee to express opinion in Parliament with the obvious intention of influencing the Secretary of State's decision? A former Lord Chancellor thought not. In the course of a debate in the House of Lords, a peer commented on the merits of an appeal then before the Minister. The Lord Chancellor rebuked him on the ground that the

---

13 1990 Act, s. 64 (determinations whether planning permission is required); s. 174 (determinations whether acts made the subject of an enforcement notice constitute development); s. 196 (appeals against refusal of certificate of established use).

14 See ch 18, below.

15 See this chapter, p. 37, above.

matter was *sub judice*.[16] The rule that there should be no comment on matters which are *sub judice* comes from the courts of law, and it can be argued that it does not strictly apply to the consideration of a planning application; indeed the Franks Committee mentioned the Minister's responsibility to Parliament as one of the reasons why the judicial view of planning decisions could not be wholly accepted.[17] But if statements can be made in Parliament with the intention of influencing the Secretary of State's decision, what happens to the principle laid down by the Franks Committee that he should only take into account information and opinions which were given at the inquiry or upon which the parties have had an opportunity to comment? Of course, there can be no objection to discussion after the Secretary of State has made his decision, but then it is too late to be of practical value.

(3) The local planning authority have granted permission. In this case there will be no appeal and no inquiry.[18] There can therefore be no objection to parliamentary discussion but it will be of little practical value unless the Secretary of State is prepared to direct the local planning authority to make a revocation order, but this can be very costly in terms of compensation.[19]

(4) The Secretary of State is called upon to give a judicial determination. Here, it is submitted, the *sub judice* principle must apply.

Where the Secretary of State has called in an application for planning permission, he can, instead of making the final decision himself, make a special development order authorising the development; the order must be laid before Parliament, thus giving the opportunity for debate. The Secretary of State has occasionally chosen that course, notably in the case of the Windscale development. This procedure may perhaps be inconsistent with the principles suggested by the Franks Committee, but there will from time to time be developments of such public concern that the final decision should be the responsibility of Parliament. It is significant that there are other instances where Parliament itself has the last word: for example the taking of land belonging to the National Trust for the construction of motorways.

Parliamentary control may to some extent have been strengthened by the Parliamentary Commissioner Act 1967. The Commissioner can investigate complaints of maladministration arising from the

16 House of Lords Debates, 1 December 1960.
17 Franks Committee Report, para 274.
18 The only person who can appeal to the Secretary of State against the local planning authority's decision on an application for planning permission is the applicant himself: 1990 Act, s. 78.
19 For revocation procedure, see ch 9, below.

exercise by the Secretary of State of any of his administrative functions. 'Maladministration', however, probably refers to the manner in which the Secretary of State reaches his decision rather than to its substance, and in some cases under the Act of 1990 the courts afford redress against this type of maladministration; unless there are special reasons, the Commissioner must not investigate complaints which can be dealt with by the courts.[20] The Secretary of State's conduct can also be reviewed by the Council on Tribunals.

Local planning authorities

At local level, the administration of town and country planning (including many of the initiatives in policy making) is the responsibility of the local planning authorities.

Prior to the re-organisation of local government in 1974, the local planning authority (outside Greater London) was usually the county or county borough council. The Minister, however, could set up joint planning boards; these might be constituted for the area, or part of the area, of two or more counties or county boroughs. In fact, only two such joint boards were set up; these were for the Lake District and Peak District National Parks.

Under the pre-1974 system a county council might delegate certain planning functions to borough and district councils, and a joint board might likewise delegate certain functions to its constituent authorities. In 1959 provision was made for the compulsory delegation of certain functions to district councils with populations of over 60,000.

The changes introduced by the Local Government Act 1972 with effect from 1 April 1974, were substantial. A comprehensive two-tier system of county and district councils was established for the whole of England and Wales, except for the Isles of Scilly, the 'all-purpose' county boroughs having been abolished, The Act divides England (exclusive of Greater London[1] and the Isles of Scilly) into six metropolitan counties and 39 non-metropolitan counties.[1] The metropolitan counties are divided into 36 metropolitan districts with populations ranging from 180,000 to 1,100,000. The non-metropolitan counties are divided into 333 non-metropolitan districts with populations mostly between 65,000 and 120,000. In Wales[2] there are eight counties divided into 40 districts.[3]

---

20 See further ch 18, below.
 1 Local Government Act 1972, Sch 1.
 2 'Wales' includes Monmouthshire: ibid, s. 20(7).
 3 Ibid, Sch 4.

These districts are in most cases much larger than the former bor-oughs and county districts, and they have been entrusted with direct (instead of delegated) responsibility for many planning matters.

The Act has brought further changes. The Greater London Council and the six metropolitan county councils have been abolished, and there is now only one tier of local government in these areas – namely in Greater London the London borough councils[4] and in the metro-politan counties the metropolitan district councils.[5] We can now consider the system of local planning authorities under two headings: England and Wales generally, and Greater London and the metro-politan counties.

England and Wales generally There are two tiers of local planning authorities; the county councils act as county planning authorities, and the district councils as district planning authorities. The Secretary of State may set up a joint board as the county planning authority for the area, or part of the area of two or more counties; and he may also set up a joint board as the district planning authority for the area, or part of the area, of two or more districts.[6]

The former joint planning board for the Peak District has been reconstituted as the planning authority for the national park. The Lake District National Park is now wholly within the area of one county – the new county of Cumbria – and the former joint planning board has been converted into a 'special planning board'. The Sec-retary of State has not so far exercised his power to establish any more joint boards.

The county planning authority are responsible for the structure plan and for certain 'county matters' in regard to development control. Since 1980 these county matters have been restricted to mineral workings and associated development; development partly within and partly without a national park; and any other development prescribed by the Secretary of State.[7]

The district planning authority will be responsible for preparing local plans for its area, unless reserved to the county planning auth-ority; the district authority will also be responsible for administering the statutory provisions relating to the control of development except of course in the case of the county matters referred to above.

4 Including, for this purpose, the Common Council of the City of London: 1990 Act, s. 336(1).
5 Ibid, s. 1(2).
6 Ibid, s. 2(1).
7 The Secretary of State has prescribed development relating to waste disposal as a county matter: T & CP (Prescription of County Matters) Regulations 1980 (SI 1980 No 2010).

In national parks, however, all planning functions will be exercisable by the county planning authority (or joint board) with only a few minor exceptions. Where there is no joint or special planning board, however, the county council must appoint a national park committee to exercise all planning functions except those relating to development plans, and the control of development which either conflicts with those plans or straddles the boundary of the park.

In the Norfolk and Suffolk Broads, the new Broads Authority is the local planning authority for the exercise of many functions under the Planning Act, such as local plans, development control, listed building control, conservation areas.[8]

Greater London and the metropolitan counties   In these areas the local planning authority will normally be the London borough council[9] or the metropolitan district council as the case may be.[10] The Secretary of State may, however, vest certain functions in urban development corporations and enterprise zones authorities.[11]

Part of the Peak District National Park is in the metropolitan county of South Yorkshire and in that part the local planning authority will be the joint planning board referred to above.[12]

In Greater London certain functions in respect of listed buildings and conservation areas can now be exercised by the Historic Buildings Commission.[13] The 1985 Act required the local planning authorities in Greater London to establish a joint committee to advise those authorities on matters of common interest relating to the planning and development of Greater London; the committee is also to inform the Secretary of State of the views of those authorities on such matters, including matters on which he has requested their advice. It has the function of informing local planning authorities in the vicinity of Greater London of the views of the authorities in London concerning matters of common interest relating to the planning and development of Greater London.[14]

Urban development areas   The Secretary of State may vest certain functions under the Planning Acts in the urban development corporations,

---

8 1990 Act, s. 5.
9 The London borough councils were constituted by the London Government Act 1963.
10 1990 Act, s. 5.
11 1980 Act, s. 149, Sch 32.
12 See p. 41, above.
13 See chs 13 and 14, below.
14 1990 Act, s. 3.

such as development control, trees, control of advertisements, listed building control and conservation areas.[15]

Enterprise zones   In an enterprise zone, the enterprise zone authority will be the local planning authority to the extent mentioned in the order designating the zone.[16]

Housing action area   Where a housing action trust is set up for a housing action area under the Housing Act 1988, the Secretary of State may make an order designating the trust as the local planning authority for certain purposes.[17]

Parish councils   The Local Government Act 1972 gave formal status in planning matters to the parish councils in England and the community councils in Wales. A parish or community council might notify the district planning authority that they wish to be consulted with regard to all applications for planning permission in their area or with regard to particular types of application.[18]

Delegation to officers

Until comparatively recently it was the almost universal rule in local government that decisions could be taken only by the council itself or by a duly authorised committee. The officers might advise but they could not take decisions even in minor matters.

However, the Act of 1968 introduced for the first time powers under which local authorities might delegate the power of decision-making in planning matters to their officers. These provisions authorised delegation to named officers of the power to decide upon applications for planning permission, for consent for outdoor advertising, for a determination under section 53 as to the necessity for planning permission, for an established use certificate, and for any approval required by the General Development Order or by a condition attached to a planning permission.

As from 1 April 1974, these powers have been replaced by a much wider power under section 101 of the Local Government Act 1972. This provides that a local authority may arrange for the discharge of

15 1990 Act, s. 7. See e g Merseyside Development Corporation (Planning Functions) Order 1981 (SI 1981 No 561); London Docklands (Planning Functions) Order 1981 (SI 1981 No 1081).
16 1990 Act, s. 6.
17 Housing Act 1988, s. 67; 1990 Act, s. 8.
18 Local Government Act 1972, Sch 16, para 20. This provision has now been repealed by the Planning (Consequential Provisions) Act 1990, Sch 1.

any of their functions by an officer of the authority. This must, however, be read subject to any other statutory provisions which in effect preclude delegation; for instance, the adoption of a local plan requires a formal resolution of the local planning authority.[19]

It is, of course, inevitable that, in the day to day conduct of affairs, landowners and developers should seek information and advice from planning officers. This is a desirable practice so long as all concerned recognise the position of the planning officer in such matters, where formal authority has not been delegated to him. Local authorities sometimes consider that they are not bound by statements made by their officers in response to requests for information or advice.

The traditional rule of local government law has been that estoppel cannot operate to prevent or hinder a local authority in the performance of a statutory duty. The local planning authority have a discretion whether or not to serve an enforcement notice,[20] but in *Southend-on-Sea Corpn v Hodgson (Wickford) Ltd*[1] the Divisional Court considered that the traditional rule applied to the exercise of a statutory discretion as well as to a statutory duty; it was held that the local planning authority were not estopped from serving an enforcement notice, even though the planning officer had written to the company saying that the land had existing use rights and that planning permission was not required.

The severity of this rule has been modified to a limited extent in *Wells v Minister of Housing and Local Government.*[2]

The applicants, who were builders' merchants and had for many years made concrete blocks, applied in December 1962 for planning permission to erect a concrete batching plant 27 feet 6 inches high. In March 1963 the council's surveyor replied that the plant could be regarded as permitted development under class VIII of the General Development Order then in force and it was therefore proposed not to take any further action on the application for planning permission. The applicants then decided to erect a plant 48 feet high. Thinking that the plant would be covered by the council's letter, they applied only for byelaw consent. The local authority granted the byelaw consent and on the official notification deleted the words 'No action should be taken hereunder until the approval of the town planning authority and licensing authority have been taken'.

The appellants erected the 48 feet high plant but the council served an enforcement notice requiring it to be taken down. The Minister upheld the enforcement notice.

The Court of Appeal decided that the letter of March 1963 was a

19 1990 Act, s. 43(1).
20 See ch 10, below.
 1 [1962] 1 QB 416, [1961] 2 All ER 46.
 2 [1967] 2 All ER 1041.

valid determination under section 53 of the Act of 1971 (now section 64 of the Act of 1990). Although there had been no application for such a determination under that section, every application for planning permission contained an implied invitation to make such a determination. As Lord Denning put it: 'a public authority cannot be estopped from doing its public duty, but I do think it can be estopped from relying on technicalities'; in his Lordship's opinion the absence of a formal application for a determination under what is now section 64 of the Act of 1990 was a technicality. But as regards the 48 feet high plant, the council had not positively stated that planning permission was not required, and there had been no application for planning permission in respect of it. The council were therefore entitled to serve an enforcement notice, but the case was remitted to the Minister to consider whether planning permission should be granted having regard to the fact that the appellants had the right (as a result of the letter of March 1963) to erect a plant 27 feet 6 inches high.

The issue of estoppel came up again in *Lever (Finance) Ltd v Westminster City London Borough Council*.[3] In that case Lord Denning (with whom Megaw LJ concurred) appeared to have considerably extended the scope of estoppel to give some protection to developers who acted upon representations made by a planning officer or other appropriate officer of a local authority. For some years thereafter estoppel was recognised by the courts and the Secretary of State as a defence to an enforcement notice.[4]

Since then, however, there has been a return to the traditional doctrine. In *Western Fish Products Ltd v Penwith District Council*[5] the plaintiffs alleged that a letter from the planning officer had amounted to confirmation that they had an existing use right which covered the uses contemplated by their scheme. The Court of Appeal held that the letter could not reasonably be understood in that sense and that accordingly no estoppel could be founded on it. That finding would have been sufficient to have disposed of the case, but the Court also held that as a matter of law that the council could not be estopped from performing their statutory duties. The Court was prepared to recognise only two exceptions. First, where the planning authority acting as such delegates to an officer authority to determine specific matters, such matters as applications under sections 64 and 192, any

3 [1971] 1 QB 222, [1970] 3 All ER 496.
4 See the decisions of the Divisional Court in *Norfolk County Council v Secretary of State for the Environment* [1973] 3 All ER 673; and *Brooks and Burton Ltd v Secretary of State for the Environment* (1976) 35 P & CR 27. For decisions of the Secretary of State see those reported in [1975] JPL 609, 614.
5 [1981] 2 All ER 204.

decision that he makes pursuant to the authority cannot be revoked. This, it is submitted, has nothing to do with the law of estoppel; the officer's decision is made on behalf of the authority and is binding on the authority even if the developer has not yet acted upon it.[6] The second exception recognised by the Court related to cases like that which arose in *Wells v Minister of Housing and Local Government*.[7] The Court insisted that there must have been (as in Wells) an application for planning permission, and were not prepared to accept any greater degree of informality.

It is difficult to reconcile this decision with the reasoning of the majority of the Court of Appeal in *Lever (Finance) Ltd v Westminster City London Borough Council*.[8] What is clear is that the Court of Appeal now regards the role of the local planning authority as 'the guardian of the planning sytem'[9] as more important than the difficulties which may be caused by insistence on compliance with formalities.

In the subsequent case of *Newbury District Council v Secretary of State for the Environment*[10] the House of Lords had to consider whether a developer who had taken up a planning permission was estopped from asserting later on that no such permission was necessary. The House of Lords decided that the developer was not estopped. It is of interest here that Lord Fraser of Tulleybelton and Lord Scarman considered that the doctrine of estoppel should not be introduced into planning law.[11] Pending any review by the House of Lords of *Lever (Finance) Ltd v Westminster London Borough City Council*[12] and *Western Fish Products Ltd v Penwith District Council*,[13] it seems that the latter case is the better authority.

6 Indeed, the Court itself seems to have doubted whether this was estoppel at all – see the judgment of the court at 29.
7 Above.
8 Above.
9 A phrase used by Romer LJ in his dissenting judgment in *Wells v Minister of Housing and Local Government* (above).
10 [1981] AC 578, [1980] 1 All ER 731.
11 At 607, 617 respectively.
12 Above.
13 Above.

Chapter 4

Development plans

One of the most important features of the planning system in this country since 1947 has been the requirement that there should be for each area a development plan to provide a basis for both positive and regulatory planning. The nature of these development plans, however, has changed fundamentally over the years. The Act of 1947 resulted in a comprehensive system of development plans prepared by county councils and county borough councils and approved in each case by the Minister. These development plans were based on detailed maps: although there was also a written statement this was more in the nature of an accompaniment to the maps.

Following the recommendations of the Planning Advisory Group[1] the Act of 1968 made provision for a quite different system of development plans consisting of structure plans which deal with strategic issues and require the approval of the Secretary of State, the local plans which do not normally require his approval. Both structure and local plans are essentially policy documents, maps and diagrams being only illustrative. Structure plans have now been completed and approved for all the counties in England and Wales and many are now being up-dated. But as late as November 1988 the coverage of local plans was described as 'patchy'. Large areas, even those parts that are under pressure for development, have no local plan.[2] As a result, parts of the old development plans will remain in force pending the completion and adoption of local plans.

However, for some of the most populous parts of the country further changes are under way. In Greater London and the six metropolitan counties structure and local plans are to be replaced by 'unitary development plans' which will combine in single plans parts corresponding to structure and local plans; unitary development plans

---

1 See ch 2, p. 12, above.
2 Planning Policy Guidance Note No 12, para 4. Local planning authorities have recently been urged to extend the area covered by local plans: ibid, paras 5 to 9.

will not normally require the approval of the Secretary of State.[3] The new unitary plans will affect a total population of some 18 million, but it remains to be seen whether their practical effect will be significantly different from that of the structure and local plans.

The old development plans

Although the old development plans made under the Acts of 1947 and 1962 have now to a considerable extent been replaced by newer types of plan, parts of the old plans remain in force for the time being.[4]

The development plan was to show the manner in which it was proposed that land in the area shall be used (whether by the carrying out of development or otherwise) and the stages by which the development was to be carried out. In particular, the plan might:

(a) define the sites of proposed roads, public and other buildings and works, airfields, parks, pleasure grounds, nature reserves and other open spaces;

(b) allocate areas of land for agriculture, residential, industrial or other purposes;

(c) designate areas of comprehensive development; these were areas which the local planning authority consider should be developed or re-developed as a whole for any of the following reasons:

    (i)   to deal satisfactorily with extensive war-damage;

    (ii) to deal satisfactorily with bad layout or obsolete development;

    (iii) to provide for the relocation of population or industry or the replacement of open space in the course of the development or re-development of any other area;

    (iv) for any other purpose specified in the plan.

The older type of development plan consisted of a basic map and written statement together with such other maps as might be appropriate.

The basic map prepared by a county borough before 1974 was to the scale of six inches to one mile; maps to this scale were referred to as 'town maps'. The basic map prepared by one of the former administrative counties was to the scale of one inch to one mile – 'county map' – but town maps might also have been prepared for particular areas which need not have been urban in character. Prior to 1965 it was necessary to submit a programme map to accompany each county map and each town map; after 1965 it was sufficient to

3 1990 Act, Part II, Chapter I.
4 1990 Act, Sch 2, Part III.

indicate in the written statement the stages by which any proposed development was to be carried out.

In addition maps would be required for special purposes such as (a) areas of comprehensive development; (b) land designated under section 232 of the Highways Act 1980 ('street authorisation maps'). All these maps were required to be to scale 1/2,500. Any area shown on a county map might also be shown on an 'inset map' to scale 1/2,500.

The written statement contained a summary of the main proposals of the development plan together with information on such matters as densities for residential development, green belts, the kind of development which would be permitted in rural areas, how it was proposed to deal with non-conforming users and so on. It also indicated the stages by which any development proposed by the plan should be carried out, and the period covered by the plan; and in relation to any comprehensive development area map a statement of the purposes for which the area was to be developed or redeveloped as a whole.

The written statement might therefore refer to a fair number of matters, but it was nevertheless a comparatively short document. The information given was usually expressed in a condensed form without any reasoning in support. There was indeed a statutory provision – which is still in force in relation to such parts of the older development plans as are still extant – that, in the event of any contradiction between the maps and the written statement, the latter is to prevail. Nevertheless the older type of development plan can fairly be described as map based.

The new system of structure and local plans

The structure and local plans are very different both in concept and presentation from the old development plans. The structure and local plans set out policies and proposals in written form, any maps and diagrams being illustrative of the text rather than the basis of the plan; they will also be much more concerned with the implementation – in land use and environmental terms – of social and economic policies.

The structure plan deals with the major planning issues for the area and sets out broad policies and proposals. Local plans elaborate these broad policies and proposals in more detail, relating them to precise areas of land and thus providing the detailed basis for both positive and regulatory planning. Structure plans require the approval of the Secretary of State; local plans do not normally require his approval.

The new system has been introduced gradually. Shortly after the

Act of 1968 was passed, the Minister invited 26 authorities[5] to prepare structure plans. Later more authorities were invited to do so,
and following local government re-organisation in 1974 the remaining county councils were likewise invited. By September 1981
all the original structure plans had been submitted to the Secretary
of State for approval and most had been approved with or without
modification. The original structure plans, except in the case of two
of the national parks, were prepared by the county councils; they
usually relate to the whole of a county. The structure plans approved
before the passing of the Act of 1990 are kept in force by section 31
of the new Act. Since local plans represent the detailed implementation of the broad policies and proposals of the structure plan, local
plans cannot normally be formally adopted before the structure plan
has been approved; it was thus only later that local plans came forward
in any significant numbers for adoption. A very large number of local
plans have now been adopted; even so as recently as November 1988
the Secretaries of State were expressing concern that 'large areas of
England and Wales are still without formally adopted and up-to-date
local plans'.[6]

   It is the intention that both structure and local plans be kept under
review; proposals for the alteration or repeal and replacement of a
structure plan can be made at any time,[7] but proposals for altering
or replacing a local plan can only be made where authorised by the
local plan scheme or by the Secretary of State.[8] The principles which
should govern the making of alterations and the procedures to be
followed are in almost every respect the same as for the making of the
original plans.

   We now turn to a more detailed examination of those principles
and procedures in relation first to structure plans and then in relation
to local plans.

THE SURVEY

Both structure and local plans must be based on the results of a survey.
It is the duty of each local planning authority to 'keep under review
the matters which may be expected to affect the development of that
area or the planning of its development', and they may at any time

5 Some of these were county boroughs under the pre-1974 system of local government.
6 Planning Policy Guidance Note No 12, para 1.
7 1990 Act, s. 32.
8 1990 Act, ss. 37(7), 38.

carry out a fresh survey examining these matters.[9] These matters are to include, inter alia, the following.[10]

(a) the principal physical and economic characteristics of the authority's area (including the principal purposes for which the land is used) and their effect on neighbouring areas;

(b) size, composition and distribution of the population (whether resident or otherwise);

(c) communications, transport system and traffic of the area and their effect on neighbouring areas;

(d) such matters as the Secretary of State may prescribe by regulations or may in any particular case direct.

Where necessary the authority must consult with neighbouring planning authorities.[11]

Structure plans

A structure plan sets out the local planning authority's[12] policy and general proposals in respect of the development and other use of land in that area (including measures for the improvement of the physical environment and the management of traffic). It must take the form of a written statement, illustrated by diagrams which are to be treated as forming part of the plan.[13] The plan is to be accompanied by an explanatory memorandum summarising their reasons for each and every policy in the plan, including the regard which they had to current national and regional policies, social considerations and the resources likely to be available.[14] This explanatory memorandum does not form part of the structure plan.

The 'proposals' in the structure plan are intended to be general in character. Thus, in relation to housing, the Secretary of State has indicated that the proposals should indicate in broad terms the scale of provision which is to be made for development in the area as a whole and in each district, and should identify those locations where provision for substantial growth is to be made; policies on residential densities should give general guidance on the densities expected but they should not attempt to restrict district planning and housing authorities to specific densities in particular areas or on particular

9 1990 Act, s. 30(1).
10 Ibid, s. 30(2).
11 Ibid, s. 30(4).
12 The local planning authority for this purpose is the county council: ibid, Sch 1, para 2.
13 Ibid, s. 31(2), (3).
14 Ibid, s. 30(4), Plans Regs, reg 7.

sites.[15] It is not the function of the structure plan to allocate specific sites.

Examples of the general policies and proposals for housing considered appropriate for a structure plan are:[16]

> Planning permission will not normally be granted for residential development at a net density of less than 80 bedspaces per hectare.
> Planning permission will not normally be granted for family housing which exceeds four storeys in height.
> In considering proposals for residential development particular regard will be given to the need for good access to existing jobs and facilities, and to whether the scale of the proposed development justifies provision being made for new employment and other facilities.

An important function of structure plans has been to indicate action areas.[17] The structure plan would indicate the general location of an action area and outline the nature of the treatment proposed for that area; the precise boundaries and the detailed proposals for the area would be dealt with in a local plan. The requirement that an action area must originate in a structure plan proposal – and thus require the approval of the Secretary of State – ceased to have effect with the passing of the Act of 1980.

It seems that the local planning authority must be able to show that the policies and proposals serve genuine planning purposes. This fundamental principle was well illustrated in *Great Portland Estates v City of Westminster*:[18]

> The City of Westminster District Plan provided for the protection of 'specified industrial activities': the plan explained that a high proportion of industrial floor space was occupied by long established firms many of which required a central location in order to maintain the services required, but this central location made them vulnerable to pressure from other more profitable uses. The council felt that the loss of those supporting industrial activities might threaten the viability of other important central London activities. Although the council could not influence matters such as the financial viability of a firm it could use its planning powers to protect these activities from disappearance in face of pressure to redevelop the sites. Great Portland Estates challenged the validity of this policy. The Court of Appeal considered that the council's real concern was the protection of existing occupiers, which was not a permissible consideration; the court therefore quashed the relevant paragraphs in the District Plan.

15 Memorandum on Structure and Local Plans, para 4.18.
16 These examples are taken from the Nottinghamshire Structure Plan approved by the Secretary of State in 1980.
17 For action areas generally see pp. 62–63, below.
18 [1984] 3 All ER 744. Some other aspects of this important case are considered at p. 65, below.

The council appealed and the House of Lords allowed the appeal. Lord Scarman said that the test of what was a material consideration in the preparation of plans or in the control of development was whether it served a 'planning purpose'; and a planning purpose was one which related to the character of the use of the land. A genuine planning purpose was stated in the plan, namely the continuation of industrial uses considered important to the character, vitality and functions of Westminster; inevitably this would mean that existing occupiers would be protected, but this was not a *purpose* of the plan though it would be a *consequence*.[19]

This emphasis on the character of the use of the land does not preclude consideration of the human factors. Lord Scarman said that the personal circumstances of an occupier and the difficulties of businesses of value to the community are not to be ignored in the administration of planning control. 'It would be inhuman pedantry to exclude from the control of our environment the human factor.' But, as his Lordship explained, these factors can be given effect as exceptional or special circumstances; the existence of such cases might be mentioned in the plan, but this would only be necessary where it was prudent to emphasise that, notwithstanding the general policy, exceptions could not be wholly excluded from consideration in the administration of planning control.[20]

Although this case concerned a local plan, it seems that the principles laid down in it apply also to structure plans.[1]

In preparing the structure plan, the local planning authority are not to work in isolation; they are specifically required to have regard to current policies for the economic planning and development of the region as a whole,[2] and they are also to state how the structure plan relates to the structure plans for neighbouring areas.[3] This latter requirement is obviously important in view of the emphasis laid on traffic management, but it also ensures that neighbouring planning authorities come to terms over such matters as overspill.

The local planning authority are also required in drawing up structure plan proposals to have regard to the resources likely to be available.[4] 'It is an essential discipline in the preparation of the plan to ensure that what is proposed is realistic, and the plan should demonstrate that, as far as can be foreseen, this is the case.'[5] This

19 Author's italics.
20 When determining an application for planning permission, the local planning authority must have regard to all material considerations: see ch 7, pp. 143 ff, below.
1 Lord Scarman used the expression 'development plans' which includes both structure and local plans.
2 1990 Act, s. 31(4)(a).
3 Ibid, s. 32(6).
4 Ibid, s. 31(4)(b).
5 Development Plans Manual, para 3.15.

emphasis on realities was not always a feature of the development plans prepared under the Act of 1947. But there is a corollary. 'In formulating their policies and general proposals, the authority should bear in mind that the use of resources implied by the proposals will represent a decision not to use those resources in other ways. Accordingly they will wish to satisfy themselves that the plan represents the best use of resources.'[6]

It is also required of the local planning authority that they shall state in the explanatory memorandum to the structure plan what regard they have had to social policies and considerations.[7] This implies, although it does not expressly require, that the needs and problems of different social groups should be taken into consideration, as well as purely physical and economic aspects. Thus regard for social considerations would clearly help to justify a policy statement that:

> In considering proposals for residential development to meet future replacement needs, particular regard will be given to locating the development as near to the area of clearance as possible.[8]

Some planning authorities, however, have seen this statutory provision as justifying the promotion of policies directed to 'social engineering'. So far this approach has received little or no encouragement from the Secretary of State. He has, for instance, deleted policy statements of the following type:

> Positive discrimination towards disadvantaged people will be exercised. Priority will be given to deprived areas in the provision of services and facilities and in schemes for environmental improvement.[9]

The question of social policies was touched upon in *R v Secretary of State for the Environment, ex p Greater London Council*.[10] The council challenged the opinion of the Secretary of State that some of their proposed alterations to the Greater London Development Plan[11] bore no relationship to a 'land use structure plan'.[12] In support of this challenge, the council relied on the speech of Lord Scarman in *Great*

---

6 The quotation is from the Memorandum on Structure and Local Plans which accompanied circular 4/79. It is not repeated in the current memorandum published with circular 22/84, but the point is still valid.

7 Plans Regs, Sch 1, Part 1.

8 Nottinghamshire Structure Plan (1978), para 5.26.

9 Nottinghamshire Structure Plan, para. 7.17.

10 [1985] JPL 543.

11 The Greater London Development Plan was prepared in pursuance of provisions in the London Government Act 1963, but is now, for the time being, the structure plan for the purposes of the 1971 Act.

12 This phrase does not denote a particular type of structure plan: it appears to be a short way of saying that a structure plan is concerned with land use.

Portland Estates v City of Westminster[13] as showing that a development plan could contain policies which did not relate wholly to the use of land but to more general matters. Taylor J considered that Lord Scarman's remarks were no authority for saying that social policy not based on planning reasons or having a planning purpose was appropriate for inclusion in a development plan.[14]

Form and content of structure plans

The structure plan is to consist primarily of a written statement describing the local planning authority's policy and general proposals.[15] It must include in addition statements about various matters prescribed by the Act or the Plans Regulations such as the regard which the local planning authority has had to regional economic policies, social policies and considerations and the availability of resources. The policy and proposals set out in the text are to be illustrated by a 'key diagram'; insets may be used to illustrate the policies and proposals for parts of the area to which the plan relates. These diagrams are to be treated as forming part of the structure plan.[16]

Before 1979 it was a requirement of the Plans Regulations that the structure plan should also contain a reasoned justification of the policy and proposals.[17] This requirement has now been replaced by a provision that proposals for altering or replacing the structure plan shall be accompanied by an explanatory memorandum. This memorandum (a) must give the local planning authority's reasons for putting the proposals; (b) must contain the information on which the proposals are based; and (c) may contain illustrative material.[18] This explanatory memorandum is not apparently to be treated as forming part of the plan. The change may be one of form rather than substance, but it means presumably that in approving the policies and proposals in the structure plan the Secretary of State does not necessarily approve the local planning authority's reasons.

The diagrams illustrating the structure plan must not be on a map base.[19] They provide in effect a pictorial index to the written text.

13 See fn 52 above.
14 At 548–549.
15 1990 Act, s. 31(2).
16 Ibid, s. 31(3).
17 1974 Plans Regs, reg 9(3).
18 1990 Act, s. 32(5), (6), (7).
19 Plans Regs, reg 8(3).

The relationship of the diagrams and other illustrative material to the written statement has been explained as follows:[20]

> The structure plan is largely concerned with long range policies that look forward over 20 or 30 years, well beyond the period within which land allocations and site definitions can be made. But where the policies are related to particular areas, illustrations can help understanding and simplify verbal descriptions. Diagrams and other illustrations will be useful in explaining the context of the plan ... They cannot settle detailed matters of the use of particular sites (which is a function of local plans), and therefore the diagrams will not have ordnance survey bases which would create a misleading impression of precision. A second limitation is that the purpose of the diagrams is to explain or illustrate the proposals in the written statement. It is therefore important that no proposals should appear on them other than those which the statement specifically mentions.

In the event of any contradiction between the written statement and any other document (including maps, diagrams, etc) forming part of the plan, the written statement is to prevail.[1]

URBAN STRUCTURE PLANS

Regulations made in 1974 (now replaced by those currently in force) made provision for 'urban structure plans' for particular urban areas; these urban plans were to form part of the general structure plan made by the county council, but provided additional treatment of the planning issues and problems of those urban areas.

The Plans Regulations now in force make no provision for further urban structure plans. Where an urban structure plan has already been approved, proposals for the alteration of the county structure plan, of which it forms part, may include proposals for the alteration or repeal of the urban structure plan; but, where the county structure plan is to be repealed and replaced, the urban structure plan will of course be repealed and it will not be replaced.[2]

PROCEDURE (A): PUBLIC PARTICIPATION

Structure plan proposals[3] will not come into force unless and until they are approved by the Secretary of State. The procedure for

20 Development Plans Manual, para 5.1.
1 Plans Regs, regs 3(1), 43.
2 Plans Regs, reg 46(3).
3 The phrase 'structure plan proposals' is used here and in the following pages to describe proposals for the alteration, or repeal and replacement, of a structure plan. The author acknowledges its source in the Department of Environment's booklet 'Structure plans: the examination in public.'

submitting the plan to the Secretary of State and for obtaining his approval is a lengthy one and is designed, inter alia, to give the public an opportunity of commenting upon the structure plan whilst it is still at a formative stage and before it is sent to the Secretary of State.

The main steps in this procedure are to be found in the Act of 1990 and in the Plans Regulations. They may be summarised as follows:

(1) Before finally determining the content of the structure plan proposals, the local planning authority must consult with district councils,[4] and they are asked to consult such other authorities and bodies as are considered appropriate.[5] District councils must be given reasonable opportunity to express their views and the local planning authority must consider any such views;[6] where other authorities and bodies are consulted, it is implicit that they should be allowed reasonable opportunity to express their views and that their views will be considered.

(2) During this formative stage the local planning authority must also ensure that adequate publicity is given to the matters which they intend to include in the structure plan proposals and to the proposed content of the explanatory memorandum. In addition they must consider what persons, or groups, are likely to want to make representations with regard to these matters and ensure that they are made aware of their right to do so. The local planning authority must allow a period of at least six weeks[7] for representations to them and they must consider any representations which are received within that time.[8] The Secretary of State has power to make regulations prescribing the detailed procedure for publicity and public participation,[9] but he has said that he prefers to rely mostly on advice rather than statutory control in this regard.[10]

(3) The local planning authority will then be in a position to determine the content of the structure plan proposals and to submit them together with the explanatory memorandum to the Secretary of State. When submitting the proposals to the Secretary of State, the local planning authority should indicate what steps they have taken to comply with the provisions for public participation as mentioned above. If the Secretary of State is satisfied on this point he will proceed to consider the structure plan proposals; but, if he is not satisfied

4 Plans Regs, reg 6.
5 Memorandum on Structure and Local Plans, para 2.27.
6 Plans Regs, reg 6.
7 Plans Regs, reg 5.
8 1990 Act, s. 33(1), (2).
9 Ibid, s. 53.
10 Circular 44/71, para 54.

he must return the proposals to the local planning authority with directions for ensuring proper publicity and consideration of representations.[11]

(4) Not later than the date on which the proposals and explanatory memorandum are submitted to the Secretary of State the local planning authority are to make copies of these documents available for inspection at various places and each copy is to be accompanied by a statement of the time within which objections to the proposals may be sent to the Secretary of State.[12]

PROCEDURE (B): EXAMINATION IN PUBLIC

When the time for submitting objections has elapsed, the Secretary of State can begin his consideration of the structure plan proposals. He is empowered to reject the proposals without formally considering the objections or holding the examination in public referred to below.[13] This is a useful time-saving provision, although it will probably not be invoked often.

If the Secretary of State does not reject the proposals at this early stage, he must consider any objections which have been received and which have not been withdrawn.

At one time, the Secretary of State had to give each objector an opportunity of being heard at a public local inquiry or other hearing, but this requirement was abolished in 1972. Since then, it has been the duty of the Secretary of State, first, to consider any objections so far as made in accordance with the Plans Regulations; secondly, to hold an examination in public of those matters which he considers should be examined in public:[14] 'The proceedings are thus designed to put more emphasis on a broad examination of strategic issues while not excluding a consideration of detailed objections.'[15] The Secretary of State may, however, dispense with an examination in public into proposals for the alteration or repeal and replacement of a structure plan if he considers that there are no issues which require examination in public.[16]

No authority or person – not even the local planning authority which prepared the proposals – will have any right to be heard at an

---

11 1990 Act, s. 33(6)–(10).
12 Plans Regs, reg 16.
13 1990 Act, s. 35(3).
14 Ibid, s. 35(3).
15 325 HL Official Report (5th series) col 762.
16 1990 Act, s. 35(4).

examination in public.[17] It is difficult to see how in practice there could be any effective examination of the strategic issues if the planning authority were not represented, and in fact they are always invited to appear; but it is perhaps worth saying that the authority are there to discuss the issues selected by the Secretary of State which are not necessarily those which they would have chosen. Moreover the Secretary of State may, and in practice does, invite objectors where their case may assist him in the examination of the plan. Indeed, in the debates on the Bill for the Act of 1972, a Government spokesman went so far as to say:

> the objections and the grounds for them will clearly be very material in the Secretary of State's consideration of which are the key issues to be examined in public and of those who would take part in the examination.[18]

The Secretary of State has power in consultation with the Lord Chancellor to make regulations with regard to the procedure to be followed at the examination in public.[19] The Secretary of State has, however, chosen not to make regulations at least for the time being. He has instead issued codes of practice.[20] This code of practice has no statutory force so that the Secretary of State is free to change the procedures from time to time without the necessity of making new regulations. There is probably little harm in that.

The 'examination in public' is a novel device in planning law, and it is very different from the traditional form of public inquiry. The Secretary of State's present code of practice states that it 'will normally be conducted by a small panel ... consisting of an independent Chairman and one or two other members'.[1] Where there are two, one will have recent experience in the regional office of a government department although it is not his role to advocate changes in the submitted proposals on behalf of that department. The other member would be a planning inspector from the Department. More significantly, perhaps, the code of practice indicates that the 'examination' should take the form of a 'probing discussion'.

In other words the examination is more inquisitorial in character, that is, the person or persons conducting the examination take the

---

17 1990 Act, s. 35(6).
18 326 HL Official Report (5th series) col 746.
19 1990 Act, s. 35(5).
20 The first such code of practice was issued in 1973. This has now been replaced by 'Structure plans: The examination in public. A guide to procedure 1984.'
 1 The independent chairman has so far been drawn from ranks of QCs versed in planning matters, retired civil servants from the Department of the Environment, retired county clerks, and in one case a professor of economics.

lead in questioning witnesses instead of leaving it in the main to examination and cross-examination by opposing advocates.

Naturally, there has been concern over the fact that objectors will have no statutory right to be heard in public. The question is whether this will in practice seriously affect landowners and such bodies as amenity societies. Land allocations and site definitions are not the concern of structure plans but of the local plans, and objectors will have a statutory right to appear at local plan inquiries.[2] But the policies laid down in the approved structure plan will in many cases effectively determine land allocations; for instance once it is decided as a matter of structure plan policy that there should be a green belt for a certain town, the issues at the local plan inquiry will be marginal ones affecting the precise boundary.

However, the new procedure has compensating advantages if it significantly shortens the period between the submission of the structure plan proposals and their approval by the Secretary of State. In particular, the public discussion of alternative strategies and the lack of precise definition in the structure plan may seriously increase the risk of planning blight with subsequent hardship to property owners; the sooner planning authorities can get ahead with the making or amendment of local plans, the quicker the uncertainties will be removed.

PROCEDURE (C): FINAL STAGES

The person or persons who have conducted the examination in public will report to the Secretary of State, who will then be able to come to a decision. In so doing, he is entitled to take into account any matters which he thinks are relevant,[3] and he may consult the local planning authority or any other person, without apparently being obliged to do so; this represents a departure for reasons of practical convenience from the rules of natural justice and would not be permitted in the absence of statutory provision.[4]

The Secretary of State may approve the structure plan proposals with or without modifications or reservations, or he may reject it;[5] he must give reasons for his decision.[6] If he proposes to modify the plan

---

2 See below.
3 1990 Act, s. 35(2).
4 Ibid, s. 35(9).
5 Ibid, s. 35(1).
6 Ibid, s. 35(10).

in any material respect, he must give notice accordingly and consider any objections which are then made.[7]

When the Secretary of State has approved the structure plan proposals, public notice will be given in the prescribed manner and arrangements will be made for enabling the public to inspect or purchase copies of the plan.[8]

The Secretary of State's decision on the structure plan proposals is final, except for a limited right of appeal in the High Court on matters of law or procedure.[9]

Local plans

The structure plan will be supplemented by a number of local plans which elaborate in more detail the broad policies and proposals set out in the structure plan. It follows of course that the local plans must be in conformity with the structure plan; where a local plan is prepared by a district council, they must obtain from the county planning authority a certificate of conformity before placing the draft plan on deposit for public inspection.[10] It may happen that the county planning authority is putting forward a proposal for amending or replacing the approved structure plan; this does not, however, preclude the preparation of a local plan in draft and the carrying out of public participation exercises before the structure plan revisions have been approved. In exceptional cases, the Secretary of State may authorise the local planning authority to go through the statutory processes leading to the formal adoption of the plan before the structure plan revisions are approved.[11]

Local plans will usually be made by the district planning authority, but some will be made by the county planning authority. It was originally the duty of the county planning authority, in consultation with the district planning authorities, to make a 'development plan scheme'. This scheme designated the authorities (whether county or district) by whom the local plans for each area are to be prepared; it specified the title and nature of each local plan, set out a programme for the preparation of the local plans, and specified those which should be prepared concurrently with the structure plan. However, to the extent that provision was not made to the contrary by the development

7 Plans Regs, reg 21.
8 1990 Act, s. 53(2)(g); Plans Regs, regs 22, 40, 41.
9 1990 Act, s. 287.
10 Ibid, s. 46(2).
11 Ibid, s. 47(2).

plan scheme, the structure plan might provide for the making of local plans by the county planning authority. As a result of the 1986 Act the development plan scheme is now replaced by a local plan scheme; this is similar to the development plan scheme but need not set out a programme or specify those plans which should be prepared concurrently with the structure plan.[12] If the district planning authority are dissatisfied with the proposals of the county planning authority, they may make representations to the Secretary of State who may amend the scheme.[13] The local plan scheme is to be kept under review and may therefore be amended.[14]

A local plan may cover any part, however small, of the local planning authority's area, but there is no requirement in either the Act of 1990 or the Plans Regulations that the whole of the county should be covered by local plans. Local plans serve a variety of purposes, and different plans may be made for different purposes for the same part of any area.[15] Until 1982 the statutory regulations relating to local plans classified local plans under three headings: district plans, action area plans and subject plans. The Plans Regulations now in force make no reference to district plans as such, but general plans for a district as a whole remain of fundamental importance; it appears to be the wish of the Secretary of State that local planning matters should as far as practicable be dealt with in general plans.[16]

General (or district) plans   A general (or district) plan may be defined as a plan based on a comprehensive consideration of matters affecting the development and other use of land in a particular area (other than an action area).[17] These general plans differ from action area plans in that they will usually cover a relatively large area and will deal with development which is likely to occur as a result of individual initiatives over a fairly long period of time. These plans provide the background for regulatory rather than positive planning.

Action area plans   An action area is one which has been selected for comprehensive treatment in the comparatively near future by means either of development, re-development or improvement or by a

---

12 See now 1990 Act, s. 37.
13 Ibid, s. 37(6).
14 Ibid, s. 37(3)–(5).
15 1990 Act, s. 36(2).
16 Planning Policy Guidance Note No 11, Appendix B, para 5.
17 This definition is in effect the same as the statutory definition of district plans in the pre-1982 Regs referred to above.

combination of these methods.[18] The concept of the action area is thus wider than that of the areas of comprehensive development under the earlier legislation. In particular the reference to 'improvement' in the definition of action areas indicates a type of activity not mentioned in the definition of areas of comprehensive development: this is no doubt a reflection on the greater emphasis placed nowadays on conservation and on improvement rather than on wholesale clearance and re-development – a change of emphasis also seen in housing legislation.

Until 1980, an action area originated by way of a proposal in the structure plan, and the Secretary of State would give his approval only on the basis that it was intended that treatment of the area by development, re-development or improvement should commence within ten years of the date on which the structure plan had been submitted to the Secretary of State. Since 1980 the local planning authority have been able to make an action area plan without a formal proposal to that effect in the structure plan; the proposed action area plan must of course be consistent with the general policies and proposals of the structure plan, and the local planning authority must intend that the treatment of the area should commence within the maximum period as prescribed in the Plans Regulations.[19]

Action area treatment may well involve substantial compulsory purchases by the local planning authority. The compulsory purchase orders will require confirmation of the Secretary of State but such orders are made under section 226 or 228 of the Act of 1990[1] and he may disregard any objection which is in effect an objection to the action area plan.[2] The fact that land is in an action area may affect the amount of compensation payable on compulsory purchase.[3]

Subject plans These are designed to enable detailed treatment to be given to particular aspects of planning, and each such plan will take the name of the subject with which it deals.[4]

Subject plans are likely to be required for a number of reasons. First, they may be required to define areas in which particular policies apply such as green belts; or where particular legal and administrative procedures apply or where special grant aid may be available such as conservation areas. Secondly, subject plans will be required to define,

---

18 1990 Act, s. 36(4), (5).
19 The prescribed period is ten years from the date on which the action area plan is placed on deposit: Plans Regs, reg 14 as amended by SI 1987 No 1760.
 1 See pp. 74, 75 below.
 2 1990 Act, s. 245(1).
 3 See the assumptions as to the availability of planning permission on valuation for compulsory purchase in the Land Compensation Act 1961, s. 16.
 4 Plans Regs, reg 11.

for the purpose of s. 232 of the Highways Act 1980, land required for proposed roads or for widening certain existing roads. Thirdly, subject plans will be useful for showing particular planning matters in areas in which there is no immediate need for either a district or action area plan. Such matters may well include mineral workings, reclamation of derelict land, recreation in a river valley or country park.

FORM AND CONTENT OF LOCAL PLANS

Local plans may, therefore, be very different in character, but the Act of 1990 and the Plans Regulations contain certain basic directions, which may be summarised as follows:

(1) A local plan is to consist of a map – called the 'proposals map' – and a written statement. The proposals map is to be prepared on an ordnance survey map base; no scale is prescribed – except for street authorisation maps which are to be scale of not less than 1/2500 – and, indeed, different scale maps may be appropriate for different plans.[5] The requirement that a local plan shall include a scale map is in contrast with the provisions as to structure plans described above.[6]

(2) The plan is to formulate, in such detail as may be considered appropriate, the local planning authority's proposals for the development, or other use of land in the area covered; alternatively, it may show the authority's proposals for any particular class of development or land use in that area. Special emphasis is laid upon measures for improving the physical environment and the management of traffic.[7] The proposals may be either site specific or more in the nature of policy statements, as may be seen from the following examples:[8]

18 hectares of land will be developed for industry and/or warehousing over and above that already with planning permission for such, including
(a) 5.3 hectares south of Watnall Road (adjacent Rolls Royce Testing Beds),
(b) 0.6 hectares beside the Ambulance Station, Watnall Road,
(c) 2.0 hectares at the junction of Watnall Road and the proposed outer by-pass, and
(d) 9.6 hectares to the south of Wigwam Lane.

Planning applications for light industry will be favourably considered on small sites and in existing buildings within Hucknall where appropriate, especially where this provides an opportunity for smaller firms to develop, subject to development control considerations.

5 1990 Act, s. 36(1); Plans Regs, reg 13.
6 See p. 55 above.
7 1990 Act, s. 36(1).
8 Hucknall (Nottinghamshire) District Plan.

(3) The written statement is to contain a reasoned justification of the proposals contained therein,[9] and it should show what regard the local planning authority have had, inter alia, to economic, social and other relevant considerations;[10] other relevant considerations will no doubt include the resources likely to be available for carrying out the proposals.

(4) The plan will be accompanied by such diagrams, illustrations and descriptive matter as the local planning authority consider appropriate.[11]

(5) In drawing up a local plan, the local planning authority must see that it conforms to the structure plan, and they are to have regard to any information and any other considerations which may appear to them to be relevant or which they are required by the Secretary of State to take into account.[12]

As we have seen earlier in this chapter,[13] the House of Lords held in *Great Portland Estates v City of Westminster*[14] that the proposals and policies in a local plan must serve planning purposes, that is, they must relate to the character and use of the land. In that case Great Portland Estates challenged the policies for office development in the district plan as well as the industrial policies mentioned earlier. The plan stated that outside the 'central activities zone' planning permission for office development would not normally be granted except in special circumstances; these special circumstances were to be dealt with by non-statutory guidance for different locations in the city.

The House of Lords quashed the relevant paragraphs in the plan. Lord Scarman said that a reference in a plan to exceptional or special circumstances was not improper, though strictly it was never necessary. But in this case the council had spoken of its non-statutory policies, and some paragraphs in the non-statutory guidelines did indeed contain matters of policy. It was the duty of the council under the Act of 1971[15] to formulate in the plan its development and land use proposals. It deliberately omitted some. There was therefore a failure on the part of the council to meet the requirement of the Act. By excluding from the plan its proposals in respect of office development outside the central activities zone, the council deprived persons such as Great Portland Estates from raising objections and securing a public inquiry.

---

9 Plans Regs, reg 12(2).
10 Planning Policy Guidance Note No 12, Appendix B, para 4.
11 1990 Act, s. 36(1).
12 Ibid, ss. 36(3), 46(1).
13 See pp. 52, 53, above.
14 [1984] 3 All ER 744, [1984] 3 WLR 1035.
15 This duty is re-enacted in the Act of 1990.

PROCEDURE FOR LOCAL PLANS

In most cases a local plan will not require the Secretary of State's approval, but he has discretion to call in any local plan for his approval. Nevertheless, in each case the local planning authority must adhere to the procedure laid down by the Act of 1990. This procedure is in many (though not all) respects similar to that for structure plans and may be summarised as follows:

(1) The local planning authority must ensure that adequate publicity is given to the matters to be included in the local plan. In addition, they must consider what persons or groups are likely to want to make representations with regard to the draft plan and ensure that they are made aware of their right to do so. The authority must allow proper time for representations to be made to them and they must consider any representations which are received within that time.[16] Where the plan is being made by a district council, they must consult the county council; a county council making a plan must consult the district councils affected.[17] The preliminary procedures for public consultation may be omitted in the case of proposals for alterations or for the replacement of an existing local plan if the local planning authority consider that the issues involved are not of sufficient importance to warrant the full procedure.[18]

(2) The local planning authority will then be able to prepare the first draft of the plan. Having done so, they must send a copy to the Secretary of State together with a statement of the steps which they have taken to comply with paragraph 1 above; and, if the Secretary of State is not satisfied on this point, he may give directions to the authority.[19]

(3) At the same time, the local planning authority must make copies of the plan available for public inspection, indicating the time within which objections may be made to the local planning authority.[20]

(4) Subject to the Secretary of State's power to call in the plan for his approval, the local planning authority will then have to consider the objections. The local planning authority must arrange for a local inquiry or other hearing into objections which have been submitted in the prescribed manner unless all the objectors have indicated in

---

16 Act of 1990, s. 39. This requirement for public participation may be omitted if the local planning authority consider it unnecessary having regard to the issues involved: ibid, s. 40.
17 Ibid, s. 39(4).
18 Ibid, s. 40(1).
19 Ibid, s. 41.
20 Ibid, s. 39(5), (6).

writing that they do not wish to appear; where objections have not been submitted in the prescibed manner, it seems that the authority will have a discretion whether or not to hold an inquiry.[1] If an inquiry or other hearing is held the inspector will in some cases be appointed by the Secretary of State; in other cases he will be appointed by the authority, but regulations may be made governing the authority's choice of inspector.[2]

(5) The inspector will report to the local planning authority. The report will be published and the authority must give due weight to the inspector's report and each separate recommendation in their consideration of the objections. They must then prepare and publish a statement of their decisions with reasons.[3] These reasons must be proper, adequate and intelligible, although they can be brief.[4]

(6) The local planning authority may then proceed to adopt the plan, either as originally prepared or as modified to take account of objections. If the authority decide to modify the plan, they must give public notice of their intentions and give an opportunity for objections.[5] There is, however, special provision for the protection of agricultural lands in that if the Minister of Agriculture has objected to the plan and the local planning authority do not propose to modify the plan to take account of the objection, the local planning authority must not adopt the plan unless the Secretary of State authorises them to do so.[6]

(7) The authority's decision is final except that there is a limited right of appeal to the High Court on matters of law and procedure.[7] Some plans have recently been challenged in this way.[8]

There has been some criticism of the procedure for dealing with objections on the ground that the local authority will be 'judge in their own cause'.[9] Although this phrase is not wholly appropriate to what is essentially an administrative procedure, there is some force in the criticism. There is a risk, once they have determined on a particular

---

1 1990 Act, s. 42(1), (2).
2 Ibid, s. 42(3), (4).
3 Ibid, s. 42(6).
4 *Great Portland Estates v City of Westminster* [1985] AC 661, [1984] 3 All ER 744.
5 Plans Reg, reg 31.
6 1990 Act, s. 43(6). It seems that the Secretary of State can authorise the adoption of the plan only if the Minister of Agriculture withdraws his objection; if not, the Secretary of State must call in the local plan: s. 44(3).
7 1990 Act, s. 287.
8 See e g the references at pp. 52, 53 above to *Great Portland Estates v City of Westminster* [1985] AC 661, [1984] 3 All ER 744.
9 See e g letter published in [1987] JPL 277; this letter includes a reference to a comment by Woolf J in *Baptist Union Corpn v Secretary of State for the Environment and St Alban's District Council* [1986] JPL 906.

course of action, the authority will close their minds to possible alternatives as suggested by the objectors or as recommended by the inspector; and, even where the authority have in fact given full consideration to possible alternatives, the public may not feel confident that this has been done. There are, however, safeguards. The Secretary of State can call in the plan at any time before the authority formally adopt it,[10] and where it is left to the authority to decide whether or not to adopt the plan, objectors may require the authority to state their reasons for doing so;[11] there is also the duty referred to above to publish a statement of their decisions on the various objections.

CALLING IN BY SECRETARY OF STATE

The Secretary of State may call in a local plan for his own approval at any time after the substantive draft has been sent to him and before it is adopted;[12] and where there is an outstanding objection by the Minister of Agriculture the Secretary of State must call in the plan.[13] Where a local plan is called in the Secretary of State must consider any objections which have been made in the prescribed manner and give objectors the opportunity to be heard at public local inquiry; he need not take these steps if the local planning authority had done so prior to the plan being called in.[14] The Secretary of State may approve the plan in whole or in part and with or without modifications or he may reject it; if he proposes to modify it he must give public notice of his intentions and allow time for objections.[15]

Unitary development plans

In Greater London and the six metropolitan counties structure and local plans are to be replaced by unitary development plans. Each local planning authority – that is in Greater London each of the 33 London borough councils[16] and in the metropolitan counties each

10 1990 Act, s. 44.
11 Tribunals and Inquiries Act 1971, s. 12; 1990 Act, s. 42(6).
12 1990 Act, s. 44. The Secretary of State has stated that this power 'will only be used in a limited range of circumstances where Central Government intervention is clearly justified': circular 22/84, 'Memorandum on Structure and Local Plans', para 3.81.
13 See fn 6 above.
14 1990 Act, s. 45(3).
15 Plans Regs, reg 34.
16 Including for this purpose the Common Council of the City of London: 1990 Act, s. 336(1).

of the 36 metropolitan district councils – is to prepare a unitary development plan.[17] The plan will be in two Parts:[18]

(a) Part I consisting of a written statement formulating the authority's general policies in respect of the development and other use of land in their area (including measures for the improvement of the physical environment and the management of traffic).

(b) Part II consisting of:
   (i) a written statement in such detail as considered appropriate (and so as to be readily distinguishable from other contents of the plan) of their proposals for the development and other use of land in their area or for any description of development or other use of such lands;
   (ii) a map showing these proposals on a geographical basis;
   (iii) a reasoned justification of the general policies in Part I and of the proposals in Part II;
   (iv) such diagrams etc as the authority think appropriate or the Secretary of State may prescribe.

The Secretary of State may prescribe other matters to be included in the plan.[19] In preparing Part I, the local planning authority must have regard to any 'strategic guidance' given by the Secretary of State, to current national and regional policies, resources likely to be available and such other matters as the Secretary of State may direct.[20]

Action areas may be designated in Part II and in that case a description must be given of the treatment proposed.[1]

Part I of a unitary development plan will thus be very similar to the structure plan for a non-metropolitan county. It seems that Part II will consist of a number of separate parts each similar in effect to a local plan. Although the structural and local elements will thus be included in a single unitary plan, it will not be necessary to defer publication and adoption of a unitary plan until every locality has been considered in detail; additional 'parts' can be added from time to time.

Two or more local planning authorities in Greater London or a metropolitan county may together prepare a joint unitary development plan;[2] this may be useful where two or more districts form a solid urban mass.

Although Part I of a unitary development plan will be the equivalent of a structure plan, a unitary development plan will not nor-

17 1990 Act, s. 12(1).
18 Ibid, s. 12(2).
19 Ibid, s. 12(3), (4).
20 Ibid, s. 12(6). See the discussion on some of these matters at pp. 51, 52 above.
 1 Ibid, s. 12(8). For action areas generally see pp. 62, 63, above.
 2 Ibid, s. 23.

mally be submitted to the Secretary of State for approval; but he has power to call in for approval either the whole or any part of such a plan; where there is an outstanding objection by the Ministry of Agriculture to a proposal affecting agricultural land he must call in the relevant part of the plan.[3]

It is the intention that unitary development plans be kept under review and proposals for the alteration or replacement of such a plan may be made at any time.[4]

THE SURVEY

As with structure and local plans, a unitary development plan must be based on a survey of physical and social conditions and other factors. The local planning authorities concerned with the preparation of unitary development plans will have inherited survey material from the former county authorities; the authorities now concerned are required to keep under review the matters likely to affect the development of their areas and may, if they think fit, institute fresh surveys.[5]

PROCEDURES

When preparing a unitary development plan the local planning authority must give adequate publicity to the matters which they propose to include in the plan and provide opportunities for public participation similar to those required in connection with structure and local plans.[6] Having considered any representations made to them by local organisations or members of the public the authority can then prepare the substantive draft plan.

The authority must then send a copy of the draft plan to the Secretary of State together with a statement of the steps which they have taken to comply with the requirements about public participation; if the Secretary of State is not satisfied with this statement he can issue directions to the local planning authority.[7]

At the same time, the authority must make copies of the plan available for public inspection indicating time within which objections may be made to the local planning authority.[8]

Subject to the Secretary of State's power to call in the plan for his

3 See p. 71, below.
4 1990 Act, s. 21.
5 Ibid, s. 11.
6 Ibid, s. 13(1), (2).
7 Ibid, s. 13(3)–(7).
8 Ibid, s. 13(3).

own consideration, it will fall to the local planning authority to consider the objections and for this purpose they must arrange for a local inquiry or other hearing at which objectors will have the right to appear.[9]

It is of course implicit that the local planning authority give proper consideration to any recommendations made by the Inspector, and they are expressly required to give reasons for their decisions.[10] There is special provision for the protection of agricultural land in that, if the Ministry of Agriculture have objected to the plan and the local planning authority do not propose to modify the plan to take account of the objection, the authority must notify the Secretary of State and must not adopt the plan unless he authorises them to do so.[11]

CALLING IN BY SECRETARY OF STATE

The Secretary of State may call in the whole or any part of a unitary development plan at any time after a copy of the substantive draft has been sent to him and before it is adopted. Moreover, where there is an outstanding objection by the Ministry of Agriculture, the Secretary of State must call in the relevant part of the plan.[12]

Where a unitary development plan or any part of it is called in the Secretary of State must consider any objections which have been made in the proper manner; he need not do so, however, if the local planning authority have already done so.[13] The detailed procedures, however, will depend on the circumstances.

(1) If the whole of the plan, or the whole or part of Part II of the plan, has been called in the Secretary of State must cause a local inquiry or other hearing to be held into the objections unless the local planning authority have already done so.[14] It is the intention that every objector shall have the right to be heard at such inquiry or hearing.

(2) If what is called in relates only to Part I of the plan, the Secretary of State may decide to have an 'examination in public'[15] into those matters which he considers should be examined in public.[16] At an examination in public only those persons invited by the

9 1990 Act, ss. 15(1), 16.
10 Tribunals and Inquiries Act 1971 s. 12; 1990 Act, s. 16(3).
11 1990 Act, s. 15(3).
12 Ibid, s. 18.
13 Ibid, s. 20(1).
14 Ibid, s. 20(2), (3).
15 As to the nature of an examination in public, see pp. 58–60, above.
16 1990 Act, s. 20(4)–(7).

Secretary of State (or by the panel of examiners) will be permitted to participate.

The Secretary of State may approve the plan, or the part which has been called in, in whole or in part and with or without modifications or reject it. Where what has been called in relates only to Part I of the plan, and the Secretary of State approves it with modifications he may direct the local planning authority to make modifications in Part II.[17]

Development plans: legal effect and implementation

The transition from the old-style development plans to the new system of structure and local plans has been lengthy; although the structure plans have been approved for England and Wales outside Greater London and the metropolitan counties, there are still many areas in which local plans are not yet in force. In Greater London and the metropolitan counties further change is under way with the introduction of unitary plans. The precise meaning of the phrase 'the development plan' as it appears in many sections of the Act of 1990 and other legislation will therefore vary from one area to another.

In England and Wales outside Greater London and the metropolitan counties 'the development plan' is to be taken as consisting of:[18]

(a) the structure plan in force for the time being together with the Secretary of State's notice of approval;

(b) any alterations in the structure plan together with the Secretary of State's notices of approval of the alterations;

(c) any local plan applicable to the district with a copy of the local planning authority's resolution of adoption (or the Secretary of State's notice of approval);

(d) any alteration to the local plan together with the resolution of adoption (or the notice of approval).

This does not, however, mean the final disappearance of the old-style development plan. It remains in force so far as it does not conflict with the structure plans and any local plans which have come into force, but the Secretary of State can expressly revoke the old-style development plan at any time.[19] These provisions for prolonging the life of the old development plan appear to be necessitated by the fact

17 1990 Act, s. 19.
18 Ibid, s. 54.
19 Ibid, Sch 2, Part III.

that in some parts of the area covered by the structure plan it may be several years before a comprehensive set of local plans is built up.

With the coming into force of unitary development plans in Greater London and the metropolitan counties, 'the development plan' for any area will consist of:

(a) the provisions of the unitary development plan in force for that area (or the relevant part of the plan) together with the local planning authority's resolution of adoption or the Secretary of State's notice of approval as the case may be;

(b) any alteration to the plan together with the resolution of adoption (or the notice of approval).[20]

Here again, there are transitional provisions preserving the effect of structure plans[1] and of local plans and old development plans pending the approval of the unitary plan.[2]

The development plan does not confer any right of development. A developer wishing, say, to build houses in an area zoned for residential development must apply for planning permission even though his proposal accords with the provisions of the plan, and there may be various reasons why permission should be refused, e g density, design, access. And although permission will probably be refused for development which does not accord with the plan, there may be good reasons why such development should be permitted. In short, the provisions of the development plan are not the only factor which the local planning authority should take into account in deciding upon an application for planning permission.[3]

Certain specific consequences, however, may result from the development plan, namely:

(1) Where it is proposed that land should be acquired by compulsory purchase under section 226 or 228 of the Act of 1990,[4] the Secretary of State may disregard any objection to a compulsory purchase order which amounts to an objection to the plan itself.[5]

(2) Where land is rendered unsaleable except at a greatly reduced price by reason of some provision of the development plan, an owner-occupier may be able to serve a purchase notice on the appropriate public authority.[6]

(3) The programming in the development plan may affect the

20 1990 Act, s. 27.
1 In Greater London, the Greater London Development Plan.
2 1990 Act, Sch 2, Parts I, II and III.
3 See ch 7, below.
4 See pp. 74, 75, below.
5 1990 Act, s. 245(1).
6 See ch 12, below.

right to compensation for refusal of planning permission under Part V of the 1990 Act.[7]

(4) The provisions of the development plan may materially affect the amount of compensation obtainable on compulsory purchase.[8]

Before 1974 the grant of working rights to mineral development under the Mines (Working Facilities and Support) Act 1966 was facilitated where the development plan provided that the land was to be used for the winning and working of minerals. This is no longer the law.[9]

COMPULSORY PURCHASE FOR PLANNING PURPOSES

The implementation of the development plan will in some cases depend upon the use of the powers of compulsory purchase for planning purposes contained in the Act of 1990. These powers are likely to be used mainly in connection with action areas, but are available for other purposes as well.

Section 226(1) of the Act of 1990 provides that a local authority may compulsorily purchase any land in their area:

(a) which is suitable for and is required in order to secure the carrying out of development, re-development or improvement;

(b) which is required for a purpose which it is necessary to achieve for the proper planning of the area in which the land is situated.

Where land is acquired under either of these paragraphs, the local authority may also compulsorily purchase (i) any adjoining land which is required for executing works to facilitate the development or use of the land which is the main subject of the compulsory purchase; (ii) to replace common land and certain other special categories of land.[10]

It will be seen that where it is proposed to acquire land under paragraph (a) above, it must be shown that the land is suitable for, as well as being required for, development, re-development or improvement. In determining the 'suitability' of the land for these purposes, regard is to be had to the following matters:[11]

(a) the provisions of the development plan;[12]

(b) whether planning permission for any development on that land is in force;

---

7 See ch 21, below.
8 See Land Compensation Act 1961, s. 16.
9 The matter is further explained in ch 15, below at pp. 284, 285.
10 1990 Act, s. 226(3).
11 Ibid, s. 226(2).
12 For the meaning of 'development plan' for this purpose, see pp. 72, 73, above.

(c) any other considerations which would be material in deciding an application for planning permission in respect of that land.[13]

Section 113 enables the Secretary of State to acquire compulsorily any land necessary for the public service.

Where land is acquired under section 226 the authority may themselves develop the land (eg by erecting buildings to let) or they may sell or lease the land for private development.[14]

There is an important provision in section 233(5)–(7) of the Act of 1990. If the authority dispose of any land acquired under section 226(1)(a), they are to have regard to the needs of persons who were living or carrying on business or other activities in the area. So far as may be practicable, any such person is to be given the opportunity to obtain accommodation in the area on terms which have regard to the price at which his property was acquired from him.[15] It does not in terms impose on the local planning authority an obligation to have regard to the possible requirements of displaced residents when drawing up their plans for the development of the area. If they have not done so, it may happen that the authority find that they cannot give the persons concerned an opportunity to acquire accommodation in the area on favourable terms.

The effect of section 233(5) is further limited in that it does not apply where the authority develop the land themselves or retain it for any other purpose.[16] Under the general law of compulsory purchase, suitable alternative accommodation must be offered to any person who is displaced from residential accommodation in consequence of acquisition by an authority possessing compulsory powers.[17] Such accommodation, however, will not necessarily be in the same area.

As regards business premises, it seems that the Secretary of State – or any other relevant Minister of the Crown – in deciding whether or not to confirm a compulsory purchase order should give due weight to objections made on the ground that it would be difficult for the occupier to find suitable alternative accommodation.[18]

---

13 For a consideration of what are material considerations in deciding upon applications for planning permission, see ch 7, pp. 143 ff, below.

14 1990 Act, ss. 233, 235. The Secretary of State's consent will be necessary if the land is not being disposed of at the best price or rent obtainable: s. 233(3).

15 The effect of the corresponding provisions of the 1962 Act was considered in *A Crabtree & Co Ltd v Minister of Housing and Local Government* (1965) 17 P & CR 232.

16 *AB Motor Co of Hull Ltd v Minister of Housing and Local Government* (1969) 211 Estates Gazette 289.

17 Land Compensation Act 1973, s. 39.

18 *CD Brinklow and Croft Bros (Sandon) Ltd v Secretary of State for the Environment* [1976] JPL 299.

Chapter 5

Definition of development

The whole system of planning control in this country depends on the definition of development. If a particular operation or change of use involves development as defined in the Act of 1990, it will (with a few exceptions)[1] require planning permission. If, however, the operation or change of use does not involve development, no planning permission is required.

For the purpose of the Planning Acts, development is defined[2] 'as the carrying out of building, engineering, mining or other operations in, on, over or under land, or the making of any material change in the use of any building or other land'.

Operations

It will be seen that there are two 'legs' to this definition of development – 'operations' and 'uses'. It is important to grasp the distinction between the two. The essence of an 'operation' was explained by Lord Parker C J in *Cheshire County Council v Woodward*;[3] it is some act which changes the physical characteristics of the land, or of what is under it, or of the air above it. 'Use' refers to the purpose to which land or buildings are devoted. The difference between the two concepts has been explained by Lord Denning as follows:

> it seems to me that the first half 'operations' comprises activities which result in some physical alteration to the land which has some degree of permanence in relation to the land itself – whereas the second half, 'use', comprises activities which are done in, alongside or on the land, but do not interefere with the actual physical characteristics of the land.[4]

Unless the context otherwise requires, the word 'use' does not

1 See ch 6, pp. 114, 115, below.
2 1990 Act, s. 55(1).
3 [1962] 2 QB 126, [1962] 1 All ER 517.
4 *Parkes v Secretary of State for the Environment* [1978] 1 WLR 1308 at 1311.

include the carrying out of building or other operations.[5] It follows
that permission for the use of land for a particular purpose does not
confer the right to erect buildings for that purpose. The point is
illustrated by the case of *Sunbury-on-Thames UDC v Mann*.[6]

> Mann had been granted permission for the continued use of certain land
> and buildings as a yard, workshop and stores until 30 October 1957. In
> May 1957, he erected a new building on the site for use in connection with
> the maintenance and repair of engineering equipment. The council served
> an enforcement notice requiring the building to be pulled down.
>
> Mann claimed that the erection of the building was permitted by what
> was then Class IV (1) of the First Schedule in the General Development
> Order, which permits the erection of buildings required in connection with
> building operations on adjoining land. Held, as Mann had permission only
> for the *use* of the land, he could not bring himself within Class IV (1) which
> refers to *operations*.

BUILDING OPERATIONS

For most purposes of the Act of 1990, the word 'building' *includes* 'any
structure or erection and any part of a building so defined, but does
not include plant or machinery comprised in a building'.[7] The use of
the word 'includes' shows that this is not intended to be a complete
definition. Its effect is to extend the ordinary meaning of the word
'building' to include structures which would not normally be regarded
as buildings such as walls, fences, hoarding, masts. Machinery in the
open will be a 'building' for the purposes of the Act of 1990 so that
its erection will be development, but not if housed in a building.

In *Buckingham County Council v Callingham*[8] it was held that a model
village of buildings constructed to scale was a structure or erection
and therefore subject to planning control. In *Cooper v Bailey*[9] the
question was whether advertisements displayed at a garage were
erected on a 'building'. The garage consisted of a central building
and petrol pumps with two walls on either side running from the
building in a curve towards the road; in front of the walls was a kerb
marking the limits of the pull-in. Some advertisement signs were fixed
to the kerb or displayed on the concrete between the kerb and the
wall. It was held that these advertisements were displayed on part of
the building or structure of the garage.

5 1990 Act, s. 336(1).
6 (1958) 9 P & CR 309.
7 1990 Act, s. 336(1).
8 [1952] 2 QB 515, [1952] 1 All ER 1166.
9 (1956) 6 P & CR 261.

It does not follow, however, that anything placed on land is to be treated as a building. Things like caravans and vending machines, which are comparatively easy to move, are not normally regarded as buildings for the purposes of planning control.[10] And in *Cheshire County Council v Woodward*[11] the Divisional Court held that the Minister was quite entitled to find that the installation of a coal hopper some 16 to 20 feet high and a conveyor was not development.

There is apparently no simple test for determining whether some object or installation is a 'building' In *Cheshire County Council v Woodward*[12] Lord Parker CJ drew an analogy with the problem frequently encountered in real property law of deciding what fixtures pass with the freehold, and concluded 'the Act is referring to any structure or erection which may be said to form part of the realty and to change the physical character of the land'. But in *Barvis Ltd v Secretary of State for the Environment*[13] the Divisional Court adopted a different approach.

The appellants – specialists in the erection of precast concrete structures – had erected at their depot a mobile tower crane some 89 feet high which ran on rails fixed in concrete. It had previously been used on contract work and they intended to use it again for contract work when required. The dismantling and re-erection of the crane was carried out by specialists; the whole operation took several days and cost about £2,000.

The Secretary of State – applying *Cheshire County Council v Woodward* – concluded that the erection of the crane with all that it entailed did alter the physical characteristics of the land and amounted to building, engineering and other operations.

The Divisional Court, in dismissing an appeal against the Minister's decision, thought it unnecessary to go so far. Bridge J giving the first judgment[14] applied criteria suggested in *Cardiff Rating Authority and Cardiff Assessment Committee v Guest Keen Baldwin's Iron and Steel Co Ltd*,[15] where the question was whether under rating legislation certain apparatus was a building or structure. These criteria may be summarised as follows:

(1) A building or structure will be something of such size that it has

10 The placing of caravans on land may, however, involve a material change in the use of the land. See ch 6, fn 9, on p. 115, below.
11 [1962] 2 QB 126, [1962] 1 All ER 517. See also *Bendles Motors Ltd v Bristol Corpn* [1963] 1 All ER 578, in which the court held that the Minister was entitled to find that the installation of a free-standing egg-vending machine in the forecourt of a garage and petrol filling station involved a material change of use and therefore constituted development.
12 Above.
13 (1971) 22 P & CR 710.
14 It is perhaps worth noting that Lord Parker CJ was a member of the Court and concurred with the judgment of Bridge J.
15 [1949] 1 KB 385, [1949] 1 All ER 27.

either been in fact or would normally be built or constructed on the site as opposed to being brought on it ready made.[16]

(2) It will have some degree of permanence; once installed it will normally remain *in situ* and only be removed by pulling down or taking to pieces.

(3) The question whether the thing is or is not physically attached to the site is relevant but not conclusive.

(4) A limited degree of motion does not prevent it being a structure.

The expression 'building operations' is also defined. It *includes* 'rebuilding operations, structural alterations of or additions to buildings, and other operations normally undertaken by a person carrying on business as a builder'.[17] The effect of this very wide definition is cut down by section 55(2)(a) of the Act of 1990 which excludes from the definition of development 'the carrying out of works for the maintenance, improvement or other alteration of any building, being works which affect only the interior of the building or which do not materially affect the external appearance of the building'.

It does not follow that something done to the exterior of a building which alters its external appearance will require planning permission; if what has been done does not amount to a building or other operation, planning permission will not be required. In *Kensington and Chelsea Royal London Borough Council v C G Hotels*[18] the owners of an hotel installed floodlights in the basement area and on the first floor balconies. The council served an enforcement notice requiring the removal of the floodlights. On appeal, the inspector quashed the enforcement notice; he decided (i) that the 'works' did not amount to building or other operations; and (ii) that in any case the floodlights were virtually invisible during daylight. The Divisional Court upheld the inspector's decision; even if the works amounted to development, they did not materially affect the external appearance. The real cause of complaint was probably the effect of the floodlighting at night, but the use of electricity is obviously not an operation within the definition of development.

It is sometimes difficult to decide whether works on an existing building are works of maintenance or improvement for the purpose

16 A thing is not necessarily removed from the category of building or structures because by some feat of engineering or navigation it is brought to the site in one piece – [1949] 1 All ER at 36. And see the rating case of *Scaife v British Fermentation Products Ltd* [1971] JPL 711 (transport in one piece of fermenting vessel weighing 13 tons and over 57 feet high).

17 1990 Act, s. 336(1).

18 (1980) 41 P & CR 40.

of section 55(2)(a) or not. The difficulty is illustrated by the case of
Street v Essex County Council.[19]

> A demolition order on a building was stayed on Street's undertaking to
> carry out repairs approved under the building byelaws. Unfortunately, he
> found it necessary to demolish the existing building down to damp course
> and to rebuild from there.
>
> The local authority served an enforcement notice alleging that Street
> had carried out development without planning permission and requiring
> him to remove what they said was a new building. The Minister upheld
> the enforcement notice. On appeal to the High Court, it was contended
> on behalf of Street that the work done did not constitute development;
> provided the design and some part, however small, of the original structure
> remained, the operations could be said to be works of maintenance.
>
> Held: whether the works could fairly be said to amount to works of
> maintenance, or were properly called reconstruction, was a matter of fact
> and degree. In the circumstances the Minister was entitled to hold as a
> matter of fact that what took place was reconstruction and as such involved
> development.

In *Street's* case, the reality was that there was no longer a building to
be maintained or improved. But where is the dividing line? The
rebuilding of one or two walls may possibly be accepted as maintenance, but it is now clear that section 55(2)(a) will not apply where
two walls are pulled down and rebuilt and then the other two are
rebuilt as part of the same programme of reconstruction. In *Larkin v
Basildon District Council*[20] the local planning authority advised the
developer that the rebuilding of two walls would not need planning
permission; having rebuilt two walls, he went on, against the advice
of the authority, to rebuild the other two. The authority served an
enforcement notice in respect of the rebuilding of all four walls. In
dismissing an appeal, the Secretary of State said:

> None of the external walls of the original building remain and new walls
> have been constructed as part of the operation and are unlike the walls of
> the original building: the construction of these walls, as distinct from
> the replacement of one or two of them, are not works of maintenance,
> improvement or other alteration of a building within the meaning of
> section [55 of the Act of 1990] since the original building has virtually
> ceased to exist.

The Divisional Court upheld the Secretary of State's decision. The
fact that the new walls were 'unlike' the originals might in itself have
put the works outside section 55(2)(a) as materially affecting the
external appearance, but that does not seem to have been the main

19 (1965) 193 Estates Gazette 537.
20 [1980] JPL 407.

point at issue. The principle that rebuilding by stages will normally be outside section 55(2)(a) has now been upheld by the Court of Appeal in *Hewlett v Secretary of State for the Environment*.[1]

These problems do not arise in connection with the restoration of war-damaged buildings because it is expressly provided that section 55(2)(a) shall not apply to war damage repairs; the result is that any war-damage repairs, however trivial, are development.[2]

The provision of additional space below ground level, if begun after 6 December 1968, is also deemed to involve development.[3]

ENGINEERING OPERATIONS

The expression 'engineering operations' includes 'the formation or laying out of means of access to highways',[4] otherwise the expression is to be given its ordinary dictionary meaning and includes building and maintenance of roads, the laying of sewers, water mains and other public utility apparatus. The removal of earth embankments has been held to constitute an engineering operation.[5]

The following are excluded from the definition of development:
(a) the maintenance or improvement of a road by the local highway authority within the existing boundaries of the road;[6]
(b) the inspection, repair and renewal of sewers, mains, cables, etc, by a local authority or statutory undertaker.[7]

MINING OPERATIONS

There is no definition of mining operations as such in the Act of 1990, but the word 'minerals' is defined as *including*[8] all minerals and substances in or under land of a kind ordinarily worked for removal by underground or surface working.[9] It is submitted that the expression 'mining operation' is to be interpreted in the light of the definition and that it would therefore include quarrying and other surface operations as well as underground mining.

1 [1985] JPL 404.
2 Until 1988 the repair of war damage was permitted development by virtue of Class XI of the previous GDOs. Class XI is not repeated in the new GDO.
3 1990 Act, s. 55(2)(a).
4 Ibid, s. 336(1).
5 See *Coleshill and District Investment Co Ltd v Minister of Housing and Local Government* [1969] 2 All ER 525. See also p. 82, below.
6 1990 Act, s. 55(2)(b).
7 Ibid, s. 55(2)(c).
8 In this case, the word 'includes' must be interpreted as 'means and includes'.
9 1990 Act, s. 336(1); peat cut for purposes other than sale is excluded.

This interpretation of mining operations is extended by section 55(4) of the Act of 1990 which provides that mining operations shall *include* (a) the removal of material of any description from a mineral working deposit, from a deposit of pulverised fuel ash etc, or from a deposit of iron, steel or other metallic slags; and (b) the extraction of minerals from a disused railway embankment.[10]

OTHER OPERATIONS

As already explained, the word 'operation' in this context means something which changes the physical characteristics of the land, or of what is under it or of the air above it.[11] There is, however, some uncertainty as to the meaning of the phrase 'other operations', since it can be interpreted in different ways.

(1) It might be taken as meaning any operation affecting the physical characteristics of the land. But in that case why does section 55(2) specifically refer to building, engineering and mining operations?[12]

(2) Another approach would be to try to apply the *ejusdem generis* rule, that is, to limit the phrase to operations of the same class or genus as building, engineering and mining. The difficulty here is to find any common genus to building, engineering and mining.[13]

(3) There is a rule of interpretation known as *noscitur a sociis*; that is, the meaning of a word can be gathered from the words with which it is associated. If this rule were applied, 'other operations' would be restricted to operations similar to building, engineering or mining, but in a less strict manner than would be required by the *ejusdem generis* rule.[14]

Even on the narrowest interpretation, the phrase 'other operations' must obviously include some matters which do not fall within the strict definitions of building, engineering or mining. The removal of topsoil (which under some circumstances would appear to be development)[15] is probably an operation of this kind.

10 This extended definition of 'mining operations' was introduced by the Minerals Act and came into force in May 1986.
11 See above.
12 See the remarks of Lord Morris of Borth-y-Gest and Lord Pearson in *Coleshill and District Investment Co Ltd v Minister of Housing and Local Government* [1969] 2 All ER 525 at 529 and 543 respectively.
13 See the remarks of Lord Guest, Lord Wilberforce and Lord Pearson, ibid, at 532, 537 and 543 respectively.
14 See the remarks of Lord Pearson, ibid, at 543.
15 The Agricultural Land (Removal of Surface Soil) Act 1953, makes it an offence to remove top-soil without planning permission in any case where such operations would constitute development.

Does the demolition of a building fall within the category of 'other operations'? For some years it was always assumed that the demolition of a building does not of itself constitute development,[16] and this view was supported by the judgment of Marshall J in *Howell v Sunbury-on-Thames UDC*.[17] But in the case of *Coleshill and District Investment Co Ltd v Minister of Housing and Local Government*[18] the House of Lords refused to say that demolition was not development and left the issue open.

The company owned a disused ammunition store which they proposed to use for storage. The buildings were surrounded by a concrete blast wall and a grass covered embankment of earth and rubble. They removed the embankment thus creating an eyesore, and the local planning authority served an enforcement notice. The company applied for a determination that the removal of the blast wall would not constitute development, but the local planning authority failed to give a determination within the prescribed period. The company appealed against the enforcement notice and the failure to give a determination. The Minister found as a fact that the blast wall and embankment were an integral part of the building; on this finding he held that the removal of the embankments was an engineering operation, and that the removal of the blast wall would constitute an alteration of the building which would materially affect its external appearance.

It was held that the Minister had not erred in law in reaching these conclusions and his decision would be upheld. Although their Lordships discussed whether demolition by itself might or might not constitute development, they did not need in the circumstances to decide the question.

Thus, demolition of part of a building may be development if it materially affects the external appearance of the building. But what if the building is totally demolished? In *Iddenden v Secretary of State for the Environment*[19] the appellants demolished three nissen huts and a lean-to shed. The Court of Appeal decided that their demolition was not development. Lord Denning explained that, whilst some demolition operations might be development (as in the *Coleshill* case[20]), the demolition of 'buildings such as these' was not development. It is not clear whether Lord Denning intended to imply that the demolition of much larger buildings would be development. There seems to be no

16 See, for example, the Minister's remarks in circular 67.
17 (1963) 15 P & CR 26. In *LCC v Marks and Spencer Ltd* [1953] AC 535, [1953] 1 All ER 1095 the House of Lords decided that demolition with a view to redevelopment amounted to 'works for the erection of a building' for the purposes of the 1947 Act, s. 78; but, it is submitted, the House of Lords did not say that such demolition constituted development.
18 [1969] 2 All ER 525.
19 [1972] 3 All ER 883.
20 Above.

logical reason why this should be so, unless the scale of the demolition is such that it might be held to be an engineering operation.[1]

Subsequently the Dobry report recommended that the demolition of buildings should be brought within the definition of development.[2] No action has been taken upon the recommendation, but the demolition of buildings in conservation areas now requires special consent.[3]

Change of use

We may now consider the second 'leg' in the definition of development – namely 'the making of any material change in the use of any buildings or other land'. The buildings or land under consideration in any particular case are often referred to as 'the planning unit'; this is usually the unit of occupation, but in some cases buildings or land in the same occupation may be divided into two or more planning units.[4] Where the occupier carries on more than one activity within the same planning unit, the 'use' of the buildings or land comprised in it will depend on the nature of the activities. It is quite common for one activity to be ancillary to a primary activity; for instance, a factory may have an office block, or part of a retail shop may be used for storage in connection with the retailing activity. The right to use buildings or land for an ancillary activity may be regarded as included in the primary use; separate planning permission is not required for the commencement of an ancillary activity[5] but the right to use land for an ancillary activity will be lost on the cessation of the primary activity.[6] The planning unit may, however, accommodate two or more activities neither of which is ancillary to the other; in such cases, the planning unit may be said to have a mixed or composite use.[7]

There will be no development unless the change of use is 'material'; that is, unless the change is of such a character that it matters having

---

1 It should not be assumed that the nissen huts were very small buildings. The nissen huts erected in large numbers in the Second World War were sectional buildings which could be constructed to any length in multiples of six feet; there were standard widths of 18 feet, 24 feet and 36 feet. They were used for such purposes as army barracks and medical wards and in some cases later converted to dwellinghouses.
2 Development Control Review: Report on the Control of Demolition (G Dobry, QC) (HMSO, 1974).
3 See ch 14, below.
4 See below.
5 *Trio Thames Ltd v Secretary of State for the Environment and Reading Borough Council* [1984] JPL 183.
6 *David W Barling v Secretary of State for the Environment* [1980] JPL 594.
7 See e g *Burdle v Secretary of State for the Environment* [1972] 3 All ER 240, [1972] 1 WLR 1207.

regard to the objects of planning control. As was said in *Marshall v Nottingham City Corpn:*[8]

> if the business of a retail dealer is being carried on in any building, it may be that there is a change of use if, for example, the business of a baker is substituted for a different business, for example, that of a grocer; but I am unable to see why or how such a change can be material from any point of view which could legitimately be taken by a planning authority.

In many cases it will be obvious that a change of use is 'material' in this sense, e g where it is proposed to use a dwellinghouse as offices or to station a large number of caravans on a field hitherto used for agriculture. In other cases, however, it is far from easy to decide whether a change of use is material or not. Is there, for instance, a material change of use if a doctor uses two rooms in a dwellinghouse for his practice? Or if a family take in a lodger? If not, in this latter case, would it be material if they took in six lodgers? Is there a material change of use if an existing use is intensified, as for instance in *Guildford RDC v Penny*[9] where the number of caravans in a field was increased over a period of years from eight to twenty-seven?

Some help with this problem is given by section 55 of the Act of 1990 which lays down specific rules for certain cases. Apart from these, however, the question whether there is a material change of use must be decided in the light of all the circumstances. We will deal first with the statutory rules laid down in section 55, and then with the general principles applicable to cases not covered by these rules.

THE STATUTORY PROVISIONS: MATTERS DECLARED TO BE A MATERIAL CHANGE OF USE

The following are specifically declared to involve a material change of use:
(a) the conversion of a single dwellinghouse into two or more separate dwellings;[10]
(b) the deposit of refuse or other waste materials, including the extension of an existing tip, if the superficial area is extended or the height is extended above the level of the adjoining ground;[11]

---

8 [1960] 1 All ER 659 at 665, per Glyn-Jones J.
9 [1959] 2 QB 112, [1959] 2 All ER 111.
10 1990 Act, s. 55(3)(a).
11 Ibid, s. 55(3)(b).

(c)   the display of advertisements on any external part of a building
not previously used for that purpose.[12]

The intention is to make it clear beyond doubt that these changes
of use constitute development and so require planning permission.
There remain, however, difficulties of interpretation. For instance,
what is meant in paragraph (a) by 'separate dwellings'?

In *Ealing Borough Council v Ryan*[13] three floors of a house were each occupied
by different families; the kitchen was shared by all the families, and it was
inferred that any bathroom and lavatory accommodation was also shared.
The corporation served an enforcement notice requiring the use of the
property as two or more separate dwellinghouses to be discontinued and
later prosecuted the owners for non-compliance. The magistrates dismissed
the case.

On appeal counsel for the corporation contended that if the people in
the house were found to be living separately, the dwellings must be separate. The Divisional Court did not accept this contention. A house might
well be occupied by two or more persons, who to all intents and purposes
were living separately, without that house thereby being used as separate
dwellings. Multiple occupation is not by itself enough to bring the statutory
rule into operation;[14] the existence or absence of any form of physical
reconstruction is also a relevant factor; another is the extent to which the
alleged separate dwellings are self contained.

The effect of these provisions should not be misunderstood. For
instance, multiple occupation of a dwellinghouse may constitute a
material change of use even though the house has not been converted
into separated dwellings; that is a matter to be decided by reference
to general principles.[15] A similar point arises with regard to the tipping
of refuse and other waste materials. Such tipping may constitute a
material change of use even though the superficial area of the existing
tip has not been extended, nor the height raised above the permitted
level. Thus in *Alexandra Transport Co Ltd v Secretary of State for Scotland*,[16]
the Court of Session considered that the backfilling of quarry refuse
had been part of the use as a quarry; use thereafter as a 'dump' was
a material change of use.

---

12   1990 Act, s. 55(4). This is not likely to be of much practical significance as all outdoor
advertisements require consent under the control of Advertisements Regulations
whether their display involves development or not – see ch 13, below.
13   [1965] 2 QB 486, [1965] 1 All ER 137.
14   See the account of *Birmingham Corpn v Minister of Housing and Local Government and
Habib Ullah* [1963] 3 All ER 668 at p. 99, below.
15   Use of a dwellinghouse by (a) a single person or people living together as a family,
or (b) not more than six residents living together as a single household, is not
development, by virtue of the Use Classes Order: see pp. 94, 95, below.
16   (1972) 25 P & CR 97.

THE STATUTORY PROVISIONS: USES EXCLUDED FROM DEFINITION OF DEVELOPMENT

Certain uses of land are specifically excluded from the definition of development.

(1) Use of buildings and land within the curtilage of a dwellinghouse The use of a building or other land within the curtilage of a dwellinghouse for any purpose incidental to the enjoyment of the dwellinghouse as such is not development.[17] It follows that the use of an existing garden shed as a garage for the owner's own car or as additional sleeping accommodation would not be development. But, since the word 'use' does not include the carrying out of building operations,[18] this paragraph does not authorise the erection of a building or shed for these purposes. This paragraph is a re-enactment of a provision originally contained in the Act of 1947. At that time the concept of the use of land had not been the subject of judicial analysis and the concept of the planning unit had not emerged, and it may have been thought important to safeguard the incidental use of the curtilages of dwelling houses. Nowadays, it is recognised that the incidental use of the curtilage of a building does not require planning permission,[19] so the above paragraph seems little more than a statutory expression of a general principle. Moreover, since the planning unit may be larger than the curtilage planning permission will probably not be necessary for the use of land outside the curtilage but within the same unit of occupation – for instance, a paddock – for purposes incidental to the enjoyment of the dwellinghouse.

(2) Use for agriculture or forestry The use of any land for the purpose of agriculture or forestry (including afforestation), and the use for any of these purposes of any building occupied with land so used, does not involve development.[20] The use of land for agriculture obviously involves the carrying out of a number of operations such as ploughing; in this context it is submitted that the word 'use' must include such operations as are essential to and inseparable from agriculture, but that it does not include such operations as the erection of farm buildings.

17 1990 Act, s. 55(2)(d).
18 See this chapter, pp. 76, 77, above; 1990 Act, s. 336(1).
19 See e g *Royal Borough of Kensington and Chelsea v Secretary of State for the Environment and Mia Carla Ltd* [1981] JPL 50: it was held in the case of a garden attached to a restaurant that planning permission was not required for the use of the garden for the purposes of the restaurant.
20 1990 Act, s. 55(2)(e).

'Agriculture' is defined as *including*:[1]

horticulture, fruit growing, seed growing, dairy farming, the breeding and keeping of livestock (including any creature kept for the production of food, wool, skins or fur or for the purpose of its use in the farming of land), the use of land as grazing land, meadow land, osier land, market gardens and nursery grounds, and the use of land for woodlands where that use is ancillary to the farming of land for other agricultural purposes.

This definition has been the subject of some precise interpretation. In *Belmont Farm Ltd v Minister of Housing and Local Government*[2] it was held that the breeding and training of horses for show jumping was not agricultural; such use was not covered by the words 'breeding and keeping of livestock' because those words were qualified by the parenthesis which refers to the keeping of creatures for the production of food. However, in *Sykes v Secretary of State for the Environment*[3] it was held that the use of land for grazing some racehorses and point-to-point ponies was agricultural because the reference in the statutory definition to the use of land as grazing land was not qualified by the words in parenthesis. The use of land for allotments has been held to fall within the statutory definition.[4]

Although the use of land for agriculture does not include operations such as the erection of buildings, it may include the placing on the land of caravans, vehicles and pieces of equipment for purposes ancillary or incidental to agriculture. In *Wealden District Council v Secretary of State for the Environment and Day*[5] D had placed a caravan on agricultural land for the purpose of providing a waterproof place for the storage and mixing of cattle food and to provide shelter for himself and his wife. The council objected, apparently because of the visual effect, and issued an enforcement notice alleging a material change of use. On appeal, the inspector quashed the enforcement notice on the grounds that the caravan was used for animal feed preparation and shelter, such uses were ancillary to the agricultural use and stationing the caravan was not a material change. The council unsuccessfully appealed to the High Court. Kennedy J pointed out:

The fact that an item which is brought on to the land is aesthetically objectionable does not of itself cast any light on the question of whether the land is being used for the purposes of agriculture and whether the item complained of is contributing to that purpose.

1 1990 Act, s. 336(1).
2 (1962) 13 P & CR 417.
3 [1981] JPL 285.
4 *Crowborough Parish Council v Secretary of State for the Environment* [1981] JPL 281.
5 [1988] JPL 268.

Kennedy J's judgment was upheld by the Court of Appeal. Ralph Gibson LJ said:

> There is, in planning law even with reference to the most beautiful parts of our countryside, no basis for excluding from the notion of ordinary equipment a useful and suitable article such as a caravan on the ground only that it was not traditional in construction or appearance for the particular purposes for which Mr Day had applied it.

Two comments may be pertinent. First, the fundamental question was whether Mr Day's use of the caravan amounted to use for agriculture: since it did, the effect of what is now section 55(2)(e) was to remove it from the definition of development. It was for this reason, it is submitted, that the question of the effect of the caravan on the amenities of neighbourhood was irrelevant; in other cases the effect on amenity may be relevant in determining whether there is a material change of use.[6] Second, had Mr Day been seen using the caravan as living accommodation and not merely for shelter whilst working, the result would probably have been very different.

(3) The Use Classes Order   No development is involved by a change of use from one purpose to another within one of the use classes specified in the use classes order made by the Secretary of State.[7] At present this means the Use Classes Order 1987. This order sets out sixteen use classes, each of which groups together a number of similar uses. We will consider first the general purpose and effect of the Use Classes Order before setting out the separate use classes.

The Use Classes Order: its purpose and effect   Where a building or other land is used for a purpose within one of the use classes specified in the Use Classes Order made by the Secretary of State, the use of that building or other land (or of part thereof[8]) for another purpose within the same use class does not constitute development.[9] Thus, a change of use from say a bookshop to a travel agency will not be development because both fall within Class A1 (shops). But a change of use from a bookshop to a shop for the sale of hot food may be development because the latter is specifically excluded from Class A1; it does not follow however that this change must be development. The Act of 1990 and the Use Classes Order say that a change from one purpose to another within the same use class does not involve development.

---

6 See pp. 101, 102, below.

7 1990 Act, s. 55(2)(f).

8 The reference to the use of part of a building is at present subject to one exception: see the discussion of Class C3 (dwellinghouse) at p. 95, below.

9 1990 Act, s. 22(2)(f).

They do not say that a change from something within a particular use class to something outside it (or vice versa) must be development; such cases must be considered in the light of all the facts, having regard to the general principles set out below.[10]

The current Use Classes Order was made in 1987, replacing that made in 1972. The use classes set out in 1972 were very similar to those originally formulated in 1948. The current order is a radical revision; by reducing the number of use classes and broadening the scope of the many of the classes, it facilitates changes of use which might otherwise be deemed to be material and thus require planning permission.

There are many uses which do not fall within any of the use classes. Some are expressly excluded. Thus, none of the use classes includes the use of buildings or other land for the manufacturing, processing, keeping or use of notifiable quantities of hazardous substances.[11] Also expressly excluded are use as a theatre, amusement arcade etc, laundrette, for the sale of fuel for motor vehicles, the sale or display of motor vehicles, taxi and car hire businesses, scrapyard, etc. Many other uses are not mentioned at all in the Use Classes Order, for instance, agriculture, transport depots.

The right to make a change of use within a particular use class does not arise until the premises have actually been used for a purpose within that class. Thus, if planning permission is granted for the use of premises as an office within Class B1, the right to change to another use such as light industry within that class does not arise until the premises have actually been used as offices. A mere token use may not be sufficient.[12]

It does not matter, however, that the initial use may have been unlawful in the sense that it was commenced without the necessary grant of planning permission. Thus, if there was an unauthorised change of use of a dwellinghouse to offices in 1963 the office use will now be immune from enforcement action and the use can now be changed to light industry;[13] if the office use commenced after the end of 1963, the use can be changed to light industry but may be the subject of enforcement action because the office use has not become immune.

When considering whether the Use Classes Order applies, it is important to distinguish between primary and ancillary uses. For

10 *Rann v Secretary of State for the Environment* (1979) 40 P & CR 113 at 117.
11 Use Classes Order, art 3(5), Notification of Installations Handling Hazardous Substances Regs 1982.
12 *Kwik Save Discount Group Ltd v Secretary of State for the Environment* (1980) 42 P & CR 166, CA.
13 Assuming that the office use is within Class B1.

instance, a farm will probably include buildings which are used for the storage of crops and farm equipment; the use of these buildings for storage is ancillary use to the primary use of the land for agriculture. Or there may be ovens for the baking of bread at the rear of a baker's shop: the baking of bread is an industrial process, but (unless the bread is also sold through other shops) is ancillary to the shop use.

It is a well established principle that where a use is ancillary to the main use, it cannot be detached and turned into an independent use.

Thus, in *G Percy Trentham Ltd v Gloucestershire County Council*[14] a firm of building and civil engineering contractors bought a farmhouse, yard and farm buildings. This firm used some of the buildings (which had previously been used for housing farm machinery, etc) for the storage of building materials for their business. The county council having served an enforcement notice, the firm appealed on the ground that both uses fell within Class X of the Use Classes Order then in force relating to wholesale warehouses and repositories. The Court of Appeal considered that the farmer's use of these buildings for housing farm machinery was not use as a repository; but even if the buildings had been a repository, they could not be severed from the rest of the farmhouse and buildings; one had to look at the unit as a whole.[15]

A similar approach was adopted by the Court of Appeal in *Brazil (Concrete) Ltd v Amersham RDC and Minister of Housing and Local Government*.[16] A builders' yard with ancillary buildings had been used for storage in connection with a building contractors's business. In 1962 the premises were bought by R Brazil & Co Ltd and this company obtained planning permission to convert a big shed in the yard to various uses including a carpenter's shop. Brazil (Concrete) Ltd – a subsidiary company – then erected a ready mix concrete plant in the yard. It was contended on behalf of the company that they were entitled to do this because the big shed was now an industrial building for the purposes of the Use Classes Order, which meant that the land used with it fell within that category by virtue of article 2(3) of the order; that being so, the company were industrial undertakers and as such entitled by virtue of the General Development Order to erect the concrete plant.[17] The Court rejected the basic contention that the

14 [1966] 1 All ER 701.
15 [1966] 1 All ER 701 at 702. The decision of the Court of Appeal that use for housing farm machinery was not use as a repository has since been disapproved by the House of Lords in *Newbury District Council v Secretary of State for the Environment* [1981] AC 578, [1980] 1 All ER 731, but there was no suggestion that the Court erred in any way in holding that the building could not be severed from the rest of the farm unit.
16 (1967) 18 P & CR 396.
17 Successive General Development Orders have given permission for certain types of development by industrial undertakers, see ch 6, pp. 124, 125 below.

big shed had become an industrial building for the purpose of the Use Classes Order; although articles were made in the carpenter's shop, that was incidental to the primary purpose of a builder's yard.

The Use Classes Order: the separate classes   Class A1 refers to use as a shop for all or any of the following purposes:
(a) for the retail sale of goods other than hot food;[18]
(b) as a post office;
(c) for the sale of tickets or as a travel agency;
(d) for the sale of sandwiches or other cold food for consumption off the premises;
(e) for hairdressing;
(f) for the direction of funerals;
(g) for the display of goods for sale;
(h) for the hiring out of domestic or personal goods or articles;
(i) for the reception or service of goods to be washed, cleaned or repaired;
where the sale, display or service is to visiting members of the public.

The purposes specified in Class A1 are very similar to those included in the definition of 'shop' for the purposes of Class I of the 1972 Order. The new Class A1 is, however, much simpler in form since it is not linked to a complicated definition of the word 'shop' as in the former Class I. Nevertheless some problems may arise; the word use in Class A1 must refer to the use of a building or other land,[19] and in the context of this particular use class this will in most cases be the use of a building. If the main activity is the sale of goods by retail, any other uses such as storage being purely ancillary thereto, the 'use' of the building is quite clearly retailing and falls within Class A1. But if another main use wholly outside the use class, such as gaming machines, is carried on as well, there would appear to be a mixed or composite use which would suffice to remove the 'use' of building from Class A1. In *Lydcare v Secretary of State for the Environment and Westminster City Council*[20] the Court of Appeal held that premises were not used for the carrying on of a retail trade or business where there was a mixed use of the sale of goods by retail and for the viewing of films in coin operated booths; although this was a decision on the definition of shop for the purposes of the 1972 Order, the principle, it is submitted, is still applicable.

18 The sale of fuel for motor vehicles and the sale or display for sale of motor vehicles are also excluded: see above.
19 See Act of 1990, s. 55(2)(f) and Use Classes Order, art 3.
20 (1985) 49 P & CR 186, CA.

Class A2 (financial and professional services) is entirely new. It refers to use for the provision of:
(a) financial services;
(b) professional services (other than health or medical services);
(c) any other services (including use as a betting office) which it is appropriate to provide in a shopping area;[1]
where the services are provided principally to visiting members of the public.

Class A2 thus embraces offices of a type – such as banks, building society branches, estate agents' offices – which the public expect to find in shopping areas.

Although offices of this type are regarded as appropriate in shopping areas, they have been assigned to a separate use class with the intention as far as possible of maintaining control over the conversion of retail shops to office uses.[2] Offices not falling within Class A2 are in Class B1 along with light industrial uses, as explained below.

Class A3 comprises use for the sale of food or drink for consumption on the premises or of hot food for consumption off the premises, e g cafes, restaurants, wine bars etc, and take-aways supplying hot food. All these uses were expressly excluded from the 1972 Order. They have now been grouped into a single use class.

Class B1 (business) is entirely new. It refers to use for all or any of the following purposes:
(a) use as an office other than a use within Class A2;
(b) for research and development of products or processes;
(c) for any industrial process;[3]
being a use which can be carried on in any residential area without detriment to the amenity of that area by reason of noise, vibration, smell, fumes, smoke, soot, ash, dust or grit.

This new use class is perhaps the most radical of the changes made by the new Use Classes Order. It brings into a single class many of the office uses and the light industrial uses which had been quite distinct classes in earlier Use Classes Orders, together with certain uses connected with research and development. It includes for instance, the development and manufacture of computers, micro-engineering, biotechnology, pharmaceutical research and manufacture – provided always that such use could be carried on without detriment to the amenities of a residential area by reason of noise, vibration, smell etc.

The proviso about detriment to the amenity of a residential area

1 Establishments for washing or dry cleaning of clothes on the premises and amusement arcades are however excluded by virtue of art 3(6): see above.
2 Circular 13/87, para 18.
3 For the definition of 'industrial process', see p. 95, below.

was an essential feature of light industrial use in the earlier Use Classes Orders, but the present Order makes one significant change. In the earlier Orders the test was whether the processes carried on or the machinery installed were such as could be carried on or installed in any residential area without detriment to the amenity of that area by reason of noise, vibration, smell etc; provided the nature of the processes or the machinery satisfied the test, the actual use might be detrimental to the activities of a residential area. The new formula is intended, apparently, to enable consideration to be given to all aspects of the use judged by the specified criteria of noise, vibration, smell, etc.[4]

The effect of the words 'which can be carried on in any residential area' was considered in *W T Properties Ltd v Secretary of State for the Environment and Crawley Borough Council*.[5] In that case an industrial use was carried on in a building near to Gatwick Airport. It was held that the proximity of the airport was irrelevant. 'One had to imagine the effect of the noise and so on from these premises were they set in the middle of a residential area. The hypothetical residential area was not one within a short distance of a busy international airport.'

Class B2 refers to general industrial use, that is, use for the carrying on of any industrial process[6] other than one falling within Class B1 or the special industrial groups B3 to B7. These classes follow the pattern of Classes III to IX of the 1972 Order, but there is one important difference. The former Classes III to IX all related to the use of a building; the new Classes B2 to B7 refer simply to use for various purposes and so may include the use of open land as well as of a building.

Class B8 refers to use for storage or as a distribution centre. This replaces the former Class X which referred to 'wholesale warehouse or repository'; the new Class B8 is apparently intended to be similar in scope and thus will not include use as a retail warehouse, but it is wider than the former Class X in that it includes the use of open land as well as of buildings.[7]

Class C1 is concerned with hotels and hostels where no significant element of care is provided, and Class C2 with various kinds of residential institutions. Class C3 is wholly new, creating for the first time a use class comprising dwellinghouses as such; it refers to use as a single dwellinghouse (whether or not as a sole or main residence)
(a) by a single person or persons living together as a family; or

4 See circular 13/87, para 20.
5 [1983] JPL 303.
6 For the definition of 'industrial process', see p. 95 below.
7 See circular 13/87, para 23.

(b) by not more than six residents living together as a single household (including a household where care is provided for residents).

Class C3 is clearly intended to facilitate change of use from a single family house to sharing by unrelated persons living together as a household, e g a group of students or other young persons or by a group of handicapped people in need of some element of care. Such a change of use would not necessarily involve development at all, but this new use class removes all doubt provided the 'household' consists of not more than six people; where there are more than six people, the question whether there is a material change of use has to be decided on general principles on each case. It is important to note that Class C3 does not derogate from the rule that the conversion of a single dwellinghouse into two or more separate dwellings is a material change of use and thus requires planning permission.[8]

Class D1 brings into a single use a variety of non-residential uses such as the provision of medical or health services (except the use of premises attached to the residence of the consultant or practitioner), day nurseries and centres, provision of education, art galleries, museums and so on. Class D2 is concerned with assembly and leisure and includes cinemas, concert halls, bingo halls, swimming baths and so on. Theatres were included in Class XVII of the 1972 Order together with cinemas, music halls and concert halls. They have been excluded from any of the use classes in the current order with the intention of protecting them from being sold off for other purposes;[9] but the question remains whether a change from theatre to, say, cinema would be a material change of use.

'Industrial process'   As we have seen, Class B1 of the current Use Classes Order includes light industrial processes, and Classes B2 to B7 are wholly concerned with various other industrial processes. An industrial process is a process for, and incidental to, any of the following purposes:[10]

(a) the making of any article (including a ship or vessel, or a film, video or sound recording);

(b) the altering, repairing, maintaining, ornamenting, finishing, cleaning, washing, packing, canning, adapting for sale, breaking up, demolition of any article;

(c) the getting, dressing or treatment of minerals.

The 'process' must be one which is carried on in the course of trade or business, that is something which is an occupation rather than a

8 See Use Classes Order, art 4.
9 See circular 13/87, para 32.
10 Use Classes Order, art 2.

pleasure.[11] It seems that a hobby, even though financially profitable, is not a trade or business; this appears to have been taken for granted in the case of *Peake v Secretary of State for Wales*.[12] But it is not essential to the concept of a business that it should be carried on with a view to making a profit; thus in *Rael-Brook Ltd v Minister of Housing and Local Government*[13] use of a building as a cooking centre by a local authority for the provision of school meals was held to be industrial, so that planning permission was not thereafter required for a change to shirt making.

It might appear from this that the court adopts a liberal approach to the definition of 'industrial building'. The court has, however, recognised the danger that amateur workshops might be turned over to commercial industrial activity without any control by the planning authority. Accordingly, a relatively severe construction is to be placed on the terms of the order. There were some important remarks to that effect in *Rael-Brook Ltd v Minister of Housing and Local Government*.[14] These remarks were followed in *Tessier v Secretary of State for the Environment*.[15]

A sculptor used a dutch barn as a studio. In the barn there were six large benches with vices, casting pits, a forge, an anvil and furnaces; stone masonry blocks of up to three-and-a-half tons would be cut out with drills, grinders, electric hammers and hand chisels. The sculptor also used the studio as a showroom and for lectures. The Secretary of State held that the use was not industrial, but *sui generis*.

Held: the Secretary of State was entitled to take the view that an artist, expressing his art form and making articles in the process, even if they were sold, was not making them in the course of a trade or business.

Difficulties sometimes arise where two or more uses are carried on together. For instance, manufacturing firms may carry on light industry in one building and general industry in a neighbouring building. Article 3(4) of the Use Classes Order, provides that land on a single site or adjacent sites is used by a single undertaking for two or more purposes within Classes B1 to B7, those classes may be treated as a single class provided the area occupied for general or special industrial purposes is not substantially increased. This facilitates changes of use within a group of buildings.

Interchangeability is also facilitated by article 3(3) which provides that a use which is ordinarily incidental to and included in a use

11 *Rolls v Miller* (1884) 27 ChD 71 at 88, per Lindley LJ.
12 (1971) 22 P & CR 889. For an account of this case, see p. 100, below.
13 [1967] 2 QB 65, [1967] 1 All ER 262.
14 Above.
15 (1975) 31 P & CR 161.

specified in the order is not excluded from that use because it is specified elsewhere in the order as a separate use. The effect of this may be seen from *Vickers-Armstrong v Central Land Board*[16] which was decided on article 3(3) of the Use Classes for the Third Schedule Purposes Order 1948.[17]

> An aviation works included an administration block; it was used partly as offices, but also by designers of blueprints and by draughtsmen, and in it technicians carried out important mechanical tests.
>
> In connection with a claim for compensation the question arose as to whether this building could have been used for general industrial purposes without planning permission.
>
> The Court of Appeal held that the building could have been so used without planning permission. 'Looked at as a whole, I should have thought that the appellants' works were clearly used as a general industrial building. It is true that the administration block was not wholly used for the carrying out of an "incidental" process, but it plainly was, I should have thought, incidental use of the works within article 3(3) of the Order. That being so, it matters not that it cannot have been said wholly to have been used for the carrying out of processes: offices are clearly incidental to the use of a general industrial building.'

GENERAL PRINCIPLES

Where the statutory rules do not apply, the question whether there is a material change of use must be decided on general principles. As we have seen, a change is 'material' if it matters having regard to the objects of planning control. In this connection the following points may arise:

(1) In most cases the first question to ask will be whether the change of use will completely alter the character of the land or buildings.

(2) Where an existing use is intensified it is necessary to ask whether there has been a complete change in the character of the land or buildings.

(3) If the change of use only partially alters the character of the land or building, it will be necessary to ask whether the change is material for some other reason.

(4) In some cases, the answer may depend on the unit of land or buildings under consideration.

(5) In some cases, it is necessary to consider whether established use rights have been lost or abandoned.

16 (1957) 9 P & CR 33.
17 This order provided a similar set of use classes, but for a different purpose (compensation).

We will consider each of these in turn.

(1) Will the change of use completely alter the character of the land or buildings?   The relevance of this test was emphasised in *Guildford RDC v Penny*.[18] On 1 July 1948 a field was used as a site for eight caravans. Over the years the number was increased to 27 and the local authority served an enforcement notice. On appeal, the magistrates held that this did not constitute a material change of use and quashed the enforcement notice. The Court of Appeal held that an increase or intensification of use might amount to a material change of use. But in this case the land had been used as a caravan site from first to last, and it could not be said that the magistrates had erred in law in finding that there had been no material change of use. The Court of Appeal was saying in effect that the increase in number was not so great that it was unreasonable for the magistrates to hold that there had been no real change in the character of the site.

It should be noted that the test is the character of the use and not the particular purpose of the particular occupier. This is illustrated by *Marshall v Nottingham City Corpn*.[19]

> From 1912 to 1957 L owned a plot of land which he used for manufacturing and selling wooden portable buildings, garages and wooden garden ornaments. The goods were made in a workshop and displayed in the open. There was a hut which he used as an office and from which he conducted sales. After 1939 the business dwindled and by 1957 was moribund though not dead.
>
> In 1957 M bought the land from L so that a company of which she was managing director could use it for selling caravans and wooden portable buildings; the company did not manufacture any goods. The corporation served an enforcement notice alleging a material change of use by using the land for the display and sale of caravans and wooden buildings.
>
> Glyn-Jones J held: (1) neither the fact that the company did not manufacture the goods which they sold, nor the fact that the company sold caravans which L had not sold, constituted a material change of use; (2) the increase in the intensity of the use had not been so great as to constitute a material change of use.

Similar considerations arose in *East Barnet UDC v British Transport Commission*.[20]

> This case concerned some 30,855 sq yards of land belonging to the British Transport Commission near a railway station. The land was divided into seven parcels. Three parcels comprising nearly 20,000 sq yds had been

18 [1959] 2 QB 112, [1959] 2 All ER 111.
19 [1960] 1 All ER 659.
20 [1962] 2 QB 484, [1961] 3 All ER 878.

used as coal stacking yards; one parcel of over 10,000 sq yds had been vacant for many years; two very small parcels consisted of buildings which had been used as workshops; the seventh parcel was a siding.

At different dates Vauxhall Motors took tenancies of all these parcels, and used the land as a transit depot for the handling and storage of crated motor vehicles nearly all of which were received and despatched by rail. In 1951 they applied for planning permission in respect of two of the parcels (one of them previously used for coal stacking, and the other the unused land) and the council granted permission subject to the condition that the use of all the land for this purpose would cease on 31 May 1958. The use continued after that date, and the council served enforcement notices.

On appeal, the magistrates quashed the enforcement notices on the ground that the use of the land did not constitute development.

The council thereupon took the case to the High Court. It was held, inter alia, that the magistrates were entitled to find that there had been no material change of use. The land had originally been a coal storage depot, the coal being brought in and taken away by rail. There would have been no material change of use if the British Transport Commission had changed the storage from coal to oil. 'The mere fact that the commodity changes does not necessarily mean that the land is being used for a different purpose nor, as it seems to me, is there any relevance in the fact that the purpose for which the land is used is effected by other hands, in this case by [Vauxhall Motors]'.[1]

Put shortly, there was no material change of use because the land was used throughout as a storage and transit depot. As regards the unused parcel, the Divisional Court said that it was proper to regard this not as a separate unit of land but merely as an unused portion of the whole unit.

That the test is the character of the use and not the particular purpose of the particular occupier has recently been confirmed by the House of Lords in *Westminster City Council v British Waterways Board*.[2]

(2) Where the existing use has been intensified, has there been a complete change in the character of the land or buildings? It is now well established that a material change in the use of a building or other land can occur through intensification of the existing use. The question is whether the existing use has been intensified to such a degree that it has become materially different from what it was before. A good illustration is the case of *Birmingham Corpn v Minister of Housing and Local Government and Habib Ullah*.[3]

1 Per Lord Parker CJ at 885.
2 [1985] AC 676, [1984] 3 All ER 737.
3 [1964] 1 QB 178, [1963] 3 All ER 668.

Two houses each of which had been in single family occupation were sold to new owners, and several familes were installed in each house. The corporation served enforcement notices alleging that there had been a material change of use by changing the use of each from single dwellinghouse to house-let-in-lodgings. The Minister considered that there had been no material change of use since the houses were still residential.

Held: the Minister had erred in law in saying that because the houses remained residential there could not be a material change of use; whether there had been a material change of use, said Lord Parker CJ, was a matter of fact and degree in each case. The court remitted the cases to the Minister for reconsideration.

Intensification may also occur through an increase in the amount of an activity. This form of intensification is illustrated by *Peake v Secretary of State for Wales*.[4]

In 1950 following the grant of planning permission, P built a private garage. From then until 1968 he used it for the repair and servicing of motor vehicles as a spare time activity or profitable hobby. In 1968 he began working full time at the garage. The local planning authority served an enforcement notice. The Secretary of State dismissing P's appeal, said that a material change of use had occurred in 1968. P then appealed to the High Court.

Held: although a change in an activity from part-time to full-time could not of itself amount to a material change of use, the Secretary of State was entitled to conclude as a matter of fact and degree that P's use of the garage prior to 1968 was incidental to its designed use as a private garage but that after that date the use escalated to a degree where it could no longer be said to be incidental to use as a private garage and involved a material change of use.

It must often be very difficult to decide at what point an intensification of use results in a material change of use, but this difficulty does not affect the general principle of law. It is worth emphasising that it is not sufficient to say that the existing use has been 'intensified'; the vital question is the degree of intensification. In the fairly recent case of *Royal Borough of Kensington and Chelsea v Secretary of State for the Environment and Mia Carla Ltd*[5] Donaldson LJ said it was much too late to suggest that the word 'intensification' should be deleted from the language of planners, but it has to be used with very considerable circumspection, and it had to be clearly understood by all concerned that intensification which did not amount to a material change of use was merely intensification and not a breach of planning control. His Lordship hoped that, where possible, those concerned with planning would get away from the term and try to define what was the material

4 (1971) 22 P & CR 889.
5 [1981] JPL 50.

change of use by reference to the *terminus a quo* (that is, the starting point) and the *terminus ad quem* (that is, the end point).

(3) Where a change of use does not completely alter the character of the land or building is the change material for any other reason? It would seem that a change of use will be 'material' if it completely alters the character of the land or building. However, there are many changes of use which only partially alter the character of the land or building. In such cases further questions must be asked. In *Guildford RDC v Penny*,[6] Lord Evershed said that a change of use might be material if it would involve a substantial increase in the burden of services which a local authority has to supply. The principle seems to be sound. Thus the conversion of large houses to multiple occupation will tend to increase the demand for services provided by public authorities, but cases of this sort will usually be considered to be material changes of use in any event by virtue of the statutory rule about the conversion of houses into more than one dwelling[7] or under the heading of intensification.[8]

Since planning control is to some extent concerned with the preservation of amenity, it may also be relevant to ask what effect a change of use will have on the neighbourhood. A change of use may well be 'material' if the nature of the use as changed is such that it is likely to involve a great increase in the number of persons calling at the premises or if it is likely to cause a great deal of noise. There have been some pronouncements which suggest that it is not permissible to take into account the effect on the neighbourhood,[9] but these seem inconsistent with the opinions of the Divisional Court. Thus in *Williams v Minister of Housing and Local Government*[10] the owner of a nursery garden had used a timber building on the land for the sale of produce grown in the nursery garden; he then began selling imported fruit as well. The Divisional Court upheld an enforcement notice: the main ground for the decision was that the planning unit was the nursery garden and not the timber building, but Widgery J also said:

> there is clearly, from a planning point of view, a significant difference in character between a use which involves selling the produce of the land itself, and a use which involves importing goods from elsewhere for sale. All sorts of planning considerations may arise which render one activity appropriate in a neighbourhood and the other activity quite undesirable.

6 [1959] 2 QB 112, [1959] 2 All ER 111.
7 See pp. 85–86, above.
8 See pp. 99 ff, above.
9 See circular 67, issued in 1948. See also remarks by Sir Douglas Frank QC (sitting as a deputy judge) in *Rann v Secretary of State for the Environment* (1979) 40 P & CR 113.
10 (1967) 18 P & CR 514.

Widgery J's point is illustrated by the recent case of *Blum v Secretary of State for the Environment and London Borough of Richmond upon Thames Council*.[11]

> The site had been used as livery stables – that is stabling for the accommodation of privately owned horses – since 1950. In 1980/81 it began to be used in addition as a riding school; an enforcement notice was issued alleging a material change of use from livery stables to riding school and livery stables.
>
> On appeal, the inspector held that there had been a material change of use. Although there were superficial resemblances, there were significant differences of purpose, function and character; the character of the use was affected by the amount of additional staff and facilities, and there would be more horse traffic, more rides out and more car traffic. He also referred to the introduction of a sanded paddock for instructional purposes.
>
> In the High Court Simon Brown J upheld the inspector's decision. Although the inspector had referred to some of the factors involved in terms of intensification, a new use had been introduced.

It seems clear enough that this was not in reality the intensification of the existing use – the livery stables – but the introduction of a new use – the riding school: in deciding whether this additional use was a material change the environmental effects were clearly very relevant.

It may also be proper to ask what is the purpose of a particular change of use, eg whether it is incidental to the existing use of the premises or whether it is the establishment of a trade or business. This test must, however, be applied with care. The doctor who uses two rooms in his private residence for the purpose of his practice and the family who take in a lodger are both doing so for the purposes of gain, but it is probably true to say that in neither case is there a material change of use.[12] Planning control is concerned with the use of land not with personal motives.

(4) What is the unit under consideration?   The Act of 1990 refers to a material change in the use of 'any buildings or other land'. This is vague and in some cases can give rise to difficulty. In *East Barnet UDC v British Transport Commission*[13] the question whether there had been a material change in the use of one parcel of land turned on whether that parcel should be regarded as a separate unit of land or merely part of a larger unit. Lord Parker CJ commented that the choice of unit was always a matter of difficulty but 'looked at *as a matter of commonsense* in the present case it seems to me that this was merely an

---

11 [1987] JPL 278.
12 See circular 67.
13 [1962] 2 QB 484, [1961] 3 All ER 878.

unused part of the unit in question'.[14] In other words there can be no hard and fast rules as to the choice of unit: one must approach the problem in each case on commonsense lines.

In the later case of *Burdle v Secretary of State for the Environment*,[15] however, the Divisional Court attempted a more precise formulation, and suggested three possible criteria for determining the planning unit. First, whenever it is possible to recognise a single main purpose of the occupier's use of his land, to which secondary activities are incidental or ancillary, the whole unit of occupation should be considered. This would seem to cover the circumstances of the *East Barnet* case. Secondly, it may be equally apt to consider the entire unit of occupation even though the occupier carries on a variety of activities, and it is not possible to say that one is incidental or ancillary to another; e g a composite use where the activities are not confined within separate and physically distinct areas. Thirdly, within a single unit of occupation two or more physically distinct areas may be occupied for substantially different and unrelated purposes. In such a case each area used for a separate main purpose (together with its incidental and ancillary activities) ought to be considered as a separate planning unit.

These criteria are not absolute rules. In *Wood v Secretary of State for the Environment*,[16] a conservatory attached to a dwellinghouse was used for the sale of produce from a smallholding. The Secretary of State, in considering an appeal against an enforcement notice in respect of this use, treated the conservatory as a separate planning unit. The Divisional Court considered that the Secretary of State had approached the matter in the wrong way. Lord Widgery CJ said that it could rarely, if ever, be right to dissect a dwelling house and to regard one room in it as a separate planning unit. In other words, the Secretary of State should have considered whether the use of the conservatory for the sale of produce amounted to a material change in the use of the whole of the premises.

Lord Widgery's dictum in *Wood*'s case is of considerable importance because of the large number of cases in which the resident occupier of a house uses one or two rooms for the purposes of his profession or business. There may, of course, be a material change of use in such cases, but the question is to be decided by looking at the house as a whole and not in separate parts.[17]

14 At 886, author's italics.
15 [1972] 3 All ER 240.
16 [1973] 2 All ER 404.
17 See for instance a decision of the Secretary of State concerning the use of part of a dwellinghouse by a veterinary surgeon for the purposes of his practice: [1976] JPL 328.

It seems that Lord Widgery's dictum is not to be extended to buildings other than single dwellings. In *Johnston v Secretary of State for the Environment*,[18] the Divisional Court considered that in the case of a block of flats in single ownership, but let to separate and different tenants, the planning unit would normally be the individual flat in question.

There will also be cases in which a large business undertaking occupies two or more geographically separate sites. Even if these separate sites could properly be described as a single unit of occupation it would not be appropriate to treat them as a single planning unit. In *Fuller v Secretary of State for the Environment*[19] the appellant farmed over 2,000 acres comprising a widely scattered number of farms. The local planning authority issued enforcement notices requiring discontinuance of the use of the land for the commercial storage of grain not grown on the appellant's own specified agricultural units. Dismissing appeals against the notices, the Secretary of State said that the separate farms could not reasonably be regarded as one planning unit; 'any more than, say, the similarly scattered retail outlets of a local chain of shops, all in the same ownership and occupation and performing the same function, would be so regarded'. In the High Court Stuart Smith J upheld the Secretary of State's decision.

Sub-division of the planning unit   There is some uncertainty as to whether the division of the planning unit into two or more separate units is a material change of use. As we have seen, the division of a single dwellinghouse into two or more separate dwellings is a material change of use by virtue of a specific statutory provision,[20] but what of other cases?

In *Wakelin v Secretary of State for the Environment*[1] a large house set in two acres of grounds had always been used as a single residential unit. In 1965 the then owner, who needed accommodation for an elderly relative was granted planning permission for 'additional residential accommodation and three garages' subject to the condition that the new building should not be occupied other than by a close relative or member of the household staff. Some years later, W, with a view to selling off the lodge, applied for planning permission for 'separate and unrelated occupancy'. Permission was refused. On appeal, the inspector concluded that changing from one unit of accommodation to two was a material change of use.[2] The Court

---

18 (1974) 28 P & CR 424.
19 [1987] JPL 584.
20 See pp. 85–86, above.
1 [1978] JPL 769.
2 The case did not fall within what is now 1990 Act, s. 55(3)(a) because the single unit of accommodation consisted of more than one building.

of Appeal held that the Inspector had quite properly concluded that the division of what was a single unit into two separate units was a material change of use.

It is clear enough that in this case the sub-division of the planning unit involved a material change of use because the use permitted in 1965 was of both buildings as a single unit. It is less certain that the Court of Appeal intended to lay down a general rule that sub-division of a planning unit would always be development; indeed Browne LJ expressly reserved his opinion on that point.

Subsequently, in *Winton v Secretary of State for the Environment*[3] Woolf J after considering the judgments in *Wakelin* said that the sub-division of the planning unit did not in itself amount to a material change of use but that it would do so if it had 'planning consequences'. The *Winton* case concerned the sub-division of an industrial building into two separate units; the previous use and the subsequent uses all fell within class IV of the then Use Classes Order. The local planning authority took enforcement action. On appeal, the Secretary of State held that there had been a material change of use and upheld the enforcement notice. Woolf J decided that the court could not interfere with the Secretary of State's decision that there had been a material change. There remained, however, the question whether this change of use was covered by the Use Classes Order; the learned judge held – perhaps surprisingly – that the Use Classes Order did not cover the division of a unit into sub-units. Since then, however, what was then section 22(2)(f) of the Act of 1971 has been amended and the sub-division of a unit into two or more units within the same use-class will not constitute development.[4]

(5) Have established use rights been lost or abandoned? The question of how far established use rights should be considered to have been lost or abandoned has caused some difficulty. The circumstances in which this may happen may be classified under two main heads: (a) extinguishment, and (b) abandonment.

Extinguishment It is a fairly obvious principle that existing use rights may be extinguished as a result of new development. In many cases the continuation of previous uses would be wholly inconsistent with the new development and often indeed impracticable. But there are cases in which the continuation of previous uses would not be impracticable. But there are cases in which the continuation of previous uses would not be impracticable and not necessarily inconsistent with the

3 (1982) 46 P & CR 205.
4 See this chapter, p. 89, above.

new development. Over the years there have been a number of cases in which previous uses have continued after some development has taken place, and it was not until the comparatively recent decision of the Court of Appeal in *Jennings Motors Ltd v Secretary of State for the Environment*[5] that a single consistent principle for deciding such cases was adopted.

It will, however, be useful to look first at some of the earlier cases. In *Petticoat Lane Rentals Ltd v Secretary of State for the Environment*[6] a cleared bomb site had been used throughout the week as a market. The entire site was redeveloped by the erection of a building; the ground floor was open, the building being supported on pillars, and was to be used as a car park and loading area. Permission was given for the use of the ground floor as a market on Sundays, but in fact it continued to be used as a market throughout the week. The Divisional Court held that the previously existing land had merged in the new building, and a new planning unit had been created which had no previous planning history; market trading was not authorised by the planning permission (except on Sundays) and was therefore a breach of planning control.

The theory of the 'new planning unit' was applied in *Aston v Secretary of State for the Environment*[7] where a building was erected on part of the original planning unit. In 1952 Aston bought some land which he began to use for the keeping of pigs and also as a base for vehicles for his transport business. In 1956 he built a large barn which he used for both these purposes. The barn was blown down in a storm in 1961 and for some years there was no use of this part of the site. However in 1969 he built a much larger barn without planning permission and claimed that he had the right to use it for the maintenance of his vehicles. The Divisional Court held that where a new building is erected on part of the land that part of the land becomes a new planning unit with no permitted uses apart from those derived from the planning permission, if any.

Alongside this theory of 'the new planning unit' another theory had emerged – that of 'a new chapter' in the planning history. It began with *Prossor v Minister of Housing and Local Government*.[8] A garage proprietor applied for planning permission to rebuild a petrol service station; permission was granted on condition that no retail sales were to take place in the new building. Afterwards the appellant claimed that he had existing use rights for selling motor cars. Lord Parker

5 [1982] QB 541, [1982] 1 All ER 471.
6 [1971] 2 All ER 793, [1971] 2 WLR 1112.
7 (1973) 43 P & CR 331.
8 (1968) 67 LGR 109.

CJ said that by adopting the permission granted in April 1964 the appellant's predecessor gave up any possible existing use rights in that regard which he may have had. 'The planning history of this site, as it were, seems to begin afresh on April 4, 1964 with the grant of this permission which was taken up and used.'[9]

This theory was later restated in *Newbury District Council v Secretary of State for the Environment*.[10] In that case temporary permission was granted for the use of two hangars as warehouses on the condition that the hangars should be removed when the temporary permission expired. Lord Lane said 'The holder of planning permission will not be allowed to rely on any existing use rights if the effect of the permission when acted on has been to bring one phase of the planning history of a site to an end and to start a new one ... In the present case there is no such break in the history.'

We can now turn to *Jennings v Secretary of State for the Environment*:[11]

The site had an established use as a taxi, car and coach hire business and for vehicle repairs and car sales. Most of the site was used for access and parking. There was a garage workshop in one corner occupying one-twelfth of the site; there was a showroom and office in another corner occupying one thirteenth of the site. There had also been a second garage workshop, but the appellants pulled it down and put up a new building notwithstanding a refusal of planning permission to do so. The new building occupied about one seventeenth of the site, and the appellants began to use it for the repair and servicing of vehicles.

The local planning authority did not take enforcement proceedings against the new building because it was better in appearance than that which it replaced. But enforcement proceedings were taken to prevent it being used for repair and maintenance work.

The Secretary of State upheld the enforcement notice. In the light of the *Petticoat Lane Rentals* case, he considered that when the new building was erected, a new planning history commenced in respect of it and the building on completion had a 'nil' use.

Held: (1) the erection of a new building did not necessarily create a 'new planning unit' nor give rise to a 'new chapter in the planning history'; (2) the question whether a new planning history was about to begin was one of fact and degree in each case; (3) in the present case there had been no change in the planning history and the appellants were entitled to the existing use rights attaching to the site inside the new building.

The Court of Appeal thus emphatically rejected the theory that the erection of a new building automatically extinguished previous use

9 There is no change in the planning history of the site if the planning permission is not taken up, and it would perhaps be more logical to have chosen the date when the development began rather than the date of the planning permission.
10 [1981] AC 578; [1980] 1 All ER 731.
11 [1982] QB 541, [1982] 1 All ER 471.

rights. The test now is whether, in the words of Lord Denning MR, 'there is a radical change in the nature of the buildings on the site or the uses to which they are put – so radical that it can be looked on as a fresh start altogether in the character of the site.'[12] This test is more flexible and, it is submitted, much fairer, but it will not always be easy to apply in practice. In the *Petticoat Lane Rentals* case the new test would have produced the same result, but different opinions have been expressed on the question whether the result would have been the same in *Aston*.[13]

Abandonment   The question whether existing use rights have been lost through abandonment arises where a use has ceased for a time and the land has not been used for any other purpose in the meantime; if the circumstances justify a finding that the use has been abandoned, the land will be deemed to have a nil use and a resumption of the previous use will require planning permission. It is not correct to say that a use has been 'abandoned' where it is immediately followed by another positive use;[14] if the latter amounts to a material change of use, it is unlikely that the previous use could thereafter be resumed without planning permission because a change from the latter to the former use would normally be a material change of use. The distinction is important because it may affect the right, given by the Act of 1990, to resume a previous use where an enforcement notice is served in respect of a subsequent unlawful use.[15]

The question whether existing use rights have in fact been abandoned is a difficult one, and can usefully be considered under a number of headings suggested by Ashworth J in *Hartley v Minister of Housing and Local Government*.[16]

(1) If the sole use to which the land is put is suspended and thereafter resumed without there being any intervening different user, prima facie the resumption does not constitute development. As Lord Parker CJ put it in an earlier case:[17] 'It is of course quite plain that a change from A to X and then from X to A does not involve development either way, if X is completely nil, no use at all.'

There are, of course, some uses of land which by their very nature are intermittent. Thus:

12 At 476.
13 Lord Denning thought that the result would have been different and that *Aston* was wrongly decided. Oliver and Watkins LJJ thought the result would have been the same.
14 *Young v Secretary of State for the Environment* [1983] JPL 465; affd [1983] JPL 677.
15 See Ch 6, p. 115, below.
16 [1969] 2 QB 46, [1969] 1 All ER 309.
17 *McKellan v Minister of Housing and Local Government* (1966) 6 May, unreported.

a racecourse is perhaps used for a few days three or four times a year, but no one would suggest that it ceases to be used as a racecourse in the closed season, or that a new development occurs on the first day of the next meeting.[18]

On the face of it Lord Parker's dictum goes wider than the case of the intermittent use and may well cover seasonal uses and cases where an activity is closed down and is then resumed after an interval.

(2) Nevertheless, there are circumstances in which the previous use will be deemed to have been abandoned. In *Hartley v Minister of Housing and Local Government*[19] Lord Denning MR said that, if the land has remained unused for a considerable time in such circumstances that a reasonable man might conclude that the previous use has been abandoned, the tribunal[20] may hold it to have been abandoned. In other words if the circumstances justify such a conclusion, it is within the competence of the court to hold that the previous use has been abandoned. Lord Denning's guidance was applied by the Divisional Court in *Ratcliffe v Secretary of State for the Environment:*[1]

> From about 1920 to 1961 a quarry had been used by a local authority for tipping refuse. Thereafter there had been some sporadic tipping, but not by the local authority who had ceased tipping when their tenancy had run out, and had mainly involved the deposit of some lorry loads of clay and earth by a purchaser of the land who had been proposing to use it for chicken farming. In 1970 the land was acquired by the appellant who applied for a determination under what is now section 64 of the Act of 1990 as to whether filling the quarry for reclamation purposes would amount to development. The Secretary of State decided that the tipping use had been abandoned in 1961 and that resumption would be a material change of use.
>
> The Divisional Court upheld the decision of the Secretary of State. Bridge J said that not only was the Secretary of State entitled so to find but applying the *Hartley* principles, he (Bridge J) could not see how he could have reached any other conclusion.

Presumably, in this case, Bridge J was saying that the 'reasonable man' looking at the circumstances would almost certainly have said that the use had been abandoned. There are, however, cases in which the intentions of the occupier must be considered. Thus in *Hale v Lichfield District Council*[2] Mrs H had spent the last 13 years of her life in hospital leaving her house empty and, it seems, no repairs

---

18 *Hawes v Thornton Cleveleys UDC* (1965) 17 P & CR 22 at 28, per Widgery J.
19 [1970] 1 QB 413, [1969] 3 All ER 1658.
20 The 'tribunal' will normally be the court or the Secretary of State.
1 [1975] JPL 728.
2 [1979] JPL 425.

were done; on her death, her personal representatives obtained a declaration that the residential use had not been abandoned.

(3) Where land is put to a composite use the issues are more complex. The cessation of one of the component uses does not of itself constitute development; nor can it be said that the change from dual use to single use is of itself a material change of use. But there may be a material change in the use of the whole site if, after the cessation of one of the uses, the continuing use absorbs some or all of the remaining land.[3] It seems that there is no need to invoke the concept of abandonment in such a case.

(4) It may happen that one of the component uses is discontinued without any subsequent intensification of the other component use or uses. If the discontinued use is later resumed without planning permission it will be necessary to consider whether that use has in fact been abandoned. Relevant considerations will include the nature of the uses, what portion of the site was devoted to the discontinued use, what use if any was made of that portion during the period of discontinuance and how long the discontinuance lasted. Ultimately, said Ashworth J, the problem will resolve itself into the question: 'When the resumption occurred, was there a material change in the use of the land?'[4]

The recent decision of the House of Lords in *Pioneer Aggregates (UK) Ltd v Secretary of State for the Environment*[5] affirms the principle that an existing use may be lost by abandonment, but it also shows that there are limits to its application. It may happen that a use was begun in accordance with planning permission and subsequently suspended in circumstances which point to the use having been abandoned. If, however, the planning permission is still in force, the use can be resumed by virtue of that permission; a planning permission cannot be extinguished by abandonment.[6]

Cases of doubt

There will obviously be many cases in which it is not clear whether an operation or use of land involves development. Section 64 of the Act of 1990 provides a relatively simple and inexpensive procedure for dealing with such cases. Any person who proposes to carry out

---

3 See *Wipperman and Buckingham v London Borough of Barking* (1965) 17 P & CR 225; *Philglow Ltd v Secretary of State for the Environment and the London Borough of Hillingdon* [1985] JPL 318.
4 *Hartley v Minister of Housing and Local Government* [1969] 1 All ER 309 at 315.
5 [1985] AC 132, [1984] 2 All ER 358.
6 See ch 8, p. 176, below.

any operation or to change the use of land may apply to the local planning authority for a determination whether the proposed operation or change of use would constitute development, and if so, whether planning permission is required, having regard to the provisions of the development order or of any enterprise zone scheme or simplified planning zone scheme.[7] The effect of the words 'having regard to the provisions of the development order' was discussed in *Edgwarebury Park Investments Ltd v Minister of Housing and Local Government*,[8] Lord Parker CJ said:

> this is a method by which the proposed developer may ascertain not only whether what he contemplates is development but also whether it is the sort of development which is covered by the blanket provision in the General Development Order, or is one for which he must apply for and get permission.

The appellants in this case, however, attempted to use this procedure to determine whether a decision of Hendon Borough Council amounted to a grant of planning permission, which Lord Parker CJ went on to say was 'right outside the contemplation of this provision'; though he added, 'there can be no conceivable reason for the appellants not being able, if they so desire, to proceed in the courts for a declaration as to the validity of the permission'.

The local planning authority must give a determination within eight weeks.[9] The application may be made concurrently with an application for planning permission if required.[10]

If the applicant is aggrieved by the determination of the local planning authority, he may appeal to the Secretary of State and will have the right to be heard by a representative of the Secretary of State.[11] Here again, it is quite common to bring this appeal concurrently with an appeal to the Secretary of State against a refusal of planning permission. There is a further right of appeal to the High Court.[12]

The section 64 procedure applies only to persons who propose to carry out operations or to make a change of use. The procedure is not available where the operations or change of use have already been

---

7 The references to enterprise zones and simplified planning zones were added by the Acts of 1980 and 1986.
8 [1963] 2 QB 408, [1963] 1 All ER 124.
9 GDO, art 23.
10 1990 Act, s. 64(2).
11 1990 Act, s. 78 applied by s. 64(3).
12 Ibid, s. 290.

carried out, nor is it appropriate for determining the effect of a purported grant of planning permission.[13]

It seems that the local planning authority may give a determination which is effective for the purposes of section 64 without a formal application having been made. In *Wells v Minister of Housing and Local Government*[14] the plaintiff applied for planning permission; the local planning authority in March 1963 wrote stating that the proposed works could be regarded as permitted development. Widgery J said that every planning application had implicit in it an invitation to the planning authority to treat the matter under section 53 if their view of the facts made it appropriate; if they could see at once that planning permission was not required, the sensible and legally appropriate action was to do what was done in March 1963. In the Court of Appeal Lord Denning MR said that once the planning authority had determined that no planning permission was necessary and had told the applicant so, that was a determination under the section; as such it was irrevocable by the planning authority 'just as is a planning permission'.[15]

A determination under section 64, that no planning permission is required may remain effective, even though the law has been changed before the person concerned has carried out the operations or made the change of use in question. In *English Speaking Union of the Commonwealth v Westminster City Council*,[16] the council determined that a change of use from residential club to hotel would not require planning permission because both uses fell within Class XI of the Use Classes Order then in force. Before the use was changed to a hotel, the Secretary of State made the 1972 Use Classes Order excluding residential clubs from Class XI. The city council now contended that there would be a material change of use,[17] but the plaintiffs were granted a declaration that the determination under what is now section 64 remained fully operative. Pennycuick V-C followed the principles laid down in *Wells v Minister of Housing and Local Government*;[18] the determination correctly made by council at the time established the rights of the plaintiffs once and for all and was as good as a planning permission.

13 *Edgwarebury Park Investments Ltd v Minister of Housing and Local Government* [1963] 2 QB 408, [1963] 1 All ER 124.
14 (1966) 110 Sol Jo 889; affirmed by the Court of Appeal [1967] 2 All ER 1041.
15 A planning permission may be revoked by an order under 1990 Act, s. 97: see ch 9, below. There is no procedure for revoking a section 64 determination.
16 (1973) 26 P & CR 575.
17 The planning officer's reasons for considering that there would be a material change of use were quoted by Pennycuick V-C and make interesting reading; but his Lordship did not in the circumstances have to decide that point.
18 Above.

Another way of ascertaining whether a particular operation or change of use involves development is to apply for a declaratory judgment of the High Court. This method may be used as an alternative to applying for a section 64 determination[19] and is also available in those cases to which section 64 does not apply.

---

19 *Pyx Granite Co Ltd v Minister of Housing and Local Government* [1960] AC 260, [1959] 3 All ER 1.

Chapter 6

Planning permission: permitted development

The basis of planning control in England and Wales is section 57(1) of the Act of 1990 which provides that 'Subject to the following provisions of this section, planning permission is required for the carrying out of any development of land'.[1]

There are certain exceptions to this rule, namely:

(1) Temporary use existing on 1 July 1948   Prior to 6 December 1968 permission was not required for the resumption of the normal use of land which on 1 July 1948 was temporarily used for another purpose. If the normal use had not been resumed by 6 December 1968, permission will be necessary.[2]

(2) Occasional use existing on 1 July 1948   Permission is not required in the case of land which on 1 July 1948 was normally used for one purpose and was also used on occasions for any other purpose, in respect of the use for that other purpose on similar occasions after that date provided the right had been exercised on at least one occasion between 1 July 1948, and the beginning of 1968.[3]

(3) Land unoccupied on 1 July 1948   Where land was unoccupied on 1 July 1948, but had before that date been occupied at some time on or after 7 January 1937, planning permission is not required in respect of any use of land before 6 December 1968, for the purpose for which it was last used before 1 July 1948.[4]

(4) Resumption of previous use   If planning permission has at any time been granted specifically for a limited period, or by a development order subject to limitations, no permission is necessary to resume the

---

1 This does not apply to development carried out before 'the appointed day', which was 1 July 1948, the day the Act came into force: 1971 Act, Sch 24, para 12; Planning (Consequential Provisions) Act 1990, Sch 3, para 3.
2 1990 Act, Sch 4, para 1.
3 Ibid, Sch 4, para 2.
4 Ibid, Sch 4, para 3.

use which was normal before that permission was granted, provided that the 'normal use' was not begun in contravention of planning control under Part III of the Act of 1990 or the corresponding provisions of the previous Acts. Nor is permission necessary to resume the previous lawful use of land when an enforcement notice has been served in respect of any unauthorised development;[5] the previous use cannot be resumed if it also was begun in breach of planning control – the fact that it was established before 1964 and is therefore no longer subject to enforcement action does not make it lawful.[6] If the previous use was unlawful, there is no right to revert to some earlier lawful use.[7]

There would appear to be little, if any, practical significance for most purposes in the distinction between these classes of development and those matters which are excluded from the definition of development. But the distinction may be of significance in certain cases, since the unexpended balance of established development value will be subject to modification in any case where new development is carried out after 1 July 1948.[8]

Except in the cases noted above[9] permission is required under Part III of the 1990 Act for all classes of development. That permission may be granted in three ways:

(a) by a development order made by the Secretary of State;
(b) by an enterprise zone scheme;
(c) by a simplified planning zone scheme;
(d) by being 'deemed to be granted' in special cases as provided in the Act of 1990;
(e) as a result of an application to the local planning authority.
    Each of these will now be considered in turn.

Permission under development order

This form of permission is provided for by section 24 of the Act of 1971. Development orders made by the Secretary of State may be either general orders applicable (subject to any exceptions specified

---

5 1990 Act, s. 57(2)–(6). For development orders, see this chapter, below. For enforcement notices see ch 10, below.
6 *LTSS Print and Supply Services Ltd v Hackney London Borough Council* [1976] QB 663, [1976] 1 All ER 311.
7 *Young v Secretary of State for the Environment* [1983] 2 AC 662, [1983] 2 All ER 1105.
8 See ch 21, pp. 348, 349, below.
9 Exceptions (2), (3) and (4) do not apply to the use of land as a *caravan site*, except where there was such use at least once during the two years ending on 9 March 1960: 1990 Act, Sch 4, para 4.

therein) to all land in England and Wales, or special orders applying only to certain specified land.

THE GENERAL DEVELOPMENT ORDER

The General Development Order is of general application and by article 3 grants permission for a wide range of developments set out in Schedule 2 to the Order. Schedule 2 is divided into 28 parts most of which are divided into different classes; for instance, Part 1 (development within the curtilage of a dwellinghouse) is divided into eight classes lettered A to H. In all, Schedule 2 sets out some 74 classes of development which can be carried out without applying to the local planning authority for express permission. Of course, this is not the same as excluding these matters from the definition of development, and nothing in the General Development Order is to operate so as to permit development contrary to a condition imposed on any other grant of permission under Part III of the Act of 1990.[10] Moreover, the Secretary of State and the local planning authority have certain powers under article 4 to withdraw in specific cases the benefit of a permission granted by the order: this power has been quite extensively used, but this would not have been possible if the matters in question had been excluded from the definition of development. Lastly, the Secretary of State can at any time make new development orders either extending or restricting the range of permitted developments.

Of the 28 categories of development permitted by the General Development Order, Parts 1 to 9, 21, 22, 27 and 28 are of general interest; the remainder concern public bodies such as local authorities and the Historic Buildings Commission, and the public utilities such as water, gas, electricity, coal, telecommunications and airports.

In many cases the permitted development is subject to limits. For example, Class A of Part 1 (development within the curtilage of a dwellinghouse) permits the extension of a house, but does not permit an extension which, inter alia, would exceed the cubic content of the original house by more than a certain amount, or which would exceed the height of the original house, or extend the house within 20 metres of the highway. This means that, if any part of the extension is in breach of any of these restrictions, the whole extension and not merely the excess is unauthorised and so liable to enforcement action.[11] In some cases, the permitted development is also subject to conditions;

10 GDO, art 3(4).
11 See ch 10, below.

breach of a condition would not, it is submitted, invalidate the whole development, but the local planning authority would be entitled to issue an enforcement notice to secure compliance with the condition.

There are some further restrictions which apply to all development permitted by the General Development Order. The Order does not authorise any development[12] which involves the formation, laying out or material widening of a means of access to a trunk or classified road, or which creates an obstruction to the view of persons using any road used by vehicular traffic at or near any bend, corner, junction or inter-section so as to be likely to cause danger to such persons.[13] Furthermore, the General Development Order does not (with certain exceptions) authorise development involving any hazardous activity, that is, the use of hazardous substances.[14]

Development within the curtilage of a dwellinghouse Part 1 makes provision for the extension of a dwellinghouse[15] and for other development within the curtilage of a dwellinghouse.

Class A permits the enlargement, improvement or other alteration of a dwellinghouse[16] within certain limits. The cubic content[17] of the original dwellinghouse[18] must not be increased:

(a) where the house is in a national park, or an area of outstanding natural beauty, a conservation area, and certain other special areas,[19] by more than 50 cubic metres or ten per cent whichever is the greater;

(b) in the case of a terraced house in any part of the country, by more than 50 cubic metres or ten per cent whichever is the greater;

(c) in the case of any other house by more than 70 cubic metres or 15 per cent whichever is the greater;

(d) in all cases by not more than 115 cubic metres.

There are several other important restrictions:

(i)   the height of the resulting building must not exceed the highest part of the roof of the original dwellinghouse;

(ii) if any part of the original dwellinghouse is within 20 metres of a

12 Except in relation to development permitted by Part 9, 11 or 13.
13 GDO, art 3(5).
14 GDO, art 3(7)–(10). For hazardous substances, see circular 9/84.
15 'Dwellinghouse' does not include a building containing one or more flats, or a flat contained within such a building: art 1(2).
16 Other than alterations to its roof, the construction of a porch to an external door, or the installation of a satellite antenna; separate provision for these forms of development is made by Classes B, C, D and H.
17 As ascertained by external measurement.
18 The 'original' dwellinghouse means the house as built on 1 July 1948 or, if built since that date, as so built: GDO, art 1(2).
19 See GDO, art 1(5).

highway bounding the curtilage, it must not be extended further
in that direction;

(iii) extensions within two metres of the boundary of the curtilage
       must not exceed four metres in height;

(iv)   only 50 per cent of the curtilage (excluding the ground area of
       the original dwellinghouse) may be covered by buildings;

(v)   if the house is in a national park, area of outstanding natural
       beauty, conservation area or other special area, cladding of the
       exterior is not permitted.

The erection within the curtilage of any building with a cubic
content of more than 10 cubic metres is to be treated as an extension
of the dwellinghouse (1) where the house is in a national park, area
of outstanding natural beauty, conservation area or certain other
special areas; (2) elsewhere if any part of that building would be
within five metres of the dwellinghouse. This will impose restrictions
on the erection of garages and greenhouses; for instance, where any
part of the dwellinghouse would be within five metres of an existing
building within the same curtilage, that building is to be treated as
part of the resulting building for the purposes of calculating cubic
content.

Furthermore, Class A does not permit the erection of any building
of whatever size in the curtilage of a listed building.[20]

Extensions to a roof of a dwellinghouse are permitted by Class B
subject to specific limits on volume – 40 cubic metres for terraced
houses and 50 cubic metres for other dwellinghouses; extension of a
roof beyond the roof face fronting a highway is not permitted. The
limits on volume count towards the total limits for the extensions
permitted by Class A. Class B does not apply in national parks, areas
of outstanding beauty, conservation areas and certain other special
areas.

Any other alteration of the roof of a dwellinghouse is permitted by
Class C provided it does not alter the shape of the roof.

Classes C to H deal with the erection of porches to external doors;
provision within the curtilage of buildings, enclosures, swimming or
other pools required for a purpose incidental to the enjoyment of a
dwellinghouse; erection within the curtilage of containers for storing
oil for domestic heating; installation of satellite antennae.

Minor operations   Class A of Part II permits the erection of gates,
fences, walls or other means of enclosure not exceeding one metre in

20 In the case of a listed building, the curtilage may include parts of the original
    curtilage which have been sold off: see ch 14, p. 251, below.

height where adjacent to a highway[1] used by vehicular traffic, or two metres in other cases. It also permits maintenance, improvement or alteration of a gate, fence etc within these limits of height or the original height, whichever is the greater.

In *Prengate Properties Ltd v Secretary of State for the Environment*[2] the Divisional Court held that the words 'gate, fence or wall' are governed by the words 'other means of enclosure'; that is, the construction of e g a wall is not authorised unless it has some function of enclosure. Lord Widgery said that the permission would not extend to someone who erected a freestanding wall in the middle of his garden in circumstances in which it did not play any part in enclosing anything. But what is meant by saying that the structure must serve some function of enclosure? It seems that in most cases, the court will regard this as a question of fact and degree to be determined, in the event of an appeal, by the Secretary of State or his inspector. In *Ewen Developments Ltd v Secretary of State for the Environment and North Norfolk District Council*[3] the court refused to interfere with an inspector's finding that some embankments within a caravan site were not enclosures for the purposes of what is now Class A of Part II even though each embankment formed a continuous ring and so in one sense did enclose land; presumably the embankments were intended merely as landscaping. The implication seems to be that, to qualify under Class A, the structure must be required as a means of preventing or restricting access to or from an area of land.

Class B of Part II permits the making of an access to a highway, which is not a trunk or classified road, where that access is required in connection with other development permitted by the General Development Order.[4]

Class C permits the exterior painting of buildings otherwise than for the purposes of advertisement, announcement or direction. The permission is only required where such painting would materially affect the external appearance of the building; in other cases it will not be development at all.[5] Perhaps the real value of Class C is that it avoids arguments as to whether development is involved.

Changes of use   As we have seen in an earlier chapter, a change of use from one purpose to another within the same use class does not

---

1 The use of the expression 'adjacent to' (instead of 'abutting upon' used in earlier GDOs) is, no doubt, intended to emphasise that the rule applies even if the structure does not touch the boundary of the highway.
2 (1973) 25 P & CR 311.
3 [1980] JPL 404.
4 Except development permitted under Part II, Class A.
5 See ch 5, p. 79, above.

constitute development and so does not require planning permission.[6]
Classes A to D of Part III of Schedule 2 of the General Development
Order permit development consisting of a change of use from one use
class to another in certain cases as summarised in the following table:[7]

Change permitted

By GDO Class	From UCO Class	To UCO Class
A	A3 (food and drink)	A1 (shops)
A	Sale of motor vehicles	A1 (shops)
B(a)	B2 (general industrial)	B1 (business)
B(a)	B8 (storage and distribution)	B1 (business)*
B(b)	B1 (business)	B8 (storage and distribution)*
B(b)	B2 (general industrial)	B8 (storage and distribution)*
C	A3 (food and drink)	A2 (financial and professional)
D	Premises within A2 (professional and financial) with display window at ground floor level	A1 (shops)

*not permitted where change of use relates to more than 235 square metres
of floor space in the building.

The phrase 'development consisting of a change of use' is significant:
the changes of use mentioned above are not excluded from the definition of development by virtue of the Use Classes Order and they will
constitute development if they amount to a material change of use. A
change of use from a warehouse (use Class B8) to a light industrial
use (which falls within use Class B1) is almost certainly a material
change of use, but is permitted within certain limits by the General
Development Order as shown above. Whether a change from a 'take
away' selling hot food (use Class A3) to an ordinary retail shop
(use Class A1) is a material change of use is arguable; the General
Development Order permits the change of use and so makes argument
unnecessary.

Class E of Part 3 introduces for the first time a measure of freedom to
change to alternative uses originally permitted by a grant of planning
permission. It has always been possible for a planning authority to
grant planning permission in a form which would enable a developer
to take up one of a number of specified uses. For example, permission
might be given for the use of a large house as offices or as an hotel; if
the developer then used it for offices, the planning permission was
implemented and would not cover a subsequent change to an hotel.

6 See ch 5, pp. 89, above.
7 From circular 22/88, para 59.

Class E now permits a change of use from one specified in a planning permission, and implemented, to any other use specified in that permission. Class E does not apply (a) if the application for the planning permission was made before 5 December 1988; (b) if the change of use would be carried out more than ten years after the grant of planning permission; or (c) if it would result in the breach of any condition, limitation or specification contained in that planning permission in relation to the use in question.

Temporary buildings and uses   Class A of Part 4 gives permission for the provision on land of buildings, moveable structures, works, plant or machinery required temporarily in connection with and for the duration of operations being or about to be carried out on, in, under or over the land or on land adjoining that land. Class A does not apply if (a) the operations referred to are mining operations, or (b) planning permission is required for those operations but is not granted or deemed to be granted. It is a condition of Class A that the buildings etc, shall be removed when the operations have been carried out and that any adjoining land be reinstated in its former condition.

Class B gives permission for the temporary use of land[8] for any purpose on not more than 28 days in any calendar year (of which not more than 14 days in total may be for the holding of markets, motor car and motor cycle racing[9]) and the provision of moveable structures on the land for the purpose of the use. The provision is often relied on for such temporary uses as fairs, markets and camping. The use of land as a caravan site is excluded from Class B; the temporary use of land for caravans is made by Part 5 of Schedule 2.

Agricultural buildings and operations   As we have seen, the use of land for agriculture is not development and so does not require planning permission.[10] The carrying out of building and other operations in connection with agriculture, however, does require planning permission because the word 'use' in the Act of 1990 does not include operations.[11] In many cases the necessary planning permission for agricultural buildings and operations is given by Part 6 of Schedule 2 to the General Development Order.

Class A of Part 6 permits the carrying out on agricultural land[12] comprised in an agricultural unit (a) of works for the erection, exten-

---

8 Class B does not apply to buildings or land within the curtilage of a building.
9 Including trials of speed and practising.
10 See ch 5, p. 87, above.
11 See ch 5, pp. 76, 77, above.
12 'Agricultural land' means land used for agriculture and which is so used for the purpose of a trade or business: GDO, Sch 2, Part 6, Class D.

sion or alteration of a building, or (b) any excavation or engineering operations, reasonably necessary for the purposes of agriculture within that unit. Class A, however, does not include the erection or alteration of a dwellinghouse, nor the provision of a building not designed for the purposes of agriculture. There are several important limitations and conditions including the following:

(1) The ground area of any building must not exceed 465 square metres, and if the building would be within 90 metres of another building (other than a house) belonging to the same farm and erected within the last two years, the area of that building must be deducted from the maximum of 465 square metres.

(2) The height of any building within three kilometres of the perimeter of an aerodrome must not exceed three metres nor 12 metres in any other case.

(3) No part of the development must be within 25 metres of the metalled portion of a trunk or classified road.

(4) There are further restrictions on the siting of buildings or excavation for the accommodation of livestock or for the storage of slurry or sewage sludge.

Where the land is within a national park or certain areas of high landscape value,[13] any person proposing to erect an agricultural building in accordance with the permission given by Class A must give the local planning authority a written description and plan of the proposed development; the authority then have 28 days in which to notify the developer that the development must not commence without prior approval of the siting, design and external appearance of the building. If the authority have not required prior approval, the development is to be carried out in accordance with the written description and plan.[14]

Class A contains a significant change of terminology from what was Class VI of the 1977 Order. The old Class VI referred to the carrying out on agricultural land comprised in an agricultural unit of building or engineering operations requisite for the use of the land for the purposes of agriculture. As we have seen in an earlier chapter, in *Fuller v Secretary of State for the Environment*[15] Stuart-Smith J held that an agricultural unit could comprise several planning units; in consequence, planning permission was required for the use of buildings on one farm for the storage of grain produced on another farm within the same agricultural unit. The reference in the new Class A to

13 These areas are specified in the GDO, Sch 1, Part 2.

14 GDO, Sch 2, Part 6, para A2(2). This replaces the Landscape Areas SDO 1950, mentioned in earlier editions of this work.

15 (1987) 56 P & CR 84, [1987] JPL 854.

the creation of buildings reasonably necessary 'for the purposes of agriculture within that unit' is apparently designed to permit storage within buildings erected under Class A of produce from other farms in the same agricultural unit. This extension of permitted development rights is likely to result in the further concentration of buildings on the 'home farm'.

The phrase 'requisite for the use of that land for the purposes of agriculture' in the former Class VI came up for consideration in *Jones v Stockport Metropolitan Borough Council*.[16] The phrase was ambiguous, one possible interpretation being that the erection of an agricultural building was permitted by the former Class VI only if its intended use was ancillary to an agricultural activity carried on on the *open* land in the agricultural unit. The Court of Appeal dismissed this narrow interpretation; the intended use could be an agricultural activity carried on wholly or substantially within the building such as intensive horticulture or battery hens. The revised wording in the new General Development Order makes no change in this respect.

Class B of Part 6 permits the excavation from agricultural land, or land held therewith, of minerals reasonably required for agricultural purposes within the same agricultural unit. Class C is concerned with the construction of fishponds and other engineering operations for the purposes of a registered business of fish farming or shellfish farming.

Forestry buildings and operations   Although the use of land for forestry is not development, the carrying out of building and other operations connected with forestry is development and requires planning permission. Part 7 permits the carrying out on land used for the purposes of forestry[17] of development reasonably necessary for those purposes consisting of:

(a) the erection, extension or alteration of buildings but not dwellinghouses;
(b) the formation, alteration or maintenance of private ways;
(c) operations on that land or land held therewith to obtain materials for the formation etc of private ways;
(d) other operations (but not engineering or mining operations).

The height of any buildings within three kilometres of an aerodrome must not exceed three metres, and no part of any development permitted by Part 7 must be within 25 metres of the metalled portion of a trunk or classified road.

Where the land is in a national park or certain areas of high

16 (1983) 50 P & CR 299, [1984] JPL 274, CA.
17 Including afforestation.

landscape value,[18] any person proposing to erect or alter a building, or to form or alter a private way, must give the local planning authority a written description and plan of the development; the authority then have 28 days in which to notify the developer that the development shall not be begun without prior approval of the siting, design and external appearance of the building, or the siting and means of construction of the private way. If the authority have not required prior approval, the development is to be carried out in accordance with the written description and plan.[19]

Industrial and warehouse development   Class A of Part 8 permits additions to industrial buildings and warehouses[20] within the curtilage of the undertaking concerned. The additions may take the form of extensions or new buildings up to certain limits of size and other limitations:

(1) In national parks, areas of outstanding natural beauty, conservation areas and certain other special areas[1] the additions must not exceed 10 per cent cubic content of the original building,[2] and the total aggregate floor space must not be increased by more than 500 square metres; elsewhere the cubic content must not be increased by more than 25 per cent and the floor space by more than 1,000 square metres.

(2) The building as extended or altered must be used for the purposes of the undertaking.

(3) The building must be used for the purpose of carrying out an industrial process[3] or, in the case of a warehouse, for storage or distribution.

(4) The height of the original building must not be exceeded, and the external appearance of the whole of the premises must not be materially affected.

(5) The extension or new building must not come within five metres of the boundary of the curtilage.

(6) There must be no reduction in the space available for parking or turning vehicles.

18 See fn 13, above.
19 GDO, Sch 2, Part 7, para A2. This replaces the Landscape Areas GDO 1950.
20 I e any building used for any purpose within Class B8 of the Use Classes Order: see ch 5, p. 94, above, but excluding a building associated with a mine: GDO, art 1(2), Sch 2, Part 8, E.
 1 See GDO, Sch 1 as amended.
 2 Ie as built on 1 July 1948 or, if built since that date, as so built: GDO, art 1(2); where two or more original buildings are in the same curtilage and are used for the same undertaking, they are to be treated as one in making any measurement.
 3 As defined in GDO, art 1(2). The definition is similar to that in the Use Classes Order: see ch 5, p. 95, above.

Part 8 also gives permission for various works and installations on land used for industry or warehousing.

ARTICLE 4 DIRECTIONS

Article 4 of the General Development Order provides that the Secretary of State or the local planning authority may direct either (i) that all or any of the developments permitted by any Part, class or paragraph in Schedule 2 of the Order shall not be carried out in a particular area without specific permission or (ii) that any particular development shall not be carried out without specific permission.[4] Such directions are often referred to as 'Article 4 directions'. An Article 4 direction by a local planning authority requires the consent of the Secretary of State unless it relates only to buildings of special architectural or historic interest[5] and does not affect certain specified operations of statutory undertakers. Directions relating to development within Parts 1 to 4 of Schedule 2 may take effect for six months without the Secretary of State's approval. Notice of a direction affecting an area of land must be published in the *London Gazette* and at least one local newspaper; where the direction is for a particular development, notice must be served on the owner and occupier.

In effect, therefore, an Article 4 direction withdraws the permission by the General Development Order and makes it necessary to apply to the local planning authority for permission. If permission is refused or granted subject to conditions, the owner is entitled to compensation on the footing that permission already granted has been revoked or modified.[6] Article 4 directions have been extensively used so as to withdraw the permission given under what is now Part 4 for temporary markets.

It would seem that an Article 4 direction may be made after the development has been commenced but not after it has been completed. In *Cole v Somerset County Council*[7] land, which before the war had formed part of a golf course, had been used since 1950 as a caravan site for members of the Caravan Club. This use was at that time permitted development under Class V of the General Development Order 1950. In 1954 the county council served on the owner of the land an Article 4 direction approved by the Minister. In 1956 the county council

---

4 Article 4 is not applicable to Class B of Part 22 or Class C of Part 23, relating to certain forms of mineral development, but a similar procedure is provided by GDO, art 6.
5 See ch 14, below.
6 1990 Act, s. 108. See ch 9, below.
7 [1957] 1 QB 23, [1956] 3 All ER 531.

served an enforcement notice requiring the owner to discontinue the use and remove the caravans. On appeal, it was held that neither the Minister nor the planning authority had power under Article 4 to withdraw permission which had already been given and acted upon. The enforcement notice was therefore invalid.

SPECIAL DEVELOPMENT ORDERS

Planning permission may also be granted by special development order. For instance, in the urban development areas[8] planning permission is granted by special development orders[9] for development which is in accordance with the general plans for those areas as approved by the Secretary of State; the permission covers both public and private development, but where the development is not being carried out by the development corporation, it may be necessary to obtain the approval of the corporation for details. Somewhat similar provision has been made for development within new towns.[10] In all these cases there is power to make directions similar to those made under article 4 of the General Development Order. These orders all facilitate development by making it unnecessary to apply to the local planning authority for express permission; in the past, some special development orders have been made to modify the effect of the General Development Order in sensitive areas such as the national parks, but these modifications are now set out in the General Development Order itself.

Some orders give permission for specific projects. The proposals for reprocessing nuclear waste at Windscale were originally the subject of an application to the local planning authority; the application was called in and, after public inquiry, the Secretary of State decided to make a special development order[11] to allow opportunity for parliamentary debate. A similar procedure was adopted with proposals for office and housing development on a very large riverside site in London.[12]

8 See ch 2, pp. 18, 19, above.
9 See e g the T & CP (Merseyside Urban Development Area) SDO 1981 (SI 1981 No 560); T & CP (London Docklands Urban Development Area) SDO 1981 (SI 1981 No 1082).
10 See the T & CP (New Towns) SDO 1977.
11 T & CP (Windscale and Calder Works) SDO 1978 (SI 1978 No 523).
12 See the T & CP (Vauxhall Cross) SDO 1982 (SI 1982 No 796).

ENTERPRISE ZONES

The concept of the enterprise zone was introduced in 1980 as a means of reviving the local economy in areas of high unemployment.

The Secretary of State may invite a district council, a new town corporation or urban development corporation to prepare a scheme for the development of an area with a view to the area being designated as an enterprise zone.[13] The authority may then prepare a draft scheme 'in accordance with the terms of the invitation': adequate publicity must be given to the draft scheme so that members of the public may make representations about it within a specified time. The authority may then adopt the scheme or modify it to take account of any representations.[14] Subject to any challenge in the High Court as to the validity of the scheme, the Secretary of State may then designate the area as an enterprise zone.[15]

The designation order grants planning permission for development specified in the scheme or for particular classes of development so specified.[16] The designation order is thus akin to a special development order by permitting the carrying out of development without the express permission of the local planning authority.

SIMPLIFIED PLANNING ZONES

A simplified planning zone (SPZ) is defined as an area in which a simplified planning zone scheme is in force.[17] The effect of such a scheme is to grant planning permission for either some specific development, or a class of development specified in the scheme; such planning permission may be unconditional or subject to conditions, limitations or exceptions.[18] These schemes have been aptly described as 'local general development orders made by local planning authorities'.[19] But the scheme must not restrict the right of any person (a) to do anything not amounting to development, or (b) to carry out development for which permission is not required or for which planning permission has been granted otherwise than under the scheme, e g by the General Development Order.[20]

13 Local Government Planning and Land Act 1980, Sch 32, para 1.
14 A scheme may not be modified in any way inconsistent with the Secretary of State's invitation; ibid, Sch 32, para 3(3).
15 Ibid, Sch 32, paras 2 to 5.
16 Ibid, Sch 32, Part III.
17 1990 Act, s. 82(1).
18 Ibid, ss. 82(2), (3), 84(1), (2).
19 House of Lords Debates, 13 October 1986.
20 1990 Act, s. 84(3).

The coming into force of the original legislation[1] imposed on every local planning authority the duty to consider, as soon as practicable, whether the making of one or more special planning zones would be desirable and thereafter to keep that question under review. Where the authority conclude that such a scheme is desirable, it becomes their duty to prepare a scheme.[2] Moreover, any person may request the local planning authority to make or alter a scheme; and, if the authority refuse or neglect to do so, refer the matter to the Secretary of State, who can then issue a direction to the authority.[3]

The content of schemes is likely to vary considerably; illustrative models are given in Planning Policy Guidance Note No 5. Mineral and waste disposal development cannot be granted permission by SPZ schemes.[4] The Planning Policy Guidance Note suggests that SPZ schemes should not be used to permit some other types of development, including the construction of buildings or the use of buildings or land for the special industrial uses B3 to B7 of the Use Classes Order.[5]

Simplified planning zone schemes cannot be made for certain environmentally sensitive areas, namely any land in a national park, conservation area, the Broads, area of outstanding natural beauty, approved green belt or an area of special scientific interest under the Wildlife and Countryside Act 1981.[6]

The procedure for the making, and adoption of, a scheme is as follows:[7]

(1) The local planning authority should notify the Secretary of State and he has power to call in the making of the scheme at any stage prior to formal adoption.

(2) The authority must give publicity to their proposals and consider any representations received within six weeks.[8]

(3) The authority then prepare the scheme, make it available for inspection indicating the time within which objections may be made.

(4) If there are objections, the authority must hold a public local inquiry or other hearing.

(5) The authority must then consider the report of the inspector who

---

1 I e the 1986 Act which came into force as regards simplified planning zones on 2 November 1987.
2 1990 Act, s. 83(1), (2).
3 Ibid, Sch 7, para 3.
4 T & CP (Simplified Planning Zones) (Excluded Development) Order 1987 (SI 1987 No 1849).
5 See ch 5, p. 94, above.
6 1990 Act, s. 87.
7 Ibid, Sch 7.
8 T & CP (Simplified Planning Zones) Regulations 1987 (SI 1987 No 1750), reg 3.

conducted the inquiry or hearing, and publish a statement of their decisions including their reasons.

(6) The authority may then resolve to adopt the scheme. Unless challenged in the High Court in the meantime,[9] the scheme will come into force six weeks thereafter.

The scheme will remain in force for ten years, but may be altered at any time.[10] The procedure for altering a scheme is the same as for the making and adoption of a scheme as set out above.[11]

Permission 'deemed to be granted' under the Act

In certain cases no application for planning permission is required because permission is deemed to have been granted under the Act of 1990. For instance, there is a deemed planning permission for the carrying out of development for which planning permission was granted after 21 July 1943 under the pre-1947 planning legislation but which had not been carried out by 1 July 1948.[12] Likewise, where works for the erection of a building had been begun but not completed before 1 July 1948 there is a deemed planning permission for the erection of the building.[13] In both cases, the deemed planning permission will now have lapsed if the development was not begun before 1 April 1974.[14] There are not likely to be many outstanding cases.

There are also deemed permissions relating to outdoor advertisements and to development authorised by a government department. We will consider each of these in turn.

The display of advertisements does not of itself constitute development, but the erection of an advertisement hoarding will be development because the hoarding is a 'building'[15] and the use for the display of advertisements of any external part of a building not normally

---

9 1990 Act, s. 288.

10 Ibid, s. 85.

11 In the case of minor alterations a somewhat shorter procedure may be used: ibid, Sch 7, para 6.

12 1962 Act, Sch 13, para 7; 1971 Act, Sch 24, para 1(3). Planning (Consequential Provisions) Act 1990, Sch 3, para 3.

13 1962 Act, Sch 13, para 8; 1971 Act, Sch 24, para 1(3). Planning (Consequential Provisions) Act 1990, Sch 3, para 3. The effect of this deemed permission was considered in *LCC v Marks and Spencer Ltd* [1953] AC 535, [1953] 1 All ER 1095 (clearance of site preparatory to erection of building held to be 'works for erection of a building').

14 1971 Act, Sch 24, para 19(1). Planning (Consequential Provisions) Act 1990, Sch 3, para 3. See ch 8, pp. 174, 175, below, as to when the development is begun.

15 See the definition of 'building' in the 1990 Act, s. 336, discussed in ch 5 at pp. 77 ff, above.

used for that purpose is a material change of use.[16] All outdoor advertisements require consent under the Control of Advertisements Regulations,[17] whether development is involved or not. The Act of 1990 provides that where the display of advertisements in accordance with the regulations involves development, planning permission shall be deemed to have been granted.[18]

Where any development by a local authority or statutory undertaker in any case requires authorisation by a government department, that department may direct that planning permission 'shall be deemed to be granted'; in other words, authorisation and planning permission are conferred simultaneously instead of separately.[19]

16 1990 Act, s. 55(4).
17 See ch 13, below.
18 1990 Act, s. 222.
19 Ibid, s. 90.

Chapter 7

Planning permission: express permission

As explained in chapter 6, there are some forms of development which do not require planning permission; some are permitted by development orders or have the benefit of deemed permission. In every other case, application should be made to the local planning authority for express permission.

WHO MAY APPLY

The applicant need not be the owner of an interest in the land, nor is it necessary to obtain the consent of the owner.[1] But whether he has an interest in the land or not, the applicant must give notice of his application to any other person who has a material interest in that land.[2]

PUBLICITY FOR APPLICATIONS

Normally, it is not necessary for the applicant to give notice to the public or to third parties but there are certain exceptions.

(1) In the case of certain kinds of development, section 65 of the Act of 1990 requires the applicant to publish a notice in the local press indicating where members of the public may inspect plans of the proposed development. He must also affix to the land a notice stating that the application is to be made. The classes of development to which section 65 applies are prescribed by the Secretary of State and are as follows:[3]

(a) construction of buildings for use as a public convenience;
(b) construction of buildings or other operations, or use of land, for the disposal of refuse or waste materials or as a scrap yard;

---

1 *Hanily v Minister of Local Government and Planning* [1952] 2 QB 444, [1952] 1 All ER 1293.
2 1990 Act, s. 66(1).
3 GDO, art 11.

(c) the winning or working of minerals or the use of land for mineral working deposits;

(d) construction of buildings or other operations (other than the laying of sewers, construction of septic tanks or cesspools serving single dwellinghouses or single buildings in which not more than ten people will normally reside, work or congregate, and works ancillary thereto) or use of land for the disposal or treatment of sewage, trade waste or sludge;

(e) construction of buildings to a height exceeding 20 metres;

(f) construction of buildings or use of land for the purposes of a slaughter-house or knacker's yard, or for the killing or plucking of poultry;

(g) construction of buildings and use of buildings for any of the following purposes – casino, funfair, bingo hall, theatre, cinema, music hall, dance hall, skating rink, swimming bath or gymnasium (not forming part of a school, college or university), Turkish or other vapour or foam bath;

(h) construction of buildings and use of buildings or land as a zoo or for the business of boarding or breeding cats or dogs;

(i) construction of buildings or use of land for motor car or motor-cycle racing;

(j) the construction of a stadium;

(k) use of land as a cemetery or crematorium.

In addition, section 65 applies with modifications whenever an application for planning permission is accompanied by an environmental statement pursuant to the Environment Effects Regulations.[4]

Any member of the public then has the right to make representations to the local planning authority within 21 days of the publication in the local press referred to above.[5]

(2) If any part of the land is included in an agricultural holding the applicant must notify the tenant[6] who then has the right to make representations to the local planning authority within 21 days of notification.[7]

(3) If any person other than the applicant has a 'material interest'[8] in the land, the applicant must notify him; if he does not know the names and addresses of all such interested parties he must give notice

---

4 Environmental Effects Regulations, reg 12. For the need to submit an environmental statement and the relevant procedures, see this chapter, pp. 138 ff, below.

5 1990 Act, s. 71(1).

6 Ibid, s. 66(4). The tenant for this purpose is the person who was such 21 days before the planning application.

7 Ibid, s. 71(2).

8 This means either the freehold or a lease with at least seven years to run: ibid, s. 66(7).

in the local press.[9] All such interested persons then have the right to make representations to the local planning authority, within 21 days of the latest notification, or of publication in the local press, whichever is the later.[10]

In each of these cases, it is the duty of the applicant to give the required notices. In the case of development affecting the setting of a listed building, or the character or appearance of a conservation area, it is the duty of the local planning authority to give public notice; any member of the public then has the right to make representations within 21 days.[11]

INDUSTRIAL DEVELOPMENT CERTIFICATES

From 1 July 1948 to early in 1982 industrial development was subject to control by central government as well as by the local planning authority. Before applying for planning permission for certain types of industrial development the applicant had to obtain an industrial development certificate from the Department of Industry that the development could be carried out consistently with the proper distribution of industry. An application which was not supported by such a certificate was of no effect and could not be considered by the local planning authority.

On granting an industrial development certificate, the Department might impose such conditions as they considered appropriate having regard to the proper distribution of industry;[12] these conditions were to be attached to the planning permission if granted by the local planning authority.

This system of control has not operated since 9 January 1982. Regulations which came into force on that date revoked the earlier regulations which had prescribed the classes of building for which an industrial development certificate was required, with the result that there were no longer any classes of building for which a certificate was required. The legislation under which the system had operated was finally repealed by the Act of 1986.

9 1990 Act, s. 66(1)–(3). For a person to be an 'owner' for the purposes of notification he must have been such 21 days before the planning application.
10 Ibid, s. 66(6).
11 LB Act, ss. 67, 73. For listed buildings and conservation areas, see ch 14, below.
12 These conditions might be of a type which could not otherwise be imposed under planning law.

OFFICE BUILDINGS

The powers of the Department of Industry in respect of industrial development derived from the Act of 1947. It was not until the passing of the Control of Office and Industrial Development Act 1965, that Whitehall was given similar powers to control office development. The relevant provisions were re-enacted in the Act of 1971, but were originally due to expire in 1972. They were extended by legislation in 1972 and 1977, but have now ceased to have effect.[13]

FORM OF APPLICATION

The application must be made on a form issued by the local planning authority and must be accompanied by a plan sufficient to identify the land and such other plans and drawings as are necessary to describe the development. The local planning authority may require the applicant to supply such further information as they need for giving a decision.[14]

Where the applicant seeks permission for the erection of a building, he may apply in the first instance for *outline* planning permission with a view to obtaining permission in principle before going to the expense of preparing detailed plans. In this case plans and particulars relating to siting, design, external appearance and means of access need not be submitted, these matters being left for subsequent approval in the event of permission being granted on the outline application.

The local planning authority may decline to entertain an outline application if they consider that the application ought not to be considered separately from siting, design, external appearance and means of access; in this event, the applicant may either furnish particulars of these details or appeal to the Secretary of State as if his application had been refused.[15] A permission on an outline application is a valid planning permission even though the applicant must obtain further approvals before acting upon it. An outline permission can be revoked only in accordance with the statutory procedures; these normally require the consent of the Secretary of State and the payment of compensation.[16]

13 See the Control of Office Development (Cessation) Order 1979 (SI 1979 No 1042).
14 T & CP (Applications) Regulations 1988 (SI 1988 No 1812), regs 3, 4.
15 GDO, art 7.
16 *Hamilton v West Sussex County Council* [1958] 2 QB 286, [1958] 2 All ER 174.

PLANNING FEES

Section 303 of the Act of 1990 enables the Secretary of State to make regulations requiring the payment of fees to the local planning authority in respect of applications for planning permission and other matters.

The regulations which the Secretary of State has made[17] provide that, with a few exceptions, every application for planning permission (or for consent for matters reserved by an outline permission)[18] shall be accompanied by the fee prescribed by the regulations. If the application is not accompanied by the requisite fee, the statutory period within which the planning authority are required to give notice of their decision on the application does not begin until the correct fee has been received.[19]

REFERENCE OF APPLICATIONS TO THE SECRETARY OF STATE

Normally, the decision on an application for planning permission will be made by the local planning authority. But, as mentioned earlier,[20] the Secretary of State has power under section 77 of the Act of 1990 to 'call in' any application for planning permission: that is, to direct that it shall be referred to him for decision. Where an application is called in, the parties have the right to be heard at a public local inquiry or other hearing.

It is entirely within the discretion of the Secretary of State whether or not an application is called in; the court will intervene only if he misconstrues his powers in some way – perhaps by taking into account some irrelevant matter – or if he exercises his discretion in a wholly unreasonable manner.[1]

The present policy of the Secretary of State is to be very selective in calling in applications. The proposed development may be of considerable national importance or it may have engendered widespread public controversy; recent examples have been the processing of nuclear waste at Windscale and coalmining in the Vale of Belvoir.

17 Town and Country Planning (Fees for Applications and Deemed Applications) Regulations 1983 (SI 1983 No 1674) as amended by SI 1985 No 1182 and SI 1987 No 101. The regulations also apply to appeals against enforcement notices, applications for established use certificates and to applications for consent under the Control of Advertisement Regulations.
18 See above.
19 GDO, art 23(2).
20 See ch 3, above.
 1 *Rhys Williams v Secretary of State for Wales* [1985] JPL 29.

But an application may also be called in because it involves a substantial departure from the development plan, or because it would involve a serious loss of agricultural land.

CONSULTATIONS BY LOCAL PLANNING AUTHORITY

On receiving an application for planning permission, the local planning authority may have to consult various government departments and other authorities. Thus, in the case of development affecting trunk roads and certain other major highways (whether existing or proposed) the local planning authority must, on receipt of the application, consult the Secretary of State[2] who may direct the authority either to refuse permission or to impose conditions.

Other consultations are prescribed by article 18 of the General Development Order or by directions made by the Secretary of State under article 18. In these cases consultation is not automatically required; the duty to consult arises if the local planning authority,' having given some consideration to the application, are minded to grant permission. For instance, the local planning authority must not grant planning permission for development within three kilometres of Windsor Castle, Windsor Great Park or Home Park or 800 metres of any other royal palace or park which might affect the amenities of that palace or park without first consulting the Secretary of State; he would presumably be able to issue a direction to the local planning authority.[3] In other cases, the local planning authority must consult with some other government department or public authority. For instance, the Secretary of State for Transport must be consulted before permission is granted for development which is likely to result in a material increase in the volume or a material change in the character of traffic entering or leaving a trunk road.[4] The Nature Conservancy Council are to be consulted before permission is granted for development in an area of special scientific interest. The government department or other public authority concerned may make representations to the local planning authority but cannot give directions.

The local planning authority must not grant permission for development involving a substantial departure from the provisions of the

---

2 GDO, art 15. These provisions apply to (a) the formation, laying out or alteration of any means of access to the highway; (b) any other development within 67 metres from the middle of the existing or proposed highway.

3 Power to issue directions restricting grant of planning permission is given to the Secretary of State by GDO, art 14.

4 It is apparently for the local planning authority to decide whether there is likely to be a material increase in volume or material change in character.

development plan without first going through the procedure laid down by the Development Plans (England) Direction 1981[5] or the corresponding direction for Wales. The Direction requires the local planning authority to advertise in the local press any application (referred to as a 'departure application') for development which they consider would conflict with or prejudice the implementation of the development plan,[6] the public must be given 21 days within which to send objections to the local planning authority.

In addition, the Secretary of State must be notified of any departure application which either:

(a) would materially conflict with or prejudice the implementation of any of the policies or general proposals of the structure plan or with a fundamental provision of an old development plan in so far as it is in force in the area concerned,[7] or

(b) would conflict with or prejudice the implementation of any provisions in a local plan introduced by way of a modification by the Secretary of State.

When notifying the Secretary of State of such a departure application, the local planning authority must send him copies of any objections received in response to the advertisement in the local press. The Secretary of State may then issue a direction to the local planning authority restricting the grant of permission or to call in the application; if he does neither, the planning authority are authorised by the Direction to grant planning permission.

What would be the position if the local planning authority granted planning permission without observing the procedures outlined above? Would such permission be valid? In *Co-operative Retail Services Ltd v Taff-Ely Borough Council*[8] Ormrod LJ and Browne LJ considered that the procedure is merely directory and not mandatory. In the subsequent case of *R v St Edmundsbury Borough Council ex p Investors in Industry Commercial Properties Ltd*,[9] the council failed to advertise a departure application. Stocker J held that the reasoning of Ormrod and Browne LJJ in the earlier case was not obiter, and held that the failure to comply with the Direction did not render the grant of planning permission null and void.

The Direction thus gives local planning authorities considerable

---

5 The text of the Direction is appended to circular 2/81.
6 The application need not be advertised in this way if it has already been advertised in pursuance of some other requirement eg under s. 65 of the 1990 Act as to which see this chapter, pp. 131, 132, above.
7 See ch 4, p. 00, above.
8 (1979) 39 P & CR 223 at 245, 246 and 253, 254, 255; affd *sub nom A-G (ex rel Co-operative Retail Services Ltd) v Taff-Ely Borough Council* (1981) 42 P & CR 1.
9 [1985] 3 All ER 234, [1985] 1 WLR 1168.

freedom to grant permission for departures from the development plan. It may be pertinent to ask, however, whether there are sufficient safeguards against the occasional abuse of that freedom, particularly in relation to departures from a local plan.

ENVIRONMENTAL IMPACT ASSESSMENT

The protection of the environment from pollution and nuisance is an obvious objective of planning control. It has been said that, in principle, the established system of control is capable in most cases of securing that the effect on the environment of any development project is evaluated before planning permission is granted. However, to comply with a European Community Directive, special requirements have been introduced for certain public and private projects.

In general, the new system is prescribed by the Environmental Effects Regulations, but there are separate regulations for special cases such as nuclear power stations. Where an environmental assessment is required under the Environmental Effects Regulations, an applicant for planning permission must submit to the local planning authority an 'environmental statement', that is, one or more documents providing specified information to enable an assessment to be made as to the likely impact of the proposed development on the environment: where significant adverse effects are identified, the statement must contain a description of the remedial measures which the developer proposes.[10] The submission of this statement will set going publicity and consultations with a view to building up a body of environmental information which must be taken into account before planning permission is granted.

The cases in which an environmental statement will be required are specified in Schedules 1 and 2 of the Regulations. Such a statement will always be necessary for development falling within Schedule 1, unless exempted by direction of the Secretary of State. Schedule 1 includes such projects as oil refineries, non-nuclear power stations, steelworks, integrated chemical installations, special roads, long distance railways, large aerodromes and various types of waste disposal.[11] Schedule 2 specifies a considerable number of categories of development in respect of which an environmental statement will be required from the developer if his particular project 'would be likely to have significant effects on the environment by virtue of factors such as its nature, size or location'; here again the Secretary of State has power to direct that a development be exempted. To mention but a few

10 Regs 2, 8, 9 and Sch 3.
11 Reg 2(1).

examples, Schedule 2 includes some forms of agricultural development such as poultry and pig rearing;[12] coal mining and other forms of mineral development; glass manufacture; various forms of food processing; development of industrial estates; holiday villages; roads and railways not mentioned in Schedule 1.

The question whether Schedule 2 applies so as to require an environmental statement will be a matter of judgment in the first instance for the local planning authority. They will have to consider whether the proposed development will have significant effects by virtue of such factors as its size, nature and location. The use of the words 'such ... as' implies that other factors may be relevant, but it seems that these must be *ejusdem generis* with those specified. Another difficulty is that the authority will have to consider whether the development would have significant effects before seeking an environmental statement, and if they decide that such a statement is necessary to give full reasons; the practical answer seems to be that they should make the best judgment on the basis of the information available to them, bearing in mind that their decision may come under review by the Secretary of State and the courts.

The question whether an environmental statement is required may come up for decision in a number of ways:

(1) The prospective developer may ask the local planning authority for their opinion. The authority should respond within three weeks or such longer period as may be agreed. If the authority fail to do so or if the developer is dissatisfied with the authority's opinion, he may apply to the Secretary of State for a direction on the matter.[13]

(2) Where the local planning authority receive an application for planning permission which is not accompanied by an environmental statement which the authority consider to be necessary, they should notify the applicant within three weeks or such longer period as may be agreed, giving their full reasons. The applicant then has three weeks in which to inform the authority either (i) that he accepts their opinion and will be submitting an environmental statement; or (ii) that he is applying to the Secretary of State for his direction on the matter.[14]

(3) An application for planning permission may have been referred to the Secretary of State for decision by him under section 77 of

12 In many cases development for poultry and pig rearing on an established agricultural holding will be permitted development by virtue of the GDO, Sch 2, Part 6: see pp. 121, 122, above. In such cases The Environmental Effects Regulations will not apply.
13 Reg 5.
14 Reg 9.

the Act of 1990,[15] or there may be an appeal to him under section 36.[16] If he considers that an environmental statement should have been submitted, he should so inform the applicant within three weeks or such longer period as he may reasonably require, giving his reasons. The applicant then has three weeks to notify the Secretary of State that he will be providing an environmental statement. Also, it may occur to the inspector appointed to decide an appeal, that an environmental statement should have been submitted, in which case, he should ask the Secretary of State for a direction on the matter.[17]

We turn now to the procedures involved in the submission of an environmental statement by an applicant for planning permission. The applicant must publish a notice in the local press stating where members of the public may inspect and, so long as stocks last,[18] obtain copies of the environmental statement, and specifying a date by which representations may be made to the local planning authority; a similar notice must be posted on the land.[19]

Various government departments and public bodies have the right to be consulted.[20] They include those whom the local planning authority are required to consult under article 18 of the General Development Order;[1] other principal councils[2] in the area; the Nature Conservancy Council and the Countryside Commission; and in some cases HM Inspectorate of Pollution. It is the duty of the local planning authority to ensure that these bodies know of their right to receive copies. The local planning authority will also send a copy to the Secretary of State;[3] presumably the intention is that he should have the opportunity to consider whether to call in the application for planning permission.[4]

The result of the publicity and consultations will be the assembly of a file of 'environmental information' comprising the environmental statement submitted by the applicant, representations made by the statutory consultees, and any representations duly made by any person about the likely environmental effects of the proposed development.[5]

15 See p. 135, above.
16 See p. 152, below.
17 Regs 10, 11
18 The applicant may make a charge for copies supplied to the public.
19 Regs 12, 13.
20 Regs 8, 14.
 1 See this chapter, p. 136, above.
 2 'Principal councils' are county councils, district councils, London Borough councils, Metropolitan district councils.
 3 Regs 8, 14.
 4 See this chapter, p. 135, above.
 5 Reg 2.

The Environmental Effects Regulations expressly prohibit the grant of planning permission by the local planning authority, or by the Secretary of State, unless they have first taken the environmental information into account. If planning permission is granted in breach of regulation 4, the validity of that permission may be challenged in the High Court by way of proceedings under section 288 of the Act of 1990.[6] Where the local planning authority fail to determine that some proposed development requires the submission of an environmental statement – either by expressly deciding that it does not or simply taking no action – it seems that the remedy would be an application to the High Court for judicial review.[7]

Finally, it should be noted that, where a local planning authority propose to carry out development to which the Regulations apply, they must prepare and publish an environmental statement and invite representations from the public and the statutory consultees mentioned above.[8]

CONSIDERATION BY LOCAL PLANNING AUTHORITY

In reaching their decision the local planning authority must, of course, comply with any directions given by the Secretary of State. They must have regard to the views of any government departments or other public authorities with whom they have been required to consult and to any representations received from interested parties under sections 65 to 67 of the Act of 1990 or section 67 or 73 of the Listed Buildings Act or in pursuance of the Development Plans Direction. Where an environmental statement has been submitted under the Assessment of Environmental Effects Regulations, the local planning authority are prohibited from granting planning permission unless they have first taken into account the environmental information which they have received.[9]

The local planning authority must always have regard to the provisions of the development plan and to any other material consideration.[10]

Provisions of the development plan   The provisions of the development plan are obviously of primary importance. Although the structure plan is concerned with general policies and proposals, the effect of

6 Reg 25, and see ch 18, below.
7 See ch 18, below.
8 Reg 17.
9 See pp. 138 ff, above.
10 1990 Act, s. 70(2).

these policies and proposals may be sufficiently clear to raise a presumption that planning permission should be granted or (as the case may be) refused. Thus if the structure plan designates a village in the countryside as a 'key' or 'growth' village, there will be a presumption in favour of residential development; if a village has not been so designated, but is in the heart of a green belt, then there is a clear presumption against any but the most limited residential development. However, where a local plan is in force, it will be the more appropriate source of guidance for development control purposes.

When considering an application for planning permission the local planning authority may also have to take account of emerging plans ie proposals for the amendments of the structure or local plan or new plans in course of preparation. It may be difficult in these circumstances to come to a decision which is fair to all concerned; if the proposed development is in accordance with the emerging plan, the authority may think it right that planning permission should be granted but to do so might pre-empt objections to the plan and the public inquiry. Some guidance on these problems has been given in *R v City of London Corpn, ex p Allan.*[11]

> The Corporation had prepared a draft local plan known as the Smithfield Local Plan. Objections had been lodged and were due to go to public inquiry. However, an application had been received for planning permission for the redevelopment of a large part of the area. The Corporation referred the application to the Secretary of State but he declined to call it in. It seemed likely that the Corporation would grant permission, so the applicants sought an order of prohibition to prevent the grant of permission at this stage.
>
> Woolf J said that once a planning authority had publicised proposals in a draft plan, the authority should have regard to that plan; if there were objections which would lead to an inquiry, the authority should take those objections into account and should consider whether it would be appropriate to deal with the application at this stage or to refuse permission on the ground that the application was premature. His Lordship concluded that there was nothing to suggest that the Corporation would not give proper consideration to the relevant matters and he dismissed the application for an order of prohibition.

Notwithstanding the obvious importance of the development plan, it has been said that the local planning authority should not 'slavishly adhere to it'. As was explained in a case arising out of the Scottish equivalent of section 70(2), the meaning of the section is plain: the

11 (1980) 79 LGR 223.

planning authority are to consider all the material considerations of which the development plan is one.[12]

Other material considerations It is an obvious principle that these considerations must be related to the objects of planning legislation. The difficulty is to say precisely what are these objects. In *Stringer v Minister of Housing and Local Government*,[13] Cooke J said that any consideration which related to the use and development of land was capable of being a planning consideration, its materiality depending on the circumstances. This dictum of Cooke J was said in the much more recent case of *Northumberland County Council v Secretary of State for the Environment and British Coal Corpn*[14] to be 'still good law'. The question whether a particular issue was or was not material has come before the courts on numerous occasions, and the courts have in general adopted a liberal approach.

Cooke J's point that the materiality of a particular issue may depend on the circumstances is well illustrated by the question whether the economics of a proposed development should be taken into account. In *J Murphy & Sons Ltd v Secretary of State for the Environment*[15] the issue was whether the cost of developing the site was a relevant consideration.

> The Camden London Borough Council proposed to build flats on a site which was far from ideal because on one side it adjoined a railway and on another adjoined Murphy's industrial works; the Council considered it could be made suitable although it would be very expensive. Murphy's wanted to acquire the site and objected to the council's proposals. The Secretary of State said that the cost of developing the site for a particular purpose was an irrelevant consideration in determining a planning application.

Ackner J in upholding the Secretary of State said 'What the planning authority is concerned with is how the land is going to be used ... The planning authority exercises no paternalistic or avancular jurisdiction over would-be developers to safeguard them from their financial follies.' That seems to be a sound approach, but the learned judge appears to have overstated matters when he held 'as a matter of law' that the Secretary of State was not entitled to have regard to

---

12 *Simpson v Edinburgh Corpn* 1960 SC at 313 and 319, per Lord Guest. These remarks were adopted in *Co-operative Retail Services Ltd v Taff-Ely Borough Council* (1979) 39 P & CR 223, CA.
13 [1971] 1 All ER 65 at 77.
14 [1989] JPL 700.
15 [1973] 2 All ER 26, [1973] 1 WLR 560.

the cost of developing the site.[16] Certainly Forbes J disagreed in *Sovmots Investments Ltd v Secretary of State for the Environment*;[17] the Secretary of State must, he said, be entitled to bear in mind the likelihood of the development being carried out: 'Cost may or may not be a relevant consideration depending on the circumstances of the case; all that the court has to do is to say that cost can be a relevant consideration and leave it to the Secretary of State to decide whether in any circumstance it is or it is not.' These remarks were adopted by Woolf J in *Sosmo Trust Ltd v Secretary of State for the Environment, London Borough of Camden*.[18] Nevertheless the Secretary of State may be overruled if his opinion as to the relevance of economic factors is unreasonable. In *Sosmo* the appellants had contended that nothing less than an office development of at least six storeys would be economically viable and that if permission were not granted the site would be left derelict; the inspector considered that the financial aspects were irrelevant and dismissed the appeal. Woolf J held that the inspector could not reasonably have come to this conclusion and remitted the case for reconsideration.

The prospective cost of development was also found to be relevant in *Niarchos (London) Ltd v Secretary of State for the Environment*.[19] The development plan provided that temporary planning permissions which had been granted for office use should not be renewed in respect of houses which could 'reasonably be used or adapted for use for residential occupation': it was held that in deciding whether the premises could *reasonably* be used or adapted, the Secretary of State should have regard to the cost of re-converting the houses to residential use.

The whole question of the relevance of financial considerations has now come before the Court of Appeal in *R v Westminster City Council, ex p Monahan*.[20]

> The trustees of the Royal Opera House (ROH) had applied for planning permission to redevelop part of Covent Garden. The central objective was to extend and improve the ROH, but the application also included the erection of office accommodation on part of the site. The modernisation of the ROH was an important feature of the local plan, but the proposal to erect offices was contrary to the plan. The City Council, albeit reluctantly, accepted the need to erect offices on the ground that the funds necessary to improve the ROH were unobtainable by any other means.

---

16 Ackner J in fact acknowledged in a later case that he 'might have stated the general proposition too widely': *Hambledon and Chiddingfold Parish Council v Secretary of State for the Environment* [1976] JPL 502.
17 [1977] QB 411, [1976] 1 All ER 178.
18 [1983] JPL 806.
19 (1977) 35 P & CR 259.
20 [1989] JPL 107.

The Covent Garden Community Association challenged the Council's decision on two grounds: first, that to permit the commercial development of part of the site for purely financial reasons, whatever their purpose, was not a material consideration which the Council was entitled to take into account; alternatively, that the Council was bound to investigate whether the erection of the offices was in fact necessary to achieve the objectives relating to the ROH.

Held: (1) the fact that the finances made available from the commercial development would enable the improvements to be carried out was capable of being a material consideration, that is, a consideration which related to the use and development of land, particularly as the proposed commercial development was on the same site as the ROH and the commercial development and the improvements to the ROH all formed part of one proposal; (2) that in fact the Council had adequately investigated the question whether the office development was necessary to achieve the improvements.

The judgments in this case must now be regarded as a definitive statement of the law on this question since the House of Lords have refused leave to appeal.

The *Royal Opera House* case thus sanctions the principle that it is lawful to grant planning permission for development 'A' in order to provide the funds necessary to carry out development 'B', although 'A' would otherwise have been refused. In the *Royal Opera House* case, development 'B' was a central feature of the local plan, and both 'A' and 'B' were included in a composite application for planning permission. But suppose there had been no physical contiguity and the sites some distance apart? That point was discussed in the Court of Appeal. Kerr LJ concluded that such a case 'would involve questions of fact and degree rather than of principle'. Staughton LJ suggested that the justification for permitting development 'B' must be that it fairly and reasonably related to development 'A'. In the subsequent case of *Northumberland County Council v Secretary of State for the Environment and British Coal Corpn*[1] the connection between 'A' and 'B' seems to be more questionable than in the *Royal Opera House* case; Mr Malcolm Spence QC, sitting as deputy judge, held that the Secretary of State had not erred in law in permitting an open cast mine because of the financial benefit to deep mining, even though no particular deep mine had been identified.

It is well established that 'other material considerations' include the Secretary of State's policy statements as contained, for instance, in the Department's circulars and the Planning Policy Guidance

1 [1989] JPL 700.

Notes.[2] There may, of course, be circumstances in which it is proper for the local planning authority to decide not to follow a particular policy statement,[3] but in that event they must give clear reasons for not doing so.[4]

A frequent bone of contention between the would-be developer and the local planning authority is whether the development is needed. Whether this issue is material depends, it is submitted, on the circumstances. The absence of need is not relevant if there are no other objections; but if there are other objections, the local planning authority may well consider whether the need for the development is sufficient to overcome those objections. Thus the need for additional farm dwellings may be sufficient to overcome the general policy objection to building isolated dwellings in the open countryside.[5]

The fact that there are permitted development rights under the General Development Order and existing planning permissions for similar, but not identical, development should be taken into account.[6]

It seems that the personal circumstances of the applicant may be a material consideration but they will only be peripheral; if there are substantial planning objections to the proposed development, those objections must obviously prevail, but where a case is more finely balanced, a genuine plea of hardship may tip the scales in the applicant's favour.[7]

It is not uncommon for the local planning authority, or on appeal the Secretary of State, to state as a ground of refusal that a grant of planning permission would create a precedent which might make it difficult to refuse a similar application. This has been recognised as a material consideration. In *Collis Radio v Secretary of State for the Environment*[8] Lord Widgery CJ said: 'Planning is something which deals with localities and not individual parcels of land and individual sites. In all planning cases it must be of the greatest importance to ask what the consequences in the locality will be – what are the side effects which will flow if such a permission is granted.' The law on this point

2 See e g *J A Pye (Oxford) Estates Ltd v West Oxfordshire District Council* (1982) 47 P & CR 125, [1982] JPL 577.

3 A good illustration is to be found in *Camden London Borough Council v Secretary of State for the Environment and PSP (Nominees) Co Ltd* [1989] JPL 613.

4 *Gransden & Co Ltd v Secretary of State for the Environment* [1986] JPL 519; affd [1987] JPL 365, CA.

5 See also the discussion in ch 2, pp. 00, 00, above.

6 *Wells v Minister of Housing and Local Government* [1967] 2 All ER 1041, [1967] 1 WLR 1000; and see the account of this case in ch 3, above.

7 *Tameside Metropolitan Borough Council v Secretary of State for the Environment* [1984] JPL 180; *Great Portland Estates v Secretary of State for the Environment* [1984] 3 All ER 744, [1984] 3 WLR 1035.

8 (1975) 73 LGR 211, 29 P & CR 390.

has now been refined to some extent. In *Poundstretcher Ltd v Secretary of State for the Environment and Liverpool City Council*[9] Mr David Widdicombe QC, sitting as deputy judge, said that mere fear or generalised concern about creating a precedent was not enough; there had to be evidence in one form or another for reliance on precedent. The learned deputy judge added, however, that in some cases the facts might speak for themselves: for instance, in the case of the rear extension of one in a terrace of houses, it might be obvious that other owners in the terrace would want extensions if one was permitted.

It is not a material consideration that planning permission has already been granted for another form of development; a landowner is entitled to make as many applications as he pleases, and the local planning authority must consider each application on its merits.[10]

The duty to consider each application on its merits is further illustrated by the case of *Stringer v Minister of Housing and Local Government*.[11] In this case there was an agreement between Cheshire County Council, the rural district council and Manchester University that development in certain areas in the neighbourhood of the Jodrell Bank telescope was to be resisted; the district council, in pursuance of that agreement, refused permission for development of a site in one of those areas. It was held that the agreement was ultra vires the planning authority and that there had been no proper determination on the application for planning permission; there would, however, have been no objection to arrangements for consulting the University provided they did not fetter the freedom of the local planning authority to have regard to all material circumstances.

The presumption in favour of development   As we have seen, it is the duty of the local planning authority to have regard to the development plan and to any other material considerations. Ministerial policy guidance over the years has emphasised that planning permission should be granted unless there are sound and clear cut reasons for refusal. Thus circular 14/85 states: 'There is always a presumption in favour of allowing applications for development, having regard to all material considerations unless the development would cause demonstrable harm to interests of acknowledged importance'.

This guidance has now been upheld by the High Court as more than mere policy, but as law. In *Cranford Hall Parking Ltd v Secretary*

9 [1989] JPL 90.
10 *Pilkington v Secretary of State for the Environment* [1974] 1 All ER 283, [1973] 1 WLR 1527.
11 [1971] 1 All ER 65, [1970] 1 WLR 1281.

of State for the Environment[12] Judge Marden said that the passage in circular 14/85 set out a correct approach reflecting the statutory position. *Cranford Hall* was a case on development in the green belt; the learned judge said that the correct approach was a presumption that planning permission would always be allowed which would be overridden where it was shown that the development would cause *demonstrable harm to the green belt policy.*[13]

THE LOCAL PLANNING AUTHORITY'S DECISION

The decision of the local planning authority may take one of three forms. They may grant permission unconditionally or they may grant permission subject to such conditions as they think fit or they may refuse permission.[14] Although the Act of 1990 permits the authority to attach such conditions 'as they think fit', such conditions must serve some useful purpose having regard to the objects of planning legislation[15] and they must not offend against the general law, eg a condition requiring a payment of money to the planning authority would be invalid.[16] Within these limits, however, the local planning authority have a very wide discretion,[17] and in particular they may attach conditions:[18]

(a) regulating the development or use of any land under the control of the applicant[19] (whether or not it is the land in respect of which the application has been made) provided the condition is reasonably related to the permitted development.

(b) requiring the permitted works to be removed or the permitted use to be discontinued at the expiry of a specified period, that is, in effect a permission granted for a limited period only.

Sections 91 to 93 of the Act of 1990 provide that each planning permission shall be subject to a deemed condition that development shall be commenced within five years. These provisions will be

---

12 [1989] JPL 169.
13 Author's italics.
14 1990 Act, s. 70(1).
15 *Pyx Granite Co Ltd v Minister of Housing and Local Government* [1960] AC 260, [1959] 3 All ER 1; *Fawcett Properties Ltd v Buckingham County Council* [1961] AC 636, [1960] 3 All ER 503.
16 *A-G v Wilts United Dairies* (1922) 91 LJKB 897.
17 For further discussion on the local planning authority's powers see ch 8, below.
18 1990 Act, s. 72(1).
19 The land need not be in the ownership of the applicant; it suffices that he has the necessary right over the land to comply with the proposed condition: *George Wimpey & Co Ltd v New Forest District Council and Secretary for the Environment* [1979] JPL 314.

considered in more detail in the next chapter,[20] but it should be noted here that the local planning authority may by express condition fix a period either shorter or longer than five years.

If the local planning authority refuse permission or impose conditions, they must state clearly and precisely their full reasons in the notice of their decision.[1] The duty to give *full* reasons was imposed as a statutory obligation for the first time in the current General Development Order, but it had in fact been required by the courts at a much earlier stage in the development of planning law that the authority should give all their reasons and not merely some of them.[2] But a developer is not entitled to claim that a condition is void merely because the local planning authority omitted to state any reason.[3]

TIME FOR GIVING DECISION

Article 23 of the General Development Order provides that the local planning authority shall notify the applicant of their decision within eight weeks, unless the applicant agrees in writing to an extension of time. If the authority do not give their decision within the proper time, the applicant can appeal to the Secretary of State as if permission had been refused.[4] Appeals are dealt with later in this chapter.

What happens if the local planning authority issue a decision out of time? The point first came up for consideration in *Edwick v Sunbury-on-Thames UDC*.[5]

The council served an enforcement notice on E requiring him to discontinue the unauthorised use of land for the display and sale of second-hand cars. Before the notice took effect, E applied for planning permission and (under the law as it then was) this had the effect of suspending the operation of the enforcement notice pending a decision on the application. More than two years later, the council notified E that permission was refused. If this decision were valid, the enforcement notice would have come into effect, but Salmon J held that the statutory direction as to the time within which the local authority should give their decision was mandatory and accordingly the notice of decision was invalid.

The law relating to enforcement notices has now been changed, and the circumstances of the *Edwick* case cannot occur again, but Salmon J's reasoning would apply to any decision of a local authority

20 See pp. 174, 175, below.
1 GDO, art 25.
2 *Hamilton v West Sussex County Council* [1958] 2 QB 286, [1958] 2 All ER 174.
3 *Brayhead (Ascot) Ltd v Berkshire County Council* [1964] 2 QB 303, [1964] 1 All ER 149.
4 1971 Act, s. 37.
5 [1962] 1 QB 229, [1961] 3 All ER 10.

on an application for planning permission. This is not likely to be of any practical consequence where the decision is in the form of a refusal, but might have serious consequences where the decision purports to grant permission.

However, in *James v Minister of Housing and Local Government*[6] the Court of Appeal disapproved of the decision in *Edwick's* case and held that the prescribed time limit was not mandatory but directory. Lord Denning MR said that a grant or refusal of permission out of time is 'not void, but at most voidable'; by that his Lordship meant that a decision out of time would not be automatically void, but that in certain circumstances it might be treated as void. In the House of Lords,[7] the decision of the Court of Appeal was in part overruled, but three of their Lordships disapproved of *Edwick* and the others did not discuss the point; no reference was made to the suggestion that a grant or refusal of permission out of time might be treated as voidable.[8]

It is clear therefore that a grant or refusal of permission out of time is not void, but the question whether it is voidable has not yet been finally resolved. Even if such a decision is voidable, the opportunities for avoiding it will be limited; for, as Lord Denning explained, it will be too late to avoid a grant of permission once it has been accepted and acted upon, or if an appeal is lodged against any conditions attached to the permission.[9] The question might, however, arise in disputes between vendor and purchaser or the assessment of compensation for compulsory purchase. It seems that the option to avoid a planning permission is for the court, not the parties;[10] in other words, the planning permission remains in force until declared void by the court.

It is submitted, however, (i) that there is no logical reason for treating a planning permission as voidable merely because the local planning authority have not complied with the provisions of what is now article 23 as to the time within which they should give notice of their decision; (ii) that the purpose of article 23 is to fix a period after which, in the absence of a decision, the applicant can appeal to the Secretary of State.

---

6 [1965] 3 All ER 602.
7 *Sub nom James v Secretary of State for Wales* [1968] AC 409, [1966] 3 All ER 964.
8 In *London Ballast Co v Buckinghamshire County Council* (1966) 111 Sol Jo 36 Megaw J said that a grant or refusal of permission out of time might be voidable: all the circumstances must be looked at.
9 [1965] 3 All ER 602, at 606.
10 *Co-operative Retail Services Ltd v Taff-Ely Borough Council* (1979) 39 P & CR 223 at 246, per Ormrod LJ.

WHEN IS PLANNING PERMISSION GRANTED?

A question of some practical importance is whether planning permission is effectively granted when the local planning authority make their decision by way of a resolution of the council or a duly authorised committee.[11] At one time it was generally assumed that planning permission was granted at that date with the result that the decision could not thereafter be changed except by making a formal order for the revocation or modification of the planning permission, which might impose upon the authority a liability for substantial compensation.[12]

However in *R v Yeovil Borough Council, ex p Trustees of Elim Pentecostal Church*[13] the Divisional Court took a different view. The Council had resolved to authorise the town clerk to grant planning permission for a youth hostel when evidence of an agreement about car parking facilities had been received. Before the town clerk had received satisfactory evidence, the council changed their mind and resolved to refuse permission. The Court held that, on the facts, there was no question of planning permission having been granted at any time before the town clerk had expressed a view with regard to the adequacy of the evidence submitted to him. This would have been sufficient to dispose of the case, but the Court also decided that there could in law be no planning permission until written notice of the council's decision had been given to the applicant. The Court appear to have relied on the decision of the Court of Appeal in *Slough Estates Ltd v Slough Borough Council* (No 2),[14] but that was a decision on the different wording of the Town and Country Planning Act 1932.

Subsequently, in *Co-operative Retail Services Ltd v Taff-Ely Borough Council*[15] the Court of Appeal adopted the same view that the planning permission does not come into existence until formal notification is given to the applicant. Here again the point was not essential to the decision in the case: the point was not expressly dealt with by the House of Lords in their decision on the case.[16]

---

11 Except where the decision is made by a duly authorised officer of the local planning authority.
12 See chs 9 and 22, below.
13 (1971) 23 P & CR 39.
14 [1969] 2 Ch 305, [1969] 2 All ER 988.
15 (1979) 39 P & CR 223.
16 *Sub nom A-G (ex rel Co-operative Retail Services Ltd) v Taff-Ely Borough Council* (1981) 42 P & CR 1.

Appeals to the Secretary of State

If the applicant is aggrieved by the decision of the local planning authority, or by their failure to give a decision within the proper time, he may appeal to the Secretary of State.[17] No one else has the right to appeal. Unless the Secretary of State agrees to an extension of time, the applicant should give notice of appeal within six calendar months of receiving the local planning authority's decision or (where the appeal is against their failure to give a decision) within six months of the date by which they should have done so.[18] The appellant must notify the persons mentioned in section 66 of the Act of 1990.[19]

The Secretary of State must offer the appellant and the local planning authority the opportunity to present their cases to an inspector at an oral hearing; this will usually take the form of a public local enquiry, although the Secretary of State may, if the issues are sufficiently straightforward, offer the parties the alternative of an informal hearing. However, if the parties agree, the appeal can be dealt with by written representations; this method is encouraged and, nowadays, most appeals are dealt with in this way.[20]

Where there is to be an inquiry, the local planning authority and the appellant must provide statements of their cases before the hearing.[1]

Until 1968 the inspector never gave a decision, but reported to the Minister whose decision was made known in due course. However, in 1968 Parliament empowered the Minister to make regulations authorising the inspector to give a decision in specified classes of appeals. The first regulations[2] authorised the inspector to give a decision in a limited number of cases, but the list was later extended[3] so that by 1981 inspectors were deciding about 80 per cent of all appeals. The latest regulations[4] delegate to the inspector the power to decide all appeals against refusal of permission or conditions attached to permissions, with the exception of some appeals by

17 1990 Act, s. 78(1), (2).
18 GDO, art 26.
19 1990 Act, s. 79(4). This applies the same procedure as in applications at first instance to the local planning authority. See this chapter, pp. 132, 133, above.
20 It should be noted that the Secretary of State retains and sometimes exercises the right to hold a public inquiry even though the parties have indicated a preference for written representations.
1 See ch 17, pp. 294, 295, below.
2 Town and Country Planning (Determination of Appeals by Appointed Persons) (Prescribed Classes) Regs 1968 (SI 1968 No 1972).
3 Town and Country Planning (Determination of Appeals by Appointed Persons) (Prescribed Classes) Regs 1972 (SI 1972 No 1652), Sch 1.
4 Town and Country Planning (Determination of Appeals by Appointed Persons) (Prescribed Classes) Regs 1981 (SI 1981 No 804).

statutory undertakers. The Secretary of State has, however, power to reserve the decision to himself in any specific instance,[5] and this will no doubt be done in appeals of exceptional importance or unusual difficulty.

The inspector is empowered to deal with the appeal as if it had to come to him in the first instance.[6] Amongst other things, this means that in the case of an appeal against a condition attached to a planning permission the inspector can attach other conditions or even refuse permission altogether.

The inspector's decision is final,[7] except for the possibility of challenge under section 288 of the Act of 1990. Section 288 enables an application to be made to the High Court on the ground either that the decision was outside the powers conferred by the Planning Acts or that some procedural requirement of these Acts had not been complied with. It should be possible therefore to question the decision on the ground that he had taken into account considerations not relevant to planning, that he had failed to take into account relevant considerations, or that he had imposed or upheld an improper condition or that there was some breach of the rules of natural justice in the handling of the appeal. The scope of section 288 is more fully considered in chapter 18, below.

Planning inquiry commissions

The usual type of public inquiry has not always proved to be the best way of dealing with the issues arising out of the siting of some large development of a national or regional character such as a nuclear power station or an airport. The matter may come before a public local inquiry in a number of ways: if the development is to be carried out by a government department, there may be a development plan amendment with related compulsory purchase orders, as in the case of the new medical school and hospital at Nottingham;[8] in other cases there may be an application for planning permission which has been either called in by the Secretary of State or has come to him on appeal. In each case, however, the inquiry is into the merits of a particular site; it is open to objectors to suggest alternative sites but the inspector cannot go very far in considering whether another specific site would

5 1990 Act, Sch 6, para 3.
6 1990 Act, s. 79(1).
7 Ibid, s. 79(5).
8 This case came before the High Court in *W J Simms, Sons & Cooke Ltd v Minister of Housing and Local Government* (1969) 210 Estates Gazette 705.

be better because the owners of that site are not before the inquiry and it may be in the area of another planning authority.

Another disadvantage of the usual type of public local inquiry is that the proposed development may raise questions of a scientific or technical character of an unusual kind, and a commission might be better equipped than a single inspector to deal with these.

The Act of 1990 (re-enacting, with some modifications, provisions originally contained in the Act of 1968) attempts to deal with these problems by providing for planning inquiry commissions. Provided there are issues of special national or regional importance or questions of an unusual scientific or technical character, the responsible Minister[9] may ask the Secretary of State to set up a planning inquiry commission to inquire into and report upon any application for planning permission which has been called in by the Secretary of State or is before him on appeal; any proposal that a government department should direct that permissions should be deemed to be granted for development by a local authority or statutory undertakers; any proposal that development should be carried out by or on behalf of a government department.[10]

The commission is to identify and investigate the issues which they consider are relevant to the question whether planning permission should be granted, and assess their importance:[11] the commission may in some cases hold a public local inquiry.[12] The commission may also arrange for the carrying out of research at the expense of the Secretary of State.[13]

The commission's function is to report to the responsible Minister; the last word rests with him.[14]

9 For the meaning of 'responsible Minister' in any particular case, see 1990 Act, Sch 8, Part II.
10 1990 Act, s. 101, Sch 8.
11 Ibid, Sch 8, para 3(1).
12 Ibid, Sch 8, paras 3(2), 5.
13 Ibid, Sch 8, para 3(3).
14 Ibid, Sch 8, para 3(3).

Chapter 8

Planning permission: further considerations

Effect of permission

A grant of planning permission, unless it provides to the contrary, enures for the benefit of the land and of all persons interested in it.[1] It is thus possible to grant permission for the sole benefit of a particular individual.

The Secretary of State considers that the use of personal permissions is seldom desirable; a personal permission may be appropriate however, where it is proposed on compassionate or other personal grounds to grant planning permission for the use of a building or land for some purpose which would not normally be allowed at the site.[2] In practice, the desired result can often be met by granting planning permission for a temporary period only.

The Secretary of State's policy may be illustrated by a number of cases.

> K lived in a large house in the Metropolitan Green Belt. He equipped and used two rooms exclusively as offices for his business, which was concerned with the sale of dehydrated foods; he employed one secretary. An enforcement notice was served. On appeal the inspector considered that there was no justification for terminating this use of the two rooms; however, the use of the rooms as offices by another organisation, or any expansion of the present business beyond these two rooms could attract additional traffic and activity. The Secretary of State granted planning permission for the use of the two rooms as an office in connection with the sale of dehydrated foods subject to conditions that the permission should enure only for the benefit of K so long as he lived there and that no other part of the dwelling house or curtilage should be so used.[3]

In another case the owner of a small holding applied for permission for a caravan required to accommodate B whose help was wanted in

---

1 1990 Act, s. 75(1).
2 Circular 1/85, para 73.
3 [1978] JPL 338.

the running of the smallholding. The Minister was satisfied that it would take some time to bring the land into production and that there were exceptional difficulties in connection with B reaching the smallholding. He accordingly allowed the appeal to the extent of granting permission for a caravan for Mr and Mrs B for a period of five years.[4]

But where a student at a theological college had taken part-time charge of a non-conformist church for the duration of his studies and needed a site for a caravan, the Minister on appeal granted permission for a caravan in the church grounds for a temporary period: it was evidently not considered necessary to make the permission a personal one.[5]

A planning permission obtained by a planning authority for their own development under the procedures introduced in 1976 is personal to that authority and does not enure for the benefit of the land.[6]

A grant of permission is effective only for the purposes of development control. It does not override listed building control. It does not relieve the developer of the necessity of complying with other legislation affecting the use or development of land such as the regulations governing the construction of buildings or the legislation relating to the control of pollution. Nor does it override restrictions imposed on the land under the general law such as easements or restrictive covenants. Although there is machinery for securing the removal or modification of restrictive covenants, the fact that planning permission has been granted is normally no ground on which a restrictive covenant can be revoked or modified.[7]

The grant of a planning permission does not revoke any previous planning permissions which have not been taken up. It has been said to be trite law that any number of planning permissions can validly co-exist for the development of the same land even though they are mutually inconsistent.[8] So where there are two or more planning permissions, none of which has been acted upon, a developer can choose which he will take up.

But what happens where there are mutually inconsistent

---

4 Ministry ref 2381/40620/122.

5 Ministry ref 781/40620/29.

6 General Regs, reg 4(7). See further ch 15, pp. 277, 278, below.

7 The principal method of obtaining the removal of a restrictive covenant is by application to the Lands Tribunal under the Law of Property Act 1925, s. 84. Less well known is the power of the county court under the Housing Act 1985, s. 610, to vary restrictive covenants affecting the conversion of a house into flats; in this case the fact that planning permission has been granted appears to be relevant.

8 *Pioneer Aggregates (UK) Ltd v Secretary of State for the Environment* [1985] AC 132, [1984] 2 All ER 358 per Lord Scarman at 365.

permissions, and one of them is acted upon? The leading case on the point is *Pilkington v Secretary of State for the Environment*.[9]

> The owner of land was granted planning permission to build a bungalow on part of it, site 'B'. It was a condition of the permission that the bungalow should be the only house to be built on the land. He built the bungalow. Later, he discovered the existence of an earlier permission to build a bungalow on another part of the same land, site 'A'. That permission contemplated the use of the rest of the land as a smallholding. He began to build the second bungalow when he was served with an enforcement notice.
>
> Held: The effect of building on site 'B' was to make the development authorised in the earlier permission incapable of implementation; the bungalow built on site 'B' had destroyed the smallholding and the erection of two bungalows on the site had never been sanctioned.

There may, however, be cases in which two planning permissions are not incompatible with each other; in some circumstances a developer may be able to rely on one permission as regards one part of the land and on another permission as regards the other part of the land. This possibility is illustrated by *F Lucas & Sons Ltd v Dorking and Horley RDC*.[10]

> In 1952 the plaintiffs were granted permission to develop a plot of land by the erection of 28 houses in a cul-de-sac layout; the layout showed 14 houses on the north side and 14 houses on the south side of the cul-de-sac. In 1957 the plaintiffs obtained permission to develop the same land by building six detached houses each on a plot fronting the main road; the plaintiffs built two houses in accordance with this permission. They then proposed to proceed with the building of the cul-de-sac and the 14 houses on the southern side thereof, relying upon the 1952 permission. The council contended that the 1952 permission was no longer valid or effective. The plaintiffs sought a declaration that it was effective and entitled them to carry out all or any of the building or other operations to which it related.
>
> Granting the declaration Winn J said that the 1952 permission was not conditional upon the developer completing the whole of the approved development; it was a permission for any of the development comprised therein.

The learned judge pointed out that section 12 of the Act of 1962 (now section 55 of the Act of 1990) forbids development without planning permission, so it is more natural and more likely to have been the intention to look at any particular development to see

---

9 [1974] 1 All ER 283. The decision of the Divisional Court in this case has been approved by the House of Lords in *Pioneer Aggregates (UK) Ltd v Secretary of State for the Environment*; see fn 8 above.
10 (1964) 17 P & CR 111.

whether or not it is unpermitted than to look at the contemplated project for the achievement of which the planning authority has granted a planning permission. This was perhaps an exceptional case, but it is important in that it shows that the taking up of a planning permission does not necessarily render other permissions incapable of implementation. The local planning authority can prevent this kind of situation arising by attaching a condition that the later permission is not to be exercised in addition to or in combination with the earlier permission.[11]

Validity of conditions

As already explained[12] the power to impose conditions on a grant of planning permission is not unlimited.

The provision in the Act of 1990 that the planning authority may impose such conditions 'as they think fit' must be read subject to the requirements of the general law. Of these perhaps the most important is the long established rule that statutory powers must be exercised only for the purpose of the statute concerned.

Thus in *Pilling v Abergele UDC*[13] the local authority refused a licence for a caravan site under section 269 of the Public Health Act 1936, on the ground that the caravans would be detrimental to the amenities of the locality; it was held that section 269 was concerned with sanitary matters, and that the authority were not entitled to consider questions of amenity.

This principle was specifically considered in relation to planning control in *Pyx Granite Co Ltd v Minister of Housing and Local Government*[14] and subsequently in *Fawcett Properties Ltd v Buckingham County Council*.[15]

The latter case provided the House of Lords with the opportunity of considering a number of points relating to the validity of conditions. As a result the following principles appear to have been established:
(1) A condition must serve some useful planning purpose.
(2) A condition must 'fairly and reasonably relate to the permitted development'.
(3) A condition must not be manifestly unreasonable.
(4) A condition may be imposed restricting the user of premises according to the personal circumstances of the occupier.

11 *F Lucas & Sons Ltd v Dorking and Horley RDC* above at pp. 118, 119.
12 See ch 7, p. 148, above.
13 [1950] 1 KB 636, [1950] 1 All ER 76.
14 [1958] 1 QB 554, [1958] 1 All ER 625; reversed in part [1960] AC 260, [1959] 3 All ER 1.
15 [1961] AC 636, [1960] 3 All ER 503.

(5) A condition may be declared invalid on the ground that its meaning is uncertain.

The first three of these principles were re-affirmed by the House of Lords in *Newbury District Council v Secretary of State for the Environment*,[16] but the others are also important and we will consider all five in turn.

CONDITION MUST SERVE SOME USEFUL PLANNING PURPOSE

This principle is based on the long standing rule that statutory powers must be exercised only for the purpose of the statute concerned. Thus, a condition which does not serve a useful planning purpose must be ultra vires. In the *Newbury* case[17] Lord Scarman explained the point by saying that 'the condition must fairly and reasonably relate to the provisions of the development plan and to planning considerations affecting the land'. His Lordship referred specifically to the duty of the local planning authority, in dealing with an application for planning permission, to have regard to the provisions of the development plan and to any other material considerations.[18]

CONDITIONS MUST RELATE TO THE PERMITTED DEVELOPMENT

A condition will be void if it does not 'fairly and reasonably relate to the permitted development'. The phrase is a dictum of Lord Denning in *Pyx Granite Co Ltd v Minister of Housing and Local Government*[19] and was adopted by the House of Lords in *Fawcett Properties Ltd v Buckingham County Council*.[20] It goes further than the simple requirement that conditions must serve the broad purposes of planning legislation.

A condition may serve some useful planning purpose, but nevertheless be invalid because it is not relevant to the particular development permitted by the planning permission.

This is well illustrated by the case of *Newbury District Council v Secretary of State for the Environment*.[1]

> In 1962 the International Synthetic Rubber Co Ltd applied for planning permission to use two hangars on a disused airfield as warehouses for the

16 [1981] AC 578, [1980] 1 All ER 731, HL.
17 Above.
18 1990 Act, s. 70(2); see discussion in ch 7, pp. 141 ff, above.
19 [1958] 1 All ER 625 at 633.
20 [1961] AC 636, [1960] 3 All ER 503.
 1 [1981] AC 578, [1980] 1 All ER 731.

storage of synthetic rubber. Planning permission was granted subject to two conditions, one being that the buildings should be removed by 31 December 1972.

ISR did not remove the buildings by that date, and the local planning authority served an enforcement notice. On appeal, the inspector was of the opinion that the hangars were large, prominent and ugly in what must have been, and could be, a pleasant rural scene, and ought to be removed.

Nevertheless, he considered that the condition was void.

The condition that two such substantial and existing buildings should be removed would appear to flow from a general wish to restore the area rather than from any planning need arising from the actual purpose for which the permission was sought. It was not necessary to that purpose, nor to the protection of the environment in the fulfilment of that purpose; it was a condition extraneous to the proposed use.

The Secretary of State accepted his inspector's opinion and quashed the enforcement notice. The case went ultimately to the House of Lords where the Secretary of State's decision was upheld.

A CONDITION MUST NOT BE MANIFESTLY UNREASONABLE

Even if conditions serve some useful planning purpose they may be quashed if they are unreasonable. But it is the well settled policy of the courts to interfere only if the condition is wholly unreasonable; that is, such as could find no justification in the minds of reasonable men.[2] Or, as it was put in another case.[3]

The task of the court is not to decide what it thinks is reasonable but to decide whether the condition imposed by the local authority is one which no reasonable authority acting within the four corners of their jurisdiction could have decided to impose.

It is impossible to give an exhaustive catalogue of what might be considered unreasonable in this sense. But it is clear that it is wholly unreasonable for a local planning authority to impose a condition which requires a developer to take on part of the authority's duties under other legislation. Two cases illustrate this particular point.

The first of these cases was *Hall & Co Ltd v Shoreham-on-Sea UDC.*[4] The company applied for planning permission to develop some land for industrial purposes. The land adjoined a busy main road, and in granting permission the council imposed a condition requiring the

2 *Kruse v Johnson* [1898] 2 QB 91 at 99.
3 *Associated Provincial Picture Houses Ltd v Wednesbury Corpn* [1947] 2 All ER 680 at 684.
4 [1964] 1 All ER 1.

company to construct an ancillary road over their own land along
the entire frontage and to give rights of passage over it to and from
the adjoining land on either side. The Court of Appeal considered
that the condition was unreasonable because it required the company
to construct a road and virtually to dedicate it to the public without
paying any compensation; 'a more regular course' was open to the
council under the Highways Act 1959,[5] that is the council should
acquire the land paying proper compensation and then construct the
road at public expense.

In *R v Hillingdon London Borough Council, ex p Royco Homes Ltd*,[6]
Royco applied for planning permission to develop land for residential
purposes. The Council granted permission but imposed conditions,
among others, that the houses when erected should be occupied at
first by persons on the council's housing waiting list, and should for
ten years be occupied by persons enjoying the protection of the Rent
Act 1968. The Divisional Court held that these conditions were
unreasonable since they were the equivalent of requiring Royco to
take on at their own expense a significant part of the duty of the
council as housing authority.

The question of unreasonableness also arises where the local planning authority wish for sound planning reasons to impose a condition
affecting land not included in the application. As we have seen,
section 72 of the Act of 1990 specifically authorises the imposition of a
condition affecting other land under the control of the applicant.[7] But
what if the land is not under the control of the applicant? In most
cases such a condition will be unreasonable. Thus in *Peak Park Joint
Planning Board v Secretary of State for the Environment and ICI*[8] Sir Douglas
Franks QC, sitting as deputy judge, upheld a decision of the Secretary
of State that a condition on a planning permission for quarrying which
would have required extensive landscaping would be ultra vires in so
far as it affected land not under the control of the applicants. In
Bradford City Metropolitan Council v Secretary of State for the Environment[9]
the Court of Appeal held that a condition of this sort will be invalid
even if the applicant has indicated a willingness to accept it.

> The council had granted planning permission for residential development
> subject to a condition requiring the widening of an existing road; it seems
> that the applicants in effect invited the condition by including the land
> required for that purpose in a revised plan. Subsequently, they appealed

5 Now the Highways Act 1980.
6 [1974] QB 720, [1974] 2 All ER 643.
7 See ch 7, p. 148, above.
8 (1979) 39 P & CR 361, [1980] JPL 114.
9 (1986) 53 P & CR 55, [1986] JPL 598.

on the ground that they did not own all the land affected by the condition. The Secretary of State held that the condition was ultra vires. The Court of Appeal upheld the Secretary of State.

Lloyd LJ explained the position in this way:

> If the proposed condition was manifestly unreasonable then it was beyond the powers of the planning authority to impose it; and if it was beyond the powers of the planning authority to impose the condition, then it was beyond their powers to agree to impose it, *even if the developer consented*.... Vires could not be conferred by consent.

The unlawfulness of this type of condition can create a dilemma since the planning authority may find it undesirable to grant planning permission for development unless, say, access to the site is improved. The difficulty has in practice often been overcome by imposing a negative condition to the effect that the development shall not be commenced until the access has been improved. The principle of the negative condition has now been approved by the House of Lords in *Grampian Regional Council v City of Aberdeen District Council*.[10]

There are grounds for thinking that a condition may be unreasonable if it enables a third party to frustrate the planning permission. In *Kingsway Investments (Kent) Ltd v Kent County Council*[11] the defendants had granted outline permission subject to the conditions (i) that detailed plans should be submitted to and approved by them before any work was begun; and (ii) that the permission should cease to have effect after three years unless within that time such approval had been notified. The plaintiffs submitted detailed plans, but they were not approved, and the three years ran out. The Court of Appeal, by a majority, held that the second condition was void. Davies LJ pointed out that the permission might lapse without any default on the part of the plaintiffs; 'the defendants are taking away with one hand that which they have purported to grant with the other and are thus evading the revocation procedure'. This, therefore, lends some support to the view that a condition is unreasonable if it puts certain matters out of the control of the developer, but it may be that in the final analysis the learned Lord Justice was basing himself on the point about the revocation procedure. Winn LJ held the condition to be invalid on different grounds, but made this significant remark:

> Nonetheless the characteristic of deprivation of ability to secure by his own efforts full enjoyment of the fruits of the permission granted to him is an important feature of the condition challenged.

10 (1984) 47 P & CR 633, HL.
11 [1969] 2 QB 332, [1969] 1 All ER 601.

The House of Lords – again by a majority – found a somewhat ingenious method of holding the condition valid thereby reversing the decision of the Court of Appeal.[12] It is submitted, however, that the reasons adduced were entirely consistent with the views quoted above.

There is also the question whether the local planning authority can impose conditions which deprive a landowner of existing use rights. Of course, there will be many cases in which the proposed development cannot be carried out without destroying existing use rights. The problem arises where the local planning authority seek to impose conditions restricting existing use rights which are not necessarily incompatible with the proposed development. The point is illustrated by *Allnatt London Properties Ltd v Middlesex County Council*,[13] in which planning permission was granted for an extension to a factory subject to conditions which restricted occupation of the existing factory to firms already established in the locality. It was held that these conditions were void as being unreasonable.

This was followed by the decision of the House of Lords in *Minister of Housing and Local Government v Hartnell*.[14]

H had owned a field of 4.7 acres; for several years he had stationed a number of residential caravans on part of this field comprising about three-quarters of an acre. In 1959 there were six caravans. When Part I of the Caravan Sites and Control of Development Act 1960 came into force he applied for a site licence to station 94 caravans on the whole field. As there was no planning permission in force, the application was treated by virtue of the Act as an application for planning permission. The local planning authority granted permission subject to a condition that not more than six caravans should be stationed on the land at any time. H appealed and the inspector reported that it had not been established that there were existing use rights for more than six caravans; the Minister dismissed the appeal.

Held: (1) H had existing use rights in respect of the smaller area of three-quarters of an acre and these were not limited to six caravans; he was entitled under his existing use rights to bring on to this part of the field such number of caravans as would not amount to making a material change of use. (2) The local planning authority was not entitled to impose conditions depriving H of these existing use rights.

The Minister had argued that, while the planning authority were not entitled to take away the whole of the owner's existing rights, they were entitled by virtue of the Act of 1960 in relation to caravans to take away without compensation anything short of the whole value by imposing conditions. The House of Lords said that a statute

12 [1971] AC 72, [1970] 1 All ER 70. And see pp. 171, 172, below.
13 (1964) 15 P & CR 288.
14 [1965] AC 1134, [1965] 1 All ER 490.

should not be held to take away private rights of property without compensation unless the intention to do so is expressed in clear and unambiguous terms.

On the basis of these authorities it seemed reasonable in some earlier editions of this book to suggest that a local planning authority should not attempt to restrict existing use rights by attaching conditions to a grant of planning permission; the more regular course would be for the authority to make an order under what is now section 102 of the Act of 1990, paying compensation accordingly.

However, it now appears that this proposition may not be correct. In the case of *Kingston-upon-Thames Royal London Borough Council v Secretary of State for the Environment*[15] Lord Widgery CJ said that there is no principle of planning law which requires a local planning authority to refrain from imposing conditions abrogating existing use rights.

> The British Railways Board applied for planning permission for the reconstruction of a railway station. Permission was granted subject to the condition that a certain piece of land should be made available at all times for car parking and should be used 'for no other purpose'.
>
> A main electric traction cable ran across this piece of land. When the Board failed to remove the cable, the council served an enforcement notice. On appeal the Secretary of State quashed the notice; the condition was ultra vires in that it prevented the lawful use of land without compensation.
>
> Held: the Secretary of State had erred in law, and the case should be remitted to him for further consideration of the merits of the condition.

This decision might appear to be quite contrary to the decision of the House of Lords in *Minister of Housing and Local Government v Hartnell*,[16] but the Divisional Court considered that that case had been decided on special facts.

As mentioned above, however, the courts will interfere only if the condition is wholly unreasonable. For instance, the courts will not consider whether a condition is unduly burdensome or whether a different condition might not have been reasonable in the circumstances. It might well be asked why the courts should not quash a condition if it is unreasonable in this more general sense. The courts will consider the question of reasonableness or the merits of some action where a statute specifically requires a public authority to act reasonably or where a statute provides a right of appeal to the courts against the decision of a local authority.[17] But where (as in the case

15 [1974] 1 All ER 193.
16 Above.
17 For example, appeals against certain decisions made under the Public Health Acts go to the magistrates; appeals against repair notices and demolition orders under the Housing Act 1985, go to the county court.

of the Planning Act and many other statutes) there is no specific mention of reasonableness, it is the general policy of the courts not to intervene. Thus, in *Associated Provincial Picture Houses Ltd v Wednesbury Corpn*,[18] the proprietors of a cinema had applied to the local authority under the Sunday Entertainments Act 1932, for a licence to open on Sundays. The licence was granted subject to a condition that children under 15 should not be admitted whether accompanied by an adult or not. The plaintiffs sought a declaration that the condition was invalid. The Court of Appeal held that it was lawful for the corporation to take into consideration matters affecting the well-being and the physical and mental health of children. That, said the court, ended the matter:

> Once that is granted, counsel must go so far as to say that the decision of the authority is wrong because it is unreasonable, and then he is really saying that the ultimate arbiter of what is and is not reasonable is the court and not the local authority. It is just there, it seems to me, that the whole argument entirely breaks down. It is perfectly clear that the local authority are entrusted by Parliament with the decision on a matter in which the knowledge and experience of the authority can best be trusted to be of value.[19]

The courts have adopted a similar policy in relation to byelaws made by local authorities. Although it is said that the validity of a byelaw may be questioned on the grounds of unreasonableness, it is clear that a byelaw will only be held to be unreasonable if it is manifestly unjust or oppressive[20] or if its application in a particular case would serve no useful purpose.[1] Byelaws made by local authorities being bodies of a public representative character entrusted by Parliament with delegated authority should be supported if possible.[2]

The idea that the local authority are likely to be the best judges of what is reasonable has been expressed in a number of cases. It is not, however, the invariable policy of the courts to trust the local authority. For instance, the court will consider whether local authority expenditure is reasonable – even where statute empowers authorities to pay such wages as 'they think fit'[3] – apparently on the ground that local authorities have a fiduciary responsibility to their ratepayers.

Finally, it may be noted that the courts are no more likely to

---

18 [1948] 1 KB 223, [1947] 2 All ER 680.
19 Per Lord Greene MR at 683.
20 *Kruse v Johnson* [1898] 2 QB 91.
 1 See for instance *Repton School Governors v Repton RDC* [1918] 2 KB 133; and *A-G v Denby* [1925] Ch 596 – both cases concerning the application of building byelaws as to space about buildings.
 2 *Kruse v Johnson*, above.
 3 *Roberts v Hopwood* [1925] AC 578.

question the reasonableness of a condition imposed by the Secretary of State (or his inspector) on a grant of a planning permission. Indeed, in *Sparks v Edward Ash Ltd*[4] – a case in which it was contended that certain traffic regulations were unreasonable – the Court of Appeal said that 'If it is the duty of the courts to recognise and trust the discretion of local authorities, much more must it be so in the case of a Minister directly responsible to Parliament'.

CONDITIONS RESTRICTING USE OF PREMISES ACCORDING TO PERSONAL CIRCUMSTANCES OF OCCUPIER

An example is the condition imposed in *Fawcett Properties Ltd v Buckingham County Council*[5] restricting the use of the cottages to agricultural occupants. The validity of such conditions was expressly upheld in that case.

It should be noticed that there is a difference in principle between a condition of this type and a personal planning permission. In the one case the permission runs with the land, although subject to a condition as to the persons who may occupy it; in the other, the permission itself is personal and does not run with the land.

CONDITIONS MAY BE VOID FOR UNCERTAINTY

A condition will be void for uncertainty 'if it can be given no meaning or no sensible or ascertainable meaning'.[6] This involves more than ambiguity; if the wording of a condition is ambiguous (that is, capable of more than one meaning) the court can determine which is the correct meaning. But a condition may be so ill worded that the court cannot resolve the doubt. Thus in *R v Secretary of State for the Environment, ex p Watney Mann (Midlands) Ltd*[7] the local justices had made an order under section 94(2) of the Public Health Act 1936 requiring the abatement of nuisance caused by music played in a public house; the order required that the level of noise in the premises should not exceed 70 decibels. The Divisional Court considered that the order was void for uncertainty because it did not specify the position where the decibel reading was to be taken.

4 [1943] 1 KB 223, [1943] 1 All ER 1.
5 [1961] AC 636; [1960] 3 All ER 503.
6 *Fawcett Properties Ltd v Buckingham County Council* [1960] 3 All ER 503 at 517, per Lord Denning.
7 [1976] JPL 368.

In *M J Shanley Ltd v Secretary of State for the Environment and South Bedfordshire District Council*,[8] in an attempt to overcome objections to development in the green belt, the appellants offered a condition that the first opportunity to buy the houses should be given to local people; the Secretary of State considered that this condition would be invalid and unenforceable. In the High Court Woolf J agreed that the condition would be invalid and unenforceable; it did not give any indication at all as to the method or terms upon which the first opportunity was to be offered.

In *Fawcett Properties Ltd v Buckingham County Council*[9] the county council had granted planning permission for two cottages in the green belt subject to the condition that 'the occupation of the houses shall be limited to persons whose employment or latest employment is or was employment in agriculture as defined by section 119(1) of the Town and Country Planning Act 1947[10] or in forestry or in an industry mainly dependent upon agriculture and including also the dependants of such persons as aforesaid'. The House of Lords, by a majority, held that the condition was not void for uncertainty. It was not necessary to the validity of the condition to identify all the persons who might at any point be eligible to occupy the cottages, the owner's obligation was to satisfy himself that any proposed occupier would come within the definition.

It seems that in the borderline cases the benefit of the doubt will be given to the local planning authority.[11]

Special types of condition

CONDITIONS RESTRICTING USE OF BUILDINGS

A grant of permission for the erection of a building may specify the purposes for which the building may be used; and if no purpose is specified, the permission is to be construed as including permission to use the building for the purpose for which it is designed.[12]

The effect of this may be illustrated by some examples. In some cases it may be sufficient to incorporate the terms of the application in the grant of planning permission; thus, permission for a dwellinghouse may state that 'the local planning authority hereby grant planning permission for the erection of a dwellinghouse in accordance

---

8 [1982] JPL 380.
9 Above.
10 Now 1990 Act, s. 336(1).
11 *Crisp from the Fens Ltd v Rutland County Council* (1950) 48 LGR 210.
12 1990 Act, s. 75(2), (3).

with the application and plans dated . . .'. However, where application is made for permission to erect a building for industrial use, the planning authority may wish to impose a condition restricting such use to light industrial purposes. But, as we have seen, in the current Use Classes Order light industry falls within Class B1 (business) which also includes offices and research and development.[13] This raises the question whether the planning authority can impose a condition to preclude the right to change from light industry to the other purposes comprised in Class B1, or even to restrict the industrial use to a particular type of manufacture such as micro-engineering. The difficulty about such a condition is that it attempts to prevent something which by the terms of the Act of 1990 is not development at all, and it might be argued that planning control cannot restrict matters which do not involve development. On the other hand, it seems reasonable that in permitting development the planning authority should be enabled to impose this type of condition provided it fairly and reasonably relates to the permitted development. This view of the matter has now been upheld by Talbot J in *City of London Corpn v Secretary of State for the Environment*.[14] In the recent case of *Camden London Borough Council v Secretary of State for the Environment*[15] it appears to have been taken for granted that a condition could be imposed to preclude the right under Class B1 to change from light industry to offices. Where such a condition is imposed, application can always be made for permission for the retention of the building or the continuance of the use without complying with the condition.[16]

CONDITIONS RESTRICTING PERMITTED DEVELOPMENT

A somewhat similar problem arises in connection with conditions restricting the right to carry out development permitted by the General Development Order. For instance, a planning authority might wish when granting permission for building a new house to impose a condition excluding the right to extend it under Part 1 of the Order. Or, on a grant of permission for mineral working, the authority might wish to impose conditions as to the siting of plant and machinery required for the treatment of the excavated mineral, thus restricting the mineral operator's rights under Part 19.

Such conditions appear to be authorised by article 3(4) of the

---

13 See ch 5, pp. 93–94, above.
14 (1971) 23 P & CR 169.
15 [1989] JPL 613.
16 1990 Act, s. 63(2).

General Development Order, which provides that 'nothing in this order shall operate so as to permit any development contrary to a condition imposed in any permission granted or deemed to be granted otherwise than by this order'. Some doubt, however, has been cast as to the meaning of this by Lord Parker CJ in *East Barnet UDC v British Transport Commission*.[17] In this case, as we have seen,[18] the Divisional Court upheld a decision of the magistrates that the change of use from a coal stacking yard to a transit depot for crated vehicles did not in the circumstances constitute development. It was also held that, even if the change did amount to development, the permission of the planning authority was unnecessary because the land was operational land of the Commission and its use was permitted by the General Development Order 1950. The condition imposed by the local planning authority requiring the use of the land to be discontinued on a certain date was therefore invalid. Lord Parker CJ said:

> It was faintly suggested by counsel for the appellants that a specific condition, such as was imposed in this case on the grant of an application, overrode any unlimited permission in a General Development Order. I find myself quite unable to accede to that argument. It seems to me that that provision is covering a case where a specific permission is followed by a General Development Order in unqualified terms. It has been suggested by counsel for the appellants that the position is really the other way round and the Justices are not entitled to quash unless it can be shown that the specific permission was a nullity. Again I cannot accede to that argument.

These remarks appear to mean that what was then article 3(2) applied only to conditions or limitations imposed on a grant of planning permission prior to the date on which the General Development Order 1950 came into operation. With respect, Lord Parker's interpretation does not follow inescapably from the wording of article 3(2), and one is entitled therefore to interpret this provision in the light of other circumstances.

It may be argued in support of Lord Parker's interpretation that conditions ought not to be imposed which circumvent the provisions of article 4 as to the withdrawal or restriction of permitted development on payment of compensation.[19] On the other hand, there may well be good planning reasons for imposing such a condition and, if it cannot be imposed, the planning authority might well feel that they must refuse permission for what may be called the primary development; for instance, where application is made for permission to work minerals, there may be strong objections on grounds of

17 [1962] 2 QB 484, [1961] 3 All ER 878.
18 See ch 5, p. 98, above.
19 See ch 6, p. 125, above.

amenity and the planning authority may quite properly consider that permission must be refused unless they can impose conditions restricting further development by virtue of the General Development Order. Moreover, article 3(2) of the 1950 Order was a re-enactment of the corresponding provision in the repealed General Development Order 1948, which came into operation on the same date as the Act of 1947. If Lord Parker's view is correct, then what is now article 3(4) of the current Order would in several cases apply only to permission 'deemed to have been granted' under Part III of the Act of 1947 (or 1990) by virtue of something done before 1 July 1948. For these reasons it is respectfully suggested that conditions imposed on a valid grant of planning permission can lawfully restrict development permitted by the General Development Order.

CONDITIONS LIMITING PERIOD OF PERMISSION

As we have seen, conditions may be imposed limiting the period for which permission is granted. The proper form of such a condition is indicated by section 72(1)(b) of the Act of 1990, namely, it should require the buildings or works to be removed or the use to be discontinued at the expiration of a specified period. This form is not always adopted in practice; for instance, the Secretary of State's decision on an appeal may state that 'the Secretary of State hereby gives permission for a period of five years'. The effect of such words was considered by the Court of Appeal in *Francis v Yiewsley and West Drayton UDC*,[20] in which the Minister on appeal granted permission for the retention of some unauthorised caravans 'for a period of six months from the date of this letter'. It was held that there was an implied condition that the caravans should be removed at the end of the six months period.

On the expiry of a temporary permission, application may be made under section 63 of the Act of 1990 for permission to retain the buildings or works or continue the use in question. Alternatively, the previous normal use of the land may be resumed without applying for permission, provided the previous use was not instituted in breach of planning control.[1]

---

20 [1958] 1 QB 478, [1957] 3 All ER 529.
 1 1990 Act, s. 57(2), (5), (6). See also ch 6, pp. 114, 115, above.

Effect of striking out conditions

Although it is clear that the courts will in suitable cases declare a condition invalid, the effect on the permission is uncertain. Does the permission remain in force shorn of the condition, or does the permission itself fall with it?

There seem to be three possible answers to this question. There are dicta which appear to suggest that, if a condition is declared void, the permission automatically falls with it. At the opposite extreme there are some dicta which suggest that the permission should always stand. But the weight of opinion appears to be in favour of an intermediate position, that is, that the permission will fall if the offending condition is of fundamental importance but not if it is trivial or unimportant.

In *Pyx Granite Co Ltd v Minister of Housing and Local Government*, Romer LJ was of the opinion that 'it would not be open for the court to leave the permission shorn of its conditions or any of them'.[2] But since the Court of Appeal were unanimous in holding that permissions were required and that the condition was proper, the point did not require decision by the court. The House of Lords subsequently held that permission was not required, so that the validity of the condition did not arise and there was no discussion on the possible effect of invalidating it.

These remarks of Romer LJ were adopted by the Court of Appeal in *Hall & Co Ltd v Shoreham-by-Sea UDC*;[3] in that case, however, it was obvious that the conditions in question were fundamental to the whole of the planning permission, and the council were granted a declaration that the permission was consequently null and void. But in some later cases, the permission has been allowed to stand. Moreover the judgments in that case recognised that it might be permissible to sever an offending condition if it were merely trivial or unimportant. So in *Allnatt London Properties v Middlesex County Council*[4] Glyn-Jones J considered himself free in the circumstances of that case to hold that the planning permission should stand, shorn of the offending conditions.

Such was the state of the authorities when the matter came up again in *Kent County Council v Kingsway Investments (Kent) Ltd*.[5] The Court of Appeal, having declared the condition void, held that the permission remained in force.[6] The condition in question related, said

---

2 [1958] 1 QB 554, [1958] 1 All ER 625.
3 [1964] 1 All ER 1.
4 (1964) 15 P & CR 288.
5 [1971] AC 72, [1970] 1 All ER 70.
6 [1969] 1 All ER 601.

Davies LJ not to the development itself but to matters preparatory or introductory to the permission; it was unimportant to the development itself. Winn LJ went further: 'if it [the condition] is void it can have no effect on the force of the permission itself'.

However, in the House of Lords, the majority of their Lordships held that condition was valid. They nevertheless went on to consider whether the permission would have stood if they had decided that the condition was void. Lord Morris of Borth-y-Gest and Lord Donovan said that there might be cases in which unimportant or incidental conditions were superimposed on the permission; if such conditions were held to be void, the permission might be allowed to survive. But in the present case the condition was not trivial or unimportant. It would seem therefore that their Lordships did not accept the distinction drawn by Davies LJ between conditions relating to the development itself and conditions of a preparatory nature. And Lord Guest seems to have thought that the permission would always fail, even apparently where the offending condition was unimportant.

To sum up: it seems that the correct approach is to consider whether the condition is fundamental to the permission; in other words would the planning authority have granted permission without the condition in question.

Limitations

A grant of planning permission may be circumscribed not only by the conditions attached to it, but also by limitations inherent in the permission itself. The principle was first recognised in relation to the permissions granted by general development orders. To take one example: Class I of the 1977 Order permitted the extension of a dwellinghouse so long as the cubic content was not exceeded by certain limits;[7] although some express conditions were attached, the restriction relating to cubic content was not a condition but was contained in the words whereby the permission was granted. (The current General Development Order uses different language to achieve the same purpose.)

The courts have since recognised that the principle applies to planning permissions granted on an application. In *Wilson v West Sussex County Council*[8] planning permission had been granted for an 'agricultural cottage . . . in the terms of and subject to compliance with the details specified in plan and application No LG/2/56a submitted to

7 See p. 117, above.
8 [1963] 2 QB 764, [1963] 1 All ER 751.

the council on July 23 1959, and any relevant correspondence'. The Court of Appeal, having regard to the wording of the planning permission and the application and correspondence specifically incorporated, held that the phrase 'agricultural cottage' limited the user of the building; the first occupant must therefore be someone engaged in agriculture. The Court was not prepared to say whether subsequent occupation by a person not engaged in agriculture would be a material change of use.

In the more recent case of *Kwik Save Discount Group Ltd v Secretary of State for Wales*[9] the Court of Appeal looked at the whole context of the application in deciding that the planning permission was subject to a limitation.

A petrol station and garage included a large building used as a workshop. Planning permission was granted for 'alterations and extensions to Swifts Service Station ... in accordance with the plan and application submitted to the council'. The application included 'Conversion of existing workshops to retail showroom ... Existing showroom to shop for retail of motor vehicle accessories and petroleum products.' No express restriction was placed on the character or nature of the goods that could be sold in the retail showroom. Subsequently the appellants acquired an interest in the workshop though not in the remaining part of the garage premises; they proceeded to use it as a retail supermarket for the sale of groceries, bread, meat etc. The Secretary of State dismissed an appeal against an enforcement notice requiring the discontinuance of the use as a supermarket.

In the Court of Appeal counsel for the Secretary of State conceded that the appeal building was not to be used for a purpose ancillary to the service station but contended that it was to be used as a constituent part of it or of the overall site.

The application had been made by Esso: it was for the use of the appeal building as a retail showroom: the plans showed that it was designed as a car showroom: what was permitted were alterations and extensions to the service station; one of those was to one building on a site that was part of a larger site with other buildings being altered and extended.

The Court of Appeal held that these items in the application and grant pointed to the permission being limited to the use of the retail showroom for the sale of cars.

The Act of 1990 expressly provides that the local planning authority may issue an enforcement notice in respect of failure to comply with any limitation subject to which planning permission has been granted.

Nevertheless, if it is the intention of the local planning authority when granting planning permission that the use of land or buildings should be restricted, it is better to impose an express condition than to rely on the limitations inherent in the permission; a well worded

9 (1980) 42 P & CR 166.

condition will prevent arguments about the interpretation of the permission and will also make it clear that the restriction is binding on subsequent occupants.

Duration of permissions

Prior to 1969 a planning permission might remain unused indefinitely unless a condition had been attached requiring work to be commenced within a specified period. Although such conditions might lawfully be imposed local planning authorities made little use of them; and in some areas unused planning permissions accumulated to the extent of becoming a serious problem. The local planning authority had no means of knowing whether the land would in fact be developed and, if so, when; developers complained that the planning authority were acting unreasonably in refusing permission to develop other land.

The Act of 1968 introduced provisions designed to overcome these problems, and these are now to be found in the Act of 1990. Every new planning permission is deemed to be subject to a condition that development shall be commenced within five years or such other period as the planning authority may expressly impose.[10] In the case of outline permissions, the deemed condition will be to the effect that application for approval of reserved matters be made within three years, and that the development must be begun within five years of the date on which the outline permission was granted or within two years of the grant of approval, whichever is the later; here again the planning authority may impose different periods.[11] Planning permissions granted before 1969 were made subject to retrospective conditions and have now lapsed if they remained unused after a transitional period.[12]

Development will be deemed to have been commenced when a start is made on any of the following 'material operations':[13]

(a) any work of construction in the course of the erection of a building;
(b) the digging of a trench which is to contain the foundations, or part of the foundations, of a building;
(c) the laying of any underground main or pipe to the foundations, or part of the foundations, of a building or to any such trench as is mentioned above;

10 1990 Act, s. 91.
11 Ibid, s. 92.
12 1971 Act, Sch 24, para 18; Planning (Consequential Provisions) Act 1990, Sch 3, para 3.
13 1990 Act, s. 56(1), (2), (4).

(d) any operation in the course of laying out or constructing a road or part of a road;

(e) any change in the use of any land, where that change constitutes 'material development'.[14]

In *United Refineries Ltd v Essex County Council*[15] planning permission for the development of 262 acres for an oil refinery was granted subject to the condition that 'the building and other operations hereby permitted' should be commenced by a specified date. The plaintiffs had constructed a temporary access road and stripped topsoil in preparation for the erection of some buildings; it was held that the plaintiffs had complied with the condition. It may even be sufficient to start digging a trench for the foundation of a building, and it is easy to imagine that there will be cases in which a trench will be dug and nothing more done for a number of years. If this happens, the local planning authority will be able to serve a 'completion notice', stating that the planning permission will cease to have effect if the development is not completed within such period as may be specified.[16]

COMPLETION NOTICES

As we have seen, a planning permission will lapse if the development is not begun within the prescribed period.[17] If the development has begun but has not been completed within that period, the local planning authority – if of opinion that the development will not be completed within a reasonable period – may serve a completion notice. The notice will state that the planning permission will cease to have effect if the development is not completed within such further period (not less than 12 months) as may be specified. The notice will take effect only if and when confirmed by the Secretary of State, and before confirming the notice he must give to the persons upon whom it has been served the opportunity of appearing at a public local inquiry or other hearing. If at the end of the period specified in the completion notice, the development has not been completed, the planning permission will be invalidated except so far as it authorises any development carried out in the meantime.[18]

14 'Material development' means (a) any development permitted by the General Development Order; (b) certain forms of development falling within Sch 3 of the 1990 Act; (c) any other development prescribed by the Secretary of State: 1990 Act, s. 56(5).

15 [1978] JPL 110.

16 See below.

17 See p. 174, above.

18 1990 Act, ss. 94, 95.

In effect, therefore, a completion notice gives the developer the choice of completing the development or of letting the planning permission lapse. It is a particularly useful procedure where a developer has kept a planning permission alive by doing only a minimal amount of preliminary work.[19] The procedure has also been used in less obvious cases; the Secretary of State has for instance confirmed a notice where one of two houses authorised by a planning permission had been built but not the other.[20] But the Secretary of State refused to confirm a notice in respect of a ten acre site because he was satisfied that, since acquiring the site, the objectors had taken reasonable steps to press forward with the development having regard to some problems with access and the uncertain state of the property market.[1]

A planning permission cannot be extinguished by abandonment. The judgments at first instance and in the Court of Appeal in *Slough Estate Ltd v Slough Borough Council (No 2)*[2] had suggested that where an owner or occupier of land had evinced an unequivocal intention to abandon planning permission, such permission would be extinguished by abandonment; the House of Lords disposed of the case in question on the ground that the document which had been relied on as a planning permission was not an effective permission, and the question of abandonment was left open. In the recent case of *Pioneer Aggregates (UK) Ltd v Secretary of State for the Environment*[3] the House of Lords have emphatically rejected the view that a valid planning permission can be abandoned.

Planning permission had been granted in 1950 to Hartshead Quarries Ltd for the mining and working of limestone on an area of land which included the appeal site. Hartshead had extracted minerals from the land from 1950 to 1966. In September 1966 they wrote to the Peak Park Joint Planning Board giving notice that they would cease quarrying by the end of that year; in 1967 the Board wrote to Hartshead informing them that the restoration conditions had to be met to their satisfaction.

In 1978 Pioneer became interested in the land and asked the Board whether planning permission to quarry was needed. The Board replied that the 1950 permission had been abandoned.

To test the matter, Pioneer fired one blast to remove some stone; the Board served an enforcement notice. On Appeal the Secretary of State upheld the enforcement notice.

The House of Lords held that there was no principle of planning law

19 See pp. 174, 175, above.
20 [1985] JPL 125. The single house was 'an unsympathetic intrusion in a street scene of high visual qualities'.
1 [1979] JPL 184.
2 [1969] 2 Ch 305, [1969] 2 All ER 988.
3 [1985] AC 132, [1984] 2 All ER 358.

that a valid planning permission capable of being implemented according to its terms can be abandoned.

Lord Scarman explained that planning control is a creature of statute; it is an imposition in the public interest of restrictions upon private rights of ownership of land. It is a field of law in which the courts should not introduce principles or rules derived from private law unless they be expressly authorised by Parliament or necessary to give effect to the purpose of the legislation.

It was the clear implication of section 33(1) of the Act of 1971 (now section 75(1) of the Act of 1990) that only the statute or the terms of the planning permission could stop the permission enuring for the benefit of the land and of all persons for the time being interested therein.

The abandonment of an existing use, Lord Scarman pointed out, was a quite separate matter which had nothing whatever to do with the extinguishment of planning permission. This distinction can be explained by saying that in cases like *Hartley v Minister of Housing and Local Government*[4] the issue is simply one of fact: what is the use of the land at the date of resumption?

4 [1970] 1 QB 413, [1969] 3 All ER 1658.

Chapter 9

Revocation or modification of existing rights

Revocation or modification of planning permission

Although a grant of planning permission is intended, in the absence of conditions to the contrary, to enure permanently for the benefit of the land,[1] in certain circumstances it may be revoked or modified. The local planning authority may, if they consider it expedient, having regard to the development plan and to any other material considerations, make an order for this purpose; with some exceptions, the order must be submitted to the Secretary of State for confirmation.[2] The Secretary of State may make such an order himself, but only after consulting and after giving formal notice to the local planning authority.[3] If the order becomes effective, the local planning authority will have to pay compensation for abortive expenditure and for the depreciation in the value of the land.[4]

It is comparatively rarely that the Secretary of State or the local authority will consider it desirable to revoke or modify a permission and the liability to compensation may deter an authority from such action even where they consider it desirable.

EXTENT OF POWER TO REVOKE OR MODIFY

The power of revocation or modification applies only to permissions granted on an application under Part III of the Act of 1990. The reference to 'an application' excludes any permission granted by a development order,[5] or any deemed permission arising under section

1 See ch 8, p. 155, above.
2 1990 Act, ss. 97, 98.
3 Ibid, s. 100.
4 See ch 22, below.
5 A permission granted under the General Development Order, however, may in effect be revoked or modified as a result of an 'Article 4 direction' (see ch 6, p. 125, above).

90 or 222 of the Act of 1990 concerning development by government departments and advertisements respectively.[6]

The power to revoke or modify applies only where the development has not been completed. This is made clear by section 97(3) of the Act of 1990, which reads:

> The power conferred by this section to revoke or modify permission to develop land may be exercised –
> (a) where the permission relates to the carrying out of building or other operations, at any time before those operations have been completed;
> (b) where the permission relates to a change of the use of any land, at any time before the change has taken place.

Furthermore, the revocation or modification of permission for the carrying out of building or other operations will not affect so much of those operations as has been previously carried out.[7]

If the local planning authority wish to remove or modify development completed in conformity with planning permission they must make a 'discontinuance order' under section 102.[8] Two procedures are available for the making of an order to revoke or modify. First, there is what may be called the standard procedure which involves submitting the order to the Secretary of State for confirmation. Secondly, there is the procedure which may be used where the local planning authority do not expect objections to the order.

The standard procedure   The local planning authority submit the order to the Secretary of State, and give notice to the owner[9] and occupier of the land and to any other person likely to be affected.

Any person receiving the notice has the right to be heard by the Secretary of State either at a public local inquiry or other hearing, before the Secretary of State decides whether or not to confirm the order.[10]

Where the Secretary of State himself makes an order, he must similarly notify the persons affected, and give them an opportunity of being heard before coming to a final decision.[11]

Procedure for unopposed orders   This procedure is available where the

6 See ch 6, pp. 129, 130, above.
7 1990 Act, s. 97(4).
8 See p. 180, below.
9 The 'owner' means a person, other than a mortgagee not in possession, who (whether in his own right or as trustee) is entitled to receive the rack-rent of the land or, where the land is not let as a rack-rent, would be so entitled if it were so let: 1990 Act, s. 336(1). And see ch 12, pp. 220, 221, below.
10 1990 Act, s. 98(3), (4).
11 1990 Act, s. 100(4)–(7).

owner and occupier of the land and all persons who, in the authority's opinion, will be affected by the order have notified the authority in writing that they do not object to the order:[12] this, of course, presupposes that the authority have given preliminary notification of their intention to make the order.

In these circumstances, the authority publish an advertisement in the local press reciting the above mentioned matters and stating that any person affected by the order may notify the Secretary of State that he wishes to be heard by a representative of the Secretary of State at a public local inquiry or other hearing. A similar notice is to be served on the very persons who have already indicated that they do not object.[13]

The authority must then send a copy of the public advertisement to the Secretary of State, who has the right to call in the order. If at the end of a specified period no person claiming to be affected has requested a hearing and the Secretary of State has not called in the order, it takes effect.[14]

The validity of an order revoking or modifying planning permission, whether made under the standard procedure or under that for unopposed orders, may be questioned in High Court proceedings under section 288 of the Act of 1990, but not otherwise.[15]

If the effect of the order is to render the land incapable of reasonably beneficial use the owner may serve a purchase notice under section 137 of the Act of 1990.[16]

Discontinuance orders

As explained earlier in this chapter the power to revoke or modify planning permission does not apply where the development has already been carried out. Section 102 of the Act of 1990 enables the local planning authority to make 'discontinuance orders' in relation to existing buildings and uses without the authority having to acquire the land.

Compensation must be paid to the owner for the loss of the rights but at least the local authority are spared the added expense of acquiring land for which they would have no particular need. This is

---

12 1990 Act, s. 99(1). This procedure cannot be used to revoke or modify a planning permission granted by the Secretary of State on a called-in application or on appeal, or to modify conditions as to the duration of a planning permission: ibid, s. 99(8).
13 Ibid, s. 99(2)–(6).
14 Ibid, s. 99(7).
15 See ch 18, pp. 316 ff, below.
16 For purchase notices, see ch 12, below.

a particularly useful method of dealing with the comparatively small objectional black spot such as 'back-garden' industry or a caravan site in the wrong place. Many such uses were of course established at a time when planning permission was not required; in some cases they have arisen since 1948 in contravention of planning control but the local planning authority have failed to serve an effective enforcement notice within the proper time.[17]

The local planning authority may take action under section 102 if they consider it desirable for the planning of their area, including considerations of amenity; regard is to be had to the development plan and to any other material considerations. An order may be made:[18]

(a) requiring any use of land to be discontinued or imposing conditions on the continuance of the use; or

(b) requiring any buildings or works to be altered or removed.

The local planning authority may be prepared to sanction some other development of the land: if so, they may include in the order a grant of planning permission for that purpose.[19] If the order would result in the displacement of residents, the local planning authority may have to secure the provision of alternative accommodation.[20]

If the Secretary of State considers that the local authority ought to have made an order he may make an order himself.[1]

An order of the local planning authority does not become effective unless and until it is confirmed by the Secretary of State.[2] Before the Secretary of State can confirm the order, the owner and the occupier of the land must be given an opportunity of being heard – usually at a public inquiry.[3] If the order is made by the Secretary of State he will give the persons affected a similar opportunity of being heard before he comes to a final decision.[4]

The Secretary of State may confirm the order with or without modifications and he may include in the order a grant of planning permission for some other purpose.[5] The validity of the order may be challenged not later than six weeks after the Secretary's confirmation

---

17 See ch 10, pp. 184, 185, below.
18 1990 Act, s. 102(1).
19 Ibid, s. 102(2), (3).
20 Ibid, s. 102(6).
 1 Ibid, s. 104.
 2 Ibid, s. 103(1).
 3 Ibid, s. 103(3)–(6).
 4 Ibid, s. 104.
 5 Ibid, s. 103.

in High Court proceedings under section 288 of the Act of 1990 but not otherwise.[6]

If the order relates to the use of the land, failure to comply is an offence punishable by fine.[7] But if it requires the removal or alteration of buildings or works the remedy is for the local planning authority to carry out the requirements of the order and recover the cost from the owner.[8]

If the effect of the order is to render the land incapable of reasonably beneficial use the owner may serve a purchase notice under section 137 of the Act of 1990.[9]

6 See ch 18, below.
7 1990 Act, s. 102.
8 Ibid, s. 103.
9 See ch 12, below.

Chapter 10

The enforcement of
planning control

A system of enforcement is required to deal with cases in which development is carried out either without planning permission or in breach of the conditions or limitations attaching to a grant of planning permission. One simple method of enforcement would have been to make a breach of planning control an offence punishable by the courts. With some minor exceptions,[1] however, Parliament decided not to make a simple breach of control a punishable offence. Instead, the local planning authority are authorised to issue an enforcement notice requiring the owner or occupier of land or premises to remedy the situation. It is when this enforcement notice is ignored that the local planning authority may prosecute the offender.

When this system was introduced by the Act of 1947, it was thought right to insist that the enforcement notice should be served within four years of the breach of planning control. If no enforcement notice were served within that time, the unauthorised development or breach of condition became immune from action; in this way a great many unauthorised changes of use have become the established use of land. However, in 1968 it was decided to remove this time limit on the service of enforcement notices in respect of unauthorised changes of use[2] occurring after the end of 1963,[3] whilst retaining the time limit in respect of building and other operations. The changes thus introduced by the Act of 1968 are now embodied in the Act of 1990.

It is very unusual not to have some time limit in civil proceedings.[4] As will be apparent from what has been said about material change

---

1 The display of advertisements without the necessary grant of consent under the Advertisements Regs and thus without any necessary grant of planning permission is an offence: 1990 Act, s. 224(3), (4). So, too, is the removal of top-soil in such circumstances as to involve development: Agricultural Land (Removal of Surface Soil) Act 1953.
2 The four year rule is retained in respect of change of use of any building to single dwellinghouse: see p. 185, below.
3 Approximately four years before the introduction of the bill for the 1968 Act.
4 Cf the Limitation Acts.

of use,[5] there are many cases in which there is genuine doubt as to what use rights attach to land or buildings; uncertainty as to whether action may be taken often makes it difficult to sell property. But there is also some advantage: where an unauthorised use of land is begun but does not cause any serious detriment to the locality, the local planning authority can monitor the situation and take enforcement action if at any time the use does become objectionable. The Act of 1981 amended the previous law about enforcement notices and appeals so as to give greater flexibility to the local planning authority in drafting enforcement notices and to the Secretary of State in dealing with appeals. A minor amendment was made by the Act of 1981 in that the local planning authority now 'issue' an enforcement notice and serve copies of it on those concerned instead as in the past 'serving' enforcement notices on those concerned.

Enforcement notices

ISSUE AND SERVICE OF ENFORCEMENT NOTICES

The law relating to the issue of enforcement notices and the service of copies on those concerned is highly technical, but it may be reduced to the following rules:

(1) The local planning authority must be satisfied that there has been a breach of planning control after the end of 1963.[6] There is a breach of planning control if either:[7]

(a) development has been carried out without permission; or

(b) a condition or limitation attached to a grant of planning permission has not been complied with.

(2) The local planning authority should not automatically issue an enforcement notice in respect of every breach of planning control. They should be satisfied that it is desirable to serve an enforcement notice having regard to the provisions of the development plan and to any other material considerations.[8] This suggests that the planning authority should ask themselves whether they would have granted planning permission had an application been made to them and, if so, whether they would have imposed conditions. If the local authority do not issue an enforcement notice the Secretary of State may himself issue such a notice.[9]

---

5 See ch 5, above.
6 1990 Act, s. 172(1)(a).
7 Ibid, s. 172(3).
8 Ibid, s. 172(1)(b).
9 Ibid, s. 182.

Recent pronouncements on behalf of the Secretary of State have emphasised the discretionary nature of the local planning authority's powers of enforcement; the present policy of the Secretary of State appears to be that enforcement action should be reserved for circumstances where the locality is seriously harmed or its proper planning would be substantially prejudiced.[10]

(3) In the following cases the enforcement notice must be issued within four years of the alleged breach of planning control:[11]

(a) carrying out without planning permission of building, engineering, mining or other operations;

(b) failure to comply with any condition or limitation relating to the carrying out of such operations and subject to which planning permission was granted for the development of the land;[12]

(c) change of use without planning permission of any building to use as a single dwellinghouse;

(d) failure to comply with a condition preventing a change of use to use as a single dwellinghouse.

(4) A copy of the notice must be served on the owner and occupier of the land and on any other person having an interest in the land which in the opinion of the local planning authority would be materially affected.[13]

'Owner' presumably means the person entitled to receive the rackrent or the person who would be entitled to receive it if the land were so let.[14] This would exclude, for instance, the owner of a freehold reversion subject to a lease at less than a rack-rent; such a person would nevertheless have an interest in the land and might be materially affected.[15]

The word 'occupier' clearly includes anyone occupying land under a lease or tenancy. And it now seems clear – in spite of some earlier

---

10 See circular 22/80, para 15 and Annex B; and Planning Policy Guidance Note No 1 (issued 1988), para 30.

11 1990 Act, s. 172(4).

12 The reference to planning permission for development appears wide enough to include planning permission for a change of use. The effect of the words about the carrying out of operations was considered by the Court of Appeal in *Peacock Homes Ltd v Secretary of State for the Environment and Epsom and Ewell Borough Council* [1984] JPL 729.

13 1990 Act, s. 172(6).

14 See definition of 'owner' in 1990 Act, s. 336(1), and *London Corpn v Cusack-Smith* [1955] AC 337, [1955] 1 All ER 302, ch 12, pp. 220, 221, below.

15 As a person interested in the land, such an owner would have the right to appeal against the enforcement notice: see p. 195, below.

doubts[16] – that it may include a licensee. In *Stevens v London Borough of Bromley*[17] the Court of Appeal rejected the proposition that an occupier for this purpose must be someone who has an interest in the land; the intention of the legislature was to ensure that anyone who might be prejudiced by an enforcement notice should be served with a copy of it.

Not all licensees will be occupiers for this purpose. Whether they are or not will depend on the circumstances. In *Stevens v London Borough of Bromley*[18] a number of caravanners occupied sites under licences from the owner of the land. These caravans were the permanent homes of their owners, and many of them made gardens on the small plots surrounding the caravans; each caravan had mains water and electricity and its drains were connected to a common cesspool. The licences could not be revoked unless one month's notice was given. It was held that the caravanners should have been served with the enforcement notice. Where, however, the arrangements are of a more transitory nature – as in *Munnich v Godstone RDC*[19] – licensees will not be regarded as 'occupiers' for this purpose, but this was obiter.

There are obvious pitfalls for the local planning authority. Failure to serve someone who should have been served with the notice may invalidate the notice altogether. (This may depend on the circumstances. In *McDaid v Clydebank District Council*,[20] the council had failed to serve the owners even though they knew of their identity: the Court of Session held that the notice was a nullity. In *R v Greenwich London Borough Council ex p Patel*[1] the Court of Appeal in England distinguished *McDaid* on the ground that the borough council did not know of the appellant's interest.) No harm is done, however, by serving someone who is not perhaps entitled to be served.

(5) The notice must specify:
(a) the alleged breach of planning control, that is the development said to have taken place without permission or the condition or limitation said to have been broken;[2]
(b) the steps to be taken to restore the land to its condition before the

---

16 Lord Denning MR suggested that a licensee could not be an occupier: *James v Minister of Housing and Local Government* [1965] 3 All ER 602 at 605; *Munnich v Godstone RDC* [1966] 1 All ER 930.
17 [1972] Ch 400, [1972] 1 All ER 712.
18 Above.
19 See fn 16, above. The report of this case does not state the degree of transience of the so-called occupiers, but Danckwerts LJ described them as 'birds of passage'.
20 [1984] JPL 579.
 1 [1985] JPL 851.
 2 1990 Act, s. 173(1).

development took place or to secure compliance with the condition or limitation alleged to have been broken;[3]

(c) the date on which the notice is to take effect;[4]

(d) the period for complying with the steps required by the notice;[5]

(e) the reasons why the local planning authority consider it expedient to issue the notice;[6]

(f) the precise boundaries of the land to which the notice relates, whether by reference to a plan or otherwise.[7]

If the rules as to service and content are not complied with, the notice may be a nullity; and, even if it is not a nullity, it may be invalid in which case it may be quashed on appeal. The distinction between 'nullity' and 'invalidity' is important because it affects the rights of persons on whom copies of the enforcement are served. If the notice is a nullity, it is 'so much waste paper';[8] it is, strictly speaking, not an enforcement notice at all, and the recipient is entitled to ignore it or, if he wishes, he can seek a declaration that it is void. If, however, the notice is invalid, it cannot safely be ignored and (with some possible exceptions) the recipient must exercise his rights of appeal under the Act of 1990.[9]

What constitutes a nullity in this context was explained by Upjohn LJ in *Miller-Mead v Minister of Housing and Local Government*.[10] It seems that a notice will be a nullity if it fails to specify one of the two periods mentioned in paragraph 5(c) and (d) above. This happened in *Burgess v Jarvis and Sevenoaks RDC*.[11]

Jarvis had built a number of houses without permission and the local authority served an enforcement notice requiring him to demolish the houses. This notice did not separately specify the period after which it was to take effect. Burgess who was the tenant of one of the houses obtained a declaration that the notice was invalid.

A notice will also be a nullity if:[12]

on its true construction it was ambiguous and uncertain so that the owner or occupier could not tell in what respect it was alleged that he had

---

3 1990 Act, s. 173(2)–(4).
4 Ibid, s. 172(5).
5 Ibid, s. 173(5).
6 T & CP (Enforcement Notices and Appeals) Regs 1981 (SI 1981 No 1742), reg 3(a).
7 Reg 3(b).
8 *Miller-Mead v Minister of Housing and Local Government* [1963] 2 QB 196, [1963] 1 All ER 459, per Upjohn LJ.
9 See p. 195, below.
10 [1963] 2 QB 196; [1963] 1 All ER 459.
11 [1952] 2 QB 41, [1952] 1 All ER 592. In the Court of Appeal, all three Lords Justices described the notice as 'invalid', but presumably they meant 'null' or 'void'.
12 *Miller-Mead v Minister of Housing and Local Government*, above, per Upjohn LJ.

developed the land without permission or in what respect it was alleged that he had failed to comply with a condition or, again, that he could not tell with reasonable certainty what steps he had to take to remedy the alleged breaches.

This dictum is illustrated by *Metallic Protectives Ltd v Secretary of State for the Environment.*[13]

> The local planning authority served an enforcement notice alleging breach of a condition in a planning permission that no nuisance should be caused to residential properties in the area by reason of noise, smell, smoke, etc. The enforcement notice required the occupier to install satisfactory sound proofing of a compressor and to take all possible action to minimise the effect created by the use of acrylic paint. On appeal, the Secretary of State accepted that the notice was far too imprecise; he therefore substituted precise requirements.
>
> Held: the enforcement notice as originally served was so defective as to be a nullity from the start: the Secretary of State could not amend it and it must be disregarded.

Although the Secretary of State's powers to amend or vary the terms of an enforcement notice have since been enlarged by the Act of 1981, it remains the law that he cannot use these powers where the notice is a nullity. Thus, in *Dudley Bowers Amusement Enterprises Ltd v Secretary of State for the Environment*[14] the local planning authority issued an enforcement notice requiring the company to discontinue the use of land for the holding of markets 'on such Sundays which fall within the period of summer time in any year'. On appeal the inspector amended the notice by substituting a reference to the Summer Time Act 1972. In the High Court Mr David Widdicombe QC, sitting as deputy judge, held the original wording was hopelessly ambiguous; the notice was therefore a nullity and there was no power to amend it.

It seems to be well enough established that the language of an enforcement notice must be given its ordinary or popular meaning and that extrinsic evidence, such as earlier planning applications and decisions are not admissible as aids to construction; where the issue is the meaning of the words used, the court will not go beyond the four corners of the notice.[15]

However, the courts are nowadays less inclined to insist on strict adherence to formalities and are willing in appropriate circumstances

---

13 [1976] JPL 166.
14 (1985) 52 P & CR 365, [1986] JPL 689.
15 *Miller-Mead v Minister of Housing and Local Government* [1963] 2 QB 196, [1963] 1 All ER 459, CA; *Dudley Bowers Amusement Enterprises Ltd v Secretary of State for the Environment* (above).

to adopt a more empirical approach. This change of emphasis is illustrated by *Coventry Scaffolding Co (London) Ltd v Parker*.[16]

The company carried on business from two premises in Crystal Palace Road, London, nos 73 and 75. Having at first warned the company not to use the rear of 73 for parking vehicles and storing equipment, the local planning authority served an enforcement notice; the enforcement notice referred to the name of the street, not the number of the property. Some years later the company were prosecuted and convicted for non-compliance with the notice.

The Divisional Court held that the omission to refer to no 73 was not a material or fundamental error so as to render the notice a nullity because the company were fully aware of the land to which it related. Kerr J, delivering the judgment of the court, said that it was not the correct view that one might only have regard to the contents of the notice within its four corners in order to decide whether it was a nullity or not.

> What had to be decided in each instance was whether, in the light of the surrounding circumstances, the recipient of the notice was sufficiently and clearly apprised of the effect of the notice, and of what he had to do pursuant to it to render it just as unjust to hold him to it.

Also, where an enforcement notice required compliance with a condition of planning permission that the occupation of a bungalow be limited to persons employed locally in agriculture, the Court of Appeal held that the word 'locally' had a perfectly intelligible meaning even if some doubtful cases might arise. The enforcement notice did not require the owner to permit occupation to persons who satisfied the provisions of the planning permission. If the proposed occupier was clearly inside or clearly outside the restriction, the owner could permit or refuse occupation as the case might be: if he was uncertain he could for his own safety refuse occupation.[17]

THE ALLEGED BREACH OF PLANNING CONTROL

The local planning authority must correctly identify the nature of the breach. The notice will be invalid (but not a nullity) if it alleges that development has been carried out without permission when in fact there has been a failure to comply with a condition or limitation. This is illustrated by *Francis v Yiewsley and West Drayton UDC*.[18]

The owner of land carried out development by using it as a caravan site.

16 [1987] JPL 127.
17 *Alderson v Secretary of State for the Environment* [1984] JPL 429.
18 [1958] 1 QB 478, [1957] 3 All ER 529.

He later applied for planning permission; on appeal, the Minister permitted the use of the land for six months from the date of his decision (February 1950). In 1952 the local authority served an enforcement notice alleging that the development had been carried out without permission. The Court of Appeal held that the notice was invalid; on the facts permission had been granted, albeit retrospectively.

This case was decided before the introduction in 1960 of the present system of appeals under which the Secretary of State can correct defects in enforcement notices provided he is satisfied that this can be done without injustice. *Francis v Yewsley and West Drayton UDC* remains good authority for the proposition that an enforcement notice will be invalid if it alleges that development has been carried out without permission when in fact there has been a failure to comply with a condition; the question nowadays will be whether the Secretary of State can amend it without causing injustice.

The importance of correctly identifying the breach of planning control is also illustrated by *Copeland Borough Council v Secretary of State for the Environment*:[19]

> Following the grant of outline planning permission for a dwellinghouse, detailed plans were submitted and approved showing that the roof was to be constructed with a particular type of slate, colour grey. In fact, buff coloured tiles were used. An enforcement notice was served alleging that building operations had been carried out without planning permission, namely the construction of the roof in buff coloured tiles, and requiring the developer to remedy the breach by removing the buff tiles.
>
> Held: where there was to be new development on virgin land the operation was to be treated as a single one; in the present case the breach of planning control consisted of the building of the whole house otherwise than in accordance with the approved plans.

When this case was decided in 1976 the Secretary of State was empowered to correct a defective enforcement notice if he was satisfied that the mistake was not material. But the Divisional Court considered that in the *Copeland* case the error could not be corrected without injustice, and the enforcement notice was quashed.

Lord Widgery CJ referred to a passage in *Miller-Mead v Minister of Housing and Local Government*[20] in which Lord Denning MR had said that the Minister can correct errors so long as, having regard to the merits of the case, the correction could be made without injustice; no error was material unless it was such as to produce injustice. Lord Widgery went on to say: 'I find it extremely hard to say that an amendment such as is contemplated here can take place without it

19 (1976) 31 P & CR 403.
20 [1963] 2 QB 196, [1963] 1 All ER 459.

being material and without giving rise to injustice ... there is no authority in this court where an enforcement notice has been saved and made effective when it failed correctly to describe the breach of planning control relied on'.

In 1981 the Secretary of State's powers of amendment were re-worded. He is now empowered to correct any informality, defect or error in the enforcement notice, or give directions for varying its terms, if he is satisfied that the correction or variation can be made without injustice to the appellant or the local planning authority.[1] The Secretary of State no longer has to be satisfied that the defect was not 'material'; instead there is explicit reference to the amendment not causing injustice either to the appellant or the authority.[2] The courts have regarded these changes as enabling the Secretary of State to amend even fundamental mistakes by the local planning authority in describing the breach of planning control. A recent example is *R v Tower Hamlets London Borough Council, ex p Ahern (London) Ltd*.[3]

> The company had planning permission for a waste skip transfer station subject to a condition that the use should cease on 31 August 1987. In September 1987 the council refused permission to continue the use and served an enforcement notice alleging a breach of planning control by making a material change of use without planning permission. On appeal the inspector decided that the notice was so defective as to be invalid and incapable of correction without injustice. He therefore quashed the notice. The company applied to the High Court to set this decision aside because they wanted a decision on the planning merits without having to go through the procedure again; they would, they said, have suffered no injustice had the substance of the appeal been dealt with, as they knew precisely what was being alleged against them and what steps the council required them to take.
>
> Roch J held that the inspector was wrong in deciding that the error in the enforcement notice was incapable of correction; he was further wrong in holding that he was unable to be satisfied that no injustice would be caused. The learned judge pointed out that in the *Miller-Mead* case the Court of Appeal had held that a misrecital did not necessarily invalidate an enforcement notice; the test, as Upjohn LJ had said, was 'does the notice tell him fairly what he has done wrong and what he must do to remedy it?'.

---

1 1971 Act, s. 88(2) substituted by 1981 Act.
2 It seems that previously an enforcement notice could be amended only in favour of the appellant.
3 [1989] JPL 757.

THE STEPS TO REMEDY THE BREACH

The Act of 1971, as originally enacted, provided that the enforcement notice must specify the steps required by the local planning authority to remedy the breach of planning control; that was either (a) in the case of development without permission, steps for the purpose of restoring the land to its previous condition; or (b) in the case of a breach of a condition or limitation, steps for securing compliance with that condition or limitation.

There was considerable doubt as to whether the local planning authority had much scope for discretion in specifying the steps to be taken. They did not have to insist on the land being restored to precisely its previous condition.[4] But, if the breach of planning control in the *Copeland* case[5] had been correctly identified, could the local planning authority have 'under-enforced' by requiring only the replacement of the offending roof tiles?[6]

Since 1981 the local planning authority has been able to be more flexible. The enforcement notice is to specify:[7]

(a) any steps which are required by the authority to remedy the breach of planning control, these being defined as steps either for restoring the land to its previous condition or for securing compliance with the conditions or limitations subject to which the planning permission was granted;

(b) such steps as the authority may require for the purpose of either (i) making the development comply with the terms of any planning permission which has been granted in respect of the land; or (ii) removing or alleviating any injury to amenity which has been caused by the development.

The new power to prescribe steps for removing or alleviating injury to amenity is no doubt intended to give the local planning authority an alternative to requiring the removal or discontinuance of the unauthorised development. Thus if a fish and chip shop has been opened without planning permission, the local planning authority may have no objection to the development in principle, but they might wish to restrict the opening hours so that they do not cause unreasonable disturbance to neighbours. Or where buildings or works have been erected without planning permission the local planning authority may be willing for them to remain provided a landscaping or tree planting scheme is carried out. Where an enforcement notice

---

4 *Iddenden v Secretary of State for the Environment* [1972] 3 All ER 883.

5 Above.

6 This question was discussed in the *Copeland* case, but it was unnecessary for the court to decide it.

7 See now 1990 Act, s. 173(2), (3), (4).

requires steps of this kind in relation to operational development, and these steps have been carried out, then planning permission will be deemed to have been granted for the purposes of the Act of 1990.[8] This does not apply, however, in relation to changes of use; thus in the example given above, the fish and chip shop would not be deemed to have planning permission.

Although the local planning authority now has more flexibility in prescribing the steps to remedy the breach of planning control, it is vital that these steps be properly defined, otherwise the enforcement notice will be void.[9]

Moreover, the steps required by the enforcement notice should not exceed what is necessary (1) to remedy the breach of planning control; or (2) to achieve the purpose of making the development comply with the terms of the planning permission or of alleviating injury to amenity. Excessive requirements do not invalidate the enforcement notice, but the Secretary of State may amend them on appeal.

An important application of the principle that the requirements should not be excessive is to be found in *Mansi v Elstree RDC*:[10]

> Land occupied by M was used as a plant nursery and contained a number of glasshouses. From 1922 onwards there was a subsidiary use of part of the land, including one of the glasshouses, for retail sales of nursery produce and other articles. In 1959 M intensified the latter use until the glasshouse became primarily a shop. The local planning authority served an enforcement notice requiring M to discontinue use for the sale of goods. On appeal the Minister upheld the enforcement notice.
>
> Held: the Minister should have recognised that a notice requiring discontinuance of all sale of goods went too far; the notice should be amended to safeguard the established right to carry on retail trade in the manner and to the extent to which it was carried on in 1959.

The 'Mansi principle' that established use rights should be safeguarded has been followed in a number of cases.[11] It is very doubtful, however, whether this principle applies where the established lesser use was begun after 1 July 1948 in breach of planning control; if, in such a case, an enforcement notice were issued in respect of the intensified use, section 57(4) of the Act of 1990 would not apply.[12]

8 1990 Act, s. 173(8).

9 *Metallic Protectives Ltd v Secretary of State for the Environment* [1976] JPL 166; see p. 188, above.

10 (1964) 16 P & CR 153.

11 See e g *Trevors Warehouses Ltd v Secretary of State for the Environment* (1972) 23 P & CR 215; *Newport v Secretary of State for the Environment and Bromley London Borough* (1980) 40 P & CR 261.

12 See ch 6, p. 115, above; see also *Denham Developments Ltd v Secretary of State for the Environment and Brentwood District Council* [1984] JPL 347.

THE DATE ON WHICH THE NOTICE TAKES EFFECT

The enforcement notice must specify the date on which it is to take effect. In specifying this date the local planning authority must have regard to section 172(6) which requires them to serve a copy of the enforcement notice on the owner and occupier and any other person likely to be affected, not later than 28 days after the date of issue and at least 28 days before the date on which the notice is to take effect.

This replaces the earlier rule that the enforcement notice should specify a period of not less than 28 days at the expiry of which the notice took effect. This rule was inconvenient in that all persons affected had to be served on the same day;[13] under the new rule those affected can be served with copies of the notice on different days.

These provisions are linked with the requirement that any appeal against the enforcement notice must be lodged with the Secretary of State before the notice takes effect; it is important therefore that anyone affected by the notice is given a minimum of 28 days in which to appeal. It seems, however, that the Secretary of State may in his discretion disregard the fact that an appellant has received less than 28 days' notice. In *Porritt v Secretary of State for the Environment*[14] an enforcement notice was issued in respect of unauthorised development but P was served with a copy of it only 27 days before the date on which it was due to take effect; however, he lodged an appeal before that date. The Secretary of State decided to disregard the procedural defect because no injustice had resulted. There was no statutory provision which authorised the Secretary of State to do so, but the court nevertheless upheld his decision; an interesting example of the extent to which the courts have moved away from insistence upon the strict observance of formalities.

THE PERIOD FOR COMPLIANCE WITH THE NOTICE

The enforcement notice must specify the period after the notice takes effect in which the steps required by the enforcement notice are to be carried out. Section 173(5) enables the local planning authority to specify different periods for the taking of different steps. There is no statutory minimum, but the period or periods specified must be reasonable having regard to what is required.

Finally a notice will be invalid if the local planning authority do not comply with the rules as to service. Thus in *Caravans and Automobiles*

---

13 *Banbury v Hounslow London Borough Council* [1966] 2 QB 204, [1966] 2 All ER 532.
14 [1988] JPL 414.

Ltd v Southall Borough Council[15] company A owned the whole of the site used for the display and sale of caravans without planning permission; company A occupied part of the site for this purpose and company B occupied the remainder of the site for the same purpose. An enforcement notice was served on company A but not on company B. It was held that both occupiers should have been served and the notice was invalid. Under the Act of 1990 the Secretary of State may disregard the fact that some person who ought to have been served with the enforcement notice has not been served, if neither the appellant nor that person has been substantially prejudiced.[16]

RIGHTS OF APPEAL

As originally enacted the Act of 1947 provided two methods by which an enforcement notice might be challenged: (a) by applying to the local planning authority for planning permission and then appealing, if need be, to the Minister against the planning authority's decision; (b) by appealing to the local magistrates on certain limited grounds of law. In addition, it was possible under the general law to apply to the High Court for a declaration on any matter of law.

These provisions were not well designed. They provided considerable opportunities for delay and evasion which were sometimes well exploited; and, owing to ambiguous drafting, there were doubts as to the precise extent of the right of appeal to the magistrates. The Caravan Sites and Control of Development Act 1960 substituted a right of appeal to the Secretary of State, both on planning and legal grounds, by any person on whom the enforcement notice had been served or by any other person having an interest in the land; these provisions, with some changes in detail, are now to be found in the Act of 1990.

Who may appeal Section 174(1) of the Act of 1990 confers a right of appeal upon any person having an interest in the land or a 'relevant occupier', whether or not a copy of the notice has been served on him; 'relevant occupier' means any person who occupies the land by virtue of a licence in writing at the date on which the enforcement notice is issued and continues to do so at the time the appeal is brought. This provision (introduced in 1984) restores the right of appeal to some of the licensees upon whom a copy of the notice ought to be served.[17]

The grounds of appeal　Section 174(2) of the Act of 1990 provides that an appeal may be brought on any of the following grounds:

(a) that permission ought to be granted for the development to which the enforcement notice relates, or the condition or limitation in question should be discharged;

(b) that the matters alleged in the notice do not constitute a breach of planning control;

(c) that the breach of planning control alleged in the notice has not taken place;

(d) in a case to which the four-year rule still applies, that that period has elapsed at the date of issue;[18]

(e) in any other case, that the alleged breach of planning control occurred before 1964;

(f) that copies of the notice have not been served as required by section 172(6);[19]

(g) that the steps required to be taken by the notice exceed what is necessary (i) to remedy any breach of planning control or (ii) for making the development comply with the terms of the planning permission or for removing or alleviating any injury to amenity;

(h) that the period specified in the enforcement notice for complying with the notice is unreasonably short.

The question of where the burden of proof lies in enforcement appeals was discussed in *Nelsovil Ltd v Minister of Housing and Local Government*.[20] Widgery J said, 'I should have thought that a person given a right to appeal on certain specified grounds is the person who has to make good those grounds and is the person on whom that onus rests.' He also said, 'I can see no sort of hardship in requiring that the onus shall lie on the appellant in such case.' In this case the point at issue was whether a material change of use had occurred more than four years before an enforcement notice was served; but the appellants failed to discharge their burden of proof, and the Minister's decision that (in effect) there was no evidence of the changed use dating back four years was upheld by the court. An appeal against an enforcement matter is a civil matter; the standard of proof is on the balance of probabilities, not the criminal law standard of beyond reasonable doubt.[1]

---

18 See p. 185, above.
19 See p. 185, above.
20 [1962] 1 All ER 423. See also *Parker Bros (Farms) Ltd v Minister of Housing and Local Government* (1969) 210 Estates Gazette 825.
1 *Thrasyvoulou v Secretary of State for the Environment* [1984] JPL 732.

PROCEDURE ON APPEAL

Notice of appeal must be given in writing to the Secretary of State before the date on which the enforcement notice is due to take effect.[2] The Secretary of State has no power to extend the time for giving notice of appeal. The appellant must submit to the Secretary of State a statement in writing specifying the grounds on which he is appealing[3] and giving such information as may be prescribed by regulations[4] made by the Secretary of State.[5] This statement may be submitted with the notice of appeal or within such time as may be prescribed by the regulations. The appellant must state the facts on which he supports each of his grounds of appeal.[6] The regulations require the local planning authority, inter alia, to submit a statement of the submissions which they propose to put forward on the appeal.[7] If the appellant fails to submit the statement required from him, the Secretary of State may dismiss his appeal forthwith; likewise, if the local planning authority fail to take the procedural steps required of them, the Secretary of State may allow the appeal.[8]

The giving of notice of appeal suspends the operation of the enforcement notice pending the final outcome of the appeal.[9] The strict procedures described above are clearly designed to prevent hardship to the public either as a result of timewasting tactics by the appellant or neglect by the local planning authority.

Subject to what has been said above, the appellant and the local planning authority have the right to be heard at a public local inquiry or other hearing.[10]

The Secretary of State may uphold, quash or vary an enforcement notice. In particular, he may grant planning permission for the development to which the notice relates; and he may determine the purpose for which the land may lawfully be used having regard to its past use and any relevant planning permission.[11]

The Secretary of State is empowered to correct any informality, defect or error in the enforcement notice provided he is satisfied that

---

2 1990 Act, s. 174(3). The notice of appeal must be received by the Secretary of State before that date: *Lenlyn Ltd v Secretary of State for the Environment and Royal Borough of Kensington and Chelsea* [1985] JPL 482.
3 Ibid, s. 174(4).
4 See T & CP (Enforcement Notice and Appeals) Regs 1981 (SI 1981 No 1742).
5 1990 Act, s. 174(4), 1981 Regs (as above), reg 5.
6 1981 Regs (as above), reg 5.
7 Ibid, reg 6.
8 1990 Act, s. 176(3).
9 Ibid, s. 175(4).
10 Ibid, s. 175(3).
11 Ibid, s. 177(1).

this can be done without injustice to the appellant or the local planning authority.[12] This power to vary the terms of a notice goes well beyond the correction of minor errors and enables the Secretary of State in most cases to put in order invalid notices provided no injustice is caused to the appellant or the local planning authority.[13]

Where the local planning authority have failed to serve a copy of the enforcement notice on a person who should have been served, the Secretary of State may disregard that fact if neither the appellant nor that person has been substantially prejudiced.[14] This, however, presupposes that an appeal has been made by a person with knowledge of the enforcement notice. In *McDaid v Clydebank District Council*[15] the local planning authority served the occupier who did not appeal but failed to serve the owner who remained in ignorance until the enforcement notice took effect: the Court of Session held that the notice was a nullity.[16]

The Secretary of State's decision on any point of law may be challenged in High Court proceedings at the instance of the local planning authority, of the appellant or of any other person on whom the enforcement notice was served; and the Secretary of State may at any stage state a case on his own initiative for the opinion of the High Court.[17]

There is an important provision in the Act of 1990 that the validity of an enforcement notice shall not be questioned in any proceedings whatsoever on any of the grounds of appeal specified in section 174(2), except by way of appeal to the Secretary of State.[18] There is one exception to this rule for the protection of previous owners of the land.[19]

This provision thus excludes the right which would otherwise be available at common law to by-pass the Secretary of State by applying to the High Court for a declaration on any point of law covered by the statutory grounds of appeal. It is now clear that this provision does not take away the right to apply for a declaration that the enforcement was a nullity on the grounds explained earlier in this chapter.[20]

12 1990 Act, s. 176(2).
13 See pp. 190, 191, above.
14 1990 Act, s. 176(5).
15 [1984] JPL 579.
16 See, however, the decision of the Court of Appeal in *R v Greenwich London Borough Council, ex p Patel* [1985] JPL 851 mentioned at p. 186, above.
17 1990 Act, s. 289(1), (3).
18 Ibid, s. 285(1). Subject, of course, to the right to test the Secretary of State's decision in the High Court under s. 289.
19 See this chapter, p. 201, below.
20 See pp. 187, 188, above.

A further point arises out of ground (h) on which appeal may be made under section 174(2). Where an appeal is brought on this ground, the local planning authority sometimes contend that, although the period is rather short, the appellant could have begun to take appropriate steps before the enforcement notice took effect. In *Mercer v Uckfield RDC*[1] the Minister accepted this argument and refused to extend the period for complying with the notice. M then appealed to the Divisional Court on the ground that the Minister was not entitled to consider the 'previous planning history'. The court upheld the Minister's right to do so.

It is by no means clear, however, that the court would take this view in every case. In *Mercer*'s case M had previously applied for planning permission and, when this was refused, had appealed to the Minister. It was only after the Minister had dismissed this appeal that the authority served an enforcement notice. M then appealed against the enforcement notice on the ground that planning permission ought to be given for the offending development as well as on the ground that the period for compliance was too short.

In many cases, however, it is not until the appeal against the enforcement notice that the Secretary of State has an opportunity of considering whether planning permission ought to be given. The appellant may also take the point (which did not arise in *Mercer*'s case) that he does not require permission. If he succeeds on either of these grounds the notice will not take effect. It would surely be unreasonable to expect an appellant to start dismantling his development until he knows whether the notice which has been served upon him will ever take effect.

EFFECT OF ENFORCEMENT NOTICE

As already explained[2] an enforcement notice requires the person on whom it is served to take specified steps to remedy the breach of planning control. The notice continues to be effective after it has been complied with.[3] Furthermore, it is effective against any subsequent owner, provided it has been registered as a local land charge.

---

1 (1962) 14 P & CR 32.
2 See p. 186, above.
3 1990 Act, s. 181(1).

ENFORCEMENT OF ENFORCEMENT NOTICE

Where the enforcement notice has not been complied with, the local planning authority's remedies vary according to the circumstances.

(1) Failure to comply with requirements other than discontinuance of a use   The local planning authority may prosecute the person who was the owner at the time the enforcement notice was served, and he will be liable to a fine.[4] If that person has ceased to be the owner at some time before the end of the period allowed for compliance, he is entitled to have the new owner brought before the court.[5] The original owner must be acquitted if he shows that no blame attaches to him; in any event, if any blame attaches to the new owner, he also may be fined.[6] If after conviction any person fails to take reasonable steps to comply with the enforcement notice, he will be liable to a further fine.[7] The defendant cannot question the validity of the enforcement notice, unless he has grounds for asserting that the notice is a complete nullity.

In addition, where any steps are required by virtue of section 173(2)(a) of the Act of 1990 – i e steps to restore the land to its original condition or to secure compliance with conditions or limitations – the local planning authority may enter the land and carry out the requisite works at the expense of the person who is then the owner of the land; the owner has the right to recover the sum involved from the person by whom the breach of planning control was committed.[8] Neither of these persons will be able to question the validity of the enforcement notice, unless there are grounds for asserting that it is a nullity.

(2) Reinstatement of buildings or works demolished or altered in compliance with an enforcement notice   Provided such reinstatement is 'development' this is a breach of the original enforcement notice.[9] The local planning authority, on giving not less than 28 days' notice, may exercise their right to enter the land to secure compliance with the enforcement notice[10] and they may also prosecute. Although the original enforcement notice still applies, nevertheless, any requirements in it concerning *demolition* or *alteration* cannot be enforced by prosecution under section 179 as a punishment for the unauthorised reinstatement or

4   1990 Act, s. 179(1), (2).
5   Ibid, s. 179(3).
6   Ibid, s. 179(4).
7   Ibid, s. 179(5).
8   Ibid, s. 178(1), (2). These provisions do not extend to steps required under s. 173(2)(b) for making the development comply with the terms of the planning permission; nor do they extend to steps requiring the discontinuance of a use.
9   Ibid, s. 181(3); even if the terms of notice 'are not apt for the purpose'.
10   Ibid, s. 181(4).

restoration work; otherwise a penalty in respect of this work could be imposed twice over, once for doing it and once for failing to undo it.[11]

(3) Failure to comply with requirements of an enforcement notice as to discontinuance of use or compliance with any condition or limitation Any person who uses the land or permits it to be used in contravention of the enforcement notice is guilty of an offence.[12] It will be observed that in this case, it is not only the owner who may be prosecuted; indeed, if he is unable to prevent somebody else – such as a tenant – from acting in contravention of the notice, he will not be guilty of an offence.[13] Here again, the validity of the notice may not be questioned on any of the grounds mentioned in section 174(2) unless the person prosecuted has held an interest in the land since before the enforcement notice was issued, was not served with a copy of the enforcement notice, and satisfies the court (i) that he did not know and could not reasonably have been expected to know that the enforcement notice had been issued; and (ii) that his interests have been substantially prejudiced by the failure to serve him with a copy of it.[14]

Where the enforcement notice merely requires the discontinuance of a use, the local planning authority have no power to enter upon the land to secure compliance with the notice; indeed, that might be impracticable. The difficulties to which this can give rise are illustrated by *A-G v Bastow*.[15] The owner of a caravan site ignored an enforcement notice requiring him to discontinue the use of land as a caravan site, he was prosecuted and fined on a number of occasions, but he still did not comply with the notice. The Attorney-General acting in the public interest then sought a High Court injunction requiring the defendant to comply with the enforcement notice. The injunction was granted. In other cases, the Attorney-General acting on behalf of the local authority has been able to bring injunctions on a county wide basis to prevent defendants escaping the effects of an enforcement notice by moving caravans from site to site.[16]

The local planning authority can now sue for an injunction in their

---

11 1990 Act, s. 181(5).
12 Ibid, s. 179(6), (7). The maximum penalties on summary conviction are £2,000 and £100 a day thereafter; on indictment there is no limit.
13 A person cannot 'permit' another person to do an act unless he has power to forbid him to do the act: *Goodbarne v Buck* [1940] 1 KB 771, [1940] 1 All ER 613.
14 1990 Act, s. 285(2).
15 [1957] 1 QB 514, [1957] 1 All ER 497.
16 See *A-G v Smith* [1958] 2 QB 173, [1958] 2 All ER 557; *A-G ex rel East Sussex County Council v Morris* [1973] JPL 429.

own name instead of invoking the aid of the Attorney-General.[17] The action must be for the promotion or protection of the interests of the inhabitants of the local authority's area. Whether an injunction will be granted will depend on the facts of each individual case.[18]

Established use certificates

The repeal of the four-year rule in relation to changes of use occurring after the end of 1963 removes some of the certainty as to the purposes for which property may lawfully be used. There are two dangers. First, where the change of use took place before 1964, the risk of enforcement action remains because the local planning authority on discovering the change of use may think it occurred more recently. Secondly, the use may have begun after the end of 1963 and the local planning authority erroneously suppose that it requires planning permission. In both cases the owner or occupier of the land would have grounds for a successful appeal if an enforcement notice were served, but to remove the uncertainty section 192 of the Act of 1990 enables any person interested in the land to take the initiative by applying for a certificate of established use. The reference to 'any person interested in the land' is doubtless intended to cover a prospective purchaser under a conditional contract.

For the purpose of the new procedure, a use of land is said to be established if either:[19]

(a) it was begun before 1964 without planning permission and has continued since the end of 1963; or

(b) it was begun before 1964 under a planning permission containing conditions or limitations which have not been complied with since the end of 1963;[20]

(c) it was begun after the end of 1963 as a result of a change of use not requiring planning permission and there has been since the end of 1963 no change of use requiring planning permission.[1]

The requirement in ground (a) that the use must have 'continued' since the end of 1963 gives rise to some problems of interpretation. At

---

17 Local Government Act 1972, s. 222. And see *Westminster City Council v Jones* (1981) 80 LGR 241.

18 *Runnymede Borough Council v Ball* [1986] 1 All ER 629.

19 1990 Act, s. 191.

20 It would appear from the reference to 'limitations' that the permission may be one granted by development order: see ch 6, above.

1 It would seem, therefore, that if in, say, 1965, there was a material change of use from A to B without permission and there was subsequently a change from B to C not amounting to a material change of use, C will not be 'established'.

one time the Secretary of State was of the opinion that the use must have continued 'on the ground', but he now considers it sufficient that the use should not have been supplanted by some other use or abandoned:[2] the latter, it is submitted, is the better view. But what is the position where a use was begun before 1964 and since then there has been a material change of use by intensification? Clearly, there is no entitlement to a certificate in respect of the intensified use, but can the local planning authority issue a certificate in respect of the lesser use? In *Hipsey v Secretary of State for the Environment and Thurrock Borough Council*[3] the applicant had applied for a certificate for the use as it existed at the time of the application, but this was refused because it was an intensified use; it was held that the Secretary of State on appeal could not issue a certificate for the lesser use because there had been no application for a certificate for that use. The court left open the question whether an amended application would have succeeded.

The decision in *Hipsey* was not followed in *Bristol City Council v Secretary of State for the Environment*.[4] In this case the Secretary of State had refused an appeal to grant a certificate to the effect that the premises had been used in multiple occupation, housing seven households with nine occupiers; but, on the evidence available, he granted a certificate for multiple occupation in the lesser amount of six households with six occupiers. Stuart-Smith J held that the Secretary of State had acted correctly. This case did not raise the question of intensification; if and when this point comes up for decision, it may well turn on the question whether the lesser use can be said to have 'continued' notwithstanding that it has become by intensification a materially different use.[5]

Application for a certificate should be made to the local planning authority;[6] normally, it will be for that authority to decide whether or not a certificate should be granted, but the Secretary of State may require the application to be referred to him. The local planning authority's decision is a purely judicial one and, if they are satisfied that the applicant's claim is made out, they must grant a certificate. The onus of proof is quite clearly on the applicant.[7] The Act of 1990

2 See decision letter of the Secretary of State quoted in *Hipsey v Secretary of State for the Environment and Thurrock Borough Council* [1984] JPL 806.

3 Above.

4 [1987] JPL 718.

5 For a discussion of intensification as a material change of use see ch 5, p. 99 ff, above.

6 1990 Act, s. 192(1). The application must be accompanied by a certificate relating to the ownership of the land: see GDO, art 29(4).

7 The principle laid down by Widgery J in *Nelsovil Ltd v Minister of Housing and Local Government* [1962] 1 All ER 423, [1962] 1 WLR 404 seems equally applicable here: see this chapter, p. 196, above.

specifically authorises the grant of a certificate for either the whole of the land specified in the application or for part of it; and, where the application specifies two or more uses, a certificate may be granted either for all or some.[8] However, it seems that the certificate should relate to the planning unit as a whole and not be restricted to part of it.[9]

If the local planning authority refuse a certificate, or if they fail to give a decision within the proper period,[10] the applicant may appeal to the Secretary of State. When a case comes before the Secretary of State (whether on appeal or a referred application) the applicant and the local planning authority have the right to a public local inquiry or other hearing.[11]

The Secretary of State's powers are wider than those of the local planning authority. He must of course act judicially in deciding whether or not the claim for an established use is made out; but if it is not made out, he may nevertheless grant planning permission for the use in question.

The Secretary of State's decision is final, but may be challenged on grounds of law under section 288 of the Act of 1990.[12]

An established use certificate is to be treated as conclusive evidence for the purposes of any appeal against an enforcement notice provided application for the certificate had been made before the enforcement notice was served.[13]

Stop notices

As we have seen, the lodging of an appeal suspends the operation of an enforcement notice until such time as the appeal is finally disposed of or withdrawn. In the meantime, the operation or change of use can continue without penalty. The Act of 1968 introduced the remedy of the 'stop notice' to prevent the continuance of operations pending the outcome of an appeal against an enforcement notice. Strangely, this procedure could not at first be used to stop a change of use, but this omission was remedied in 1977.

---

8 1990 Act, s. 194(2).
9 *Cullmore v Monmouth Borough Council* (unreported).
10 The prescribed period is two months unless the applicant agrees to an extension of time: GDO, art 29(10).
11 1990 Act, s. 196(1).
12 See ch 18, p. 316, below.
13 1990 Act, s. 192(4). See also *Broxbourne Borough Council v Secretary of State for the Environment* [1980] QB 1, [1979] 2 All ER 13; *Vaughan v Secretary of State for the Environment and Mid-Sussex District* [1986] JPL 840.

A stop notice is essentially a supplement to an enforcement notice, and cannot be served until an enforcement notice has been issued. The local planning authority are entitled to decide at one and the same time to take enforcement action and to serve a stop notice.[14] Furthermore, although a strict interpretation of section 183(1) suggests otherwise, the Court of Appeal has decided that the enforcement notice and the stop notice can be served simultaneously.[15]

A stop notice may prohibit any activity complained of in the enforcement notice.[16] There are, however, three types of 'activity' which may not be prohibited by a stop notice:[17]

(1) the use of any buildings as a dwellinghouse;
(2) the use of any land as the site of a caravan occupied by a person as his only or main residence;
(3) the taking of any steps required by the enforcement notice to remedy the breach of planning control alleged in the enforcement notice.

Moreover, a stop notice cannot be served in respect of an activity which began more than 12 months earlier unless it is, or is incidental to, building, engineering, mining or other operations, or the deposit of refuse or waste materials.[18] A problem which arises here is whether the period of 12 months is the time during which the activity in question has been carried on in fact or the period during which it has been carried on in breach of control. In *Scott Markets Ltd v Waltham Forest London Borough Council*[19] a temporary planning permission, granted in 1975, for the use of land as an open-air market expired on 30 June 1978. The use continued after that date and shortly afterwards the council informed the plaintiffs that they intended to serve enforcement and stop notices. The plaintiffs were granted a declaration that the council were not entitled to serve a stop notice because the use had begun more than 12 months previously, although of course, there had been no breach of planning control until after 30 June 1978.

Although a stop notice depends for its validity upon an enforcement notice, the stop notice can be served upon any person interested in the land or carrying out any activity specified in the stop notice; a stop notice may therefore be served on a contractor as well as on the owners and occupiers of the land. The local planning authority may also put up a site notice.[20]

---

14 *Westminster City Council v Jones* (1981) 80 LGR 241, [1981] JPL 750.
15 In *R v Pettigrove* (1990) Independent, 31 May.
16 1990 Act, s. 183(1).
17 Ibid, s. 183(3).
18 Ibid, s. 183(5).
19 (1979) 38 P & CR 597.
20 1990 Act, s. 183(6).

It is obviously very important that the wording of a stop notice should state clearly what activities are prohibited. But, where a stop notice relates to a change of use, absolute precision may be difficult to achieve, as was illustrated in *R v Runnymede Borough Council, ex p Seehra*.[1]

> The council issued an enforcement notice alleging a material change in the use of Mr Seehra's house to mixed residential and religious purposes, and prohibiting the use of the land for the purposes of religious devotion 'otherwise than as incidental to the enjoyment of the dwellinghouse as such'. The council also served a stop notice requiring the premises to cease to be used for purposes other than those incidental to a dwellinghouse.
>
> The problem here was that participation in religious devotions by visitors to the house may up to a point be incidental to the enjoyment of a private house. Mr Seehra complained that the stop notice left it to him to decide how to behave; if he came to the wrong judgment he might be prosecuted or, alternatively, he might act so carefully that he was being deprived of something which he would be entitled to do.
>
> Schiemann J said that these were well founded worries; he nevertheless held that the notices were not void and did, within the spirit of the decided cases, give an indication to the applicant of what he had and had not to do.

There is no appeal against a stop notice, and failure to comply with it is a punishable offence.[2] But it is not an offence under the stop notice procedure to continue the prohibited activity after the enforcement notice has come into effect; and of course the stop notice will cease to have effect if the enforcement notice is quashed or withdrawn.[3]

There is one important safeguard. If the enforcement notice is quashed or withdrawn, the local planning authority may be liable to pay compensation to owners or occupiers of the land for any loss or damage directly attributable to the stop notice; this compensation will include any damages payable to contractors.[4]

In *J Sample (Warkworth) Ltd v Alnwick District Council*[5] the claimants were a building firm who had contracted to build a house for a Mr & Mrs W at a fixed price. The council served an enforcement notice alleging that the erection of the house had been undertaken without planning permission and requiring it to be demolished. A stop notice served on the same day prohibited any further building on the site.

---

1   (1986) 151 JP 80, 53 P & CR 281.
2   The maximum penalty on summary conviction is the statutory maximum and a daily fine of £200; there is no limit on indictment. 1990 Act, s. 187; Criminal Law Act 1977, s. 28(2).
3   1990 Act, s. 183(7).
4   Ibid, s. 186.
5   [1984] JPL 670.

The council subsequently granted planning permission but did not withdraw the enforcement notice or the stop notice. The enforcement notice was subsequently quashed on appeal and as a result the stop notice ceased to be effective.

The Lands Tribunal awarded compensation to the claimants for (1) cost of idle time when the work force was taken off construction of the house; (2) work needed to rectify deterioration caused by the delay; (3) loss of interest on the purchase price of the house pending the delay in completion; (4) a payment made by the claimants to Mr & Mrs W for temporary accommodation.

The council had contended that some of these items were not reasonably forseeable, but the Lands Tribunal held that compensation was payable for any loss directly attributable to the stop notice.

Where the enforcement notice turns out to be a nullity, it follows that the stop notice was also a nullity. Strictly speaking, therefore, there never was a stop notice upon which a claim for compensation could be based. The remedy here would seem to be to seek an injunction ordering the local planning authority to withdraw the stop notice.[6]

---

6 *Clwyd County Council v Secretary of State for Wales and Welsh Aggregates* [1982] JPL 696; affirmed on other grounds by the Court of Appeal *Welsh Aggregates Ltd v Secretary of State for the Environment and Clwyd County Council* [1983] JPL 50.

Chapter 11

Planning by agreement

The statutory system of planning control described in previous chapters is supplemented by provision for voluntary agreements between landowners and local planning authorities. Section 106 of the Act of 1990 (re-enacting section 52 of the Act of 1971) provides that a local planning authority may enter into an agreement with any person interested in land in their area for the purpose of restricting or regulating the use of the land either permanently or for a limited period only.

From 1948 to 1968 such agreements could be made only with the approval of the Minister. The Act of 1968 removed the need to obtain the Minister's approval, and there followed a great increase in the number of agreements made under what is now section 106. Furthermore the scope of the agreements entered into has been much wider, and in recent years there has been much controversy about these agreements.

Provision for voluntary agreements between local authorities and landowners began with the Act of 1932. Section 34 of that Act enabled a local authority to enter into an agreement with a landowner whereby the latter agreed to restrict the development or use of the land in 'any manner in which these matters might be dealt with by or under a scheme' under that Act. The purposes for which an agreement could be made were thus limited to matters which could be included in a planning scheme and these matters were precisely defined in the Act.[1] Section 34 was clearly a helpful supplement to the planning control provisions of the Act of 1932. A local authority might, it has been suggested, keep 'green fields free from buildings without having to pay compensation, the landowner had his *quid pro quo* when he was allowed to develop other land without having to meet a claim for betterment'.[2] It has also been suggested that a section 34 agreement

---

1 For planning schemes under the 1932 Act, see ch 1, above.
2 W Wood 'Planning and the Law: A Guide to the Town and Country Planning Act 1947' cited J Jewell 'Bargaining in Development Control' [1977] JPL 423.

could make it easier for a local authority to enforce the terms of an interim development permission pending approval of the scheme.[3]

With the introduction of a comprehensive system of planning control by the Act of 1947 the need for such agreements was less apparent and their role less clear. The objects of planning control were no longer limited to certain closely defined matters as in the Act of 1932. Nevertheless during the 1950s planning was generally regarded as being concerned with the control of land uses, consideration of amenity and similar matters. The idea that planning might also be concerned with wider social and economic policies was to develop later.

During the period from 1948 to 1968 the number of agreements was quite small.[4] There were, for instance, agreements to discontinue the sale of petrol from a badly sited garage on the opening of a new filling station under the same ownership, to restrict the use of holiday chalets to the summer months and to prevent their being used as permanent residences, and to regulate the use of caravan sites. A particularly interesting agreement related to a windmill in Kent. The windmill was subject to a building preservation order but was falling into disrepair; the county council agreed to carry out repairs at their own expense in return for undertakings to restrict the use of the property to agricultural and private residential purposes, to keep the mill clean and to protect it from damage, and to allow members of the public to visit it.[5]

With the removal of ministerial control in 1968 many local planning authorities saw the opportunity to obtain 'gains' for the 'community' which could not be secured by means of conditions attached to a grant of planning permission. There entered into the business of granting planning permission an element of bargaining, and in the development boom of the late sixties and early seventies many developers were ready to make concessions rather than court a refusal of permission and incur the delay involved in exercising the right of appeal to the Secretary of State. The type of 'gain' achieved in this way included such matters as dedication of land to public use; provision of community buildings in large developments; to provide the local authority with land for local authority requirements or to construct housing suitable for local authority requirements.[6] Gains of this kind represent

3 *Ransom and Luck Ltd v Surbiton Borough Council* [1949] Ch 180, [1949] 1 All ER 185.
4 The total number of agreements approved by the Minister in the four years 1956–59 was 83: the number approved in the 1960s was rather higher, but did not exceed 157 in any one year: see Jewell, above, at 416.
5 Ministry of Housing and Local Government Report 1957, p. 81.
6 Jewell, above.

purposes going well beyond traditional land use and amenity considerations.

Section 106 can be and often is used, however, for the benefit of the developer. A proposed development may require improved means of access, provision of new sewers or other forms of infrastructure which involve the carrying out of work on land which is not under the control of the applicant for planning permission.[7] Under a section 106 agreement the developer can give enforceable undertakings to carry out the necessary work when he has obtained the power to do so or to reimburse the appropriate public authority for doing the work under statutory powers.

It now seems likely that section 106 will be used in a more restrained manner. The controversy engendered by the use and abuse of what is now section 106 resulted in the Secretary of State asking his Property Advisory Group to review the matter. The Group in their report[8] urged that, with some exceptions, the practice of bargaining for planning gain should be regarded as unacceptable and recommended that it be discouraged. As a result the Secretary of State issued circular 22/83 pointing out that it is a matter of law as well as of good administration that planning applications should be considered on the merits having regard to the provisions of the development plan and any other material considerations, and that they should be refused only where this serves a clear planning purpose and the economic effects have been taken into account. The question of imposing a condition or obligation should only arise where it is considered that it would not be reasonable to grant a permission in the terms sought without such condition or obligation. 'A wholly unacceptable development should not of course be permitted just because of extraneous benefits offered by the developer.'[9]

Circular 22/83 set out in some detail the tests which should apply in formulating agreements, but the Secretary of State has now announced his intention of issuing a revised circular. Moreover, there has now been some very important guidance from the courts as to what is permissible in section 106 agreements. In *Bradford City Metropolitan Council v Secretary of State for the Environment*[10] the council had imposed a condition requiring the widening of an existing road; this would have required the carrying out of works on land not owned or controlled by the developers. On appeal the Secretary of State held that the condition was illegal and expressed the view that the council

7 See ch 7, p. 148, above.
8 'Planning Gain' 1981.
9 Circular 22/83 para 4.
10 [1986] JPL 598, CA.

should either have refused permission altogether or attempted to negotiate an agreement under what is now section 106. The Court of Appeal held that the condition was manifestly unreasonable.[11] Commenting on the possible use of what is now section 106 Lloyd LJ said that, if the condition was manifestly unreasonable and so beyond the powers of the planning authority to impose it, whether or not the developers consented, it had to follow that it was also beyond the powers of the planning authority to include it in a section 106 agreement. But, said Lloyd LJ, there might be a case for a more limited agreement under section 106. A contribution towards the cost of widening the road might well have been reasonable, due to the increased use of the road resulting from the development and the benefit to the occupiers of the residential development. 'There was all the difference in the world between a provision of a section [52] agreement requiring a contribution from a developer toward the cost of widening a highway and a provision which required the entire works to be carried out at his risk and expense.'

Likewise, in *R v Westminster City Council, ex p Monahan*[12] Kerr LJ said:

> Section [52] agreements undoubtedly facilitated the formulation of quali-
> fied planning permissions in comparison with the imposition of express
> conditions, and no doubt they also simplified the procedural aspects of the
> planning process in many ways ... But if a particular condition would be
> illegal – on the ground of manifest unreasonableness or otherwise – it could
> not acquire validity if it was embodied in a section [52] agreement whether
> at the instance of the applicant himself or not. That in effect was equally
> the conclusion of Lloyd LJ in *Bradford*.

The remarks of both Lloyd and Kerr LJJ were obiter, but they afford substantial authority for the proposition that – as with conditions in planning permission – a local authority cannot under section 106 lawfully require or agree to a provision that is manifestly unreasonable.[13] It also seems that a section 106 agreement must satisfy the test applied to conditions that the provisions must serve a planning purpose. In *R v Gillingham Borough Council, ex p Parham Ltd*[14] Roch J referred to the decision of the House of Lords in *Newbury District Council v Secretary of State for the Environment*[15] where Lord Scarman had said that 'a condition must fairly and reasonably relate to the provisions

---

11 The Court of Appeal followed the earlier decision *Hall & Co Ltd v Shoreham-on-Sea UDC* [1961] 1 All ER 1, [1964] 1 WLR 240, CA; see ch 8, p. 160, above.
12 [1989] JPL 407, CA. See ch 7, pp. 144, 145, above.
13 For the meaning of 'manifestly unreasonable' in the context of conditions, see ch 8, pp. 160 ff, above.
14 [1988] JPL 336.
15 [1981] AC 578, [1980] 1 All ER 731, HL.

of the development plan and to planning considerations affecting the land'; that test, said Roch J, applied also to section 106. In relation to conditions there is a further test namely that they must fairly and reasonably relate to the permitted development, that is, it must be related to planning needs arising from the actual purpose for which the permission has been granted;[16] Roch J held that this test did not apply to section 106 agreements.

The facts in the *Gillingham* case were that when negotiating for planning permission for residential development the developer (Flaherty) agreed at the request of the local planning authority to the construction of a road on their own land going beyond that required for their own development in order to facilitate the development of adjoining lands including land owned by Parhams; the road would not extend to the boundary so leaving a ransom strip. The requirement to extend the road beyond that required for Flaherty's development could not be imposed by a condition of the planning permission and was embodied in a section 106 agreement. Parhams sought a judicial review of the agreement because they wished to include Flaherty's land in a comprehensive planning application for all the land in the vicinity.

Roch J upheld the agreement; it was not manifestly unreasonable and a section 106 agreement could go beyond what fairly and reasonably related to the particular development. Since the result of the agreement was to leave a ransom strip, Flaherty would recoup far more than the cost of providing the requirement extension. The fact would seem to justify Roch J finding that the agreement was not manifestly unreasonable. However, it seems to have been his opinion that it would not have been unreasonable for the local planning authority to have asked Flaherty to have extended the road up to the boundary; that conclusion does not seem wholly consistent with earlier decisions unless it be argued that Flaherty could still have imposed some form of ransom payment for access from the adjoining land.

In the later case of *R v Wealden District Council, ex p Charles Church South East Ltd*[17] Popplewell J agreed with the opinion of Roch J in *Gillingham* that a section 106 agreement did not have to satisfy the requirement imposed on conditions of fairly and reasonably relating to the permitted development.

The judgments of Roch and Popplewell JJ on this particular point represent a broader view of the scope of section 106 than was adopted by the Secretary of State in circular 22/83.

---

16 See the account of *Newbury District Council v Secretary of State for the Environment*, at ch 8, p. 159, above.
17 [1989] JPL 837.

ENFORCEMENT OF AGREEMENTS

The local planning authority should have no difficulty in enforcing the agreement against the landowner who entered into it. Agreements by local authorities and other public bodies are normally made by deed and, if this has been done, the agreement will be enforceable even if the landowner has not given any consideration.

There may be difficulty, however, in enforcing the agreement against successors in title to the original owner. For this reason, section 106 provides that the local planning authority may enforce the agreement against persons deriving title from the original owner as if the agreement had been made for the benefit of adjoining land owned by the authority. This means that *restrictive* covenants will be enforceable.[18] It is doubtful however whether *positive* covenants – that is, those requiring the expenditure of money or labour by the owner – could be enforced against successors in title.[19]

These difficulties have now been overcome to some extent. Prior to the introduction of general legislation in 1974 some local authorities obtained local Act powers which enabled them to enforce both positive and negative covenants. However, there is now general legislation regarding the enforcement of covenants in agreements made between local authorities and landowners under various statutory powers. Section 126 of the Housing Act 1974 provided for the enforcement of agreements made between a local authority and a landowner for the purpose of securing the carrying out of works on, or of facilitating the development of, the land concerned. To be effective for this purpose, however, it had to be specifically declared that section 126 of the Housing Act applied to the agreement; it follows that the provisions of this section will not assist local authorities in enforcing positive covenants in section 52 agreements made before 1974.

Section 126 of the Housing Act 1974 has now been replaced by section 33 of the Local Government (Miscellaneous Provisions) Act 1982. The section is wider in scope than section 126; in particular, it provides for the enforcement of covenants regulating the use of land as well as those relating to the carrying out or facilitating the development of land. Here again, it must be specifically declared that section 33 is to apply; the agreement must be registered in the land charges register.

The owner of the land will be able to enforce the agreement both in respect of positive and restrictive covenants since the authority were parties to the original agreement. In the case of agreements entered

18 *Tulk v Moxhay* (1848) 2 Ph 774.
19 *Austerberry v Oldham Corpn* (1885) 29 ChD 750.

into before 1 April 1974 – the date on which the new system of local government came into force – the new successor authority will be liable on the covenants by virtue of section 254(3) of the Local Government Act 1972.

Section 106(4) provides, however, that nothing in the agreement is (i) to prevent the exercise by any Minister or authority of their powers under the Act of 1990 so long as those powers are exercised in accordance with the provisions of the development plan, or (ii) to require the exercise of powers otherwise than in accordance with the development plan.

The precise meaning of section 106(4) is unclear. It is a general rule of law that a public authority cannot by agreement restrict the future exercise of its statutory powers, and this rule was specifically applied by the Court of Appeal in *Windsor and Maidenhead Royal Borough Council v Brandrose Investments Ltd.*[20]

> In January 1976 the defendants and the council entered into two agreements, namely, an agreement for the exchange of adjoining pieces of land and an agreement under what is now section 106 to enable both parties to develop their sites. In October 1976 the council granted the plaintiffs outline permission to develop their site along the lines contemplated by the two agreements, but in 1978 the council designated a conservation area, which meant that the demolition of buildings would require special consent.[1] In 1979 the defendants started to demolish the buildings on their site without the consent of the council. The council sought an injunction to restrain the defendants from demolishing the building.
>
> Held: (1) there was nothing in what is now section 106 or in the agreement to inhibit the council from including the site in a conservation area; (2) what is now section 106(4) did not empower the council to bind itself not to exercise its powers to designate a conservation area; (3) the developers were not entitled to demolish the buildings without consent.

It was not necessary for the court to consider the full implications of the references in what is now section 106(4) to the exercise of powers in accordance with the development plan. It seems quite clear that the local planning authority cannot commit themselves by means of a section 106 agreement to grant planning permission not in accordance with the development plan. Moreover, it is doubtful whether the local planning authority could commit themselves to grant planning permission even in accordance with the development plan; other considerations apart, to do so in some cases would pre-empt the right of members of the public to make representations.[2] A developer may,

---

20 [1983] 1 All ER 818, [1983] 1 WLR 509.
1 See ch 14, p. 268, below.
2 See ch 7, pp. 131 ff, above.

of course, be reluctant to enter into commitments unless he is sure of planning permission, but this problem can be met by making the operation of the agreement conditional upon the grant of permission.

Chapter 12

Purchase notices

Although planning control often prevents the landowner putting his land to the most profitable use, normally his only remedy – and this is not always available – is to claim compensation under Part IV or Part V of the Act of 1990.[1] This is reasonable enough: in the normal case, there remains a profitable use for the land, and the owner can either continue to use it for this purpose or sell the land to someone else at a reasonable price. To take an obvious example: however disappointing a refusal of planning permission for building development may be to the owner of agricultural land he can continue to use it for agriculture or sell it to someone who is prepared to use it for agriculture.

There are however some cases of hardship in which the Planning Acts recognise the need for some further remedy. For instance, there may be no profitable use for the land unless planning permission can be obtained for its development; a common example is the site of a building destroyed by fire. Such land is said to have become incapable of reasonably beneficial use, and Chapter I of Part VI of the Act of 1990 enables the owner in certain circumstances to serve a purchase notice requiring the appropriate local authority to purchase his interest.

Hardship may also arise where land is designated, say, in the development plan for some purpose which will ultimately involve its compulsory acquisition. The designation does not render the land incapable of reasonably beneficial use, but the threat of compulsory purchase may make it virtually unsaleable. This hardship is remedied to some extent by Chapter II of Part VI of the Act of 1990 which enables certain owner-occupiers to serve a purchase notice in these circumstances; this type of purchase notice is called a 'blight notice'.

1 See chs 20 and 21, below.

Adverse planning decisions

Chapter I of Part VI of the Act of 1990 applies where (a) planning permission has been refused or granted subject to conditions as a result of an application to the local planning authority; or (b) planning permission is revoked or modified; or (c) a discontinuance order is made under section 97.[2]

In the first two of the above cases any owner of the affected land may serve a purchase notice if the following conditions are satisfied:[3]

(a) the land has become incapable of reasonably beneficial use in its existing state; and

(b) if permission was granted subject to conditions, that the land cannot be rendered capable of reasonably beneficial use by carrying out development in accordance with these conditions; and

(c) in any case (ie whether permission was refused or granted subject to conditions) that the land cannot be rendered capable of reasonably beneficial use by carrying out any development for which permission has been granted or for which either the local planning authority or the Secretary of State have undertaken to grant permission.

If a discontinuance order has been made, the conditions for the service of a purchase notice are:[4]

(a) that by reason of the order the land has become incapable of reasonably beneficial use; and

(b) that it cannot be made capable of reasonably beneficial use by the carrying out of any development for which planning permission has been granted whether by that order or otherwise.[5]

The expression 'beneficial use' was explained by Widgery J in *Adams and Wade Ltd v Minister of Housing and Local Government*[6] as follows:

> The purpose of section 129 [of the Act of 1962] is to enable a landowner whose use of his land has been frustrated by a planning refusal to require the local authority to take the land off his hands. The reference to 'beneficial' use must therefore be a reference to a use which can benefit the owner or a prospective owner and the fact that the land in its existing state confers some benefit or value upon the public at large would be no bar to the service of a purchase notice.

In many cases, therefore, the test will be an economic one – is the land in its existing state capable of yielding a reasonable return to its

2 Or under Sch 9, para 1: see ch 15, p. 282, below.
3 1990 Act, s. 137(2), (3).
4 Ibid, s. 137(2), (4).
5 For grant of planning permission by discontinuance order, see ch 9, p. 181, above.
6 (1965) 18 P & CR 60.

owner? In some cases – for example the site of a former building – it will usually be quite clear that there is no beneficial use in this sense. Where there is *some* beneficial use, it will be necessary to decide whether that use is reasonably beneficial. In the event of dispute, this will be largely a question of fact for the Secretary of State, and the court is not likely to interfere with his findings if he has applied the right tests. Thus, in *General Estates Co Ltd v Minister of Housing and Local Government*,[7] the company owned a site of about eleven acres. About half was let to a sports club at a rent of £52 a year; the rest was vacant but could be let for grazing at about £20 a year. The Minister concluded on these facts that the land had not become incapable of reasonably beneficial use. The company applied to the High Court for an order to quash the Minister's decision. The application was dismissed; it could not be said that the Minister's findings were so perverse as really to be outside his powers.

In deciding what is a reasonably beneficial use it may be helpful to compare the value of the land in its existing state with the value it would have if developed in accordance with planning permission. There have been some expressions of doubt as to whether comparisons of this sort are legitimate. Thus in *Brookdene Investments Ltd v Minister of Housing and Local Government*[8] Fisher J asked:

> How can a use which would involve the carrying out of a development be relevant to an inquiry as to whether land has become incapable of reasonably beneficial use *in its existing state?*

However, it now seems clear that it is permissible to compare the value of the land in its existing state with the value which it would have if planning permission were granted for the limited range of development comprised in Schedule 3[9] to the Act of 1990. That seems to follow from section 138(1) and (2) which provide that, for the purpose of deciding whether the basic conditions for the service of a purchase notice have been satisfied, no account is to be taken of any 'unauthorised prospective use' of the land that is either (a) new development, or (b) Schedule 3 development in excess of certain limits.

The effect of what is now section 138(1), (2) of the Act of 1990 was considered by the High Court in the recent case of *Gavaghan v Secretary of State for the Environment and South Harris District Council*.[10]

The claimant had been refused planning permission to erect a

7 (1965) 194 Estates Gazette 202.
8 (1970) 21 P & CR 545.
9 See ch 20, below.
10 [1989] JPL 596.

dwellinghouse on some land adjoining a residential property known as Lower Court. He served a purchase notice on the council, but the council served a counter notice that they were unwilling to comply with it. On the matter being referred to the Secretary of State, he decided that the land could be rendered capable of reasonably beneficial use, because he considered it reasonable to conclude on the evidence that the owner of Lower Court was a prospective purchaser of the land to use it as curtilage land; the council had given an undertaking to grant planning permission for the change of use to curtilage land.

The claimant challenged the Secretary of State's decision that the ground that the change of use to curtilage land would be new development and so must be disregarded under what is now section 138(1), (2); further there was no evidence that the owner of Lower Court was a prospective purchaser.

Mr Lionel Read QC, sitting as deputy judge, held that a prospective use involving new development was not to be disregarded in determining whether the basic conditions were satisfied. But the Secretary of State had acted irrationally in concluding on the evidence that there was a prospective purchaser, and he should therefore have confirmed the purchase notice.

Thus, it seems that the effect of section 180(2) is to disallow comparison with the value of the land with permission for new development.

Does it follow that land is incapable of reasonably beneficial use if in its existing state it is of substantially less value than it would be if permission were granted for Schedule 3 development? The question came before the Divisional Court in *R v Minister of Housing and Local Government, ex p Chichester RDC*.[11]

A piece of coastal land of about $2\frac{1}{2}$ acres was subject to considerable erosion, and a large sum of money would be required to prevent further erosion. There were 14 bungalows on part of the land, and the remainder was divided into 17 plots which were let as caravan sites during the summer under temporary planning permissions. The owner applied for permission to develop the land for residential purposes; on this being refused he served a purchase notice. The Minister confirmed the notice on the ground that 'the land in its existing state and with the benefit of temporary planning permissions is of substantially less use and value to its owner than it would be if planning permission had been granted (without limitation as to time) for the rebuilding of the buildings which formerly stood there and have been demolished since January 7th, 1937'.

The Chichester RDC applied to the High Court for an order to quash the Minister's confirmation of the purchase notice.

Held: the reason given by the Minister was not valid because the question was whether 'the land has become incapable of reasonably beneficial use in its existing state' and not whether the land was of less use to the owner in its present state than if developed.

The Divisional Court did not, however, go so far as to say that there should be no comparison of the value of the land in its existing state with the value which it would have after Schedule 3 development. Where the Minister erred in the *Chichester* case was in accepting the comparison with Schedule 3 as conclusive. The correct approach seems to be that approved, albeit somewhat reluctantly, by Fisher J in *Brookdene Investments Ltd v Minister of Housing and Local Government*[12] – namely, that a comparison with Schedule 3 values may be made; but, if it is made, it must be made along with other relevant facts, and it is for the Secretary of State to decide in each case how much weight is to be given to such comparison.

'ANY OWNER'

A purchase notice may be served by 'any owner of the land' who considers that the above conditions are satisfied. Section 336 of the Act of 1990 provides that for this purpose the word 'owner' is to mean:

> a person, other than a mortgagee not in possession, who, whether in his own right or as trustee for any other person, is entitled to receive the rack-rent of the land or, where the land is not let at a rack-rent, would be so entitled if it were so let.

Although rack-rent is not specifically defined, this definition clearly excludes the owner of a reversion expectant on the termination of a long lease at a ground rent. For this reason, it was contended in *London Corpn v Cusack-Smith*[13] that the context required a different meaning for the word 'owner'.

> Land in the City of London was held by H on 99 years' lease at a ground rent. Following the destruction of the buildings H disclaimed liability for the rent under the Landlord and Tenant (War Damage) (Amendment) Act 1941, until the premises were rebuilt. Planning permission was subsequently refused for rebuilding and H served a notice under what is now section 137 requiring the Corporation to purchase his interest; this notice was confirmed by the Minister.
> Subsequently the freeholders served a notice requiring the purchase of their interest, but the Corporation contended that the freeholders were not within the definition of owner in section 119 of the Act of 1947 (now section 336 of the Act of 1990). The House of Lords (reversing a decision of the

12 (1970) 21 P & CR 545.
13 [1955] AC 337, [1955] 1 All ER 302.

Court of Appeal) held that the word 'owner' must be given the meaning ascribed by section 119(1).

The hardship in this case occurred because the lessees had exercised their right under the Act of 1941 to suspend payment of the ground rent and the Corporation had refused to permit rebuilding: a similar situation might arise where a building is destroyed by fire, and the lease contains a clause permitting abatement of the ground rent. In other cases, however, there will be less hardship, because the freeholder will be entitled to the ground rent even if the lessee's interest is acquired by a public authority.

PROCEDURE

In the cases of adverse planning decisions, a purchase notice is served on the district council (or the London borough) for the area in which the land is situate.[14] If the council are willing to comply with the purchase notice, or if they have found another local authority or statutory undertaker who are willing to comply with it, they serve a notice to that effect; the authority in question are then deemed to have served notice to treat for the interest of the owner who served the notice.

If the council are not willing to comply with the notice and have not found another authority or statutory undertaker who would be willing to comply with it, the council must within three months forward the purchase notice to the Secretary of State and notify the owner accordingly. If the Secretary of State considers that the basic requirements are satisfied, he will either:

(a) confirm the notice, in which case the council are deemed to have served notice to treat;

(b) grant permission for the development in respect of which the application was made; or, if permission was granted subject to conditions, amend the conditions so far as is necessary to render the land capable of reasonably beneficial use;

(c) grant permission for some other development of either the whole or part of the land;[15]

(d) substitute another local authority or statutory undertaker for the council on whom the notice is served, in which case that authority or statutory undertaker are deemed to have served notice to treat.

A special situation arises where the land forms part of a larger

14 1990 Act, s. 137(2).
15 If he considers that this would make it capable of reasonably beneficial use: 1990 Act, ss. 141(2), 142(3).

area for which planning permission has been given; there may be a condition that the particular piece of land in question is to remain undeveloped or is to be laid out as amenity land, or the application for permission may show that this was contemplated. In these circumstances, the Secretary of State may in his discretion refuse to confirm the notice.[16]

Whatever action the Secretary of State proposes to take he must give notice to the person who served the purchase notice, to the council on whom it was served, to the local planning authority, and to any other local authority or statutory undertaker whom he proposes to substitute for the council. Any of these parties then has the right to be heard at a public local inquiry or other hearing. This procedure also applies where the Secretary of State decides not to confirm a notice on the ground that the basic requirements have not been satisfied, but not apparently if he decides that the purchase notice should not be confirmed on the ground that the person who served it is not an 'owner'.

The Secretary of State must give his decision during the 'relevant period'; that is, nine months from the date of service of the purchase notice or within six months of the date on which a copy of the purchase notice was forwarded to him, whichever is the earlier. If he fails to do so, or if he fails to take any of the other courses of action open to him (see (b) and (c) above), the purchase notice is deemed to have been confirmed.[17]

Adverse planning proposals: blight notices

Blight notices relate to land which has become difficult to sell because of 'planning blight', that is, the threat of compulsory purchase implicit in some planning proposal. The scheme was first introduced by the Act of 1959, but it has been considerably extended since then: there are now far more cases in which a blight notice can be served, and the conditions have been relaxed. There are, however, two important limitations. First, only certain classes of owner-occupier can serve a blight notice. Secondly, at least some part of the owner-occupier's land must be under threat of compulsory purchase; the scheme affords

---

16 1990 Act, s. 142 re-enacting a provision originally introduced by the 1968 Act and designed to deal with the position revealed in *Adams and Wade Ltd v Minister of Housing and Local Government* (1965) 18 P & CR 60.

17 1990 Act, s. 143(2); in *Ealing Borough Council v Minister of Housing and Local Government* [1952] Ch 856, [1952] 2 All ER 639, the Minister purported to modify a purchase notice, but since his modification was void, the original notice was 'deemed to be confirmed' after six months.

no protection to the person whose land is depreciated in value by a threat of compulsory purchase hanging over neighbouring land.

A blight notice may be served in respect of an hereditament or agricultural unit consisting wholly or partly of land falling within any of the following cases.

1 STRUCTURE PLANS

Land indicated in a structure plan either as:[18]
(a) land which may be required for the purposes of any of the functions of any government department, local authority or statutory undertakers or of the British Coal Corporation or a public telecommunications operator; or
(b) land which may be included in an action area.

A blight notice under this heading may be served at any time after the plan (or proposals for its alteration) has been submitted to the Secretary of State, but not after the plan has been withdrawn for any reason.

A blight notice cannot be served under this heading after a local plan has come into force allocating land for any of the purposes mentioned in sub-paragraph (a) above.

2 LOCAL PLANS

Land allocated by a local plan for the purposes of any of the functions mentioned in paragraph 1(a) above. The blight notice may be served at any time after the local planning authority have formally published the plan (or proposals for its alteration), but not after it (or the proposals for its alteration) has been withdrawn for any reason.

3 UNITARY DEVELOPMENT PLANS

Land which is either (i) indicated in a unitary development plan as land which may be required for the purposes of any of the functions mentioned in para 1(a) above; (ii) indicated in such plan as land which may be included in an action area; or (iii) allocated by such plan for the purposes of any of the functions mentioned above. The blight notice may be served at any time after the local planning authority have formally published the draft plan, but not after it has been withdrawn for any reason.

18 1990 Act, Sch 13.

4 LAND AFFECTED BY RESOLUTION OF LOCAL AUTHORITY OR DIRECTIONS OF THE SECRETARY OF STATE

Land earmarked by resolution of local authority or by a direction of the Secretary of State as land which may be required for the purposes of any functions of a government department, local authority of statutory undertaker.

5 COMPULSORY PURCHASE UNDER SPECIAL ACT

Land authorised to be acquired by special Act.

6 NEW TOWNS

Land within an area designated as the site of a new town. The blight notice may be served at any time after the draft designation order has been published. If subsequently the Secretary of State decides not to make the designation order, or modifies it so as to exclude the land in question, a blight notice cannot thereafter be served.

7 SLUM CLEARANCE

Land which is either included in a clearance area under section 289 of the Housing Act 1985, or is land surrounded by or adjoining a clearance area which the local authority have determined to purchase.

8 GENERAL IMPROVEMENT AREA

Land indicated by information published under section 257 of the Housing Act 1985 as land which the local authority propose to acquire as part of a general improvement area.

9 HIGHWAYS PROPOSALS IN DEVELOPMENT PLAN

Land indicated in a development plan (otherwise than in paragraph 1 or 2 above) as required for the construction or improvement of a highway.

In this context the expression 'development plan' means, it is submitted, a plan approved by the Secretary of State or, in the case of a local plan, one formally adopted by the local planning authority.

10 ORDERS OR SCHEMES FOR TRUNK OR SPECIAL ROADS

Land indicated in an order or scheme under the Highways Act 1980 for the construction, alteration or improvement of a trunk or special road, or under section 22 of the Land Compensation Act 1973 for mitigating the adverse effects of a trunk or special road.

11 COMPULSORY PURCHASE ORDER UNDER HIGHWAY LAND ACQUISITION POWERS

Land subject to a compulsory purchase order under section 250 of the Highways Act 1980 for the acquisition of rights over highway land, but notice to treat has not yet been served. The blight notice can be served at any time after the order has been submitted to the appropriate Minister for confirmation; or, where the order is proposed by the Minister, after the draft order has been published. If the order is subsequently not confirmed or, in the case of a draft order is not made, a blight notice cannot thereafter be served.

12 LAND AFFECTED BY NEW STREET ORDERS

Land affected by an order made under section 188 of the Highways Act 1980 or section 30 of the Public Health Act 1925 regarding the minimum widths of new streets or highways declared to be new streets.

13 LAND IN URBAN DEVELOPMENT AREAS

Land in an urban development area designated by the Secretary of State under the Act of 1980.

14 COMPULSORY PURCHASE ORDERS

Land subject to a compulsory purchase order, but notice to treat has not yet been served.[19]

The blight notice may be served at any time after the compulsory purchase order has been submitted to the appropriate Minister for confirmation; or, in the case of compulsory purchase by a government department, after the draft order has been published. If subsequently

---

19 A compulsory purchase order ceases to have effect if notice to treat is not served within three years of the date on which the order became operative: Compulsory Purchase Act 1965, s. 4.

the compulsory purchase order is not confirmed (or, in the case of a government department, the order is not made) a blight notice cannot thereafter be served.

These categories of land are referred to in the Act as 'blighted land'.[20]

WHO MAY SERVE NOTICE

A blight notice under these provisions may be served by a person having an interest 'qualifying for protection'[1] namely:
(a) the resident owner-occupier of any hereditament;
(b) the owner-occupier of any hereditament with a net annual value not exceeding the prescribed limit – at present £2,250,[2]
(c) the owner-occupier of an agricultural unit.[3]

For this purpose 'owner-occupier' includes a lessee with at least three years to run as well as a freeholder.[4] 'Resident owner-occupier' is defined as 'an *individual* who occupies the whole ... of the hereditament',[5] and for this reason in *Webb v Warwickshire County Council*[6] the Lands Tribunal held that the interest must be a strictly personal one abating on death with the result that a personal representative could not serve a blight notice.

The effect of this decision is modified by section 161 of the Act of 1990 which provides that a personal representative may serve a blight notice if the deceased owner would have been entitled to serve such a notice at the date of his death. It is a further condition that one or more individuals (to the exclusion of any body corporate) shall be beneficially interested in the proceeds of sale.

'Hereditament' means the land comprised in a hereditament included in the valuation list for rating purposes. As agricultural land is not included in the valuation list, the Act speaks in this connection of an agricultural unit, and this means land which is occupied as a unit for agricultural purposes.[7]

In certain circumstances a mortgagee of such an interest may serve a blight notice.[8]

It will be appreciated that a blight notice can only be served in

20 1990 Act, s. 149(1).
 1 Ibid, s. 149(2), (3).
 2 The present limit is prescribed by the Town and Country Planning (Limit of Annual Value) Order 1973 (SI 1973 No 425).
 3 As defined in 1990 Act, s. 171.
 4 1990 Act, s. 168(4).
 5 Ibid, s. 168(3).
 6 (1971) 23 P & CR 63.
 7 1990 Act, s. 171(1).
 8 Ibid, s. 162.

respect of business and other essentially non-residential premises if the net annual value does not exceed £2,250 or if the owner occupies some part of the premises as a dwelling. Investment owners have been excluded because:

> the value of an investment is affected by many factors. It would be well nigh impossible to determine whether the value of an investment property had changed because of some blighting effect of local authority proposals or because of some change in the market. Local authorities might therefore find themselves forced to buy an interest in property which had not really been blighted by their proposals. Moreover, the time when the interest in property was offloaded on the local authority would be likely to depend, not upon any genuine need to realise capital, in order to enable a man to find a new roof for his head, as in the other case, but merely because at that particular date the changes in the market were such that the money might be more profitably invested in something else.[9]

In *Essex County Council v Essex Incorporated Congregational Church Union*,[10] the House of Lords had to consider an appeal concerning an attempt to serve a blight notice in respect of a church and church hall. The actual decision was that, in the circumstances, the Lands Tribunal had at the outset no jurisdiction to decide whether the respondents' interest in the property was 'qualified for protection' by purchase notice, and consequently that the Court of Appeal and the House of Lords had no jurisdiction either. The Lands Tribunal and Court of Appeal had, however, considered that they possessed this jurisdiction, and had decided that since the property was marked 'exempt' in the rating list this included it in the category of premises with a net annual value not exceeding the prescribed limit. The House of Lords stated that this decision, though there was in any case no jurisdiction to give it, was wrong.

SERVICE AND EFFECT OF NOTICE

The blight notice is to be served on the 'appropriate authority' – namely, the government department, local authority or other body who are likely to acquire the land.[11]

The person serving the notice is known as the claimant and he must serve a notice in the prescribed form.[12] This will state that the whole or some part of the hereditament or agricultural unit is 'blighted

---

9 Speech of Lord Chancellor on 27 April 1959 (215 HL Official Report (5th series) cols 1041–1042).
10 [1963] AC 808, [1963] 1 All ER 326.
11 1990 Act, s. 169.
12 For the prescribed form, see the General Regulations.

land',[13] that the claimant is entitled to an interest which qualifies for protection in the hereditament or unit, that he has made reasonable efforts to sell that interest, and that he has been unable to sell it except at a price substantially lower than he might reasonably have expected but for the threat of compulsory purchase.

In the case of a hereditament, the notice must require the appropriate authority to purchase the whole of the claimant's interest. This applies even if part only of the hereditament is blighted; only where the claimant does not own the whole can the notice refer to less than the whole hereditament and even then it must require the authority to take the whole amount owned by the claimant.[14]

In the case of an agricultural unit, the rules are different. The threat of compulsory acquisition may extend only to a small part of the farm and might not cause difficulty in selling the farm as a whole. If, however, the effect is to render the farm unsaleable at a reasonable price, a blight notice may be served in respect of the 'affected area', that is, so much of the farm as is blighted land.[15] If the claimant can show that the whole or a part of the 'unaffected area' would not be viable as a separate unit, then that land may also be included in the blight notice.[16]

If the appropriate authority are not willing to purchase the land they may within two months serve a counter notice specifying their objections.[17] There are in effect three main grounds on which the authority may object:

(1) that the conditions laid down in the Act of 1990 have not been satisfied;

(2) that they do not intend to acquire any part of the hereditament or (in the case of any agricultural unit) any part of the affected area;

(3) that they do not intend to acquire any part of the hereditament or any part of the affected area within the next 15 years, but this only applies where the blight arises from the provisions of the structure plan or local plan or unitary plan or in certain cases in which the land is indicated in the development plan for the construction or improvement of a highway.

In the case of an agricultural unit the authority may also object on the ground that they propose to acquire part only of the affected area.[18]

13 See pp. 223 ff, above.
14 1990 Act, s. 150(1), (2), (3).
15 Ibid, s. 158(1).
16 Ibid, s. 158(2).
17 Ibid, s. 151.
18 Ibid, s. 158.

The claimant may require the objections to be referred to the Lands Tribunal; unless the objection falls within class (2) or (3) above, it is for him to satisfy the Tribunal that the objection is not well founded. If the Tribunal are satisfied the objection is not well founded, they will declare the notice valid. If the authority upholds an objection that the authority intend to acquire part only of the affected area the Tribunal will declare the notice valid in relation to the part only.[19]

If no counter-notice has been served or if the notice has been declared valid, the appropriate authority will be deemed to have served notice to treat in respect of the hereditament or (in the case of an agricultural unit) either the affected area or such less area as the authority intended to acquire in any event.[20]

19 1990 Act, s. 153.
20 Ibid, s. 154.

Chapter 13

Special forms of control

One of the objects of town and country planning is the preservation and enhancement of amenity – that is, the pleasant features of town and countryside. This is achieved partly through the control of development as described in earlier chapters; that is, the planning authority may refuse permission for development which would be detrimental to amenity or they may attach conditions designed to safeguard amenity. In addition to this general power of control planning legislation provides a number of special forms of control which are mainly concerned with preserving or improving the pleasant features of the town and country. The Act of 1990 provides for the preservation and planting of trees; control over the display of outdoor advertising; the proper maintenance of waste land; and the disposal of abandoned vehicles and other refuse. In addition the Hazardous Substances Act provides for the control of hazardous substances.

Tree preservation

The felling of trees is not development as defined in the Act of 1990, but where it is considered desirable in the interests of amenity the felling or lopping of trees or woodlands can be controlled by making tree preservation orders under section 198 of the Act. A tree preservation order may apply to a single tree, a group of trees or to a substantial woodland. It may prohibit the felling, lopping, uprooting, wilful damage or wilful destruction of the trees without the consent of the local planning authority; and in the case of woodlands, it may contain provisions as to the replanting of any area which is felled in the course of forestry operations permitted under the order.[1]

What is a tree? There is no definition of 'tree' in the Act of 1990, but the use of the word 'tree' probably excludes bushes and shrubs and hedgerows as such;[2] a hedgerow, however, may include trees. A

1 1990 Act, s. 198.
2 See circular 36/78, para 44.

gardening encyclopaedia[3] defines a tree as a 'a woody plant normally with one stem at least 12 to 15 feet tall in maturity'. The same work defines a shrub as 'a perennial woody plant, branching naturally from its base without a defined leader (a single main shoot) and not normally exceeding 30 feet high. In *Kent County Council v Batchelor*[4] Lord Denning said in *woodland* a tree 'ought to be something over seven or eight inches in diameter'; on that view, it would apparently not be an offence to fell smaller trees in a woodland covered by a tree preservation order. However, in *Bullock v Secretary of State for the Environment*,[5] Phillips J treated Lord Denning's remark as obiter and declined to follow it; he held that there was no reason why anything which would ordinarily be called a tree should not be a 'tree' for the purposes of the legislation, and no reason why a coppice should not be the subject of a tree preservation order.

It seems that a tree may be 'wilfully destroyed' by negligence as well as deliberate intent. In *Barnet London Borough Council v Eastern Electricity Board*,[6] contractors laying electric cables damaged the root systems of six large trees all of which were subject to a tree preservation order; as a result, the life expectancy of the trees was shortened and they had been rendered less stable and a potential danger. The council prosecuted the Board but the magistrates dismissed the case on the ground that the reduction of the life expectancy of the trees by an uncertain period could not amount to destruction. The Divisional Court, however, held that a person wilfully destroyed a tree if he inflicted on it so radical an injury that in all the circumstances any reasonable forester would decide that it must be felled.

A tree preservation order will normally be made by the local planning authority[7] but in exceptional cases the Secretary of State may make an order.[8] Tree preservation orders no longer require the approval of the Secretary of State, but the local planning authority must give notice of the making of the order and consider any objections.[9]

There are restrictions on the making of tree preservation orders where a Forestry Dedication Covenant is in force or where the Forestry Commissioners have made a grant under the Forestry Acts. In these circumstances an order may be made only if there is not in force some working plan approved by the Forestry Commissioners and they

---

3 *Encyclopaedia of Gardening* (Marshall Cavendish).
4 (1976) 33 P & CR 185.
5 (1980) 40 P & CR 246, [1980] JPL 461.
6 [1973] 2 All ER 319.
7 1990 Act, s. 198.
8 Ibid, s. 202.
9 Ibid, s. 199.

consent to the making of the order.[10] Moreover, a tree preservation order cannot prohibit the cutting down of trees which are dying or dead or have become dangerous, nor may it prohibit felling in order to comply with a statutory obligation or to abate a nuisance.[11]

In making and administering a tree preservation order the planning authority are concerned solely with considerations of amenity; they are not concerned with such matters as the economic value of the trees. Control over felling in the interests of the national economy was introduced, however, by the Forestry Act 1951 (now the Forestry Act 1967). Under that Act it is an offence to fell any tree without the consent of the Forestry Commissioners, except in certain specified cases.[12] The cutting down of a tree may therefore require the consent of the local planning authority under a tree preservation order and/or the consent of the Commissioners under the Forestry Act 1967.

MAKING THE ORDER

A tree preservation order is to be in the form (or substantially the form) prescribed by the Tree Preservation Regulations. The position of the trees or woodlands must be defined on a map attached to the order.[13] In order to prevent felling before the order can be confirmed, the local planning authority may include in the order a direction under section 201 of the Act of 1990 that the order shall take effect provisionally on a specified date and this direction will continue in force for a maximum of six months.[14]

Notice that the order has been made must be served on the owners and occupiers of the land affected by the order and on any other person known to be entitled to work minerals in the land or to fell any of the trees.[15] Any of these persons has the right to make objections and representations within 28 days by notice in writing to the local

---

10 1990 Act, s. 200.
11 Ibid, s. 198(6).
12 The exceptions are to be found partly in the Forestry Act 1967, s. 9, and partly in the Forestry (Exceptions from Restriction of Felling) Regs 1951. They include the cutting down of small trees and felling which is necessary for the purpose of carrying out development in accordance with planning permission.
13 Tree Preservation Regs, reg 4.
14 Further provision is made for the protection of trees in conservation areas by the 1990 Act, s 211; see ch 14, p. 269, below.
15 Tree Preservation Regs, reg 5.

planning authority.[16] If there are objections or representations the local planning authority will have to consider them before deciding whether to confirm the order.[17] If the order is confirmed by the local planning authority, its validity can be questioned in High Court proceedings under section 288 of the Act of 1990.[18]

CONSENTS UNDER THE ORDER

The procedure for obtaining consent to fell or top trees protected by a preservation order varies according to whether the Forestry Act 1967, also applies.

If the Forestry Act 1967 does not apply, the procedure will be that laid down in the tree preservation order and this procedure will be modelled on the provisions of the Act of 1990 for obtaining planning permission. Application for consent must be made to the local planning authority, and the authority may refuse consent or grant it either unconditionally or conditionally.[19] The authority must give their decision within two months. If they fail to do so, or if the applicant is aggrieved by their decision he may appeal to the Secretary of State who will deal with the matter in the same way as an appeal against refusal of planning permission.

If the Forestry Act 1967 applies, application is made to the Forestry Commissioners. If the Commissioners propose to grant a licence, they must consult the local planning authority; if that authority objects, the application will be referred to the Secretary of State who will deal with it as if it had been referred to him under section 77 of the Act of 1990. If the Commissioners propose not to grant a licence, they need not consult the local planning authority and the applicant has no right of appeal, though he may have a right to compensation under the Forestry Act. The Commissioners may decide not to deal with the application themselves but to refer it to the local planning authority in which case the procedure laid down in the tree preservation order applies.[20]

If the matter comes before the Secretary of State in any of the ways mentioned above, his decision may be challenged in High Court proceedings under section 288 of the Act of 1990.[1]

16 Tree Preservation Regs, regs 5 and 7.
17 Ibid, reg 8.
18 See ch 18, below.
19 The conditions may require the replacement of any tree or trees on site or in the near vicinity.
20 Forestry Act 1951, s. 13.
 1 See ch 18, below.

The local planning authority may revoke or modify any grant of consent under the tree preservation order. The procedure is similar to that described in an earlier chapter for the revocation or modification of planning permission.[2] The planning authority will be liable to pay compensation for abortive expenditure.

COMPENSATION

No compensation is payable for the making of a tree preservation order. In general, compensation is payable for loss or damage resulting from a refusal of consent or for the imposition of conditions.[3] But compensation will not be paid if the local planning authority, when refusing consent or imposing conditions, certify that the refusal or conditions are in the interests of good forestry or that the trees have a special or outstanding amenity value; there is a right of appeal to the Secretary of State.[4]

REPLACEMENT OF TREES

As we have seen, a tree preservation order may contain provisions as to the replanting of any area felled in the course of forestry operations permitted under the order. In the case of trees not forming part of a woodland, the local planning authority, in granting consent to fell, may impose conditions as to the replacement of the trees.[5]

Further provisions as to replacement of trees are contained in section 206 of the Act of 1990. This section applies where a tree is removed or destroyed in contravention of the preservation order or is removed or destroyed or dies at a time when its cutting down is authorised without express consent because it is dead or dying or dangerous. In these circumstances the owner of the land must plant another tree of an appropriate size and species at the same place as soon as he reasonably can – unless, on his application, the local planning authority dispense with the requirement. The new tree will be subject to the original preservation order.

In the case of woodlands, it will suffice to plant the same number

2 See ch 9, above.

3 Prescribed form of tree preservation order, arts 9, 10. See also *Cardigan Timber Co v Cardiganshire County Council* (1957) 9 P & CR 158.

4 See prescribed form of tree preservation order, art 5 (as amended by SI 1988 No 963) and Third Schedule, para 23.

5 There is no express provision to this effect in the 1990 Act or in the prescribed form of tree preservation order, but reference to such conditions is made in art 7 of the prescribed form and in s. 207(1) of the Act.

of trees on or near the land on which the trees stood or on such other land as may be agreed, and in such places as may be designated by the local planning authority.[6]

ENFORCEMENT

The effective enforcement of tree preservation orders has caused some difficulty. The Act of 1947 provided that contravention of a tree preservation order should be an offence punishable by fine, and this was re-enacted in the Act of 1962; the penalties were small and were not always an effective deterrent. Some early tree preservation orders provided for the service of enforcement notices requiring replanting, and this might well have proved an effective deterrent, but in 1953 the Minister advised local authorities that it was doubtful whether these enforcement provisions could be validly included in preservation orders. However, when the Civic Amenities Act 1967 was passed penalties were increased and express provision made for enforcement notices.

The relevant provisions are now to be found in the Act of 1990 and may be summarised as follows:

(1) If any person contravenes a tree preservation order by cutting down, uprooting or wilfully destroying a tree, or topping or lopping it in such a manner as to be likely to destroy it, he may be charged under section 102 and may be fined the statutory amount or twice the value of the tree, whichever is the greater. If the defendant is indicted before the Crown Court, the court may impose whatever fine it considers appropriate, and they may have regard to any financial benefit which accrued to the defendant.[7] The offence is absolute in that knowledge of the order is not a requirement of the offence.[8]

(2) Any other contravention of a tree preservation order is an offence punishable by fine not exceeding level 4 of the standard scale; if the contravention is continued after conviction, the offender is liable to a daily fine of £5.[9]

(3) If a landowner fails to comply with the requirements of section 206 as to the replacement of trees, he is not guilty of any offence but

6 1990 Act, s. 206(3).
7 1990 Act, s. 210(1), (2), (3).
8 *Maidstone Borough Council v Mortimer* [1980] 3 All ER 552. No offence is committed if the defendant's ignorance is due to the failure of the authority to place a copy of the order on deposit for inspection: *Vale of Glamorgan Borough Council v Palmer and Bowles* (1982) 81 LGR 678. The owner is liable for the acts of his servants but not for an independent contractor who had been expressly told not to touch the tree: *Groveside Homes Ltd v Elmbridge Borough Council* [1988] JPL 395.
9 1990 Act, s. 210(4), (5).

the local planning authority may serve an enforcement notice under section 207 requiring him to plant a tree or trees of such size and species as may be specified in the notice. An enforcement notice under section 207 may also be served if a landowner fails to comply with any conditions of a consent given under a tree preservation order requiring the replacement of trees, although this might also be an offence under section 210. An enforcement notice under section 207 must be served within four years,[10] and there is a right of appeal to the Secretary of State.[11]

PLANTING OF NEW TREES

The provisions so far described are concerned with the preservation of existing trees and their replacement when felled or destroyed. The Civic Amenities Act introduced for the first time provisions designed to secure the planting of new trees. These provisions are now contained in section 197 of the Act of 1990. Under this section it is the duty of the local planning authority when granting planning permission for any development to consider whether it would be appropriate to impose conditions for the preservation and planting of trees and to make tree preservation orders in connection with the grant of planning permission.

Outdoor advertising

The Act of 1947 brought all outdoor advertising under control by introducing – as a general rule – that any outdoor advertisement required consent even if its display does not involve development. This system of control is now continued by the Act of 1990. Advertisements displayed prior to 1 July 1948 were also brought under control, the local planning authority being empowered to 'challenge' any such advertisement by requiring the persons responsible for its display to make application for its retention. Provision is also made for areas of special control in which only certain limited classes of advertising are permitted, and the planning authority has no power to grant consent for anything outside these classes.

The system of advertising control is embodied in regulations made

10 1990 Act, s. 207(2).
11 Ibid, s. 208.

by the Secretary of State under section 220 of the Act of 1990.[12] The definition of advertisement for the purposes of the Act and of these regulations is extremely wide and includes much else besides ordinary commercial advertising. The full definition is as follows:

> any word, letter, model, sign, placard, board, notice, device or represen- tation, whether illuminated or not, in the nature of, and employed wholly or partly for the purposes of, advertisement, announcement or direction, (excluding any such thing employed wholly as a memorial or railway signal), and (without prejudice to the preceding provisions of this defin- ition) includes any hoarding or similar structure used, or adapted for use, for the display of advertisements.[13]

Thus the legend 'Samuel Short, Family Butcher' on a shop fascia, or 'John Jones, Dental Surgeon' on a door plate will be advertisements as well as the large poster advertising a well-known national product. So will road traffic signs and election posters.

PRINCIPLES OF CONTROL

The powers of control conferred by the Act of 1990 are to be exercised only in the interest of amenity and public safety.[14]

There is an express ban on any condition amounting to censorship of the subject matter of any advertisement; and the consent is to be the use of the site rather than for particular advertisements. There is however one exception: where application is made for the display of a particular advertisement, the authority may consider its contents so far – but only so far – as is necessary from the point of view of amenity and public safety.[15]

It is clear from all this that the planning authority is not entitled to consider such controversial questions as the economic value or social desirability of advertisements, nor even the substantial rates payable to the local authority in respect of many commercial adver- tisements.

In considering questions of amenity, the local planning authority are to consider the general characteristics of the locality, and special consideration is to be given to features of historic, architectural, cultural or similar interest. Under the heading of public safety they

12 The current regulations are the Control of Advertisements Regulations 1989 (SI 1989 No 670).
13 1990 Act, s. 336(1). For the purposes of the Regulations, however, 'advertisement' does not include anything employed wholly as a memorial or as a railway signal: reg 2(1).
14 1990 Act, s. 220(1); Advertisements Regs, reg 4(1).
15 Advertisements Regs, reg 4(3), (4).

are to consider the safety of persons using any road, railway, waterway (including coastal waters), docks, harbour or airfield likely to be affected by the display of advertisements; and in particular whether they are likely to obscure or hinder the interpretation of traffic signs, etc.[16]

Under the Regulations there are in effect three categories of advertisements. First, there are ten types of advertisement which are not subject to the general rule that outdoor advertising requires consent. Second, there are many advertisements which require consent, but are deemed to have received consent under the Regulations themselves. Finally there are those which do not come within either of the first two categories and thus require express consent from the local planning authority. We will deal with each of these categories in turn.

ADVERTISEMENTS EXCEPTED FROM CONTROL

Some ten types of advertisements are excepted from the general rule that all advertisements require either deemed or express consent. This status is different from deemed consent, in that excepted advertisements cannot be 'challenged' by the local planning authority as described below.

The ten classes of excepted advertisements are as follows:[17]

Class A: displayed on single captive balloon, not more than 60 metres above ground, on a site for a maximum of ten days in a calendar year so long as the site is not in an area of outstanding natural beauty, a conservation area, a national park, the Broads, or an area of special control.
Class B: displayed on enclosed land and not readily visible outside the enclosure, or from any part of it over which the public has a right of way or a right of access.
Class C: displayed on or in a vehicle or vessel, unless it is being used primarily for the display of advertisements (rather than for conveying people or goods).
Class D: incorporated in and forming part of the fabric of a building, not excluding an advertisement fixed to or painted on a building.
Class E: displayed on goods for sale (including a gas as liquid) or their container, provided it refers to the article for sale, is not illuminated, and does not exceed 0.1 square metres in area.
Class F: relating specifically to pending Parliamentary, European Commission or local government elections.

16 Advertisements Regs, reg 4(1).
17 Ibid, Sch 2.

Class G: required by standing orders of either House of Parliament or by enactment.

Class H: approved traffic signs.

Class I: display of any national flag on a single flagstaff.

Class J: displayed inside a building not principally used for the display of advertisements and not within one metre of any external doors, windows or other opening through which it is visible from outside.

It is important to note that, although excepted from the provisions relating to consent, all the above classes of advertisements are subject to the standard conditions set out in Schedule 1 to the Regulations.[18]

DEEMED CONSENT

All advertisements (other than those falling within the excepted classes set out above) require consent under the Regulations, but some 14 classes of advertisements have the benefit of deemed consent; some of these classes are sub-divided with the result that large numbers of advertisements have deemed consent. The classes of advertisements with deemed consent are set out in Schedule 3 in the Regulations. They include, inter alia:

(1) Functional advertisements of local authorities, statutory and public transport undertakings.[19]

(2) Advertisements relating to the premises on which they are displayed, namely advertisements for identification, direction or warning, subject to a maximum size of 0.75 metres or 0.3 square metres in an area of special control and other conditions;[20] business and professional name plates subject to a maximum size of 0.3 square metres and other conditions;[1] advertisements relating to religious, educational, recreational, medical and other institutions, hotels, public houses subject to a maximum size of 1.2 square metres and other conditions.[2]

(3) Temporary advertisements relating to the sale or letting of premises,[3] sale of goods or livestock,[4] building work being carried out on the land,[5] local events of a non-commercial character;[6] each of these categories is subject to a variety of conditions.

18 Advertisement Regs, reg 3(2).
19 Ibid, Sch 3, class 1.
20 Ibid, Sch 3, class 2A.
 1 Ibid, Sch 3, class 2B.
 2 Ibid, Sch 3, class 2C.
 3 Ibid, Sch 3, class 3A.
 4 Ibid, Sch 3, class 3B.
 5 Ibid, Sch 3, class 3C.
 6 Ibid, Sch 3, class 3D.

(4) Advertisements on business premises with reference to the business carried on, the goods sold or services provided; in the case of shops there are some conditions including a requirement that the advertisement must be on a wall containing a window.[7]

(5) Advertisements on the forecourts of business premises; here again there are conditions.[8]

The Secretary of State may in effect withdraw deemed consent by issuing – following a proposal by the local planning authority – a direction that the display of an advertisement of a class or description in Schedule 3[9] may not be undertaken in any particular area, or in any particular case, without express consent. Before making such a direction the Secretary of State must publish statutory notices and give notice to persons likely to be affected, and he must consider any objections received within a specified period.[10]

Furthermore, the local planning authority may 'challenge' an advertisement displayed with deemed consent by issuing a discontinuance notice requiring the discontinuance of the display of an advertisement or the use of the site for that purpose. The person on whom it is served may apply to the local planning authority for express consent and, if consent is refused, appeal to the Secretary of State; the discontinuance notice will not take effect pending the outcome of these proceedings.[11]

EXPRESS CONSENT

Unless an advertisement is excepted from control or has deemed consent under the Regulations, application must be made to the local planning authority for express consent.[12] The authority may grant consent subject to certain standard conditions[13] and any other conditions they think fit or they may refuse consent; if they refuse consent or impose conditions, they must state their reasons for so doing.[14] Each consent will be for a period of five years unless the local planning authority specify either a longer or shorter period; if they specify a shorter period, they must state their reasons for so doing.[15]

If the local planning authority refuse consent or attach conditions,

---

7 Advertisement Regs, Sch 3, class 5.
8 Ibid, Sch 3, class 6.
9 Other than class 11B, 12 or 13.
10 Advertisements Regs, reg 7.
11 Ibid, reg 8.
12 Ibid, reg 9.
13 Ibid, Sch 1.
14 Ibid, regs 13, 14(2).
15 Ibid, regs 13(5), 14(2).

the applicant may appeal to the Secretary of State, but he may refuse to entertain an appeal against the standard conditions.[16] The procedure for appeals is based on that for appeals against refusal of planning permission.[17]

The proposed display may involve development as defined in section 55 of the Act of 1990. It is not necessary to apply for planning permission – this is deemed to be granted by the consent under the Regulations.[18]

The Regulations contain provisions for the revocation or modification of consent similar to those in the Act of 1990 for the revocation of planning permission.[19]

ENFORCEMENT OF CONTROL

Any person who displays an advertisement in contravention of the Regulations is guilty of an offence punishable by a fine not exceeding level 3 on the standard scale and a daily fine of £40.[20] The persons displaying an advertisement are deemed to include not only the person who puts it up, but also the person whose land it is displayed on and the person whose goods or business are advertised; in the latter two cases, however, it is a defence to show that the advertisement was displayed without knowledge or consent.[1]

AREAS OF SPECIAL CONTROL

The Act of 1990 provides for the definition of areas of special control which may be '(a) a rural area, or (b) an area which appears to the Secretary of State to require special protection on the grounds of amenity'.[2] The language is curious since the purpose of defining a special area (whether rural or not) will be the protection of amenity rather than public safety. Perhaps the meaning is that rural areas may be freely defined as areas of special control, but there must be some really pressing reason for imposing special control in an urban area. By 1989 rather more than 45 per cent of the total land area of England and Wales had been defined as being within an area of

16 Advertisement Regs, reg 15, Sch 4.
17 The detailed provisions are set out in the Advertisements Regs, Sch 4.
18 1990 Act, s. 222. See ch 6, pp. 129, 130, above.
19 Advertisements Regs, regs 15, 16, Sch 4.
20 1990 Act, s. 224(3).
 1 Ibid, s. 224(4), (5). *John v Reveille Newspapers Ltd* (1955) 5 P & CR 95.
 2 1990 Act, s. 221(3).

special control.[3] The effect of special control is that only the following classes of advertisement may be displayed.[4]

(a) *without express consent*
   (i)   advertisements within classes B to J of the excepted classes;[5]
   (ii) advertisements specified as having deemed consent, with the exception of illuminated advertisements on business premises.[6]
(b) *with express consent*
   (i)   structures for exhibiting notices of local activities;
   (ii) announcements or directions relating to nearby buildings and land, eg hotels and garages;
   (iii) advertisements required for public safety;
   (iv) advertisements which would be permitted under (a)(ii) above but for infringing the conditions as to height, number or illumination.

If the local planning authority consider that any area should be made subject to special control, they make an order to this effect. The order will require the Secretary of State's confirmation and, if there are any objections, the Secretary of State will hold a public inquiry before deciding whether or not to confirm the order.[7]

Where an order defining an area of special control is in force, it is the duty of the local planning authority to consider at least once in every five years whether it should be revoked or modified.[8]

Land adversely affecting amenity of neighbourhood

The powers of local planning authorities to secure the tidying up of unsightly pieces of land have recently been considerably strengthened. The Act of 1971, as originally enacted, enabled the local planning authority to deal with any 'garden, vacant site or other open land' which was in such a condition that it 'seriously injured the local amenities'. This was replaced by new provisions now to be found in section 215 of the Act of 1990. These enable the local planning authority to secure the tidying up of *any* land in their area which is in such a condition that it 'adversely affects' the amenity of the neighbourhood. In such a case the authority can serve a notice on the

3 Circular 15/89.
4 Advertisements Regs, reg 19.
5 See pp. 238–239, above. The conditions for the specified classes are in some cases more stringent than in areas not subject to special control.
6 See pp. 239–240.
7 1990 Act, s. 221(6); Advertisements Regs, Sch 5.
8 Advertisements Regs, reg 18(4).

owner[9] and occupier requiring him to take the steps specified in the notice for remedying the condition of the land. Subject to a right of appeal to the local magistrates,[10] failure to comply with the notice is a punishable offence[11] and the planning authority may also enter upon the land and carry out the work at the expense of the defaulter.[12]

If a local authority consider that any land in their area is derelict, neglected or unsightly, they have power under the National Parks and Access to the Countryside Act 1949, to carry out work to bring the land into use or to improve its appearance; these powers apply throughout England and Wales and not only in national parks.[13]

Abandoned vehicles and other refuse

When Parliament enacted the Civic Amenities Act 1967, to strengthen the powers of planning authorities with regard to the conservation of areas and buildings of special interest and with regard to tree preservation, the opportunity was taken to introduce new provisions as to the disposal of abandoned vehicles and other refuse. These provisions, which are to be found in Part III of the Civic Amenities Act, do not strictly speaking form part of planning law and procedure, but, since they are concerned with the preservation of amenity, they deserve a brief mention. Broadly speaking, Part III deals with the growing problem of abandoned vehicles and other refuse by (a) requiring local authorities to establish places where local residents may deposit refuse, other than business refuse, free of charge; (b) making it an offence to abandon a motor vehicle, or any other thing brought there for the purpose, on any land in the open air without lawful authority; and (c) giving local authorities powers and duties in relation to abandoned vehicles and other refuse.

Hazardous substances

The normal processes of planning control provide some opportunities for regulating the presence on land of hazardous substances. Thus, on an application for planning permission for industrial use or for storage

9 For definition of owner, see pp. 220, 221, above.
10 1990 Act, s. 217. Section 218 gives both the appellant and the local planning authority a right of appeal from the magistrates to the crown court.
11 Ibid, s. 216(2).
12 Ibid, s. 219.
13 National Parks and Access to the Countryside Act 1949, s. 89, as amended by the Local Authorities (Land) Act 1963, s. 6, and the Derelict Land Act 1982.

the local planning authority could refuse permission or impose conditions controlling the presence of hazardous substances; however, the lengthy procedures for enforcement might well result in delays which would be unacceptable where hazardous substances were concerned. Moreover, once an industrial or storage use has been established, the introduction of hazardous substances would not be development at all.

In 1979 the Advisory Committee on Major Hazards recommended that development control under the Planning Acts should be extended to cover the use of hazardous substances; the Committee recommended this method of control in preference to a specialised system exercisable by the Health and Safety Executive because control by local planning authorities was perceived as involving the community.

The first legislative steps were taken in 1983 by amendments to the Use Classes and the General Development Orders then in force and these amendments are now incorporated in the current Orders.[14]

Comprehensive provision for controlling the presence of hazardous substances was made by the Act of 1986 which added some new sections to the Act of 1971. These provisions are now to be found in the Planning (Hazardous Substances) Act 1990. The Act will come into force on a date to be prescribed by the Secretary of State.[15]

WHAT ARE HAZARDOUS SUBSTANCES?

There is no definition of 'hazardous substances' in the Hazardous Substances Act. It will be for the Secretary of State to specify by regulations the substances which are to be subject to control.[16]

The presence of any hazardous substance on, over or under land will require hazardous substances consent.[17] Consent will not be needed where the aggregate amount of the substance on the land and on other sites within 500 metres under the same control[18] is less than the controlled quantity.[19]

Where hazardous substances consent is required it will be necessary to apply to the hazardous substances authority for express consent,[20] but there are two forms of deemed consent.[1]

---

14 See ch 5, p. 90 and ch 6, p. 117, above.
15 No regulations had been made for this purpose when this edition went to press.
16 Hazardous Substances Act, s. 5.
17 See pp. 245–246, below.
18 Two or more companies within the same group may be treated as a single person for this purpose: Hazardous Substances Act, s. 39(3).
19 Ibid, s. 4(1), (2). The controlled quantity is to be specified by regulations.
20 See p. 245, below.
 1 See p. 246, below.

HAZARDOUS SUBSTANCES AUTHORITIES

Generally, the hazardous substances authority will be the district or London borough council. The county council will be the authority in respect of land which is used for mineral working or refuse disposal in a national park in a non-metropolitan county; however, where there is a joint or special planning board for a national park, that board will be the hazardous substances authority. The Boards Authority, those urban development corporations which are vested with full planning powers and some housing action trusts will be hazardous substances authorities.[2] In most cases therefore the hazardous substances authority will be the local planning authority under another name.[3]

In the case of operational land of statutory undertakers and land which they hold or propose to acquire for operational purposes, the hazardous substances authority will be the appropriate Minister.[4]

EXPRESS CONSENT

The procedure for obtaining express consent is to be prescribed by regulations. These regulations may require the applicant or the authority or both to give publicity to the application; for the owner to give certificates of ownership (similar to those required by section 66 of the Act of 1990[5]); for the authority to consult the Health and Safety Executive and other bodies.

When considering an application the authority are to have regard to any material considerations and in particular to:
(a) any current or contemplated use of the land;
(b) the way in which land in the vicinity is used or likely to be used;
(c) any planning permission that has been granted for development of land in the vicinity;
(d) the development plan;
(e) any advice given by the Health and Safety Executive.[6]
The authority may then grant consent either unconditionally or subject to such conditions as they think fit, or they may refuse consent. If granting consent the authority must include a description of the land to which it relates, a description of the hazardous substance or substances to which it relates, and in respect of each hazardous

---

2 Hazardous Substances Act, ss. 1, 3.
3 See ch 3, pp. 40 ff, above.
4 Hazardous Substances Act, s. 2.
5 Ibid, ss. 7, 8.
6 Ibid, s. 9(2).

substance to which it relates a statement of the maximum quantity allowed at any one time.[7]

If the authority refuse consent or grant it subject to conditions the applicant will be entitled to appeal to the Secretary of State. The Secretary of State must offer the appellant and the authority the opportunity of a public local inquiry or other hearing. The decision on the appeal may be given by the Secretary of State or delegated to the inspector. The Secretary of State has power to call in an application before it is determined by the authority.[8]

DEEMED CONSENTS

Section 11 provides for deemed consent for hazardous substances present on the land during the 'establishment period', that is the 12 months immediately preceding the relevant date. The relevant date is the date on which the Hazardous Substances Act comes into force. The owner of the land will have to submit a claim for the deemed consent, and this claim will have to be submitted within six months of the relevant date.

Section 12 provides that where the authorisation of a government department is required for development by a local authority or statutory undertakers,[9] the department in giving the authorisation may direct that hazardous substances consent is deemed to have been granted.

REVOCATION OF CONSENT

The hazardous substances authority may make an order to revoke or modify a hazardous substances consent if they consider it expedient so to do and also in certain defined circumstances.[10] The order will not take effect unless and until confirmed by the Secretary of State,[11] and there are provisions for compensation.[12] Furthermore, a hazardous substances consent is revoked if there is a change in the person in control of part of the land to which it relates unless application for continuation of the consent has previously been made to the authority. On such an application the authority may modify the consent in any way they think appropriate or they may revoke it, but there is

7 Hazardous Substances Act, s. 9(1), (4).
8 Ibid, s. 20.
9 As to authorisation by government department, see ch 6, p. 130, above.
10 Hazardous Substances Act, s. 14.
11 Ibid, s. 15.
12 Ibid, s. 16.

provision for compensation to the person who was in control of the whole of the land.[13]

ENFORCEMENT

Contravention of hazardous substances control will be an offence punishable on summary conviction by a fine not exceeding the statutory maximum or on indictment by a fine; if the offence continues thereafter, there may be a daily fine.[14]

The hazardous substances authority may also issue a contravention notice similar to an enforcement notice under the Act of 1990.[15]

---

13 Hazardous Substances Act, ss. 17, 18, 19.
14 Ibid, s. 23.
15 Ibid, ss. 24, 25. As to enforcement notices, see ch 10, above.

Chapter 14

Buildings of special interest and conservation areas

Buildings of special interest

The preservation of buildings of special architectural or historic interest has long been regarded as an important objective of town and
country planning. Thus schemes under the Act of 1932 could provide
for the preservation of such buildings. The Act of 1947 enabled local
authorities to make building preservation orders with the approval of
the Minister. A building preservation order prohibited the demolition
of, or the making of specified alterations to, the building without the
consent of the local authority. Before approving the order, the Minister
had to consider any objections or representations made by interested
persons and, if need be, hold a public local inquiry. The system was
thus fair and open, the case for giving the building special status was
fully tested at the time, and thereafter the owner knew exactly what
was prohibited without consent. The Act of 1947 also provided for
the listing of buildings by the Minister; where a building was listed,
it became an offence to demolish or alter it without first giving notice
to the local planning authority who could then consider whether to
make a preservation order.

All this was changed by the Act of 1968. The provisions as to
building preservation orders were repealed, and instead it became an
offence to demolish or alter a listed building without first obtaining
'listed building consent' from the local planning authority or the
Minister.[1]

The system thus introduced in 1968 was continued under the Act
of 1971 with some significant changes under later Acts. The legislation
has now been consolidated in the Listed Buildings Act.

---

1 Buildings subject to preservation orders under the old law are now deemed to be
listed.

LISTING OF BUILDINGS

The listing of buildings of special architectural or historic interest is the responsibility of the Secretary of State. He may compile lists of such buildings or he may give his approval (with or without modifications) to lists complied by the Historic Buildings and Monuments Commission or by other persons or bodies.[2] In compiling his own list the Secretary of State may act on his own initiative,[3] but he may – and often does – receive suggestions from the local planning authority and sometimes even from private individuals.

When considering whether to list a building the Secretary of State may consider not only the building itself but also: (a) the contribution which its exterior makes to the architectural or historic interest of a group of buildings and, (b) the desirability of preserving any features fixed to the building or contained within its curtilage;[4] the reference to features undoubtedly includes chattels such as portrait panels and carvings inside the building provided they have been affixed to the premises so as to become part thereof.[5]

Before including buildings in the lists, the Secretary of State must consult the Commission[6] and such other persons as he may consider appropriate as having a special knowledge of, or interest in, such buildings.[7]

The Secretary of State has placed a very wide interpretation on the words 'buildings of special architectural or historic interest'. The selections have not been limited to buildings of obvious aesthetic quality or those associated with well known characters or events, but may include architecture typical of a certain period or illustrative of the work of particular architects.[8]

Listed buildings are in practice (though not as a matter of statutory requirement[9]) classified as Grade I, Grade II* or Grade II. Grade I buildings are buildings of 'exceptional interest'. Grade II* buildings are 'particularly important buildings of more than special interest'; and Grade II buildings are 'buildings of special interest which warrant every effort being made to preserve them'.[10]

---

2 Listed Buildings Act, s. 1(1).
3 There is an interesting account of the workings of the system in *Amalgamated Investment and Property Co Ltd v John Walker & Sons Ltd* [1976] 3 All ER 509.
4 Listed Buildings Act, s. 1(3).
5 *Corthorn Land and Timber Co Ltd v Minister of Housing and Local Government* (1965) 63 LGR 490.
6 The requirement to consult the Commission does not apply in Wales.
7 Listed Buildings Act, s. 1(4).
8 See circular 8/87, Appendix I.
9 There is a reference to Grade II buildings in the Listed Buildings Regs, reg 5.
10 Circular 8/87, Appendix I.

The Secretary of State is not required to notify the owner of a building that it is intended to list it and there is no opportunity at this stage for objections; but on appeal against a refusal of listed building consent, the appellant may contend that the building is not of special architectural or historic interest and ought to be excluded from the list.[11] If he decides that a building should be listed, the Secretary of State will notify the local planning authority who must then give notice to the owner and occupier;[12] the listing will also be recorded in the register of local land charges.[13]

The secrecy with which buildings can be listed can create problems for intending purchasers and developers. Some protection is now afforded by section 6 of the Listed Buildings Act. Where planning permission has been made, or permission has been granted, for development involving the demolition or alteration of a building, application may be made to the Secretary of State for a certificate that he does not intend to list the building; if he gives such a certificate, he is precluded from listing the building within the next five years.

The purpose of listing is to give guidance to local planning authorities in the performance of their functions under the Listed Buildings Act and also under the Act of 1990 as well as to prohibit demolition or alteration;[14] this means that the local planning authority will be expected to give special consideration to listed buildings in deciding whether to give planning permission for nearby development and in the preparation of action area plans, etc.

There appear to be no restrictions on the types of building which may be included in such lists, but the prohibition on demolition or alteration does not apply to ecclesiastical buildings nor to ancient monuments.[15] Moreover, in view of the wide meaning given to the word 'building' in section 336 of the Act of 1990[16] (applied by section 91(2) of the Listed Buildings Act), it would seem that such structures as village pumps, lych gates and milestones may be included in such lists.

---

11 See p. 256, below. The Secretary of State has indicated that he is willing to consider requests from owners for 'de-listing': see circular 8/87, para 40.
12 Listed Buildings Act, s. 2(3).
13 Ibid, s. 2(2).
14 Ibid, s. 1(1).
15 Ibid, ss. 60, 61. A building used by a minister of religion wholly or mainly as a residence from which to perform the duties of his office is deemed for this purpose not to be an ecclesiastical building; this special provision overrides the decision of the Court of Appeal in *Phillips v Minister of Housing and Local Government* [1965] 1 QB 156, [1964] 2 All ER 824. Some redundant churches are exempted from this prohibition on demolition: ibid, s. 61(7).
16 See ch 5, pp. 77 ff, above.

WHAT IS A LISTED BUILDING?

Section 1(5) of the Listed Buildings Act provides that, in addition to the building itself, the following are to be treated as part of the building:

(a) any object or structure fixed to the building;
(b) any object or structure within the curtilage of the building which, although not fixed to the building, forms part of the land and has done so since before 1 July 1948.

This definition has caused some problems.

In the *Calderdale* case[17] a terrace of mill cottages was linked by a bridge to a mill which had been listed. At the date of listing, the mill and the cottages were in common ownership, but in 1973 the cottages had passed into the ownership of the borough council who now wished to demolish them. The question was whether the cottages were structures within the curtilage of the mill. The judgments in the Court of Appeal seem to have taken it for granted that the terrace, and each cottage within it, were structures for the purposes of what is now section 1(5). The court concentrated on two questions: whether the cottages were 'fixed' to the mill and whether they remained within the curtilage notwithstanding the division of ownership. It was held (1) that the terrace was a single structure and fixed to the mill by the bridge; (2) that the terrace had not been taken out of the curtilage by reason of the changes that had taken place.

The apparently wide ranging effects of this decision have been considerably narrowed as a result of the more recent decision of the House of Lords in *Debenhams plc v Westminster City Council*.[18]

Debenhams were the owners of two buildings, the 'Regent Street building' and the 'Kingly Street building'. They were separated by a street but linked by a tunnel and a bridge. The Regent Street building had been listed, but not the other. In order to claim certain exemptions for unoccupied listed buildings under the General Rate Act 1967, Debenhams claimed that the Kingly Street building fell within the definition of listed building in what is now section 1(5) of the Listed Buildings Act.

The House of Lords considered that the important question was the meaning of 'structure' in section 1(5). Lord Keith of Kinkel said that in its ordinary significance 'structure' certainly embraced anything built or constructed and so would cover any building; but in the present context 'structure' was intended to convey a limitation to such structures as were ancillary to the listed building itself, for example the stable block of a mansion house or the steading of a farm house, either fixed to the main building or within its curtilage.

17 *A-G (ex rel Sutcliffe) v Calderdale Borough Council* (1982) 46 P & CR 399, [1983] JPL 310, CA.
18 [1987] AC 396, [1987] 1 All ER 51, HL.

> Held: The Kingly Street building was not ancillary to the Regent Street building, and so was not included in the listing.

Although the House of Lords interpreted the word 'structure' in this context in a much narrower sense than that assumed by the Court of Appeal in the *Calderdale* case, that case is still good authority on the question of what is the curtilage of a listed building. Moreover, the actual decision in *Calderdale* might, in the very unusual circumstances of that case, have been correct since the cottages might be regarded as having originally been ancillary to the mill itself.[19]

LISTED BUILDING CONSENT

Section 55 of the Act of 1971 makes it an offence to execute, without first obtaining listed building consent, any works for the demolition of a listed building or for its alteration or extension in a manner which would affect its character as a building of special architectural or historic interest; as we have seen, any object or structure fixed to the building and certain other objects or structures forming part of the land comprised within the curtilage are to be treated as part of the building.[20] In addition, where it is proposed to demolish a building, notice must be given to the Royal Commission on Historical Monuments to enable them to inspect and record details of the building.[1]

Special provision is made for cases in which it is urgently necessary to execute works in the interests of safety or health or for the preservation of the building. The legislation does not expressly authorise such works, but provides that in the event of a prosecution for carrying out works without consent it shall be defence to prove all of the following matters: (a) that the works were urgently necessary in the interests of safety or health or for the preservation of the building; (b) that it was not practicable to secure safety or health or, as the case may be, to preserve the building by works of repair or works for affording temporary support or shelter; (c) that the works were limited to the minimum necessary; (d) that notice in writing justifying in detail the carrying out of the works was given to the local planning authority as soon as reasonably practicable.[2]

The prohibition against works which would affect the character of

---

19 See the comments in *Debenhams plc v Westminster City Council* (above) of Lords Keith of Kinkel and Mackay of Clashfern.
20 See above.
 1 It seems that this provision may apply to partial demolition required to alter or extend a listed building: *R v North Hertfordshire District Council, ex p Sullivan* [1981] JPL 752: see p. 254, below.
 2 Listed Buildings Act, s. 9(3).

the building as one of special architectural or historic interest extends to works which do not fall within the definition of development[3] or which are permitted development.[4] Thus the painting of the exterior of a building is permitted by the General Development Order[5] but may be held to affect the character of a listed building.[6] The prohibition also extends to works to the interior of the building if they affect the special character of the building.[7] There is no formal machinery by which the owner or occupier of a building can secure a formal determination as to whether his proposed works would affect the character of the building.[8] In the last resort, the question will be one of fact for the Secretary of State on appeal against a listed building enforcement notice or for the magistrates on a prosecution. In cases of doubt it may be helpful to discuss the matter with the local planning authority, but since the decision in *Western Fish Products Ltd v Penwith District Council*[9] it is by no means clear that the advice of the planning officer would be binding on the authority. The only really safe course seems to be to apply for listed building consent. If the planning authority return the application on the ground that consent is unnecessary the authority would thereafter, it is submitted, be estopped from taking any action by way of prosecution or enforcement; even so, it would still be open to a private individual to prosecute.[10]

Originally, a planning permission for development involving the demolition or alteration of a listed building might be so worded as to make it unnecessary to make separate application for listed building consent. This provision has now been repealed with the result that where development involves the demolition or alteration of a listed building, separate applications must be made for planning permission and listed building consent.

3 See ch 5, pp. 79 ff, above.
4 See ch 6, pp. 115 ff, above.
5 GDO, Sch 2, Part 2, Class C.
6 *Windsor and Maidenhead Royal Borough Council v Secretary of State of the Environment* (1987) 86 LGR 402, [1988] JPL 410.
7 Listed Buildings Act, s. 1(5).
8 The Secretary of State is under no statutory obligation to consider the point if taken on an appeal against refusal of listed building consent, but there appears to be nothing in law to prevent his doing so.
9 [1981] 2 All ER 204, (1978) 38 P & CR 7.
10 *Wells v Minister of Housing and Local Government* [1967] 2 All ER 1041.

PROCEDURE FOR OBTAINING CONSENT

The procedure for obtaining listed building consent is modelled on that for obtaining planning permission, but there are some additional requirements as to publicity and consultation with the Secretary of State which illustrate the importance which is now attached to the preservation of buildings of special interest.

Any person may apply for listed building consent; but, whether or not he has an interest in the land, he must give notice of his application to every other person who has a sufficient interest[11] in the land.[12]

The application should be made on a form obtainable from the local planning authority.[13] If the application involves either the demolition or (with minor exceptions) the alteration of a listed building the applicant must advertise the application stating where plans may be inspected; a notice to the same effect must also be displayed on or near the land. Any member of the public then has a period of 21 days in which to make representations.[14]

The Secretary of State has directed that in the case of demolition, the local planning authority must give notice of the application to certain national organisations.[15] The Secretary of State has also directed that the local planning authority must notify the Historic Buildings and Monuments Commission of all applications for listed building consent to alter, extend or demolish any Grade I or Grade II* buildings.[16] It seems that these requirements are mandatory and not merely directory; failure to comply with them may result in a grant of listed building consent being quashed. In this connection it should be noted that an application for alterations or extension may involve some demolition: unless the amount of demolition would be *de minimis*, the authority must notify the specified organisations accordingly.[17]

The Secretary of State may give directions calling in the application;[18] in any event, if the local planning authority propose to grant consent, they must notify the Secretary of State of their intention, and

---

11 Ie the fee simple or a tenancy with at least seven years to run: Listed Building Regs, reg 6(5).
12 Ibid, reg 6(1),(2).
13 Ibid, reg 3.
14 Ibid, reg 5.
15 The direction is contained in circular 8/87, para 81.
16 See circular 8/87, para 81.
17 *R v North Hertfordshire District Council, ex p Sullivan* [1981] JPL 752.
18 Listed Buildings Act, s. 12.

he then has a period of 28 days in which to consider whether or not to call in the application.[19]

In considering whether to grant listed building consent for any works, or whether to grant planning permission for development which affects a listed building or its setting, the Secretary of State and the local planning authority are required to have special regard to the desirability of preserving the building or its setting or any features of special interest which it possesses.[20] It is clearly the intention of Parliament that the desirability of preserving the building or its setting or special features should be the primary consideration, but it is also clear that it cannot be the sole consideration. For instance, the economics of restoring a listed building has been recognised as a relevant consideration.

In *Kent Messenger Ltd v Secretary of State for the Environment*[1] the applicants had appealed against the local planning authority's refusal of consent to demolish a listed building. The inspector accepted that restoration and repair would be uneconomic and recommended that consent be granted for demolition. The Secretary of State disagreed but failed to give adequate reasons for doing so. In the High Court Forbes J quashed the decision and remitted the case to the Secretary of State for re-consideration.

However, in considering whether the restoration of a listed building would be an economic proposition, the Secretary of State is entitled, on the basis of evidence given at the inquiry, to take into account the extent to which the cost of restoration could be recouped by the redevelopment of the remainder of the site.[2]

There is some uncertainty as to whether, on an application for consent to demolish a listed building, it is relevant to consider the quality of the building which the developer wishes to erect in its place. In *Kent Messenger Ltd v Secretary of State for the Environment*[3] Forbes J left the question open, and there is still no direct authority on the point. It may well be that, where the listed building is in a conservation area, the quality of the proposed replacement building is a relevant consideration, because the planning authority are required to have

---

19 Listed Buildings Act, s. 13. In London, the local planning authority should notify the Historic Buildings and Monuments Commission: s. 14.
20 Listed Buildings Act, s. 16(2).
 1 [1976] JPL 372.
 2 *Godden v Secretary of State for the Environment* [1988] JPL 99.
 3 Above.

special regard to the desirability of preserving or enhancing the character or appearance of the area.[4]

If the Secretary of State does not call in the application, the local authority may grant consent with or without conditions or they may refuse consent.[5] Where consent is granted for demolition of a listed building, the local planning authority may impose a condition that demolition shall not take place until a contract for carrying out works of redevelopment has been made, and planning permission has been granted for the redevelopment for which the contract provides.[6] Every listed building consent (whether for demolition or alterations) must contain a condition to the effect that the consent will lapse if it is not acted upon within five years or such other period as may be stated in the consent.[7] If consent is refused or granted subject to conditions, the applicant may appeal to the Secretary of State;[8] so too, if the authority fail to give a decision within the prescribed period.[9] The Act expressly provides that the grounds of appeal may include a claim that the building is not of special architectural or historic interest;[10] this is of considerable importance because, as noted earlier in this chapter, the owner or occupier cannot object to the listing of his building. Where a case comes before the Secretary of State (whether on appeal or on calling in) the applicant and the local planning authority have the right to a hearing.[11] The Secretary of State's decision is final except that it can be challenged in High Court proceedings under section 63 of the Listed Buildings Act.

REVOCATION AND MODIFICATION

A listed building consent may be revoked or modified. The local planning authority may make an order for this purpose if they consider it expedient having regard to the development plan and any other material considerations; or the Secretary of State may make the order himself. It is to be noted, however, that the power to revoke or modify

---

4 Listed Buildings Act, s. 72. The quality of the proposed replacement building was held to be a relevant consideration in the case of an application for conservation area consent for the demolition of an unlisted building in *Richmond-upon-Thames London Borough Council v Secretary of State for the Environment* (1978) 37 P & CR 151, [1979] JPL 175: see p. 268 below.

5 Ibid, s. 16(1).

6 Ibid, s. 17(3).

7 Ibid, s. 18.

8 Ibid, s. 20(1).

9 Ibid, s. 20(2). The prescribed period is two months: Listed Building Regs, reg 3(4).

10 Ibid, s. 21(3).

11 Ibid, s. 22(2).

only applies where the works authorised by the listed building consent have not been completed.[12]

In the normal case, the local planning authority must submit the order to the Secretary of State for confirmation, and he will if need be hold a public local inquiry or other hearing before deciding whether or not to confirm the order.[13] But there is an alternative procedure which may be used where the persons affected have notified the local planning authority that they do not object to the order.[14]

Where listed building consent is revoked or modified, the local planning authority are liable for compensation for abortive expenditure and for any other loss or damage directly attributable to the revocation or modification.[15] Compensation is not payable where the persons affected by the order had notified the local planning authority that they did not object to the order.

ENFORCEMENT

The demolition or alteration of a listed building without consent, or in breach of the conditions attached to consent, is an offence punishable by fine and/or imprisonment:[16] it is similarly an offence to demolish a listed building without giving notice to the Royal Commission on Historical Monuments.[17] Usually, of course, the actual work will be done by a contractor, but the owner will also be guilty of an offence if it can be shown that he caused the work to be done.

In *R v Wells Street Metropolitan Magistrate, ex p Westminster City Council*[18] the Divisional Court held that the offence was one of strict liability, that is, the prosecution did not have to prove that the accused knew that the building was listed. The court considered that the issue was one of social concern and that the creation of strict liability would promote the objects of the legislation by encouraging greater vigilance; fears of injustice were all capable of being allayed by the discretion whether to prosecute or not and the discretion of the court to refrain from punishment.

---

12 Listed Buildings Act, s. 23.
13 Ibid, s. 24.
14 Ibid, s. 25.
15 Ibid, s. 28. The claim for compensation should be made to the local planning authority within six months of the date of the order: Listed Buildings Reg, reg 8.
16 On conviction on indictment, the court in imposing a fine is to have regard to any financial benefit accruing from the offence: ibid, s. 9(5). A fine may thus be more suitable than imprisonment: see *R v Chambers* reviewed at [1989] JPL 229.
17 Listed Buildings Act, s. 9.
18 [1986] 3 All ER 4, [1986] 1 WLR 1046.

In addition, the local planning authority may issue a 'listed building enforcement notice' specifying the steps to be taken:

(i)   for restoring the building to its former state; or

(ii) where such restoration would not be reasonably practicable, or would be undesirable, such further works as the authority consider necessary to alleviate the effect of the works carried out without consent;

(iii) for bringing the building to the state it would have been in if the terms and conditions of listed building consent had been complied with.[19]

Copies of the notice are to be served on the owner and occupier of the building and on any person having an interest in the building which is materially affected by the notice.[20] Any of these persons may appeal to the Secretary of State on a number of specified grounds; these grounds include: (a) that the building is not of special architectural or historic interest and (b) that the matters complained of do not constitute a contravention of section 9, for instance that they do not affect the special character of the building.[1] There is a further right of appeal to the High Court on matters of law.[2]

Failure to comply with an enforcement notice is an offence punishable by fine not exceeding the statutory maximum on summary conviction or an unlimited fine on indictment.[3] The local planning authority may also carry out the work themselves and recover the cost from the owner of the land.[4]

COMPENSATION AND PURCHASE NOTICE

Refusal of listed building consent or the imposition of conditions may have two serious consequences for the owner of the building. It may cause him substantial loss at least in the sense of preventing him realising some development value; and where the land has become incapable of reasonably beneficial use, it may prevent him from rendering it capable of beneficial use. These possibilities are recognised to some extent by the Listed Buildings Act.

---

19 Listed Buildings Act, s. 38(1), (2). The effect of sub-para (ii) was considered in *Bath City Council v Secretary of State for the Environment and Grosvenor Hotel (Bath) Ltd* [1983] JPL 737 (roof of building in disrepair and patched with unsuitable materials before unauthorised repair works).

20 Ibid, s. 38(4).

 1 Ibid, s. 39(1).

 2 Ibid, s. 65.

 3 Ibid, s. 43. On subsequent convictions for non-compliance a daily fine may be imposed.

 4 Ibid, s. 42.

The Act gives no general right of compensation for refusal or conditional grant of listed building consent. Compensation is payable, however, where the following conditions are satisfied:[5]

(a) the Secretary of State, either on appeal or on a called-in application, has refused consent for the alteration or extension of the building or has granted it subject to conditions;

(b) the works do not constitute development or, if they do, are development permitted by development order;[6]

(c) the value of the claimant's interest is less than it would have been if consent had been granted unconditionally.

There is thus no compensation for refusal of consent to demolish a listed building.

If the land has become incapable of reasonably beneficial use, the owner may be able to serve a 'listed building purchase notice' on the planning authority. This procedure is available where listed building consent has been refused or granted subject to conditions or revoked or modified, and the owner claims that the following conditions are satisfied:[7]

(a) that the land has become incapable of reasonably beneficial use in its existing state;[8]

(b) if consent was granted subject to conditions (or modified by the imposition of conditions) that the land cannot be rendered capable of reasonably beneficial use by carrying out the works in accordance with these conditions;

(c) in any case (ie whether consent was refused or granted subject to conditions or revoked or modified) that the land cannot be rendered capable of reasonably beneficial use by carrying out any other works for which listed building consent has been granted or for which the local planning authority or the Secretary of State has undertaken to grant consent.

The procedure for the service of such purchase notices and the powers of the Secretary of State are similar to those for purchase notices in connection with refusal of planning permission.[9]

5 Listed Buildings Act, s. 27(1), (2).
6 For permission by development order, see ch 6, pp. 115 ff, above.
7 Listed Buildings Act, s. 32.
8 For the significance of this phrase see ch 12, pp. 217 ff, above.
9 See ch 12, pp. 221, 222, above.

BUILDING PRESERVATION NOTICE

A building preservation notice may be served to protect a building which is considered to be of special architectural or historic interest but which has not yet been listed as such and is in danger of being demolished or altered.[10] The notice remains in force for a maximum period of six months,[11] and whilst it is in force the building is protected in the same way as if it had been listed.[12]

Before serving the notice the local planning authority must request the Secretary of State to consider the listing of the building. They then serve notice on the owner and occupier explaining the position.[13] In cases of urgency, they may affix a notice to the building itself instead of serving notice on the owner and occupier.[14]

The notice ceases to have effect as soon as the Secretary of State decides to list the building or tells the local planning authority that he does not intend to list it. If he does not reach a decision within six months the notice automatically lapses.[15]

Application for listed building consent may be made whilst the building preservation notice is in force. And, if consent is refused or granted subject to conditions, a claim for compensation may be submitted, although the compensation will not be paid unless and until the building is listed.[16]

If the Secretary of State decides not to list the building or allows the building preservation notice to lapse, the local planning authority are liable for compensation in respect of loss or damage directly attributable to the making of the building preservation notice, and it is specifically provided that this compensation shall include damages payable for breaches of contract caused by the necessity of discontinuing or countermanding works to the building.[17]

---

10 Listed Buildings Act, s. 3(1).
11 Ibid, s. 3(3).
12 Ibid, s. 3(5).
13 Ibid, s. 3(2).
14 Ibid, s. 4.
15 Ibid, s. 3(3), (4).
16 Ibid, ss. 3(5), 27(5).
17 Ibid, s. 29. It seems that loss or damage is not limited to what could reasonably have been foreseen but may include any loss or damage which is directly attributable to the building preservation notice: *J. Sample (Warkworth) Ltd v Alnwick District Council* [1984] JPL 670; see ch 10, pp. 206, 207, above.

REPAIR AND ACQUISITION OF LISTED BUILDINGS

The listing of a building does not impose any direct obligation on the owners or occupiers for the repair of the building. But the Secretary of State and local planning authority have two remedies if the building falls into disrepair. First, section 54 of the Listed Buildings Act[18] enables the local planning authority to take emergency action where a listed building is wholly or partly unoccupied and is in urgent need of repair; in such a case the authority can enter the building after giving seven days' notice[19] to the owner[20] and themselves carry out the necessary work.[1] The authority may subsequently serve notice on the owner to recover the cost; the owner may appeal against this notice to the Secretary of State on a number of grounds including hardship.

The Secretary of State has power to take action to secure the repair of any listed building[2] which is unoccupied which is in urgent need of repair. In England (as distinct from Wales) he will authorise the Historic Buildings and Monuments Commission to do the work.[3]

Secondly, where a listed building (whether occupied or unoccupied) is not kept in a reasonable state of preservation, either the Secretary of State or a local authority may, under section 47 of the Listed Buildings Act, acquire the building by compulsory purchase, together with any adjacent buildings required for preserving the listed building.[4] The power of compulsory purchase does not extend to ecclesiastical buildings and ancient monuments.[5]

Before starting the compulsory purchase the Secretary of State or the local authority must have served, at least two months previously, a repairs notice on the owner[6] of the building specifying the works

---

18 In London the Historic Buildings and Monuments Commission has concurrent powers with the London borough council: Listed Buildings Act, s. 54(7).

19 The notice must specify the works which the authority intend to carry out: ibid, s. 54(6). It seems that the purpose of giving seven days' notice is to enable the owner to discuss the matter with the local authority and perhaps to volunteer to do the works for himself: *R v Secretary of State for the Environment, ex p Hampshire County Council* (1980) 44 P & CR 343, [1981] JPL 47, at 48 per Donaldson LJ.

20 The word 'owner' has the same meaning as in the 1990 Act, s. 336: Listed Buildings Act, s. 91(2). See ch 12, pp. 220, 221, above.

1 But only to the unoccupied parts: Listed Buildings Act, s. 54(4).

2 Listed Buildings Act, s. 76(1).

3 Ibid, s. 59(2)(a).

4 Ibid, s. 47(7). In London, the Historic Buildings and Monuments Commission may be authorised to use these powers.

5 Ibid, ss. 60, 61.

6 The word 'owner' has the meaning given by the 1990 Act, s. 336. See above.

considered necessary for the proper preservation of the building.[7] The notice does not impose any obligation on the owner to carry out the specified works, and it is presumably for this reason that there is no statutory provision for challenging it; the notice has been described as the 'harbinger of a compulsory purchase order and a useful checklist for the Secretary of State when he had to decide under section 114 [of the Act of 1971] whether or not reasonable steps had been taken for the proper preservation of the building and thus whether he should confirm a compulsory purchase order'.[8] The act does not expressly state that neither the Secretary of State nor the authority can proceed with compulsory purchase if the repairs are carried out, but it is submitted that this is the case.

Where a local planning authority draw up a repairs notice they must specify only such works as are reasonably necessary for the preservation of the building; and in deciding whether to confirm a compulsory purchase order, the Secretary of State must consider whether the items specified in the repairs notice form a proper basis for a compulsory purchase order. However, in *Robbins v Secretary of State for the Environment*[9] the Court of Appeal held that such works might include items of restoration; whether restoration was reasonably necessary was one of fact and degree, but to include the restoration of some feature which had disappeared at, say, the date of listing would probably be unreasonable.

In making a compulsory purchase order, the Secretary of State or the authority must go through the procedure laid down in the Acquisition of Land Act 1981, and the owner and any lessees will have the usual rights of objection under that Act.[10] In addition, there is a right of appeal to the magistrates on the ground that reasonable steps are being taken for properly preserving the building; if the magistrates are satisfied on this point, any further proceedings on the compulsory purchase order will be stayed.[11]

There are two bases of compensation for the compulsory acquisition of a listed building. Under what may be called the standard basis, it may be assumed for the purpose of assessing compensation that listed building consent would be granted[12] for (a) the alteration or extension of the building; or (b) the demolition of the building for the purpose of carrying out any development specified in Schedule 3 of the Act of

7 Listed Buildings Act, s. 48.
8 *Robbins v Secretary of State for the Environment* [1988] JPL 824, CA, per Glidewell LJ.
9 Above.
10 Ibid, s. 47(2).
11 Ibid, s. 47(4).
12 Ibid, s. 49.

1990.[13] These assumptions cannot be made if listed building consent has been previously refused or granted subject to conditions so as to give rise to a claim for compensation.[14] This standard basis applies to any compulsory purchase of a listed building whether under section 47 of the Listed Buildings Act or some other statutory powers.

These provisions place the owner of a listed building in a less favourable position than other owners whose land is compulsorily acquired. Of course, the owner of a listed building need not ask for compensation to be assessed on the basis of assumptions about demolition and redevelopment; he can claim if he wishes the value of his building as it stands.

There is also a penal basis of compensation. The amount of compensation will be reduced where the building has been deliberately allowed to fall into disrepair for the purpose of justifying its demolition and the redevelopment of the site or any adjoining land. In these circumstances the acquiring authority may include in the compulsory purchase order a 'direction for minimum compensation'. There is a right of appeal to the magistrates, who may quash the direction for minimum compensation. In any event, the Secretary of State must be satisfied that the direction is justified. Where a direction for minimum compensation is confirmed, it is to be assumed in assessing compensation that planning permission would not be granted for development of the site and that listed building consent would not be granted for development of the site and that listed building consent would not be granted for demolition or alteration of the building. This penal basis of compensation can only be applied to compulsory purchase under section 47.[15]

Conservation areas

Conservation areas are a more recent innovation. Prior to 1967, the emphasis was on the preservation of individual buildings as distinct from areas. Of course, under general planning powers, the local planning authority might, when considering an application for planning permission, consider the effect of the proposed development on the character of the surrounding area, and it would be wrong to belittle what had been done by many authorities to prevent unsuitable developments. But until 1967 no positive duty had been laid upon local planning authorities to take specific steps to safeguard the character of areas of special architectural or historic interest.

13 For development falling within Sch 3, see ch 20, below.
14 Listed Buildings Act, s. 49.
15 Ibid, s. 50.

The Civic Amenities Act 1967 imposed such a duty for the first time; local planning authorities were required to determine which parts of their areas were of special architectural or historic interest, the character or appearance of which it was desirable to preserve or enhance, and to designate such areas as conservation areas. The relevant provisions of the Civic Amenities Act have been considerably extended over the years. The legislation is now contained in the Listed Buildings Act.

DESIGNATION OF CONSERVATION AREAS

It is the duty of the local planning authority to determine from time to time which parts of their area should be treated as conservation areas.[16] In shire counties the local planning authority for this purpose is the district council, but the county council may also designate conservation areas. In Greater London, the Historic Buildings and Monuments Commission has concurrent powers with the London borough council.[17] The Secretary of State may also designate conservation areas but will probably do so only in exceptional cases.[18] It is also the duty of the local planning authority from time to time to review the past exercise of their functions in this respect and to consider whether new areas should be designated.[19]

The procedure for the designation of a conservation area is comparatively simple. The district local planning authority determine – presumably by resolution of the council – that a specified area is a conservation area.[1] Where a county planning authority propose to designate a conservation area they must first consult the district authority.[2] The Secretary of State's approval is not required, but the local planning authority must give him formal notice of the designation of any area as a conservation area, and they must publish notice in the *London Gazette* and the local press;[3] notice must also be entered in the local land charges register.[4] There are no provisions for the making of objections or representations at this stage by interested

16 Listed Buildings Act, s. 69(1).
17 Ibid, s. 70(1).
18 Ibid, s. 69(3).
19 Ibid, s. 69(2).
1 Ibid, s. 69(1). In London, the Historic Buildings and Monuments Commission also has power to designate conservation areas but must first consult the London borough council: ibid, s. 70(1), (2).
2 Ibid, Sch 4, para 4(2).
3 Ibid, s. 70(5), (8). In England (as distinct from Wales) notice must also be given to the Historic Buildings and Monuments Commission.
4 Ibid, s. 69(2).

parties.[5] It seems that the local planning authority may subsequently cancel the designation of an area as a conservation area.[6]

Although there is no statutory requirement to this effect, local planning authorities have been recommended to establish conservation area committees and many authorities have done so; these committees are advisory to the authority, and the intention is that they should mainly consist of people who are not members of the council.[7]

THE CONSEQUENCES OF DESIGNATION

The designation of a conservation area has a number of direct legal consequences: the local planning authority must prepare a conservation area plan; there are special procedures for applications for planning permission, control of demolition of buildings and felling of trees, possible stricter controls over outdoor advertising. These matters are discussed later in this chapter. In addition, section 72 provides that special attention shall be paid to the desirability of preserving or enhancing the character or appearance of the conservation area in the exercise, with respect to any buildings or other land in the area, of any powers under the Listed Buildings Act and some other legislation. The importance of this section has recently been highlighted by the decision of the High Court in *Steinberg v Secretary of State for the Environment*.[8]

> The local planning authority had refused planning permission for the erection of a dwellinghouse on a small piece of unused, derelict and overgrown land in a conservation area. On appeal, the inspector identified as one of the main issues 'whether the proposed development would harm the character of the conservation area'. On this issue the inspector considered that the condition of the site detracted considerably from both the residential amenity and the visual character of the locality. The inspector allowed the appeal.
>
> Two members of a neighbourhood association applied to the High Court to set aside that decision. Mr Lionel Read QC, sitting as deputy judge, held that the inspector had misdirected himself on a point of law. There was, said the learned deputy judge, a world of difference between the issue which the inspector had identified for himself – whether the proposed

5 See, however, the provisions mentioned below for the calling of a public meeting to consider the local planning authority's detailed proposals for safeguarding and enhancing the conservation area.
6 Listed Buildings Act, s. 70(5).
7 See circular 8/87, para 68.
8 [1989] JPL 258.

development would 'harm' the character of the conservation area – and the need to pay special attention to the desirability of preserving or enhancing the character or appearance of the area. The concept of avoiding harm was essentially negative. The underlying purpose of what is now section 72 seemed to be essentially positive. The case was remitted to the Secretary of State.

The judgment is important because it emphasises the positive nature of the duty imposed by section 72 on the Secretary of State and local planning authorities to pay special attention to the desirability of preserving or enhancing the character or appearance of the conservation area. Moreover, it seems from this judgment that in deciding whether or not to grant planning permission for development in a conservation area the Secretary of State must be seen from the terms of his decision letter to have paid special attention to the specified conservation aims. This does not, it is submitted, relieve the Secretary of State – or the local planning authority – of the duty when determining an application for planning permission to have regard to any other material considerations,[9] but conservation aims are the most important consideration.

Section 277(8) appears to specify four separate aims: preservation of the character of the area, enhancement of its character, preservation of its appearance, enhancement of its appearance. In *Steinberg v Secretary of State for the Environment*[10] the judge left open the question whether the statutory duty could be discharged by considering only whether development would preserve the character of the area, and granting permission if it would.

CONSERVATION AREA PLAN

The local planning authority are required to prepare proposals for the preservation and enhancement of the character and appearance of the conservation area.[11] This requirement was introduced by the Act of 1974 and, it is submitted, applies to conservation areas designated before the passing of that Act as well as to new conservation areas.

The proposals must be published and submitted to a public meeting in the area concerned; and, before finalising the proposals the local

9   See ch 7, pp. 141 ff, above.
10   Above.
11   Listed Buildings Act, s. 71(1).

planning authority must have regard to any views expressed by persons attending that meeting.[12]

The proposals put forward by the local planning authority are likely to involve the use of various powers under the Planning Acts, e g listing of buildings of special architectural or historic interest, the making of article 4 directions to restrict permitted development,[13] and the making of discontinuance orders to remove or modify non-conforming uses.[14] There is nothing to prevent the local planning authority putting forward schemes which would involve the use of powers given by other statutes: for instance, they might propose a traffic regulation scheme under the Road Traffic Regulation Act 1967.

The effective treatment of a conservation area may also involve issues which ought to be dealt with in the context of the development plan, and for that reason the preparation of a local plan may well be desirable;[15] this would of course involve the formal procedures for the making and adoption of local plans.[16]

CONTROL OF DEVELOPMENT

Designation of an area as a conservation area does not preclude the possibility of new development within the area; what is important is that new developments should be designed in a sensitive manner having regard to the special character of the area. Section 73 of the Listed Buildings Act requires the local planning authority to advertise applications for planning permission for any new development which is likely to affect the character or appearance of a conservation area; it is for the local planning authority to decide whether the development would be of such a character and thus whether to advertise the application or not. The advertisement will take the form of a notice in the local press and the display of a notice on or near to the land to which the application relates. The public will then have the right to inspect the details of the application and to make representations to the local planning authority. In England (as distinct from Wales) the local planning authority must also send a copy of the notice to the Historic Buildings and Monuments Commission.[17] When considering

12 Listed Buildings Act, s. 71(2), (3).
13 See ch 6, p. 125, above. The Secretary of State's policy with regard to art 4 directions in conservation areas is set out in circular 8/87, para 64.
14 See ch 9, above.
15 Development Plans Manual, para 10.3.
16 See ch 4, above.
17 Listed Buildings Act, s. 67(3) applied by s. 73(1).

the application, the local planning authority must pay special attention to the desirability of preserving or enhancing the character or appearance of the area.[18]

CONTROL OF DEMOLITION

The local planning authority may well see fit to protect some of the buildings in a conservation area by listing them as being of special architectural or historic interest under section 1 of the Listed Buildings Act.[19] There will, however, be many buildings in a conservation area which do not merit listing, but their demolition might detrimentally affect the general appearance of the conservation area. Sections 74 and 75 prohibit (with some exceptions) the demolition of any building in a conservation area without special consent. For the purpose of controlling demolition, section 74 applies many of the provisions of the Listed Buildings Act relating to listed buildings, and until 1987 consent to demolish an unlisted building in a conservation area was known as listed building consent; it has now been re-named 'conservation area consent'. Section 74 does not apparently extend to works of alteration, but it probably does prohibit the demolition of part of a building without consent.[20] Many of the provisions relating to listed building consent apply to conservation area consent. Thus, section 16(3) of the Listed Buildings Act, which requires the Secretary of State or the local planning authority to have special regard to the desirability of preserving the building or its setting,[1] will also apply to applications for conservation area consent to demolish an unlisted building. Moreover, as we have seen, there is always the duty imposed by section 72 to pay special attention to the desirability of preserving or enhancing the character or appearance of the area.[2] The effect of this was illustrated in *Richmond-upon-Thames London Borough Council v Secretary of State for the Environment*[3] where the Secretary of State had refused consent to demolish an unlisted building on the ground that the proposed new building would intrude to an unacceptable degree into the conservation area; the High Court upheld the Secretary of State's decision: the function described in what is now section 72 could

18 See pp. 265, 266, above.
19 See pp. 249, 250, above.
20 The word 'building' includes part of a building: 1990 Act, s. 336(1) applied by Listed Buildings Act, s. 91(2). It is therefore permissible to treat part of a building as a separate building. In any event demolition of part of a building may be a building operation requiring planning permission: see ch 5, pp. 83, 84, above.
1 See ch p. 255, above.
2 See pp. 265, 266, above.
3 [1979] JPL 175.

not be performed without seeing what was to be substituted and how it would fit into the conservation area.

Where consent is granted for demolition, the local planning authority may impose a condition that demolition shall not take place until a contract for carrying out works of redevelopment has been made, and planning permission has been granted for the redevelopment for which the contract provides.[4]

The local planning authority have power to prosecute and to issue an enforcement notice for breach of section 74 as in the case of listed buildings.[5] If consent to demolish is refused, the owner may be able to serve a purchase notice.[6]

Section 74 does not apply to ecclesiastical buildings[7] or ancient monuments. Furthermore, the Secretary of State may make a direction exempting certain classes of building.[8] He has in fact made a direction exempting some eleven classes of building: these include inter alia small buildings of up to 115 cubic metres, and buildings which the owner is required to demolish as a result of a statutory order.[9]

TREES IN CONSERVATION AREAS

Under section 211 of the Act of 1990, anyone who wishes to cut down, top, lop, uproot, wilfully damage or wilfully destroy[10] any tree in a conservation area must give notice of intention to the local planning authority. The authority then have six weeks in which to consider making a tree preservation order. The person concerned must not proceed with his intentions during this period of six weeks unless the authority have given specific consent in the meantime.[11]

The Secretary of State has power to specify exemptions from section 211. Some five cases are currently exempted by the Trees in Conservation Areas Regulations.[12]

---

4 Listed Buildings Act, s. 17(3) applied by s. 74(3).
5 See pp. 257–8, above.
6 See p. 259, above.
7 See p. 250, above.
8 Listed Buildings Act, s. 74(3).
9 Circular 8/87, para 97.
10 For 'wilful destruction' of a tree, see the account at p. 231, above of *Barnet London Borough Council v Eastern Electricity Board* [1973] 2 All ER 319.
11 1990 Act, s. 211(3).
12 T & CP (Tree Preservation Order) (Amendment) and (Trees in Conservation Areas) (Excepted Cases) Regs 1975 (SI 1975 No 148), reg 3.

ADVERTISEMENTS IN CONSERVATION AREAS

Section 63 of the Act of 1971 (as amended by the Act of 1986) enables the Secretary of State to make special provision in the Advertisement Regulations with respect to advertisements in conservation areas. To date no special regulations have been made with respect to advertisements in conservation areas.[13] The local planning authority may ask the Secretary of State for an order designating the whole or part of a conservation area as an area of special control,[14] if they feel that there are compelling reasons.[15] To some extent, however, section 72 of the Listed Buildings Act may result in a higher standard of control in conservation areas because, in considering any application for express consent, the local planning authority must pay special attention to the desirability of preserving or enhancing the character or appearance of the area.

FINANCIAL ASSISTANCE FOR CONSERVATION AREAS

Special financial assistance from central government is available for the preservation or enhancement of conservation areas.

The Historic Buildings and Monuments Commission (in Wales the Secretary of State) may make a loan or grant for work which has made or will make a significant contribution towards preserving or enhancing the character or appearance of a conservation area or part of such an area.[16] In practice such loans or grants are made: (a) for works to a building in a conservation area of particular architectural or historic interest for which the local authority has been invited by the Commission (or the Secretary of State) to submit a programme of conservation work; (b) where there is a 'town scheme' in operation;[17] (c) for a scheme of conservation work prepared by local authorities, amenity societies, preservation societies, or a group of private owners.[18]

Provision for 'town schemes' in conservation areas is made by section 79 of the Listed Buildings Act. These are in effect partnership agreements between the Historic Buildings and Monuments Commission (in Wales the Secretary of State), the district council and/or the county council. Under the partnership agreement the Commission

---

13 In conservation areas and certain other areas advertisements falling within the Advertisement Regulations, Sch 2, class A and Sch 3, classes 4 and 8 require express consent, but these are exceptions to the general provisions: see ch 13, pp. 238, 239, above.
14 See ch 13, pp. 241, 242, above.
15 Circular 15/89, paras 23 et seq.
16 Listed Buildings Act, s. 77.
17 For town schemes, see below.
18 See circular 21/81 para 35.

(or the Secretary of State) and the local authorities concerned will set aside a specified sum of money to be used over a period of years for making grants for the repair of the buildings included in the town scheme.

Chaper 15

Special cases

Crown land

It is a general rule of English law that the Crown is not bound by a statute unless the statute so provides, either expressly or by necessary implication.[1] Thus, where Parliament intends that a particular statute shall not apply to the Crown, it is normally unnecessary to make any specific provision to that effect. In passing the Act of 1947, the intention of Parliament was that planning control should not apply as a matter of law to the Crown, but since it is possible under the English system of land tenure for the Crown and private persons to hold interests in the same land, it was necessary to make special provision as to Crown land.

'Crown land' is defined[2] as any land in which an interest belongs to Her Majesty in right of the Crown or of the Duchy of Lancaster or the Duchy of Cornwall, or belongs to a government department or is held in trust for Her Majesty for the purposes of a government department. The boards of nationalised industries and other public corporations – such as the British Broadcasting Corporation and the new town development corporations – are not government departments and cannot claim the privileges of the Crown.[3] The National Health Service is in a somewhat different position, all the land and buildings are vested in the Department of Health and are thus 'Crown land'.[4]

The application of the Act of 1990 to Crown land is as follows:
(1) A development plan may include proposals relating to the use of the land.[5]
(2) A government department does not require planning permission in order to carry out development on land in which they have

1 *Magdalen College, Cambridge Case* (1615) 11 Co Rep 66b.
2 1990 Act, s. 293(1).
3 The British Transport Commission, a nationalised body, was held not to be a Crown servant in *Tamlin v Hannaford* [1950] 1 KB 18, [1949] 2 All ER 327.
4 National Health Service Act 1946, ss. 6 and 58.
5 1990 Act, s. 296(1)(a).

an interest and no enforcement notice can be served on the department. Other persons having an interest in Crown land, such as a lease from the Crown Estates Commissioners, who wish to carry out development may apply for planning permission in the ordinary way; if the appropriate authority agree,[6] an enforcement notice may be served on any such person.[7]

(3) Buildings on Crown land may be listed as buildings of special architectural and historic interest, but a government department does not require listed building consent to demolish or carry out works on such buildings, and no listed building enforcement notice may be served on the department. Any other person having an interest in the land must obtain listed buildings consent; and, if the appropriate authority agree, a listed building enforcement notice may be served on any such person.[8]

(4) The powers of compulsory purchase for planning purposes conferred by the Act of 1990 may be exercised in relation to any interest in the land, other than a Crown interest, provided the appropriate authority agree.[9]

(5) The owner of an interest in Crown land may serve a purchase notice but only if he has first offered to sell it to the appropriate authority and that offer has been refused.[10]

Although government departments are exempt from planning control, they are expected to consult local planning authorities before carrying out major development. The arrangements for such consultation are set out in circular 18/84. Government departments will consult the local planning authority in respect of any development for which a private developer or a local authority would require specific permission, and also in respect of development in motorway service areas and similar developments in connection with trunk roads,[11] and, even where consultation would not be required on this basis, government departments will notify the local planning authority of proposals likely to be of special concern, e g development affecting conservation areas. Proposals for development by government departments will usually be given publicity in the same way as for private

---

6 The 'appropriate authority' is defined in s. 293(2) of the 1990 Act, and means the particular government department which controls the land in question, or the Crown Estates Commissioners, or the Duchy of Lancaster, or the Duchy of Cornwall, according to circumstances (with the Treasury deciding any disputed cases).

7 1990 Act, s. 296(1)(c), (2).

8 Listed Buildings Act, s. 83.

9 1990 Act, s. 296(1)(b), (2), (3).

10 Ibid, s. 296(1)(c), (2).

11 Proposals for trunk roads are subject to statutory procedures, but these procedures do not apply to such ancillary developments as service areas.

developments, and opportunity given for representations by members of the public.

The local planning authority cannot veto development by government departments; but, where there is disagreement, the matter may be referred to the Secretary of State and he may hold a public inquiry. Such inquiries have been held in the past into the use of land by service departments, and, because of the feelings of local residents, into proposals for prisons and mental homes.

All these arrangements are, of course, subject to modification where national security is involved.

PLANNING PERMISSION ETC. IN ANTICIPATION OF DISPOSAL OF CROWN LAND

Although the Crown does not require planning permission for its own development and the owner of a private interest in Crown land may apply for planning permission, there is a special problem where the Crown wishes to sell land for private development. In the past the Law Officers of the Crown have always advised that it is not open to the Crown nor to any third party to apply for planning permission; that of course precluded prospective purchasers of Crown land from applying for planning permission. The Secretary of State, as the minister responsible for town and country planning, attempted to deal with the problem by recommending that, where a government department wished to dispose of land, an opinion be sought from the local planning authority as to whether planning permission would be forthcoming if a formal application were made; if the local planning authority and the government department could not agree, the Secretary of State would be willing to give an opinion.[12]

This informal procedure was not entirely satisfactory. It did not bind the local planning authority or the Secretary of State in the event of a subsequent application or appeal; so the purchaser by whom an application or appeal would have to be made was still at some risk. Moreover, in so far as the procedure was effective it deprived local people of their right in certain cases to make representations. Ultimately the procedure was held to be unlawful in *R v Worthing Borough Council, ex p Burch*[13] in that it constrained the local planning authority in the exercise of its powers and precluded local people from making representations.

Following the decision in that case, the Town and Country Planning

12 Circular 49/63.
13 [1984] JPL 261.

Act 1984 was passed, inter alia, to enable Crown land to be sold or leased with planning permission already granted under proper statutory procedures; the relevant provisions are now contained in the Act of 1990, and the Listed Buildings Act. The new procedure applies only where there is no existing private interest in the land;[14] holders of existing private interests have always been able to apply for planning permission and their right to do so is not affected by the new Act.[15] Under the new Act the appropriate authority[16] on behalf of the Crown, or any person authorised by that authority in writing, may now make application for planning permission, listed building consent or conservation area consent.[17] All the statutory procedures for the making and determination of any such application will apply as if the land were not Crown land.[18] A planning permission granted by virtue of the Act of 1984 will apply to (a) development carried out after the land has ceased to be Crown land; (b) so long as the land remains Crown land to development carried out by virtue of a private interest in the land;[19] it seems that the reference to a private interest must be to one created after the grant of planning permission. Listed building consents and conservation area consents also apply only after the land has ceased to be Crown land or a new private interest has been created.[20]

The new Act contains a useful provision enabling the local planning authority to make a tree preservation order in anticipation of the disposal of Crown land. The local planning authority must obtain the consent of the appropriate authority. The order does not require confirmation at this stage; but, on the land ceasing to be Crown land or the grant of a private interest in it, it will take immediate effect as a provisional order, subject to confirmation.[1]

SPECIAL ENFORCEMENT NOTICES

As we have seen, where a person owning a private interest in Crown land carries out unauthorised development, the local planning authority can issue an enforcement notice provided the appropriate

---

14 1990 Act, s. 299; Listed Buildings Act, s. 84.
15 See pp. 272, 273, above.
16 See p. 273, fn 6, above.
17 I e consent to demolish a building in a conservation area.
18 1990 Act, s. 299(1), (2).
19 Ibid, s. 299(3); some additional requirements are imposed by the Crown Land Applications Regs.
20 Listed Buildings Act, s. 84(3).
 1 1990 Act, s. 300; for the effect of a provisional tree preservation order and the procedure for confirmation see ch 13, pp. 232, 233, above.

authority agree.[2] But unauthorised development may be carried out on Crown land when no person is entitled to occupy it by virtue of a private interest; a common example is the stationing of mobile snack bars or refreshment vans on trunk road lay-bys.[3] The Act of 1990 enables the local planning authority with the consent of the appropriate authority to issue a 'special enforcement notice'. Copies of the notice are to be served on the person alleged to have carried out the development (except where, after reasonable inquiry, the local planning authority cannot identify or trace him), on any person occupying the land when the notice is issued and on the appropriate authority. There is a right of appeal to the Secretary of State but only on the grounds that the matters alleged in the notice have not taken place or do not constitute development.[4]

CONTINUANCE OF USES INSTITUTED BY THE CROWN

Since the Crown is not subject to planning legislation, any use of land begun by the Crown can lawfully be continued by a third party such as a purchaser of the land. The Act of 1990 enables a local planning authority and the appropriate authority to enter into an agreement whereby a use of the land instituted by the Crown is to be deemed to have been authorised by a planning permission granted subject to a condition requiring its discontinuance when the Crown ceases that use. The effect is that planning permission will normally be required for the continuance of the use by any one other than the Crown.[5]

Development by local authorities and statutory undertakers

Local authorities and statutory undertakers are subject to planning control and must therefore obtain planning permission for any development which they propose to carry out. But the system of planning control is modified in three special types of case: development by a local planning authority within their own area; development carried out on operational land by a statutory undertaker; development by a local authority or statutory undertaker which requires the authorisation of a government department.

2 See pp. 272, 273, above.
3 Trunk roads are owned by the Department of Transport and are thus Crown land.
4 1990 Act, ss. 294, 295; T & CP (Special Enforcement Notices) Regs 1984 (SI 1984 No 1016).
5 1990 Act, s. 301.

OBTAINING OF PLANNING PERMISSION BY LOCAL PLANNING AUTHORITIES

Section 316 of the Act of 1990 authorises the Secretary of State to make regulations governing the grant of planning permission for (a) development by the local planning authority of land within their area; (b) development by other persons of land owned by the local planning authority. New procedures were introduced in 1976.

Where a local planning authority propose to carry out a development on land within their area, they should (unless the development is permitted by the General Development Order)[6] pass a resolution 'to seek permission for that development'.[7]

Having passed the resolution they must take a number of steps:[8]

(a) they must place a copy of the resolution and plans in the public register of planning applications;

(b) they must give notice to all persons having a 'material interest' in the land;[9]

(c) if any of the land is comprised within an agricultural holding, they must give notice to the tenant;

(d) if the development is 'bad neighbour' development, as specified in article 11 of the General Development Order,[10] they must publish notice in the local press;

(e) if the development would affect the character and appearance of a conservation area, they must publish notice in the local press and display a notice on or near the land;

(f) if the development is a departure from the development plan, they must comply with the Development Plans Direction;[11]

(g) if the authority seeking permission is the county council, they must consult the district council; similarly the district council must consult the county council;

(h) in the case of development affecting a trunk or special road, they must give notice to the Secretary of State.

After all the necessary notices have been served or published, the local planning authority must wait until the expiry of the period allowed for the making of representations. If any representations are received, the authority must of course give them proper consideration. There is apparently no obligation upon the authority to notify the Secretary of State, except in the case of a departure from the

6 For the General Development Order, see generally ch 6, pp. 116 ff, above.
7 General Regs, reg 4(1).
8 Ibid, reg 4(2), (3), (4).
9 I e either the freehold or a lease with at least seven years to run.
10 See ch 7, pp. 131, 132, above.
11 See ch 7, pp. 136, 137, above.

development plan or in the case of development affecting a trunk or special road.[12] Provided the Secretary of State has not called the matter in for his own consideration, the local planning authority may then pass a resolution to carry out the development. This second resolution takes effect as a planning permission deemed to have been granted by the Secretary of State. This deemed planning permission will, however, be personal to the local planning authority and may be implemented only by that authority.[13]

A similar procedure should be followed where the local planning authority wish to obtain planning permission in respect of land which they own but do not propose to develop themselves. Such planning permission may be either an outline or a detailed permission; and, since the development is to be carried out by other persons, the resolution authorising the development may include such conditions as the authority think fit.[14]

These procedures cannot be used to obtain planning permission for work involving the alteration or extension of a listed building.[15]

An authority may wish to arrange for the function of obtaining a deemed planning permission to be exercised by an officer. In that case, a written notice given to the authority by the officer concerned will take the place of a resolution of the authority.[16]

The procedures described above are mandatory. In *Steeples v Derbyshire County Council*[17] the council failed to enter their resolution to seek planning permission on the register; Webster J held that the subsequent purported grant of planning permission was ultra vires and void. In *R v Lambeth Borough Council ex p Sharp*[18] the council proposed to carry out development in a conservation area; notice was published in a local newspaper, but it contained a number of irregularities. Croom-Johnson LJ quashed the subsequent grant of planning permission.

---

12 There is nothing to prevent other persons drawing the Secretary of State's attention to the matter.
13 General Regs, reg 4(5), (6), (7).
14 Ibid, reg 5. The words 'such conditions as the authority think fit' must be read subject to the requirements of the general law: see ch 7, p. 148 and ch 8, pp. 158 ff, above.
15 Ibid, regs 4(1), 5(1). For listed buildings, see ch 13, above.
16 General Regs, reg 6.
17 [1984] 3 All ER 468.
18 (1984) 50 P & CR 284.

DEVELOPMENT BY STATUTORY UNDERTAKERS

For the purposes of the 1990 Act, the expression 'statutory undertaker' means 'persons authorised by any enactment to carry on any railway, light railway, tramway, road transport, water transport, canal, inland navigation, dock, harbour, pier or lighthouse undertaking, or any undertaking for the supply of hydraulic power and a relevant airport operator (within the meaning of Part V of the Airports Act 1986).[19] Public gas suppliers, water and sewerage undertakers, the National River Authority, the Post Office, the Civil Aviation Authority, and the holders of licences under the Electricity Act 1989 are also deemed for certain purposes to be statutory undertakers.[20] A local authority may be a statutory undertaking; e g some local authorities provide public transport services and some are authorised to extend such services beyond their own boundaries.

Statutory undertakers who propose to carry out development must apply to the local planning authority for planning permission, but in relation to the operational land of statutory undertakers, some modifications are made by Part XI of the Act of 1990.

If the application comes before the Secretary of State (either because it is called in under section 77 or on appeal against the decision of the local planning authority) the Secretary of State must act jointly with the Minister responsible for the type of undertaking in question, e g in the case of railways the Secretary of State for Transport.

DEVELOPMENT REQUIRING AUTHORISATION OF A GOVERNMENT DEPARTMENT

In many cases development by a local authority or statutory undertaker will require (apart from planning control) the authorisation of a government department, e g the confirmation of a compulsory purchase order or consent for the borrowing of money. Section 90 of the Act of 1990 enables the government department concerned to direct that planning permission shall be deemed to be granted. In practice, however, local authorities are expected to obtain planning permission by applying in the ordinary way.[1]

19 1990 Act, s. 262(1).
20 Ibid, s. 262(3)–(7).
 1 See this chapter, pp. 277 ff, above.

Minerals

As explained in an earlier chapter, the winning of minerals whether by underground or surface working constitutes development. As a physical operation, however, mineral working differs from other forms of development. In the erection of a building, for instance, the digging of foundations or the laying of bricks are only of value as part of the whole building; in mineral working, however, the removal of each separate load is of value. As Lord Widgery CJ put it,[2] 'each shovelful or each cut by the bulldozer is a separate act of development'. Because of the special characteristics of mineral working, the Secretary of State is authorised to make regulations adapting and modifying the provisions of the Act of 1990 in relation to mineral development.[3] The current regulations were made in 1971 prior to the coming into force of the Act of 1971. The regulations refer therefore to various provisions of the Acts of 1962 and 1968, but they have been kept in force by virtue of provisions in the Acts of 1971 and 1990 and references in the regulations to specific provisions of the Acts of 1962 and 1968 should now be read as references of the corresponding provisions of the Act of 1990.

Another feature which distinguishes mineral working from other kinds of development is the physical damage to the land and the injury to the environment. The general power to impose conditions on the grant of planning permission has not always proved adequate to deal with the problems created by mineral working. As a result several new provisions were added to the Act of 1971 by the Minerals Act; these provisions are now to be found in the Act of 1990.

SPECIAL PROVISIONS RELATING TO MINERAL DEVELOPMENT

Mineral planning authorities   Many of the powers and duties of the local planning authority under the Act of 1990 are exercisable in relation to minerals by the 'mineral planning authority', namely: (1) in a non-metropolitan county, the county planning authority; (2) in a metropolitan county or Greater London, the local planning authority which (except in a national park) is the metropolitan district council or the London borough council.[4]

---

2 *Thomas David (Porthcawl) Ltd v Penybont RDC* [1972] 1 All ER 733; affirmed by the Court of Appeal [1972] 3 All ER 1092, (1972) 24 P & CR 309.
3 1971 Act, s. 264.
4 1990 Act, s. 1(4).

Grant of temporary permission Section 72 of the Act of 1990 provides that, on a grant of planning permission, a condition may be imposed requiring the removal of a building or works or the discontinuance of any use of land at the expiration of a specified period. This provision does not apply to mineral workings, but is replaced by special provisions namely: (a) where the planning permission was granted before 22 February 1982, the development must cease not later than 60 years from that date; (b) in the case of a permission granted after that date, the development must cease (unless some other period is specified) not later than 60 years from the date of the permission.[5]

Duration of planning permission The normal rule is that a grant of planning permission will lapse if development is not commenced within five years. In the case of minerals, the permission will lapse if development is not commenced within ten years; for this purpose development is to be taken as having commenced on the earliest date on which any of the mining operations to which the planning permission relates began to be carried out.[6]

Aftercare conditions Ever since the modern system of planning control was introduced in 1948, it has been standard practice of local planning authorities when granting permission for mineral workings to impose conditions relating to the restoration of the site after the minerals have been extracted. Since 1982 the mineral planning authority has had further powers; where planning permission is granted subject to a restoration condition, the authority may also impose an 'aftercare condition'. This is a condition requiring that such steps be taken as may be necessary to bring the land to the required standard for whichever of the following uses is specified in the condition: (1) use for agriculture, (2) use for forestry, (3) use for amenity. The condition may also specify an aftercare period during which the required steps are to be taken.[7]

Reviews of mineral workings It is now the duty of every mineral planning authority to carry out periodical reviews of every site in their area in which operations for the winning and working of minerals are being carried out, or have been carried out during the previous five years, or are authorised by planning permission but have not yet begun.[8] The essence of such reviews is that the mineral planning

5 1990 Act, Sch 5, para 1.
6 Minerals Regs, regs 6, 7.
7 1990 Act, Sch 5, para 2.
8 Ibid, s. 105.

authority should consider whether it would be appropriate to make a discontinuance order or a prohibition order, or a suspension order.

Discontinuance orders   Section 102 of the Act of 1990 enables a local planning authority to make a 'discontinuance order' in respect of any use of land i e an order requiring a use of land to be discontinued, or imposing conditions on the continuance of the use, or requiring the removal or alteration of buildings etc.[9] In relation to minerals, section 102 enables the mineral planning authority to make an order revoking a planning permission for mineral workings, or modifying it by imposing new conditions, and these conditions may specifically include a restoration condition and an aftercare condition.[10] A discontinuance order will not take effect unless and until confirmed by the Secretary of State; there are the usual procedures for the making and hearing of objections.[11]

Prohibition orders   Where it appears to the mineral planning authority that mineral working has permanently ceased, they may make a prohibition order. The authority may assume that mineral working has permanently ceased only (1) where there has been no substantial working on the site of which the land forms part for at least five years; and (2) it appears on the available evidence that a resumption is unlikely. The order may prohibit the resumption of working and may impose any of the following requirements:
(a) removal of plant or machinery;
(b) to take specified steps for removing or alleviating injury to amenity;
(c) compliance with the conditions of the original planning permission;
(d) a restoration condition and an aftercare condition.
   The order does not take effect unless and until confirmed by the Secretary of State; there are the usual procedures for the making and hearing of objections.[12]

Suspension orders   Where it appears to the mineral planning authority that the winning and working of minerals has been temporarily suspended, they may make a suspension order; the authority may assume that working has been suspended only (a) where there has been no substantial working on the land of which the site forms part for at

9 See ch 9, p. 180.
10 1990 Act, Sch 9, paras 1, 2.
11 Ibid, s. 103. See ch 9, pp. 181, 182, above.
12 Ibid, Sch 9, paras 3, 4.

least 12 months, but (b) it appears likely on the available evidence that working will be resumed. The order will require that steps be taken for the protection of the environment. These steps may be for the purpose of:

(1) preserving the amenities of the area during the period of suspension;
(2) protecting that area from damage during that period; or
(3) preventing any deterioration in the condition of the land during that period.[13]

Provision is made for supplementary suspension orders. These may be made either for the purpose of imposing further requirements for the protection of the environment or revoking the suspension order or any previous supplementary order.[14]

A suspension order or supplementary suspension order will not take effect unless confirmed by the Secretary of State; opportunity must be given for objections and the Secretary of State will if need be hold a public local inquiry or other hearing. A supplementary suspension order which merely revokes the suspension order or a previous supplementary order does not require confirmation.[15] Suspension orders and supplementary orders must be registered as land charges.[16]

A suspension order does not prohibit a resumption of mineral working but a person intending to recommence must give notice to the mineral planning authority.[17]

It will be the duty of the mineral planning authority to review suspension orders and supplementary suspension orders every five years.[18]

Enforcement notices An enforcement notice may require the demolition or alteration of any unauthorised buildings or works or the discontinuance of any use of land.[19] The Minerals Regulations treat mineral development as a use for this purpose, and also for the purposes of what is now section 179 of the Act of 1990 so that the mineral operator can be prosecuted if he fails to comply with the enforcement notice.[20] Where mining operations are carried out without planning permission, the enforcement notice must be served

---

13 1990 Act, Sch 9, para 5.
14 Ibid, Sch 9, para 6.
15 Ibid, Sch 9, para 7.
16 Ibid, Sch 9, para 8.
17 Ibid, Sch 9, para 10.
18 Ibid, Sch 9, para 9.
19 See ch 10, above.
20 Minerals Regs, reg 3.

within four years of the development being carried out.[1] But in the event of non-compliance with a condition, the Regulations provide that an enforcement notice may be served at any time within four years *after the non-compliance has come to the knowledge of the local planning authority.*[2]

The Minerals Regulations do not apply to the working of minerals vested in the British Coal Corporation nor to the winning and working of minerals in connection with agriculture.[3] There may therefore be difficulty in imposing time limits upon these forms of mineral working and in serving enforcement notices.

WORKING RIGHTS BY ORDER OF THE HIGH COURT

The power to obtain working rights to facilitate mineral development has existed, quite independently of planning legislation, since 1923. In the first place it has been found that minerals might be left unworked because the land was or had been copyhold land or was subject to a lease or some restriction, or because the minerals were owned in such small parcels that they could not be conveniently worked. Secondly, even where these difficulties did not apply, a mineral operator might require some ancillary working right such as the right to let down the surface, to construct airways and shafts, or to obtain a water supply.

The Mines (Working Facilities and Support) Act 1966 (replacing earlier legislation) provides machinery by which such working rights can be obtained. The applicant, wishing to search for or work minerals, must first approach the Department of Energy who will if satisfied that there is a prima facie case refer it to the High Court.[4]

Right to work minerals　The Act of 1966 enables the High Court to make an order granting to the applicant the right to work minerals provided:
(a) that the applicant has an interest in the minerals or, if the minerals are owned in small parcels, in minerals adjacent to them;
(b) that there is a danger for certain reasons of the minerals being left permanently unworked;

1　1990 Act, s. 172(4). Since 'each shovelful or each cut by the bulldozer is a separate act of development', the four-year rule does little more than protect the mineral operator from any liability to restore the land; it certainly does not prevent the service of an enforcement notice to restrain further unauthorised working: *Thomas David (Porthcawl) Ltd v Penybont RDC*, above.
2　Minerals Regs, reg 4.
3　1990 Act, s. 315(4).
4　Originally the Railway and Canal Commission.

(c) that it is not reasonably practicable to obtain the necessary rights by private negotiation;

(d) that it is expedient in the national interest that the rights should be granted.

The working of minerals may also be impeded by restrictions in a mining lease or other documents of title. Under the Act of 1966, as originally enacted, the court might grant the right to work certain specified minerals free from these restrictions if this result could not be achieved by private negotiation and would be in the national interest. The Mines (Working Facilities and Support) Act 1974 extends this provision to all minerals other than coal.

Ancillary rights   The Act of 1966 also enables the High Court to make an order for the grant of ancillary rights provided conditions (c) and (d) are satisfied.

Section 265 of the Act of 1971 (re-enacting provisions in the Acts of 1947 and 1962) authorised the Secretary of State to make regulations to facilitate the making of orders conferring the right to work minerals where the land was allocated for mineral working in the development plan. The regulations provided that where the development plan allocated any land for mineral working and there was danger for any reason that the minerals would be left unworked, the court might grant the necessary working rights; and for this purpose it was to be assumed that the working of the minerals would be in the national interest.

Section 265 of the Act of 1971 has now been repealed by the Mines (Working Facilities and Support) Act 1974. It follows that the development plan can no longer be relied on as conclusive evidence that the working of the minerals would be in the national interest.

Chapter 16

Highways and planning

The general law of highways is a subject of some complexity and, in any event, is outside the scope of this book. But some aspects of planning law are concerned with highways and in order to understand these it will be helpful to begin with a brief general account of the law of highways.

What is a highway?

A highway is usually defined as land whether made or unmade, over which all Her Majesty's subjects have the right to pass and to repass. The fact that all members of the public have this right of passage distinguishes a highway from various private rights of way (such as easements) and rights of way for the benefit of a limited section of the public (such as a churchway to enable the inhabitants of a village to go to and from church).

A highway is not necessarily open to vehicles. At common law highways may be either:

(a) footpaths;
(b) bridleways over which there is also the right to ride or lead a horse;
(c) drift-ways over which there is in addition the right to drive animals; and
(d) carriageways over which in addition to all the above there is the right to drive vehicles.

The right of the public to use a carriageway for foot passage and for horses and other animals may be restricted on motorways and trunk roads by order of the Secretary of State under legislation now embodied in the Highways Act 1980. This Act also recognises a further category of highway – namely a cycle track.[1]

---

1 Highways Act 1980, s. 329(1).

CREATION OF HIGHWAYS

At common law the normal method of creating a highway is by 'dedication and acceptance'; that is, the owner of the land dedicates it as a highway and the public accept it. Dedication and acceptance may be formal but are often implied as where a landowner permits the public to use a road for a long period without counter-measures[2] to rebut the presumption that he intends dedication; or where an estate developer lays out a road communicating at both ends with existing highways.

Nowadays many highways are created by public authorities under statutory authority; for example, where the Minister of Transport builds a trunk road or a local authority lays out roads as part of a housing estate.

Highways created before 1835 were automatically 'repairable by the inhabitants at large'; that is, at the public expense. With the rapid growth of population and towns in the nineteenth century, this could have imposed a serious burden on the public authorities who had no control over the creation of highways. The Highway Act 1835, made no change in the law relating to the creation of highways but provided that no new highway should become repairable by the inhabitants at large unless it was made up to the satisfaction of the public surveyor of highways. Then, in 1875 came the first of the 'private street works codes'.

Section 150 of the Public Health Act 1875 enabled any urban authority to require the owners of properties adjoining any unadopted highway or private street to carry out specified works for making up, sewering and lighting the street; if any frontager failed to do so, the authority might carry out the work at his expense. This was followed by the Private Street Works Act 1892, under which the authority gave each owner notice of their intention to do the work and to charge him for it in proportion to the length of his frontage.[3]

Section 150 of the Act of 1875 continued in force in some areas until 1974. The code introduced by the Act of 1892 is now the standard code for all areas: the relevant provisions are now contained in Part XI of the Highways Act 1980.

---

2 For example, by displaying a notice or by periodically closing gates.
3 The authority may modify this to take account of the 'degree of benefit' derived by any particular owner.

THE NATIONAL HIGHWAY SYSTEM

Prior to 1936, all roads in Great Britain were the responsibility of the local authorities. The Minister of Transport was empowered to make grants to local authorities for the construction and maintenance of highways, but he had no power to undertake construction and maintenance. In 1936 the first Trunk Roads Act was passed. It specified a number of major roads which were henceforth to be trunk roads and vested them in the Minister of Transport as highway authority; more roads were declared to be trunk roads under an Act of 1946. In addition, the Minister of Transport was empowered to direct that any existing road should be a trunk road and he was given power to construct new trunk roads. He might also direct that any existing trunk road should cease to be a trunk road.

The next step in the creation of a national highway system was the passing of the Special Roads Act 1949. This enabled highway authorities in pursuance of schemes, either made by the Minister of Transport as a highway authority or made by the local highway authority with the approval of the Minister of Transport, to provide roads restricted to use by particular classes of traffic only. It is in pursuance of these powers that the motorways have been constructed.

The greater part of the Trunk Road Acts and of the Special Roads Act has been replaced by the Highways Act 1980, but there is no material change in the earlier provisions.

The siting of trunk roads and special roads is of fundamental importance to the planning of town and countryside, and it is not surprising that the Secretary for Transport is required to give consideration to 'the requirements of local and national planning including agriculture'.[4]

When the Secretary for Transport proposes to make a trunk road order or a scheme for a special road, he must publish notice in the *London Gazette* and in local newspapers and he must allow time for objections to be lodged. If there are any objections, the Secretary for Transport must (except in certain specified circumstances) cause a public local inquiry to be held. Thereafter, he will decide whether to make the order or scheme, either in its original form or with modifications.[5]

The fact remains, however, that in preparing development plans the local planning authority will have little or no control over the siting of trunk and special roads. The Act of 1990 provides that neither the Secretary of State nor the local planning authority shall be obliged

4 Highways Act 1980, ss. 10(2), 16(8).
5 Ibid, Sch 1.

to consider representations or objections which are in substance representations and objections with respect to orders and schemes for trunk and special roads.[6]

LOCAL HIGHWAYS

Highways, other than trunk roads and special roads vested in the Secretary for Transport, are the responsibility of the local highway authorities. Since 1 April 1974, the local highway authority is the county council. District councils, however, may exercise certain functions in respect of footpaths, bridleways and urban roads which are neither trunk roads nor classified roads; certain powers are also given to parish councils.

Most applications for planning permission will, however, be determined by the district council; since many applications for planning permission involve highway considerations, the district council may need to consult the Secretary of State for Transport or the county council as highway authority, and in some cases the Secretary of State for Transport may issue directions to the district council.[7] The county council no longer has the power to issue directions.

Where land is defined in a development plan[8] as the site of a new road, or as being for a road-widening, the highway authority must purchase the land they actually require for the construction or widening of the road. At the same time, the new or widened road may confer considerable benefits on adjoining landowners. Section 232 of the Highways Act 1980 enables the authority, in certain circumstances, to charge the expense of construction (as distinct from the cost of the land) to the owners of adjoining property. The circumstances are:

(a) that the land has been defined in the development plan as the site of a new road, or as being required for the widening of a road of less than byelaw width; and

(b) it must have been designated in the development plan as land to which section 232 of the Highways Act 1980, is to apply.

When the development plan has been confirmed the appropriate council may make an order declaring the land (including in the case of a street widening, the existing street) to be a 'private street'. This has the effect of bringing into operation the private street works code for that district (that is, either the code of 1875, the code of 1892 or any local enactments) together with certain modifications made by

6 1990 Act, ss. 24, 49.
7 GDO, arts 15, 18.
8 See ch 4, pp. 72, 73, above.

the Construction and Improvement of Private Streets Regulations. When the street has been made up or widened to the satisfaction of the authority, it becomes a highway maintainable at the public expense.[9]

Stopping up and diversion of highways

The common law rule is 'once a highway, always a highway'. The effect is that in common law there is no power whatever to stop up or divert an existing highway. There are, however, various statutory powers, some of which specifically relate to the requirements of good planning.

STOPPING UP BY THE SECRETARY OF STATE

Under section 247 of the Act of 1990, the Secretary of State may make an order to stop up or divert a highway if it is necessary to do so in order to enable development to be carried out in accordance with a grant of planning permission or by a government department.

The order may require the provision of an alternative highway or the improvement of an existing highway, and for this purpose the Secretary of State or a local highway authority may compulsorily acquire the necessary land. The order may also require any other authority or person to pay or contribute towards (a) the cost of any works required by the order, (b) the repayment of any compensation paid by the highway authority under the Restriction of Ribbon Development Act 1935, in respect of the highway to be stopped up or diverted. The persons likely to be charged in this way are, of course, the persons responsible for the development to be assisted by the stopping up or diversion. Thereafter, however, the new or improved highway may become maintainable at the public expense.

Under section 251, the Secretary of State may make an order to stop up any public right of way over land held for planning purposes by a local authority (not necessarily the local planning authority); he must be satisfied that an alternative right of way has been or will be provided, or that an alternative right of way is unnecessary.

The procedure for orders by the Secretary of State under section 247 or 251 is prescribed by section 252. The Secretary of State must publish notice of the proposed order in the *London Gazette* and the local

9 Town and Country Planning (Construction and Improvement of Private Streets) Regs 1951 (SI 1951 No 2224), reg 10.

press, and a copy of the notice must be prominently displayed at each end of the stretch of highway which is to be stopped up or diverted. Time must be allowed for objections; if objections are received from any local authority, statutory undertaker or from any person apparently affected by the order, the Secretary of State must hold a public inquiry unless in the special circumstances an inquiry is unnecessary. Thereafter the Secretary of State will decide whether or not to make the order either in its original form or subject to modifications. If the order requires any person to pay or contribute towards the cost of a new or improved highway or to repay compensation paid on an earlier occasion, that person may require the order to be subject to special parliamentary procedure.

In the case of mineral development, the order may provide for the stopping up or diversion for a limited period, after which the original highway is to be restored.[10]

At one time no steps could be taken until planning permission had actually been granted. Now, however, the Secretary of State may in certain cases (eg where there is an appeal in connection with the application for planning permission) make the draft order before the actual grant of planning permission. This enables the two matters to be dealt with concurrently and thus save possibly many months of delay; but the Secretary of State cannot make the final order until planning permission has been granted.[11]

STOPPING-UP AND OTHER ACTION BY LOCAL AUTHORITIES

Under section 257 of the Act of 1990 a footpath or bridleway may be stopped up or diverted by order of the local planning authority for the purpose of enabling development to be carried out in accordance with a grant of planning permission or by a government department.

Section 258 enables a local authority (not necessarily the planning authority) to make an order stopping up any footpath or bridleway over land held by them for planning purposes; the authority must be satisfied that an alternative right of way has been or will be provided, or that an alternative right of way is unnecessary.

Before making an order under either of these sections, the authority concerned must publish a notice stating the effect of the order and indicating the time and manner in which representations and objections may be made. If there are no representations or objections, the

10 1990 Act, s. 261.
11 Ibid, s. 253.

authority may themselves confirm the order. Otherwise, the order must be submitted to the Secretary of State who will hold a public local inquiry or other hearing before deciding whether or not to confirm the order.[12]

Local planning authorities also have powers to convert highways used by vehicles into footpaths. These powers may be used where the local planning authority have adopted a proposal for improving the amenity of part of their area,[13] eg convert a highway into a pedestrian precinct; having taken this preliminary step, the authority apply to the Secretary of State for an order.[14] Thereafter the procedure is the same as for orders by the Secretary of State for the stopping up or diversion of a highway.[15] The local planning authority are liable in compensation for injurious affection to any person having lawful access to the highway.[16]

---

12 1990 Act, s. 259; Sch 14.
13 Ibid, s. 249(1). This power cannot be used over a trunk road or a road classified as a principal road.
14 Ibid, s. 249(2).
15 See pp. 290, 291, above.
16 1990 Act, s. 250. Injurious affection can be mitigated by exercise of the Secretary of State's power to authorise the use of the footpath or bridleway by specified vehicles: ibid, s. 249(3).

Chapter 17

The conduct of a planning inquiry

The powers and duties of planning authorities cover a very wide field, but they can conveniently be classified under three main heads: (i) the making of schemes of various kinds (including the development plan); (ii) giving a decision on applications put forward by landowners or developers; (iii) enforcement notices.

Where a planning authority (whether the local planning authority or the Secretary of State) make a scheme, the persons likely to be affected by it have the right to make objections or representations; any person putting forward an objection or representation will usually have the right to be heard at a public local inquiry or at least a private hearing by a person appointed for the purpose, that is, an inspector. There is an exception to this rule in the case of structure plans where the Secretary of State will hold an 'examination in public' at which no one will have any statutory right to be heard.

Where the local planning authority give a decision on an application, the applicant has the right to appeal to the Secretary of State, who must consider the appeal unless it is clear that the local planning authority could not in law have given any other decision: the applicant always has the right to make representations to the Secretary of State and usually has the right to be heard by a person appointed by the Secretary of State. If the application has been referred to the Secretary of State for decision – for instance under section 77 of the Act of 1990 – the applicant and the local planning authority always have the right to make representations before the Secretary of State gives his decision and usually the right to ask for a hearing.

Where an enforcement notice or listed building enforcement notice has been issued, any person having an interest in the land or building to which it relates has the right to appeal to the Secretary of State; if there is an appeal both the appellant and the local planning authority have the right to ask for a hearing.

What form a hearing shall take is decided by the Secretary of State, but usually it is a public local inquiry. At a public local inquiry, the inspector has power to require evidence on oath, to subpoena witnesses and to require the production of documents;[1] these powers are not available at a hearing.

The great majority of public local inquiries and hearings relate to appeals against planning decisions, and appeals against enforcement notices. Considerable importance also attaches to inquiries into development plans and major highway schemes. We will consider each of these in turn.

Appeals against planning decisions

PRELIMINARY

As we have seen, the great majority of appeals against planning decisions will now be determined by the inspector;[2] in such cases the Determination by Inspectors Rules apply. Where the decision is reserved to the Secretary of State, the Inquiries Procedure Rules apply. The procedure is similar in either case up to the close of the inquiry or hearing.

The current Rules in each case were made in 1988, and make some important changes to the pre-inquiry procedure: the inspector may hold a pre-inquiry meeting in order to facilitate the efficient running of the inquiry itself; the appellant must now in all cases furnish a written statement of case, and third parties may be required to do so, and a timetable is laid down for the successive steps in the procedure. The timetable is based on the 'relevant date', that is, the date of the written notice informing the local planning authority that an inquiry is to be held.

The local planning authority must send a written statement of their case (a) to the appellant, and (b) to every person who has made representations to the Secretary of State under section 66 of the Act of 1990;[3] where the Determination by Inspectors Rules apply, this must be done not later than six weeks from the relevant date. Where the Inquiries Procedure Rules apply, the statement must be furnished within six weeks of the relevant date unless a pre-inquiry meeting is held, in which case the statement must be furnished within four weeks of the conclusion of that meeting.[4]

The local authority's statement of their case is to deal with four matters:[5]

1 Local Government Act 1972, s. 250(2)–(5) applied by 1990 Act, s. 320.
2 See ch 7, pp. 152, 153, above.
3 See ch 7, pp. 132, 133, above.
4 Inquiries Procedure Rules, r. 6; Determination by Inspectors Rules, r. 6.
5 Ibid.

(1) It must contain a statement of the submissions which they propose to put forward at the inquiry.
(2) It must include a list of all the documents (including maps and plans) to which they intend to refer at the inquiry; and it must be indicated where and when these documents can be inspected and copied.
(3) It must mention any relevant direction given by the Secretary of State and must include a copy of the direction and the reason given for its making.
(4) It must include any expressions of views given by any government department or other local authority that planning permission should be refused or if granted subject only to conditions.

The appellant must now submit his written statement of case not later than nine weeks from the relevant date, except where a pre-inquiry meeting is held under the Inquiry Procedure Rules in which must be submitted within four weeks. The Secretary of State may require any person who has notified an intention to appear at the inquiry to serve a statement of case.[6]

Any member of the public has the right to inspect the statements of case.[7]

The inspector may permit any person[8] to add to or alter his statement of case at the inquiry, but he must allow every other party adequate opportunity to consider any fresh matter or document and for this purpose he may adjourn the inquiry.[9]

The new Rules have introduced an important new requirement about the giving of evidence. A party who intends to give or call evidence by reading a written statement must now send a copy of that statement to the inspector at least three weeks before the date of the inquiry,[10] and the inspector may require a written summary of it.[11]

PROCEDURE AT THE INQUIRY

The procedure at a public local inquiry into an appeal against a planning decision is as follows:

(1) The inspector opens the proceedings by stating the purpose of the inquiry. The appellant and the local planning authority then

---

6 Inquiries Procedure Rules, rr 6(3), (13); Determination by Inspectors Rules, rr 6(3), 14.
7 Inquiries Procedure Rules, r. 6(9); Determination by Inspectors Rules, r. 6(9).
8 'Person' includes the local planning authority.
9 Inquiries Procedure Rules, r. 14(8); Determination by Inspectors Rules, r. 15(8).
10 Or the date on which the evidence is due to be given, if fixed at a pre-inquiry meeting.
11 Inquiries Procedure Rules, r. 13; Determination by Inspectors Rules, r. 14.

'enter their appearance': that is, the advocate for each party states his name and indicates what witnesses he proposes to call. The inspector then asks if any other interested parties wish to be heard.

(2) Unless the inspector directs otherwise,[12] the appellant 'opens'. The appellant's advocate makes an opening speech in which he will summarise the history of the case to date, the more important facts on which he intends to rely and the arguments in favour of the appeal being allowed.

(3) The appellant's advocate then calls his witnesses. The inspector has the power to require evidence to be given on oath, but this is rarely done at an inquiry of this sort. The rules of evidence are less formal than in a court of law; although admissible as a matter of law in planning inquiries,[13] hearsay evidence is unsatisfactory and may well be disregarded by the inspector. The evidence may be given as in a court of law by question or answer; but, what would not be allowed in a court of law, it may be given instead by the witness reading his proof of evidence. The matters on which evidence may be required are discussed later in this chapter. Each witness may expect to be cross-examined by the advocate for the local planning authority and by any person who has made representations under section 66 or section 79(4) of the Act of 1990;[14] the inspector has a discretion to allow other interested persons to ask questions of the witness. The advocate for the appellant will then re-examine his witness. Questions may also be asked by the inspector; sometimes the inspector reserves his questions until after re-examination, but it is more appropriate for such questions to be put prior to re-examination.

(4) It is also permissible to put in letters and other documents supporting the appellant's case, but it should be remembered that such documents (unless agreed by the local planning authority) are not so impressive as oral evidence by a witness which is open to cross-examination.

(5) The advocate for the local planning authority then calls his witnesses who will, of course, be subject to cross-examination and to questions from the inspector. After calling his witnesses he makes his speech on behalf of the authority.

(6) Persons who have made representations under section 66 or section 79(4) of the Act of 1990[15] then have the right to state their case and the inspector may allow other interested persons to make

12 Inquiries Procedure Rules, r. 10(2); Determination by Inspectors Rules, r. 12(2).
13 *T A Miller v Minister of Housing and Local Government* [1968] 2 All ER 633.
14 See ch 7, pp. 132, 133, 152, above.
15 See fn 14, above.

statements. This may be done by a lawyer or professional representative or by the interested persons themselves.

(7) The advocate for the appellant then makes his final speech.

(8) The inspector closes the inquiry and inspects the site in the company of representatives of the appellant and the local planning authority.

HEARINGS

The procedure at a hearing is the same as at a public local inquiry except that members of the public will not normally be present, or if present, will not be permitted to take part in the proceedings.

THE SECRETARY OF STATE'S DECISION

Although the great majority of appeals will now be determined by the inspector, it will be useful to consider first the procedure where the decision is reserved to the Secretary of State.

The inspector must in his report set out specific findings of fact and his recommendations; he is free not to make a recommendation, but in that case he must give his reason for not doing so.[16] In addition, the inspector invariably includes in his report a paragraph headed 'Conclusions'; these are the opinions which the inspector has drawn from his findings of fact, and it is upon these conclusions that his recommendation will be based.

The inspector's duty to record findings of fact was considered in *Continental Sprays Ltd v Minister of Housing and Local Government*.[17] The appellants contended that the inspector should make findings on all the principal material issues of fact arising from the evidence given at the inquiry. Without deciding whether the inspector should have done so, Megaw J held that the court was not entitled to review the evidence and decide what were the principal material issues of fact arising therefrom.

This decision was followed by Willis J in *William Boyer & Sons Ltd v Minister of Housing and Local Government*[18] and again in *W J Simms, Sons and Cooke Ltd v Minister of Housing and Local Government*.[19]

The Secretary of State may disagree with the inspector on a finding

---

16 Inquiries Procedure Rules, r. 16(1).
17 (1968) 19 P & CR 774.
18 (1968) 20 P & CR 176.
19 (1969) 210 Estates Gazette 705. This was a case arising out of the Minister's decision on a development plan amendment and related compulsory purchase orders.

of fact; he may receive some new evidence (including expert opinion on a matter of fact); or he may take into consideration issues of fact not raised at the inquiry. If, in any of these circumstances, he is minded to disagree with the inspector's recommendation he must inform the appellant, the local planning authority and all persons who have made representations under section 66 or 79(4) of the Act of 1990.[20] Any of these persons then has 21 days in which to make either written representations or to require the inquiry to be re-opened.[1] The Secretary of State is not obliged to notify the parties and give them the opportunity of making further representations where he disagrees with the inspector's conclusions; but he should consider whether what the inspector has described as a conclusion is really a finding of fact.[2]

The Secretary of State is to notify his decision with his reasons to the appellant, the local planning authority, the persons who made representations under section 66 or 79(4) of the Act of 1990[3] and any other person who attended the inquiry and asked to be notified. The Secretary of State usually sends a copy of the inspector's report with his decision letter; if he does not do so, any of these persons may ask for a copy.[4] Instead of formally setting out his reasons, the Secretary of State may adopt the inspector's conclusions. This is an acceptable procedure; but, where the inspector's conclusions were so worded as to be meaningless, the court held that the Secretary of State had failed to give any reasons and quashed his decision.[5]

THE INSPECTOR'S DECISION

Where the inspector himself gives the decision, there will be no report to the Secretary of State and the inspector is under no statutory obligation to record findings of fact. However, if he proposes to take into account new evidence (including expert opinion on a matter of fact) or any new issue of fact, he must not come to a decision without first notifying the appellant, the local planning authority and the persons who made representations under section 66 or 79(4) of the

20 See fn 14, above.
 1 Inquires Procedure Rules, r. 16(3).
 2 *Lord Luke of Pavenham v Minister of Housing and Local Government* [1968] 1 QB 172, [1967] 2 All ER 1066, overruling the decision of Lawton J at first instance.
 3 See fn 14, above.
 4 Inquiries Procedure Rules, r. 17.
 5 *Givaudon & Co Ltd v Minister of Housing and Local Government* [1966] 3 All ER 696.

Act of 1990.[6] Any of these persons then has 21 days in which to make further representations or to ask for the inquiry to be re-opened.

The inspector will notify his decision in the same manner as the Secretary of State.[7] The decision letter must enable the appellant to understand upon what grounds the appeal had been decided and be in sufficient detail to enable him to know what conclusions the inspector had reached on the principal issues in controversy.[8]

APPEAL BY WRITTEN REPRESENTATIONS

Most planning appeals are nowadays dealt with by way of written representations and other documents. Since 1987 the procedure for written representations has been governed by statutory regulations,[9] the effect of which may be briefly summarised as follows:

(1) Where the appellant informs the Secretary of State that he wishes the appeal to be dealt with in this way, he should set out his case in full in his notice of appeal.

(2) On receipt of the notice of appeal, the Secretary of State will notify the appellant and the local planning authority of the starting date.

(3) On receiving notification of the appeal, the local planning authority are required to give written notice to any authority or person who was notified of or consulted about the original application for planning permission together with any other persons who made representations about it.

(4) The local planning authority will pass on to the Secretary of State any representations made by those parties about the original application other than any submitted in confidence. Those parties then have 28 days in which to tell the Secretary of State to disregard those representations and/or to make further representations.

(5) The local planning authority must within 14 days send to the Secretary of State their answers to a questionnaire issued by him; they must at the same time send to the appellant a copy of the completed questionnaire and all other documents which they have submitted to the Secretary of State.

---

6 Determination by Inspectors Rules, r. 17(2). And see fn 14, above.

7 Ibid, r. 18.

8 *Ellis v Secretary of State for the Environment* (1974) 31 P & CR 130; *Hope v Secretary of State for the Environment* [1975] JPL 731; *Bosies Ltd v Secretary of State for the Environment* (1983) Times, 10 May.

9 T & CP (Appeal) (Written Representations Procedure) Regs 1987 (SI 1987 No 70).

(6) The authority may choose to treat the above-mentioned documents as their representations on the appeal, or they may submit further representations within 28 days of the starting date.

(7) The appellant then has a further 17 days in which to submit further representations by way of reply to the representations of the local planning authority.

This procedure is based on a very tight timetable, although the Secretary of State has power to grant extensions of time. It is clearly prudent for the appellant to begin preparation of his case well before the last date for giving notice of appeal, because he is required to set out his case in his notice of appeal.

Finally, it should perhaps be emphasised that, even if the appellant is willing to proceed by written representations, the local planning authority may insist on a hearing and at any stage the Secretary of State may decide to hold an inquiry or other hearing.

Listed building consent and conservation area consent appeals

The procedure at public inquiries into these types of appeal[10] is governed by the Inquiries Procedure Rules and the Determination by Inspectors Rules described earlier in this chapter.

Enforcement notice etc inquiries

The procedure at an inquiry into an appeal against an enforcement notice is very similar to that at an inquiry into an appeal against a planning decision. But the evidence is often on oath; and, because there may be some difficult questions of law of a kind which do not usually arise at an inquiry into an appeal against a planning decision, the inspector sometimes sits with a legal assessor.

There are now inquiries procedure rules relating to appeals under section 174 against enforcement notices, appeals under section 195 in connection with certificates of established use and appeals under section 39 of the Listed Buildings Act against listed building enforcement notices.[11] These rules are similar in many respects to the inquiries procedure rules for appeals against planning decisions, as described earlier in this chapter;[12] it is unnecessary to go into them in detail

10 See ch 14, pp. 256, 268, above.
11 See the T & CP (Enforcement) (Inquiries Procedure) Rules 1981 (SI 1981 No 1743).
12 See pp. 294 ff.

again but in practice reference should always be made to the actual rules.[13]

Structure and local plan inquiries

It was explained in an earlier chapter that, when a structure plan proposal is submitted to the Secretary of State, he will hold an 'examination in public' into selected issues, and he will decide whom to invite to appear at the examination; the procedure is governed by a code of practice issued by the Secretary of State.[14] The procedure for considering objections to the new unitary plans depends on whether all or any part of the plan has been called in by the Secretary of State.[15]

As regards local plans, the local planning authority will be under a duty to hold a public local inquiry for the purpose of considering objections which have been duly submitted.[16] The objectors will have the right to appear at this inquiry.

Although the inquiry is for the purpose of considering objections, it would be appropriate for the local planning authority to 'open'. That is to say, the advocate for the local planning authority would make an opening speech and call evidence in support of the plan generally. There may be some cross-examination on general issues of the authority's witnesses at this stage. The objectors would then present their respective cases. If there are many objections, a programme might be arranged so that each objector may know when his case will be heard. At the public inquiries into the older type of development plan, the manner in which an objection was heard was often arranged between the planning authority and the objector; in some cases the objector opened, but in others the local planning authority opened. Whatever arrangements are made, the objector needs to support his case by proper evidence and the local planning authority will probably call evidence with regard to the particular objection. Otherwise, it may be expected that the inquiry will follow much the same lines as an inquiry into a planning appeal.

In exceptional cases, the Secretary of State may call in a local plan for consideration by himself. It follows that the Secretary of State may hold a public inquiry instead of the local planning authority doing

---

13 The Secretary of State is empowered to delegate the decision on these appeals to the inspector, but so far has not made regulations for that purpose.
14 See ch 4, p. 59, above.
15 See ch 4, pp. 70 ff, above.
16 1990 Act, s. 42. And see ch 4, pp. 66 ff, above.

so. A public inquiry held on behalf of the Secretary of State is likely to follow the pattern described above.

Highways inquiries

A public inquiry must be held where there are objections to highway schemes put forward by the Secretary of State or by the local highway authority under the Highways Act 1980. These highway schemes will, of course, include proposals for new motorways and trunk roads. Some public inquiries have engendered a good deal of controversy and some have been disrupted by angry objectors.

Since 1976 there have been Highways Procedure Rules;[17] they apply to inquiries into highway schemes whether proposed by the Secretary for Transport or by the local highway authority.

The rules give procedural rights to certain categories of objector described in the rules as 'statutory objectors'. They include objectors who own or occupy land which may be required for the carrying out of the scheme and objectors who are likely to be entitled to claim compensation under Part I of the Land Compensation Act 1973 in respect of the use of the new highway.[18]

Where the scheme is put forward by the Secretary for Transport himself, he must not later than 28 days before the inquiry is held send a statement of his case to each statutory objector together with a list of documents, maps and plans which are to be referred to at the inquiry.[19] If he intends to rely on the views of any other government department, a statement of those views must be included in the rule 5 statement.[20]

The Secretary for Transport must make available a representative to give evidence at the inquiry in elucidation of the rule 5 statement; and, if any other government department is supporting the scheme, they must also provide a representative to give evidence. These departmental representatives are to be subject to cross-examination except that the inspector is to disallow any question which he considers is 'directed to the merits of government policy'.[1] It seems that the need for a particular motorway or trunk road is a matter of government policy.[2]

---

17 SI 1976 No 721.
18 Highways Procedure Rules, r. 3(1).
19 Ibid, r. 5(1), (3).
20 Ibid, r. 5(2).
 1 Ibid, rr. 6 and 7.
 2 *Bushell v Secretary of State for the Environment* [1981] AC 75, [1980] 2 All ER 608.

There are somewhat similar rules for inquiries into schemes put forward by local highway authorities.

Preparing the evidence

The outcome of a planning inquiry may well depend on the care with which the evidence is prepared; for this reason, the preparation of the evidence should not be left to the last moment. Evidence should be given on the following matters:

(a) any fact which may possibly be disputed by the other side;
(b) any questions of technical or expert opinion which may assist the inspector and/or the Secretary of State in coming to a conclusion;
(c) any intentions which the landowner or developer may have as to the future use or development of the land.

We will consider each of these in turn.

EVIDENCE OF FACTS

Any facts which may be disputed by the other side should be proved by proper evidence. On the other hand, there is no need for witnesses to give evidence of facts which have already been agreed by the other side, and it is quite unnecessary for the appellant's surveyor and for the planning officer to include in their evidence details of the application and of the planning authority's grounds of refusal; the inspector has been supplied with copies of these documents before the inquiry and in a properly conducted case they will have been sufficiently referred to by the appellant's advocate in his opening speech.

Where evidence of facts is given, care should be taken to see that it is both reliable and pertinent. For instance, the local planning authority may allege that the extension of the appellant's factory would attract a great number of vehicles and in support of this may give evidence of the number of vehicles parked on a certain day in the road outside the existing premises; the figure given by the planning officer may be perfectly correct, but it is of little value unless there is some evidence to connect these vehicles with the appellant.

Although hearsay evidence is admissible,[3] it must be reliable. This point is illustrated by *French Kier Developments Ltd v Secretary of State for the Environment*[4] where it was held that figures in an interim development control policy document were of insufficient evidentiary value

3 See p. 296, above.
4 [1977] 1 All ER 296. See also *Knights Motors v Secretary of State for the Environment and Leicester City Council* [1984] JPL 584.

as the local planning authority were unable to explain where the document had come from and had called no evidence about it.

TECHNICAL AND EXPERT EVIDENCE

The foundation of a sound case is the evidence of fact, but evidence of a different kind – that is, technical or expert evidence – may be required as well. The need for technical or expert evidence may be considered under the following headings:

(1) Interpretation of facts   The facts given in evidence or admitted by the other party may require interpretation. Thus, the report of the survey may contain data about the future of industry in the area (eg figures relating to trade, employment, factory space, industrial trends) and the local authority may claim that these data indicate the need for certain specific planning proposals. A suitably qualified person – eg an economist – might show, however, that the data support other conclusions.

(2) Special problems   Planning inquiries sometimes involve consideration of a question of a highly technical nature; for example, the Essex chalkpit inquiry involved consideration of the amount of dust likely to result from certain quarrying operations and the effect of such dust on agriculture. Such evidence is likely, of course, to be both factual and interpretative, but it can only be given by specialist witnesses.

(3) Questions of design and amenity   A planning inquiry may involve questions as to the design of buildings and other forms of visual amenity. These are more matters of opinion rather than of fact, but it may be appropriate to call architects and similar experts whose opinions may be of assistance to the inspector.

(4) Planning policy   The ultimate arbiter of planning policy is, of course, the Secretary of State, but here again there are acknowledged experts whose opinions will carry weight.

EVIDENCE OF INTENTIONS

In many cases there is no need for the landowner or prospective developer to give evidence; the evidence necessary to support the case may be given more appropriately by other witnesses. There are, however, cases in which it is necessary to refer to the intentions of the landowner or developer as to the future use or development of the site; in such cases that person ought to be available to give evidence. A mere statement by counsel of his client's intentions unsupported by evidence, is unsatisfactory because counsel cannot be cross-examined. This is illustrated by *Re London (Hammersmith) Housing Order, Land Development Ltd's Application:*[5]

> At a public local inquiry by the Minister to consider the confirmation of a compulsory purchase order in respect of part of the White City, counsel for the owners of the land sought to state the intentions of his clients as to the future use of the property. He had already stated that he did not intend to call any evidence. The inspector refused to allow the statement as to intentions to be made. Held: the inspector was right.

Although the case referred to an inquiry into objections to a compulsory purchase order, it is submitted that the rule in this case would apply equally to development plan inquiries. On an appeal against a refusal of planning permission it is not necessary for the landowner or prospective developer to give evidence that he intends to use the land for the purposes for which he has applied for permission, but he may need to give evidence of his intentions in other respects. Thus, on the hearing of an appeal against a refusal of permission for the retention of an unauthorised caravan site, a director of the appellant company stated that they proposed to provide access roads and other improvements; cross-examination revealed, however, that the cost of these improvements would be likely to be beyond the company's financial resources.

CROSS-EXAMINATION

Each witness must expect to be cross-examined. The purpose of cross-examination is to test the accuracy of facts given by the witness, the inferences which he has drawn from the facts and the soundness of any opinions he has put forward. It is both the right and the duty of the cross-examiner to be as searching as possible, and the witness should not resent this. On the other hand, the witness has the right to be treated with courtesy: as a judge once reminded an over-zealous young advocate, to cross-examine does not mean to examine crossly. Some witnesses, however, forfeit respect and may annoy the inspector and the cross-examiner by evasiveness or by unwillingness to admit even simple points.

The important of adequate cross-examination is illustrated by the

5 [1936] 2 All ER 1063.

recent decision in *Gabbitas v Secretary of State for the Environment*[6] in which it was held that an inspector is not entitled to reject unchallenged evidence without good reason.

There is a further aspect of cross-examination which is not always fully understood at planning inquiries. In cross-examination, an advocate who has not yet presented his own case ought to put to the witness any points of substance on which he proposes to lead evidence in due course; this enables the witness to comment on the points in question. This does not mean, of course, that the advocate must put the whole of his case to every witness whom he cross-examines; what he should do is put his points to the most suitable witness.

THE ROLE OF THE PLANNING OFFICER

At many inquiries, the only witnesses for the local planning authority are the planning officer (or one of his deputies) and other servants of the council. There is some confusion as to their role and the kind of evidence which they ought to give. And their position is sometimes delicate because their professional opinions do not always coincide with the views of the council. The fundamental issue seems to be whether the planning officer is there simply to give evidence as to the facts and considerations which led the council to their decision, or whether he is also there to give expert evidence on the issues involved.

On at least one occasion the Minister has taken the view that the planning officer's role is limited to explaining the council's position. In one appeal, counsel for the appellant in his cross-examination asked the council's witness for his personal opinion; the witness was reluctant to give his own opinion, and the inspector refused to press him to do so. The Minister in his decision letter said that the inspector had acted quite properly 'since the views of individual officers of the council are not considered to be relevant to the issue before the Minister'.[7]

This is hardly satisfactory; indeed, one learned journal has described the Minister's statement as 'one of the most extraordinary ever to appear in a planning appeal decision'.[8] If expert evidence has any relevance at a planning inquiry, the planning authority should be liable to call such evidence and it seems illogical to suggest that they cannot call their own professional officers for that purpose. Moreover, what is the position if the other side call expert evidence, but the views

6 [1985] JPL 630.
7 [1968] JPL 708.
8 Ibid.

of the council's professional officers are considered to be irrelevant? How in these circumstances is the inspector to evaluate the evidence?[9]

It seems that it is not for the planning officer to decide which questions he will answer in cross-examination; that is a matter for the inspector.[10]

---

9 For the views of the Town Planning Institute on the position of the planning officer see a statement issued in 1961 and reprinted in [1961] JPL 94.
10 *Accountancy Tuition Centre v Secretary of State for the Environment and London Borough of Hackney* [1977] JPL 792.

Chapter 18

The role of the courts and the ombudsmen

It will be appreciated from previous chapters that the Planning Acts invest both the local planning authority and the Secretary of State for the Environment with wide discretionary powers in the making of decisions. Such discretion is subject to the powers of review and supervision of the High Court. The court is not concerned with the merits, on planning grounds, of any particular decision but rather with the question of legality – substantive or procedural.[1] In reviewing legality, the court applies the doctrine of 'ultra vires' by which actions beyond the powers of the enabling statute will be quashed or declared to be a nullity and of no effect. The application of the doctrine to the planning field is dealt with in this chapter.

In most cases the Act of 1990 provides for an appeal against decisions of the local planning authority by the applicant himself.[2] Before reaching his decision, the Secretary of State shall, unless the parties waive the right to a hearing and confine themselves to written representations, appoint an inspector to hold a public inquiry.[3] In nearly all cases now, however, the inspector will make the decision himself[4] and currently over 80 per cent of appeals are dealt with by way of written representations. The decision of the Secretary of State (or his inspector with power to determine) in a planning appeal is expressed to be 'final'[5] but the Act of 1990 has a statutory machinery whereby its legality may be challenged in the High Court on specified grounds amounting to substantive or procedural ultra vires within six weeks of the decision by any 'person aggrieved' by it.[6]

---

1 See *Seddon Properties Ltd v Secretary of State for the Environment* (1978) 42 P & CR 26n, [1978] JPL 835 and *Centre 21 v Secretary of State for the Environment* [1986] JPL 914.
2 1990 Act, s. 78.
3 See ch 17, above.
4 See ch 7, pp. 152, 153, above.
5 1990 Act, s. 79(5).
6 1990 Act, s. 288. Actions may also be brought in the High Court under s. 287 (validity of structure or local plans) and s. 289 (validity of enforcement notices). See chs 4 and 10.

Apart from the statutory machinery for quashing a decision of the Secretary of State it is now accepted that the legality of decisions of the local planning authority may be challenged in the High Court as part of that court's supervisory jurisdiction.[7] The method of challenge is provided at common law by the prerogative orders of certiorari, mandamus and prohibition and the private law remedies of declaration and injunction. All these methods of challenge may be obtained by an application for judicial review which requires the applicant to have a sufficient interest in the matter concerned ('locus standi').[8]

This chapter will deal with first, the grounds for judicial review and secondly the methods by which decisions may be brought before the courts as mentioned in the two previous paragraphs. Finally we will examine briefly the role of the Parliamentary and Local Commissioners ('ombudsmen'), who have powers to investigate maladministration by government departments and local authorities respectively.

Grounds for review

The circumstances in which discretionary decisions under the Planning Acts may be challenged in the courts cannot be neatly categorised; most of the decided cases fall into more than one of the categories listed below. Nevertheless, it is suggested that a decision may be challenged if:

(1) It exceeds the statutory powers conferred on the body making it; 'substantive' ultra vires.
(2) There has been a disregard of some procedural requirement causing substantial prejudice; 'procedural' ultra vires.
(3) There has been a breach of the rules of natural justice.
(4) There has been an abuse of discretionary power.
(5) There is an error of law.

These grounds will now be considered in turn.

SUBSTANTIVE ULTRA VIRES

Here an act is done in excess of a statutory power. Thus the local planning authority in *Stringer v Minister of Housing and Local Government*[9] acted ultra vires in entering into an agreement with Manchester

---

7 *R v Hillingdon London Borough Council, ex p Royco Homes Ltd* [1974] QB 720, [1974] 2 All ER 643.
8 See generally, Garner, *Administrative Law*, ch VI.
9 [1971] 1 All ER 65, [1970] 1 WLR 1281, and see ch 7, p. 147, above.

University to resist development in the vicinity of Jodrell Bank. The authority had no express or implied power to fetter their decision in such a manner. Where an officer of the local planning authority grants planning permission without authority to do the same, the purported grant is ultra vires and of no effect.[10]

If a body's primary purpose in exercising a power is intra vires, incidental benefits gained may be disregarded. In *Westminster Corpn v London and North Western Railway Co*,[11] a case involving compulsory purchase, the corporation was expressly empowered to construct public conveniences. Underground conveniences were designed so as also to provide a pedestrian subway for crossing the street. In the absence of evidence of bad faith, the House of Lords refused to restrain the corporation from continuing the work.

Ultimately, whether or not a power has been exceeded is a matter of statutory interpretation. The court may have to consider the purpose that Parliament was seeking to achieve in drafting the particular provision.[12]

PROCEDURAL ULTRA VIRES

The failure to observe procedural requirements laid down by the planning legislation may invalidate the purported exercise of a power. The position is usually said to depend upon whether the requirement in question is regarded as mandatory or directory. If the former, all subsequent proceedings are a nullity; if the latter, the subsequent proceedings do not necessarily fail.[13]

The clear cut distinction referred to above has left the court with the difficulty of deciding into which category a particular requirement falls. More recently the courts have been prepared to adopt a more flexible, discretionary approach and in some instances have rejected the mandatory/discretionary distinction altogether.[14] In *Main v*

10 *Co-operative Retail Services Ltd v Taff-Ely Borough Council* (1979) 39 P & CR 223, CA.
11 [1905] AC 426, HL.
12 See, for example, *Chertsey UDC v Mixnam's Properties Ltd* [1965] AC 735, [1964] 2 All ER 627, HL.
13 The distinction is explained in *Howard v Secretary of State for the Environment* [1975] QB 235, [1974] 1 All ER 644. See also *Steeples v Derbyshire County Council* [1984] 3 All ER 468, [1981] JPL 582; *R v St Edmundsbury Borough Council, ex p Investors in Industry Commercial Properties Ltd* [1985] 3 All ER 234, [1985] 1 WLR 1168.
14 *London and Clydeside Estates Ltd v Aberdeen District Council* (1979) 39 P & CR 549 at 555, per Lord Hailsham LC; *Main v Swansea County Council* (1985) 49 P & CR 26, [1985] JPL 558, CA; *R v Carlisle City Council* [1986] JPL 206; *R v Lambeth London Borough Council, ex p Sharp* [1987] JPL 440; *R v Doncaster Metropolitan District Council, ex p British Railways Board* [1987] JPL 444.

Swansea District Council[15] the Court of Appeal held that the certification procedure under what is now section 66 of the Act of 1990, whereby owners must be notified of planning applications, was mandatory but the court exercised its discretion to refuse relief largely on the ground of the applicant's delay in bringing proceedings. Significantly the court stressed that the mandatory/directory distinction was not crucial.[16] In a later case, *R v Lambeth London Borough Council, ex p Sharp*,[17] the authority proposed to construct a synthetic athletics track in a conservation area (a deemed planning permission) but failed in their newspaper advertisement to specify the period for objections. The Court of Appeal quashed the permission and did not consider it necessary to consider whether the requirement was mandatory or directory. Rather the court asked how important or fundamental was the procedural requirement and whether it should exercise its discretion to quash. In the instant case the proposed development had aroused intense public concern in the locality.

Under the statutory machinery for challenging a decision of the Secretary of State, the court will only quash for a procedural defect where the applicant has suffered 'substantial prejudice'.[18] Further, it should be noted that procedural breaches may, in certain very limited circumstances, be cured by estoppel.[19]

BREACH OF NATURAL JUSTICE

There are two rules of natural justice, (i) the right to a hearing ('audi alteram partem') and (ii) no person shall be judge in his own cause or the rule against bias ('nemo debet esse index in propria causa'). The rules, as applicable to planning appeals, are now regarded as consisting of a general 'duty to act fairly' and the House of Lords has referred to the need for an objector to feel he has had 'a fair crack of the whip'.[20]

We will now consider the application of the two rules in turn.

The right to a hearing   The requirements of this branch of the rule will

---

15 (1984) 49 P & CR 26, [1985] JPL 558, CA.
16 Cf *R v Bradford-on-Avon UDC, ex p Boulton* [1964] 2 All ER 492, [1964] 1 WLR 1136.
17 [1987] JPL 440.
18 1990 Act, s. 288(5)(b); *Miller v Weymouth and Melcombe Regis Corpn* (1974) 27 P & CR 468; *Davies v Secretary of State for Wales* (1976) 33 P & CR 330, [1977] JPL 102.
19 *Wells v Minister of Housing and Local Government* [1967] 2 All ER 1041, [1967] 1 WLR 1000, but see *Western Fish Products Ltd v Penwith District Council* [1981] 2 All ER 204, CA.
20 *Fairmount Investments Ltd v Secretary of State for the Environment* [1976] 2 All ER 865, [1976] 1 WLR 1255, HL.

be satisfied providing a party (a) knows the case against him and (b) is given a fair opportunity to state his views. For this reason an oral hearing is not necessarily required and the planning legislation provides for planning appeals to be dealt with by way of written representations.

In the conduct of planning appeals, the requirements of the 'audi alteram partem' rule are reflected in the Inquiries Procedure Rules.[1] Although the rules are an expression of natural justice, they do not replace it, rather they complement it.[2] Nevertheless, where the Rules have not been breached, it appears that there is a heavy burden of proof on the party alleging unfairness.[3] Disregard of the Rules will not automatically render a decision ultra vires in the absence of substantial prejudice[4] but where such disregard amounts to a substantive breach of natural justice, the court will quash the decision.[5] It is not easy to extract from the case law on this aspect of natural justice a coherent set of principles, but the following are suggested.

First, each party must have had a 'fair crack of the whip'. In *Performance Cars Ltd v Secretary of State for the Environment*,[6] the applicant was provided with documents containing the authority's case only on the morning of the inquiry and he requested an adjournment of 30 days to consider them. The inspector offered him a long lunchbreak to consider them; the Court of Appeal held that the procedure was unfair despite the absence of substantial prejudice. Further, it might be asked whether the right to cross-examine is a requirement of natural justice. Certainly the Rules confer a right of cross-examination on the main parties, but other parties may only cross-examine to the extent permitted by the inspector; his discretion here must be exercised fairly.[7]

Secondly, and this is one aspect of the need for a fair crack of the whip, the decision must not be based on a ground which was not before the parties and upon which they have had no opportunity to comment. Thus in *Fairmount Investments Ltd v Secretary of State for*

---

1 SI 1988 No 944. See ch 17, above.
2 *Hyndburn Borough Council v Secretary of State for the Environment* [1979] JPL 536.
3 *Rea v Minister of Transport* (1982) 47 P & CR 207, [1982] JPL 508.
4 *Reading Borough Council v Secretary of State for the Environment* (1985) 52 P & CR 385, [1986] JPL 115.
5 Even here the court may be reluctant to grant relief in the absence of substantial prejudice, see for example *Swinbank v Secretary of State for the Environment* (1987) 55 P & CR 371, [1987] JPL 781.
6 (1977) 34 P & CR 92, [1977] JPL 585. And see *R v Bickenhill Parish Council, ex p Secretary of State for the Environment* [1987] JPL 773; *Wilson v Secretary of State for the Environment* [1988] JPL 540.
7 See *Bushell v Secretary of State for the Environment* [1981] AC 75, [1980] 2 All ER 608, HL. Cf *Nicholson v Secretary of State for Energy* [1978] JPL 39.

the Environment,[8] a case under the Housing Act 1957, the inspector recommended, after a site visit, that the objectors' houses were structurally unsound and that rehabilitation would not be financially viable. This observation had not been made before or at the inquiry and the objectors had not had an opportunity to comment on it. The House of Lords held that a breach of natural justice had taken place.[9] This principle is reflected in the present Inquiries Procedure Rules which provide that if the Secretary of State disagrees with the inspector's findings of material fact and is for that reason disposed to disagree with an inspector's recommendation he must invite the parties who were entitled to appear and did appear to make representations. In cases where new evidence or facts have been taken into account he must reopen the inquiry if requested to do so by the appellant or the local planning authority. In other cases he has a discretion to reopen the inquiry which is subject to the rules of natural justice.[10] Where the Secretary of State disagrees with his inspector on a finding of fact, but no evidence was adduced at the inquiry upon which he could reasonably have based his decision, the court will overturn the decision.[11]

Thirdly, proper, adequate and intelligible reasons should be given for the decision. This requirement is not technically one of natural justice but is required by legislation in the case of planning inquiries.[12] The reasons can be briefly stated.[13] In a number of cases over recent years the courts have warned against scrutinising too closely the wording of decision letters,[14] but nevertheless the most common ground of challenge remains the adequacy of the reasoning contained in the decision letter.

The rule against bias   This rule of natural justice, that no man shall be

---

8 [1976] 2 All ER 865, [1976] 1 WLR 1225, HL.

9 And see *Furmston v Secretary of State for the Environment and Kent County Council* [1983] JPL 49.

10 Rule 16(4); Rule 17. As to the distinction between questions of fact and questions of policy opinion see *Bushell v Secretary of State for the Environment* [1981] AC 75, [1980] 2 All ER 608, HL; *R v Bickenhall Parish Council, ex p Secretary of State for the Environment* [1987] JPL 773.

11 *Coleen Properties Ltd v Minister of Housing and Local Government* [1971] 1 All ER 1049, [1971] 1 WLR 433, CA.

12 Tribunals and Inquiries Act 1971, s. 12; *Givaudan & Co Ltd v Minister of Housing and Local Government* [1966] 3 All ER 696, [1967] 1 WLR 250; *Wycombe District Council v Secretary of State for the Environment* (1987) 57 P & CR 177, [1988] JPL 111.

13 *Bradley & Sons Ltd v Secretary of State for the Environment* (1983) 47 P & CR 374, [1982] JPL 43.

14 A recent example is *West Midlands Co-operative Society Ltd v Secretary of State for the Environment* [1988] JPL 121.

a judge in his own cause, has only limited application in planning. Certainly it is true that there should be no pecuniary interest or conflict of interest manifest in the circumstances in which a decision is made. Here the appearance of bias is sufficient to invalidate. In *R v Hendon RDC, ex p Chorley*,[15] a member of the council committee dealing with a planning application was an estate agent acting for the applicants in connection with the property the subject matter of the application. He was present at the meeting that resolved to permit development, although apparently he took no part in the discussion. Certiorari was granted to quash the decision on the ground, inter alia, of bias.

In *Steeples v Derbyshire County Council*[16] the county council contractually bound itself to a development company whereby the council would use its best endeavours to obtain planning permission for a leisure centre. Webster J accepted that the council's decision to grant permission had been fairly made. However, to the reasonable man, who would be taken to know of all relevant matters including the council's potential liability in damages if permission were not granted, it would appear that the contract would have had a significant effect on the planning committee's decision. The judge held that the decision was voidable or void on the ground of a failure to comply with natural justice.[17] A political predisposition in favour of a proposed development will not amount to bias.[18]

ABUSE OF DISCRETIONARY POWER

A decision may amount to an abuse of discretionary power where it is so unreasonable that no reasonable authority could have arrived at the decision.[19] Discretion may also be abused where an authority takes an irrelevant matter into account in arriving at a decision;[20] likewise

---

15 [1933] 2 KB 696.
16 [1984] 3 All ER 468, [1981] JPL 582.
17 Cf *R v St Edmundsbury Borough Council, ex p Investors in Industry Commercial Properties Ltd* [1985] 3 All ER 234, [1985] 1 WLR 1168 where a test of actual bias seems to have been applied.
18 *Franklin v Minister of Town and Country Planning* [1948] AC 87, [1947] 2 All ER 289, HL; *R v Amber Valley District Council, ex p Jackson* [1984] 3 All ER 501, [1985] 1 WLR 298.
19 *Associated Provincial Picture Houses Ltd v Wednesbury Corpn* [1948] 1 KB 223, [1947] 2 All ER 680, CA. As to reasonableness in the context of planning conditions, see ch 8, above.
20 As to material considerations, see ch 6 above.

where there is a failure to take relevant matters into account.[1] Further a discretion must not be effectively surrendered to some other body. In *H Lavender & Son Ltd v Minister of Housing and Local Government*[2] it was the policy of the Ministry of Housing not to release land for mineral working without the consent of the Ministry of Agriculture. Willis J quashed a decision made in accordance with this policy on the basis that the decision 'while purporting to be that of the Minister (of Housing), was in fact, and improperly, that of the Minister of Agriculture'. It should be noted that a decision may also be quashed if it was made in circumstances of bad faith or fraud. Nevertheless, the statutory time limit in section 288 of the Act of 1990[3] may operate to prevent a decision reached in bad faith from being challenged.

ERROR OF LAW ON THE FACE OF THE RECORD

Where a body which is under a duty to decide questions of law fails to direct itself properly on the law, the decision may be set aside by the court. The error of law must be clear and obvious from the record of the proceedings of the inferior agency. The error makes a decision voidable; the remedy is usually certiorari. Some of the examples of ultra vires decisions we have dealt with in this chapter may be explained in terms of 'error of law'. The language of error of law is particularly prevalent in the judicial review of enforcement appeals.[4]

Method of review

The decision on appeal against a refusal or conditional grant of planning permission is said by the Act of 1990 to be 'final',[5] and it 'shall not be questioned in any legal proceedings whatsoever'.[6] However, section 288 of the Act of 1971 gives a limited right to challenge the decision on a planning appeal in the High Court within six weeks of the decision by any 'person aggrieved' by it. The scope of this section and the court's common law jurisdiction to review the

---

1 *Ashbridge Investments Ltd v Minister of Housing and Local Government* [1965] 1 WLR 1320, CA; *Wycombe District Council v Secretary of State for the Environment* (1987) 57 P & CR 177, [1988] JPL 111.
2 [1970] 3 All ER 871, [1970] 1 WLR 1231.
3 See pp. 316 ff, below.
4 See, for example, *Kingston-upon-Thames Royal London Borough Council v Secretary of State for the Environment*, [1974] 1 All ER 193, [1973] 1 WLR 1549.
5 1990 Act, s. 79(5).
6 1990 Act, s. 284. The same applies to most of the other decisions, directions and orders within the Secretary of State's jurisdiction.

legality of decisions of the local planning authority will be considered below.

SECTION 288

The grounds of challenge under section 288 fall into two branches. First, a decision may be challenged if it is not within the powers of the Act. This includes decisions ultra vires in the sense we have discussed, breaches of natural justice and the abuse of discretionary power. The second branch refers to a failure to comply with 'the relevant requirements'; this extends to procedural requirements not necessarily to be found in the Act itself, such as the Inquiries Procedure Rules. This branch covers therefore procedural defects and errors of law. The two branches clearly overlap but the main difference between them is that under the second branch the defect must have resulted in 'substantial prejudice' to the applicant.[7]

The courts' powers under section 288 are limited to quashing the decision. There is no power to substitute its own decision or to modify or vary the Secretary of State's decision. Further the whole decision is quashed and it was held in *Kingswood District Council v Secretary of State for the Environment*[8] that the Secretary of State is under a duty to deal with the matter 'de novo', with, as it were, a clean sheet. He might therefore have to have regard to any further material considerations arising subsequently to his original decision. The Inquiries Procedure Rules deal with this possibility by requiring the Secretary of State to give the parties an opportunity to make further representations.[9]

The right to challenge under section 288 is extinguished after six weeks from the date of the decision. The courts have interpreted such time limits strictly. Thus in *Smith v East Elloe RDC*,[10] the House of Lords held that an identically worded provision relating to a compulsory purchase order prevented a person aggrieved by the order from challenging its validity after the expiry of the time limit in circumstances where it had been made in bad faith. Some years later, a majority of the same court took the view that such privative clauses could not prevent an application to the court out of time where a

---

7 See above, pp. 310, 311. Even where a decision is ultra vires under the first branch it seems that the court still has a discretion whether or not to quash; *Miller v Weymouth and Melcombe Regis Corpn* (1974) 27 P & CR 468.
8 (1987) 57 P & CR 153, [1988] JPL 249.
9 Rule 18; Rule 9.
10 [1956] AC 736, [1956] 1 All ER 855, HL.

decision was ultra vires.[11] More recently, however, the Court of Appeal has followed *Smith v East Elloe RDC*,[12] and in *Griffiths v Secretary of State for the Environment*[13] the House of Lords held, Lord Scarman dissenting, that the six-week period runs from the date when the decision is made by the Secretary of State and not from when notice of it is received by the aggrieved person. It seems that the decision is made by the Secretary of State on the date stamped on the decision letter; in the case itself the letter took five days to arrive, thus reducing the time within which an application might be made to the High Court. The potential injustice to individuals of the six-week bar is obvious; nevertheless it serves a useful purpose in preventing delay and uncertainty. Where the bar causes injustice there would seem to be no possibility of obtaining redress except (a) through the ombudsman[14] or (b) where the bar confers an unimpeachable planning permission, it might be possible to persuade the local planning authority to change its policy by revoking the planning permission or making a discontinuance order.

Only 'persons aggrieved' by the Secretary of State's decision have locus standi under section 288. It is arguable whether these words were ever intended to import a requirement of standing in the legal sense, but historically the courts have taken a narrow view of the words. Thus in *Buxton v Minister of Housing and Local Government*,[15] Salmon J held that adjoining landowners were not persons aggrieved; the words were confined to persons with a *legal* grievance.[16] Later, in *Turner v Secretary of State for the Environment*,[17] it was held that if, at the inquiry, the inspector exercises his right under the Inquiries Procedure Rules to invite third parties to appear and make representations, such persons may be persons aggrieved. In that case, Ackner J held that a local preservation society who had appeared at the inquiry at the grace of the inspector had sufficient locus standi under section 288.

---

11 *Anisminic Ltd v Foreign Compensation Commission* [1969] 2 AC 147, [1969] 1 All ER 208, HL.

12 *R v Secretary of State for the Environment, ex p Ostler* [1977] QB 122, [1976] 3 All ER 90, where the Court of Appeal distinguished *Anisminic* on the ground, inter alia, that it referred to a judicial decision. And see *R v Secretary of State for the Environment, ex p Kent* (1988) 57 P & CR 431, [1988] JPL 706.

13 [1983] 2 AC 51, [1983] 2 WLR 172, HL.

14 See pp. 319 ff, below.

15 [1961] 1 QB 278, [1960] 3 All ER 408. For the full background to the case see [1961] JPL 359.

16 Salmon J's interpretation of person aggrieved was, in effect, restricted to the applicant for planning permission and s. 66 parties.

17 (1973) 28 P & CR 123. And see *A-G of Gambia v N'Jie* [1961] AC 617, [1961] 2 All ER 504.

Subsequent first instance decisions have continued the same liberal approach.[18]

AT COMMON LAW

The case of *R v Hillingdon London Borough Council, ex p Royco Homes Ltd*[19] established beyond doubt that certiorari will lie to bring up and quash a decision of the local planning authority.[20] In that case, Lord Widgery CJ stressed that certiorari will only go where there is no other equally effective remedy; so far as the applicant for planning permission is concerned, in most cases the appeal to the Secretary of State will be more effective since the Secretary of State can deal not only with matters of law but with the merits of the case; indeed with all the issues that may arise out of a planning application. Certiorari provides a cheap, efficient and quick remedy where the decision is clearly wrong in law. Another advantage of this procedure is that it is not subject to the strict six weeks' time limit of section 288 – however the application must be made promptly once the grounds of review have arisen.

The locus standi requirements have always been generous, extending to such parties as adjoining landowners and ratepayers, and the liberal approach has been given a strong stimulus by a reform in the Rules of Court introduced in 1977[1] and by the tenor of certain speeches in a House of Lords decision of 1981.[2] Under Order 53 of the reformed Rules of Court, there is a uniform procedure for applying for judicial review under which a party can apply to the High Court for all or any of the prerogative orders of certiorari, mandamus and prohibition and also the private law remedies of declaration and injunction. Under the Rules, leave to apply for judicial review must be obtained; leave will not be granted unless the applicant has a 'sufficient interest' in the matter to which the application relates.[3]

---

18 *Bizony v Secretary of State for the Environment* [1976] JPL 306; *Hollis v Secretary of State for the Environment* (1982) 47 P & CR 351, [1983] JPL 164. And see *Wilson v Secretary of State for the Environment* [1988] JPL 540.
19 [1974] QB 720, [1974] 2 All ER 643.
20 Mandamus and prohibition may also lie in an appropriate case.
 1 Rules of the Supreme Court (Amendment No 3) 1977 (SI 1977 No 1955), as amended by RSC (Amendment No 4) 1980 (SI 1980 No 2000). Supreme Court Act 1981, s. 31(3).
 2 *R v IRC, ex p National Federation of Self-Employed and Small Businesses Ltd* [1982] AC 617, [1981] 2 All ER 93, HL. See, in particular, the judgment of Lord Diplock at 640.
 3 *R v Hammersmith and Fulham Borough Council, ex p People Before Profit Ltd* (1981) 45 P & CR 364, [1981] JPL 869; *R v Westminster City Council, ex p Monahan* [1989] JPL 407. And see *R v Secretary of State for the Environment, ex p Royal Borough of Kensington and Chelsea* [1987] JPL 567.

The locus standi requirements for declarations and injunctions have, historically, been restrictive; in *Gregory v Camden London Borough Council*,[4] Paul J held that a neighbour did not have standing to obtain a declaration that a grant of planning permission relating to adjoining property was ultra vires. Locus standi depended upon the deprivation of some legal right belonging to the plaintiff and 'in the matter of a declaration, only the rights of the plaintiff and defendant are involved, and not the rights of all the persons who might be governed by the order made'.[5] However, since 1977, declarations and injunctions may be sought by means of an application for judicial review under Order 53 to which the strict test in *Gregory v Camden* does not apply.

Where declarations and injunctions are sought by way of ordinary civil proceedings, the cases differ as to whether the *Gregory v Camden* test applies[6] and in another group of cases it is suggested that Order 53 is the appropriate form in which decisions of local authorities should be challenged so that an ordinary civil application might be struck out as an abuse of process.[7] Finally, it should be noted that where a party has questionable standing to bring proceedings in his own name, an alternative is to seek the *fiat* of the Attorney General to start a relator action in his capacity as guardian of the public interest.[8]

The ombudsman remedy

PARLIAMENTARY COMMISSIONER FOR ADMINISTRATION

In the 1950s there was a widespread feeling that parliamentary control was an insufficient safeguard against maladministration by government departments. To allay such fears, the Parliamentary Commissioner Act 1967 created the office of Parliamentary Commissioner for Administration or 'ombudsman',[9] appointed by the

---

4 [1966] 2 All ER 196, [1966] 1 WLR 899.
5 The judge relied heavily on *Buxton v Minister of Housing and Local Government* [1961] 1 QB 278, [1960] 3 All ER 408. See p. 317, above.
6 *Steeples v Derbyshire County Council* [1981] JPL 582. Cf *Covent Garden Community Association Ltd v Greater London Council* [1981] JPL 183 and *Barrs v Bethell* [1982] Ch 294, [1982] 1 All ER 106.
7 *Irlam Brick Co Ltd v Warrington Borough Council* [1982] JPL 709; *O'Reilly v Mackman* [1983] 2 AC 237, [1983] 3 All ER 680. But see *Davy v Spelthorne Borough Council* [1984] AC 262, [1983] 3 All ER 278, HL.
8 See *Co-operative Retail Services Ltd v Taff-Ely Borough Council* (1979) 39 P & CR 223.
9 'Grievance-man'. The 1967 Act does not define 'maladministration' but it would seem to relate to the way in which a decision is arrived at; *R v Local Comr for Administration for the North and East Area of England, ex p Bradford Metropolitan City Council* [1979] QB 287, [1979] 2 All ER 881, CA.

Crown and responsible to Parliament. His function is to investigate individual complaints of injustice in consequence of maladministration by government departments and produce a report in each case. There is a select committee appointed by Parliament to examine his reports.

There has been criticism that his powers are too limited. Thus he cannot, in the absence of special reasons, investigate actions in respect of which the complainant may take action in the courts. Complaints must be made via a Member of Parliament and generally must be brought within 12 months from the date the citizen first became aware of the maladministration. He has no power to order that a decision be altered or to award damages and in many cases, where maladministration is found, his report produces nothing more than an apology. Nevertheless, an adverse report may put pressure on the Department of the Environment to improve its procedures for the future. Where there is no maladministration, he cannot question a decision on its merits, even where it is based on a mistake of fact or is unreasonable.[10]

A considerable number of complaints have been brought against the Department of the Environment and its predecessor. The reports reveal that where maladministration has been found, the greatest single cause for complaint has been delay, followed by, inter alia, complaints concerning the handling of planning inquiries, the refusal to award costs, failures to enforce planning control and refusals to call in planning applications.

LOCAL COMMISSIONERS FOR ADMINISTRATION

The Local Government Act 1974 introduced two Commissions for Local Administration, one for England and one for Wales, with responsibility for providing Local Commissioners ('Local Ombudsmen') on a regional basis. Their function is to investigate complaints by members of the public of injustice as a consequence of maladministration by local authorities.

The Local Ombudsmen are specifically excluded from dealing with matters where the complainant has a right of appeal to a tribunal or Minister or a right of redress in the courts.[11] They cannot investigate actions of local authorities which affect all or most of the inhabitants of the authority concerned. There is, as in the case of the Parliamentary Commissioner, a 12 month limitation period. In the first instance,

10 1967 Act, s. 12(3).
11 1974 Act, s. 26(6).

a complaint must be made to a member of the authority alleged to have caused injustice; the Local Ombudsman may, if he thinks fit, proceed to investigate a complaint where a councillor refuses to refer it to him.[12] The Act of 1974 requires that reports of investigations should be publicised by various means at the local level.[13]

Of the many matters that have been found to be maladministration causing injustice by local planning authorities, unreasonable delay, the giving of incorrect information or misleading advice and poor liaison between the various agencies in local authorities figure strongly. Maladministration may be found where a council departs from a well-established practice to the prejudice of a complainant. Thus in one report, a landowner who was refused planning permission alleged, inter alia, that a councillor who spoke strongly against her application failed to declare to the planning sub-committee that he was her relative. This was in breach of a local government code of practice. The Local Commissioner recommended that the council should make a small 'ex gratia' payment to the complainant and draw its members attention to the relevant code of practice.[14] In another complaint relating to a planning application in a conservation area, the complainant was an adjoining owner, whom the council had notified. The complainant inspected the plans, but the planning officer failed to draw his attention to certain errors in the plans affecting amenity. As a result, the complainant had not objected. The council was urged to apologise and make an 'ex gratia' payment.[15] Another report found that inconvenience and distress had been caused to the complainant because, due to the council's failure to ascertain the proper facts, an extension to adjoining property had not been built in accordance with the original planning permission.[16] Again, the council was urged to apologise and to consider reimbursing the complainant's professional costs.

The Local Commissioners' powers are only persuasive; if a complainant is not satisfied by the action a council has taken, the

---

12 The Court of Appeal have held that the Local Commissioners' discretion here is subject to judicial review and should not therefore be abused; see the *Bradford* case (fn 9, above). The case also reveals that in the case of the Local Ombudsman the 12 month limitation period will not be enforced strictly.

13 The government have proposed certain improvements to the local ombudsman system: see [1988] JPL 739.

14 Complaint No 3034. Since 1978, local authorities have had a power to pay compensation, as opposed to payments on an 'ex gratia' basis: Local Government Act 1978.

15 Complaint No 665/H/79.

16 Complaint No 2439.

Commissioner may issue further reports. Not infrequently, as the reports show, a council is slow to provide the suggested redress, particularly where it is required to make payments to the complainant.

Part Two

Financial provisions

Chapter 19

The nature of the
financial problem

So far in this book we have dealt with the purposes and machinery
of planning control. But planning control involves certain financial
problems which are called the 'Compensation – Betterment Problem'.
Put quite simply, this is the problem of what is to be done about (a)
owners whose property is reduced in value by action taken under
planning legislation; and (b) owners whose property is increased in
value by such action. It is scarcely too much to say that the twin
problem has bedevilled planning control ever since 1909.

The historical background

COMPENSATION FOR PLANNING RESTRICTIONS

English law has adopted two contrasting principles with compensation
for the deprivation of rights over land. On the one hand, the courts
have insisted that property shall not be compulsorily acquired without
full compensation – unless Parliament provides to the contrary. As
was said in *A-G v De Keyser's Royal Hotel Ltd.*[1]

> It is a well-established principle that, unless no other interpretation is
> possible, justice requires that statutes should not be construed to enable
> the land of a particular individual to be confiscated without payment.

Or, as it was put more recently in *Belfast Corpn v OD Cars Ltd.*[2]

> The intention to take away property without compensation is not to be
> imputed to the legislature unless it is expressed in unequivocal terms.

On the other hand, compensation is not payable for restrictions on
the user of property unless Parliament expressly so provides. Through
the Public Health Acts and similar legislation, Parliament has either
directly restricted the user of land or authorised local authorities to

1 [1920] AC 508.
2 [1960] AC 490, [1960] 1 All ER 65.

do so. In only a few cases, however, has it been thought necessary to provide for the payment of compensation.[3]

Strictly, speaking, the restrictions imposed by planning legislation fall within the second category: in other words, planning legislation restricts an owner's use of his property but it does not take away the property from him. On the other hand, some of the restrictions imposed or authorised by the Planning Acts go far beyond anything in, say, the Public Health Acts. They can be fairly said to take away rights in property. The building regulations may restrict the way in which a man develops his land, but under planning legislation the appropriate authorities may forbid him to develop at all.[4]

Until 1947 at least, Parliament recognised that many planning restrictions were in effect confiscatory of property rights. For the purposes of compensation planning restrictions were divided into those which were confiscatory and those which were merely regulatory and thus akin to public health restrictions.

The Acts of 1909 to 1925 provided for compensation to any person 'injuriously affected' by any provisions in any planning scheme subject, inter alia, to the following exceptions:

(a) no compensation was payable for any provision in a scheme which could have been imposed as a byelaw without payment of compensation;

(b) provision might be made in the scheme itself for excluding compensation in respect of restrictions on the density, height or character of buildings, if the Minister was satisfied that it was reasonable to exclude compensation having respect to the situation and nature of the land.

The same approach was adopted in the Act of 1932. Compensation was payable to persons whose property was injuriously affected by any provisions in the scheme or by the carrying out by the responsible authority of any work under the scheme. As under earlier legislation, the scheme might exclude compensation for certain restrictions; the list of matters in respect of which compensation could be excluded was extended to restrictions on the use of land or buildings if these were needed for the protection of health or the amenities of the neighbourhood.

---

3 See *Belfast Corpn v OD Cars Ltd*, above.
4 Building regulations may prevent development where the site is too small to satisfy the requirements as to space about buildings, but this is exceptional.

BETTERMENT

'Betterment' has been defined as 'any increase in the value of land (including the buildings thereon) arising from central or local government action, whether positive, eg by the execution of public works or improvements, or negative, eg by the imposition of restrictions on other land'.[5] The word 'betterment' is sometimes used to describe not only the increase in value of the property but also the amount of such increase in value recovered from the owner.

Betterment resulting from positive action by a public authority can be recovered in a number of different ways:

(1) A direct charge on the owner of any property bettered by the public works. Thus an Act of 1662 provided for the widening of certain streets in London and for the recovery of a contribution for 'melioration' (ie betterment) from owners and occupiers of property the value of which was enhanced by widening.

Between 1890 and 1894, the London County Council, when promoting local bills authorising various public works, unsuccessfully attempted to obtain power for the recovery of betterment. In 1894, however, the House of Lords appointed a Select Committee on Betterment. The Committee reported that the principle 'is not in itself unjust' but that it would be difficult to assess the effect of public works in raising the value of neighbouring lands. Thereafter, the London County Council obtained a betterment clause in a number of local Acts passed between 1895 and 1902. The experiment was not a success; the trouble and expense involved were found to be out of all proportion to the amounts received.[6]

(2) Set off In assessing compensation for lands compulsorily acquired, regard must be had to any increase in value of other lands belonging to the same owner which will result from the carrying out of the work for which the land is being acquired.

Under this method it is possible to recover betterment only from persons directly affected by a compulsory purchase. The principle of set off was introduced into the early Housing Acts in connection with slum clearance schemes,[7] and it has been adopted in a few other cases. By virtue of the Land Compensation Act 1961, it now applies to all compulsorily purchased land.[8]

---

5 Final Report of the Expert Committee on Compensation and Betterment (Uthwatt Committee), para 260.
6 Report, paras 267–269.
7 See now the Housing Act 1957.
8 Section 9.

(3) Recoupment   The purchase and re-sale by the authority of land adjoining a public improvement and likely to be increased in value by it: if the property does in fact increase in value, the authority secures the whole of the increase. Recoupment clauses have been included in local Acts authorising road improvements by the London County Council.

The advent of planning legislation in 1909 raised the problem of betterment in a new form. Earlier statutes had been concerned only with betterment resulting from positive action in the form of public works. Planning control, however, produces betterment in a different way. If building is prohibited or restricted on certain land – for instance, land to be kept in a green belt or open space – two results may follow. First, adjoining land on which building is to be permitted may be increased in value because of the amenity created by the green belt or open space. Secondly, the restriction on the amount available for development may intensify the demand for land on which building will be permitted.

Without the compulsory purchase of large areas of building land, betterment resulting from planning control can only be recovered by a direct charge on the land concerned; that is, the first of the methods described above. The Acts of 1909 to 1925 adopted this method and authorised the recovery of one-half of any increase in the value of property due to the coming into operation of a scheme. This was no more successful than the London County Council's experiment; it is believed that no betterment was ever recovered under these Acts.

The Act of 1932 went further and provided for the recovery of 75 per cent of any increase in value due either to the coming into operation of a scheme or the execution of works by the responsible authority under the scheme.

THE UTHWATT REPORT

The Act of 1932 had not been in force seven years when the Second World War broke out, and by 1942 only 5 per cent of England and 1 per cent of Wales were subject to operative schemes. It is difficult to judge whether the Act of 1932 would have been a success over a longer period, and whether enough could have been raised by way of betterment to meet the liability for compensation. The historical precedents in relation to betterment were certainly not encouraging, and the liability to compensation deterred authorities from full use of their powers of planning control.

In short, now that the law empowered local authorities to limit an owner's right to make whatever use of his land he wished, the authorities were finding that to use such powers, though they wished to do so, was too expensive a process. It was said to be prohibitively expensive on two grounds. In the first place, the compensation often arose in the interests either of the nation as a whole, or of the people in a very wide area, while it had to be borne by a local authority. Restrictions were often most needed round the fringe of towns, and the authorities concerned were usually those of small rural areas whose resources were very limited. Even with the large authority the size of the prospective compensation bill alarmed them. Secondly, compensation was said to include inflationary elements which made the amounts to be paid excessively large. On the other hand, while in theory such authorities could recoup all or part of such expenses by means of betterment, it was said that in practice they could rarely secure it.

It was this state of affairs that led the Barlow Commission to say that 'the difficulties that are encountered by planning authorities under these provisions are so great as seriously to hamper the progress of planning throughout the country'.[9] The Commission accordingly recommended that 'the Government should appoint a body of experts to examine the questions of compensation, betterment, and development generally'.[10]

Acting on this advice, the government in January 1941, appointed what came to be known as the Uthwatt Committee to consider a number of matters including compensation and betterment. The committee considered that the burden of compensation was greatly increased by two particular factors which they described as 'floating value' and 'shifting value'. These concepts are important because right or wrong they have profoundly influenced the policies of successive governments, and they may fairly be described as the basis of the present system of compensation for planning restrictions.

'Floating value' This concept was noted by an earlier government committee,[11] and their explanation is as simple as any:

> If all building except agricultural is permanently prohibited over wide areas, compensation must be paid for the loss of potential building value over these areas. It may be that on any reasonable estimate that can be formed not more than 100 houses are likely to be built in a 100,000-acre rural zone in the lifetime of the scheme, so that over the whole zone the loss of 'potential building value' on prohibition of any building would be

9 Barlow Report, para 248.
10 Ibid, para 250.
11 Report on the Preservation of the Countryside (1936) from the Minister of Health's Town and Country Planning Advisory Committee.

only 100 houses. But potential building value is necessarily a 'floating value' and it is practically impossible to predict where it will settle. Hence, if the 100,000 acres are held in many ownerships, and claims by individual owners for loss of potential building value come to be separately adjudicated (as under the present system they must be), the total resulting bill for compensation is likely to be enormous, and greatly to exceed in the aggregate the amount of the real loss.

Or, as it was put by the Uthwatt Committee:[12]

Potential development value is by nature speculative. The hoped-for building may take place on the particular piece of land in question, or it may take place elsewhere; it may come within five years, or it may be 25 years or more before the turn of the particular piece of land to be built upon arrives. The present value at any time of the potential value of a piece of land is obtained by estimating whether and when development is likely to take place, including an estimate of the risk that other competing land may secure prior turn. If we assume, a town gradually spreading outwards, where the fringe land on the north, south, east and west is all equally available for development, each of the owners of such fringe land to the north, south, east and west will claim equally that the next development will 'settle' on his land. Yet the average annual rate of development demand of past years may show that the quantum of demand is only enough to absorb the area of one side within such a period of the future as commands a present value.

Potential value is necessarily a 'floating value', and it is impossible to predict with certainty where the 'float' will settle as sites are actually required for purposes of development. When a piece of undeveloped land is compulsorily acquired, or development upon it is prohibited, the owner receives compensation for the loss of the value of a probability of the floating demand settling upon his piece of land. The probability is not capable of arithmetical quantification. In practice where this process is repeated indefinitely over a large area the sum of the probabilities as estimated greatly exceeds the actual possibilities, because the 'float', limited as it is to actually occurring demands, can only settle on a proportion of the whole area. There is therefore over-valuation.

'Shifting value'   This concept was explained by the Uthwatt Committee as follows:[13]

The public control of the use of land, whether it is operated by means of the existing planning legislation or by other means, necessarily has the effect of shifting land values; in other words, it increases the value of some land and decreases the value of other land, but it does not destroy the land values. Neither the total demand for development nor its average annual rate is materially affected, if at all, by planning ordinances. If, for instance,

12 Uthwatt Report, paras 23, 24.
13 Ibid, para 26.

part of the land on the fringe of a town is taken out of the market for building purposes by the prohibition of development upon it, the potential building value is merely shifted to other land and aggregate values are not substantially affected, if at all. Nevertheless, the loss to the owner of the land prohibited from development is obvious, and he will claim compensation for the full potential development value of his land on the footing that but for the action of the public authority in deciding that development should not be permitted upon it, it would in fact have been used for development. The value which formerly attached to his land is transferred and becomes attached to other land whose owners enjoy a corresponding gain by reason of the increased chance that their land will be required for development at an earlier date.

A similar shift of value takes place if part of the land is taken out of the market for building purposes by being purchased for a public open space or other public purpose.

In an attempt to solve these problems, the Uthwatt Committee recommended what was in effect the nationalisation of the development rights in land outside built up areas. The land would remain in private ownership, but development would require the consent of the state which would thereupon acquire the land, if necessary by compulsory purchase, either for development by a public authority, or for re-sale or lease to a private developer.[14]

THE 1947 ACT SOLUTION

The Act of 1947 in some respects went even further than the Uthwatt Committee had recommended. In effect, it nationalised the development rights in all land, including land in built up areas. On the other hand, it did not provide for the acquisition by the state of all land required for development purposes. Although extensive powers of compulsory purchase were conferred upon public authorities, land required for private development would not normally be acquired by the state; instead, the existing owner would, so to speak, re-acquire the development rights by paying a 'development charge'.

The word 'nationalisation' was not used in the Act of 1947; nor indeed was it expressly provided that the development rights in land should be transferred to the state. But the transfer of development rights to the state was clearly enough the underlying theory. In practice this was achieved in the following ways:
(a) development must not be carried out without planning permission;
(b) if permission was refused or granted subject to conditions, the

14 Uthwatt Report, para 56.

owner of the land was not entitled to compensation because he no longer possessed the development rights;

(c) if permission was granted for development, the owner would pay a development charge representing the difference in the value of the land with the benefit of that permission and its existing use value;

(d) if the land were compulsorily acquired, the compensation would be limited to existing use value;

(e) as a measure of compensation for the loss of development rights landowners were entitled under Part VI of the Act of 1947 to make a claim for a once-for-all payment from the government.

Although the financial provisions set out in paragraphs (b) to (e) have been drastically changed, it is necessary to consider the claims under Part VI of the Act of 1947 in rather more detail.

PART VI CLAIMS

Two types of claim were possible under Part VI of the Act of 1947. Section 58 provided for a global sum of £300 million as compensation for landowners generally for loss of development value. Section 59 provided for additional payments in respect of certain war damaged land.

Under section 58, the owner of a freehold or leasehold interest could submit a claim for compensation for loss of development value representing the difference between the 'unrestricted' and 'restricted' values of his interests on 1 July 1948. The unrestricted value was that which the interest would have had if the Act of 1947 had not been passed; the restricted value was its value on the assumption that permission would not be granted for any development other than Third Schedule development (which is described below).

The claims as agreed or determined by the Lands Tribunal were to be paid by the Treasury in stock not later than 1 July 1953. If the amount of the claims were to exceed £300 million, then it would not be possible to pay them all in full. Certain claims relating to land considered 'near ripe' for development were to be given priority and paid in full; the non-priority claims were to be paid *pro rata* to the residue of the £300 million. In fact, the total approved claims amounted to £340 millions of which approximately £100 million represented priority claims; the non-priority claims would then have been met at 16s in the £.

The claims were not, in fact, paid out in this way because the new government which came into office in 1951 decided to replace the financial provisions of the Act of 1947 by a different scheme; this was effected by the Acts of 1953 and 1954.

THE SECTION 59 SCHEME

The War Damage Act 1943, provided government compensation for war damaged land and buildings. If the damage was capable of repair, the owner of the property received a cost of works payment when the repairs were done. If, however, the building were a total loss the owner received a 'value payment' representing the difference between the before and after damage value of the property. This value payment was assessed on the assumption that the owner would be able to realise any development value which the site might possess. Thus where an old dilapidated building was totally demolished by a bomb and there was the prospect of a profitable future development, the development value might be considerable. In such a case the then development value would increase the after-damage value of the site and thus reduce the war damage payment. The Act of 1947, however, took away this development value, and to avoid double loss on the part of the owner, section 59 of the Act of 1947 provided supplementary compensation for loss of development value in such cases. This compensation was paid in full in cash. The fact that such a payment was made may still be of significance as will be explained in later chapters.

THIRD SCHEDULE DEVELOPMENT

Lastly, in this review of the financial provisions of the 1947 Act, it must be noticed that certain forms of development, considered to be within the existing use of land, were exempted from the 'nationalisation' scheme. These developments were set out in detail in the Third Schedule to the Act of 1947 and for this reason were originally referred to as 'Third Schedule development'. The Third Schedule to the Act of 1947 became the Third Schedule to the Act of 1962, then Schedule 8 of the Act of 1971, but in the Act of 1990 it is Schedule 3; it will therefore be referred to henceforth in this book as 'Schedule 3 development'. Schedule 3 development may be described as development consistent with, or required for the existing use of the land or building in question. For instance, the conversion of a large house into flats is development and requires planning permission,[15] but the house remains in residential use. Or again, a farmer wishes to erect barns or cowsheds; this involves development and requires planning

15 1990 Act, s. 55(3)(a).

permission, but they are developments required for the existing use of his farm in contrast to a general building development.

It must be emphasised that Schedule 3 development requires planning permission. But under the Act of 1947 it did not attract development charges and in assessing loss of development value any potential development of this kind was included in the existing use or restricted value of the land. Moreover, even under the Act of 1947, compensation was payable if planning permission was refused or granted subject to conditions for certain forms of Schedule 3 development.[16]

THE 1954 ACT SOLUTION

The financial provisions of the Act of 1947 were unpopular and widely criticised. Among the more informed sources of criticism were the Law Society, the Royal Institution of Chartered Surveyors and the Chartered Auctioneers and Estate Agents Institute.

All these bodies criticised the financial provisions as discouraging to development. It is difficult to judge how far the liability to development charge did in fact discourage development. At that time, development was restricted by the post-war shortage of labour and materials and a strict system of building licensing was in force. It seems likely that development was proceeding as far as the country's resources would permit.

There seems little doubt, however, that the development charge increased the cost of development. The framers of the Act of 1947 supposed that the liability to development charge would result in land changing hands at existing use value, and the Central Land Board were given powers of compulsory purchase to deal with cases where landowners were not willing to sell at existing use value. In fact, land was generally bought and sold at prices substantially in excess of existing use value, and to that extent the development charge operated as a kind of tax; the Central Land Board made little use of their powers of compulsory purchase.

In November 1952, the government published a White Paper announcing a drastic revision of the financial provisions of the Act of 1947. The government proposed in effect to hand back to private ownership the development rights in land as they existed immediately before the Act of 1947, but not as altered for better or worse by the operation of planning control since that date. The government appear in this to have been influenced by the doctrine of shifting value explained earlier in this chapter.

16 See ch 20, below.

These proposals were put into effect by the Act of 1953 – an emergency measure to deal with the more urgent problems – and by the Act of 1954. These two Acts did not affect the powers of control over development provided by the Act of 1947, but the financial consequences of granting or refusing permission were altered. If permission were granted, the owner no longer had to pay development charge.[17] If permission were refused or granted subject to conditions, then (with some exceptions) owners of legal interests in the land were entitled to compensation, provided a claim for loss of development value had been established under section 58 of the Act of 1947. Similarly, if land were compulsorily acquired, the compensation was to include the amount of the section 58 claim as well as the existing use value. In consequence of all this, the obligation to pay the £300 million in one lump sum was abolished, the full amount of the established claim being available to provide compensation as and when a loss of development value was actually incurred – namely, when planning permission was refused or granted subject to conditions or when land was compulsorily acquired.

Provision was also made for compensating landowners or developers who had suffered loss in consequence of the operation of the Act of 1947 prior to 1 January 1955 – the date on which the Act of 1954 came into force. Part I of the Act of 1954 provided a complicated scheme of payments for dealing with some of these cases – notably, where land had changed hands at less than its full value because of the developers' prospective liability to development charge or where land had been compulsorily acquired at existing use value. These payments could be made only if a claim had been established under section 58 of the Act of 1947, and the making of the payment reduced the amount of the established claim.

Loss might also have been suffered under the Act of 1947 by the refusal of planning permission or the imposition of conditions, or by the revocation or modification of permission already granted. In these cases, a claim for retrospective compensation might be made under Part V of the Act of 1954, provided a section 58 claim had been established and was still subsisting; that is, had not been extinguished under Part I. (As an alternative to paying compensation under Part V, the Minister was authorised to give permission for the development in question or for some other profitable development.) Any compensation paid under Part V reduced the amount of the established claim.

The established claim, or what was left of it after payments under Parts I and V, was then converted into an 'unexpended balance of

17 This liability was abolished by the 1953 Act with effect from November 1952.

established development value'. This provides the basis of compensation for restrictions on development (other than Schedule 3 development) imposed on or after 1 January 1955. Compensation for restrictions on Schedule 3 development continues to be payable under the rules originally established by the Act of 1947. There are now, therefore, two sets of rules for compensation for planning restrictions – namely, one scheme for restrictions on Schedule 3 development, and another more complex scheme for restrictions on what is now known as 'new development', that is, development outside Schedule 3.

Compensation for restrictions on new development is payable only if there is an unexpended balance and this will exist only if a claim was established under section 58 of the Act of 1947, and the amount of the compensation will not exceed the unexpended balance. No new claims may be made under section 58, and there is no provision for increasing the amount of the established claims to take account of the decline in the value of money. And, of course, the landowner is denied any increase of development value resulting from the development plan zoning – often a very substantial item indeed.

For these reasons the Act of 1954 was in its turn subjected to a good deal of criticism, and in 1959 Parliament decided to revert to full market value (including the benefit of any enhancement due to the development plan) as the basis of compensation for compulsory purchase. The Act of 1954, however, is left untouched in relation to compensation for planning restrictions.[18]

THE LAND COMMISSION

Following the General Election of 1964, a fresh attempt was made to deal with the compensation–betterment problem. The Labour Party's election programme contained a proposal to set up a Land Commission which would acquire all land about to be developed – a proposal similar to the recommendation of the Uthwatt Committee.[19] The Commission would pay existing use value plus an increment to the owner, but not the full market value.

The new Labour Government subsequently came to the conclusion that it would be administratively impracticable for the proposed Land Commission to take over all land required for development. In a White Paper published in September 1965[20] the Government announced that they would introduce legislation to set up a Land Commission with power to acquire land for development at current use value plus a

18 The relevant provisions are now contained in the 1990 Act.
19 See p. 331, above.
20 The Land Commission, Cmd 2771.

part of the development value. But if land not acquired by the Commission were to change hands on an unrestricted basis there would be a two-tier price system; one price for land acquired by the Commission and another for land bought by other persons whether public authorities or private developers. To avoid this situation the White Paper explained that a betterment levy would be imposed on development value when realised by sales or leases of land, and to the extent that development value has not been realised in previous sales or leases when it is realised by actual development of the land. The levy would be fixed in the first instance at the rate of 40 per cent of the net development value and would be collected by the Commission and paid into the Exchequer. A landowner would thus realise the same net amount from the sale of his land whether he was selling to the Land Commission, another public authority or to a private purchaser.

These proposals were given effect in the Land Commission Act which received the Royal Assent on 1 February 1967. Most of the provisions came into effect on 6 April 1967. No betterment levy was payable on development commenced before 6 April 1967, and for this development was deemed to have commenced if a start had been made on road works or sewers for a project or if a trench for foundations had been dug. As a result the amount of betterment levy collected in the three years following the passing of the Act was comparatively small: and, following the change of government in 1970, the Land Commission Act was repealed.

COMMUNITY LAND AND DEVELOPMENT LAND TAX

The Labour Government which came into office in 1974 made yet another attempt to deal with the problem of land values. This latest attempt was embodied in the Community Land Act 1975, and the Development Land Tax Act 1976. This new legislation was concerned not only with the recoupment of betterment. It was also designed to enable local authorities to plan more positively and to decide where development took place. The new legislation thus had two main objectives. As set forth in a White Paper,[1] these were:

(a) to enable the community to control the development of land in accordance with its needs and priorities; and

(b) to restore to the community the increase in value of land arising from its efforts.

The first objective implied two things: that there was a need for

1 Cmd 5730, para 16.

more positive planning and that the powers available under other legislation – such as the Planning Acts and the New Towns Act – were insufficient. The White Paper asserted that the existing system of planning control was largely negative.

> The community, via its elected local authority and, in the final analysis central government, can veto proposals for development, but the initiative is left largely in private hands. The community does not at present have sufficient powers always to plan positively, to decide where and when particular development should take place.[2]

The White Paper proposed, therefore, that major development of land should take place only after the land has passed through public ownership. To this end, local authorities would for a period of some years following 'the first appointed day'[3] be *enabled* to acquire land needed for 'relevant development', that is all development other than comparatively small developments. At any time, however, the Secretary of State might make an order – usually known as a 'duty order' – imposing upon the appropriate authorities a *duty* to acquire all land required for specified classes of development. And after 'the second appointed day' it would be the duty of all local authorities to acquire all land needed for relevant development. Planning permissions granted after the first appointed day might be suspended pending a decision on whether or not the land was to be brought into public ownership.

The second objective – restoring to the community the increase in value due to its efforts – was to be achieved in the first instance by means of the development land tax. This was payable wherever development value was realised – typically on the sale of land for development. Where land was compulsorily purchased – whether under the Community Land Act or under other powers – development land tax would be deducted from the compensation so that the acquiring authority would pay the net amount. But where an authority subsequently disposed of land held under the Community Land Act, they would normally charge full market value.

The development land tax was intended to be an interim measure only. After the second appointed day compensation for compulsory purchase was to be restricted to 'current use value' thus excluding development value altogether.

The Community Land Act was repealed in 1980 following the return of a Conservative Government, but the development land tax was retained. However in the economic climate of the early 1980s it

2 Cmd 5730, para 3.
3 This was 6 April 1976.

was considered to be a discouragement to development, and in his 1985 Budget speech the Chancellor of the Exchequer announced its abolition in respect of all chargeable transfers and events arising on or after 19 March 1985.

Chapter 20

Compensation for restrictions on Schedule 3 development

The concept of Schedule 3 development, that is development which for certain purposes is deemed to be within the existing use of land – has been explained in the previous chapter. It is now necessary to consider Schedule 3 in more detail.

As originally enacted, it dealt only with development deemed to be within the existing use of land or buildings on 1 July 1948; it did not apply to buildings erected[1] or uses commenced after that date. The Act of 1954 extended Schedule 3 to refer also to buildings erected and uses begun after 1 July 1948. In this form the Schedule was re-enacted in the 1962 Act. Early in 1963, however, the government came to the conclusion that the fear of liability to compensation for restrictions on rebuilding or extension of existing premises– notably offices – was deterring planning authorities from exercising proper control. The Act of 1963 was passed to deal with this problem by amending the Schedule.

Some paragraphs of Schedule 3 refer to 'a material date'; this is either 1 July 1948, or the date on which the Schedule has to be applied in any particular case.[2] For instance, where the Schedule has to be applied for the purpose of section 114 of the Act of 1990, the material date would presumably be the date of the planning decision which gives rise to the claim for compensation.

The extension of the Schedule to buildings erected or uses begun after 1 July 1948, may apply even where the development has been carried out in contravention of planning control. If at the material date the planning authority have not issued an effective enforcement notice in respect of the offending development, the landowner is entitled in most cases to claim benefit of the Schedule.[3]

---

1 Except for buildings substituted for previously existing buildings in accordance with para 1 of Sch 3.
2 1990 Act, Sch 3, para 12(1).
3 Ibid, Sch 3, para 12(2).

Where the development was the subject of a temporary permission, the extension of the Schedule is limited to the period of the permission.[4]

Classes of development

Schedule 3 specifies the following classes of development:

PART I. DEVELOPMENT NOT RANKING FOR COMPENSATION UNDER SECTION 114

(1) The rebuilding, as often as occasion may require, so long as the cubic content[5] of the original building is not exceeded by more than the prescribed amount of –
(a) any building in existence on 1 July 1948;
(b) any building destroyed or demolished between 7 January 1937 and 1 July 1948;
(c) any building in existence at a material date.

Where the original building was erected after 1 July 1948, no increase in cubic content is permitted. In every other case the prescribed amount is one-tenth or 1750 cubic feet whichever is the greater, in the case of a dwellinghouse: one-tenth in the case of any other building.

It is also to be assumed that the right of rebuilding and alteration would be subject to the restrictions on floor space introduced by the Act of 1963 and now to be found in the Act of 1990. The effect is that where the building in question is the original building the amount of gross floor space used for any purpose must not be increased by more than ten per cent; where the building is not the original building (i e it has already been rebuilt or altered) no increase in the amount of gross floor space used for any purpose is permitted for the purposes of the Schedule.[6]

(2) The use as two or more separate dwellings of any building used at a material date as a single dwelling.

---

4 1990 Act, Sch 3, para 9.
5 As ascertained by external measurement: where two or more buildings in the same curtilage are used as one unit for the purposes of any institution or undertaking, the cubic content of the original building is to be taken as the total cubic content of these buildings; ibid, para 10.
6 Ibid, Sch 10.

PART II, DEVELOPMENT RANKING FOR COMPENSATION UNDER SECTION 114

(3) The enlargement improvement or other alteration, as often as occasion may require, of any such building as mentioned in paragraph 1 – or of any building substituted for it – subject to the same restriction as to increase in cubic content and floor space.

Even with these restrictions on the amount of floor space, local planning authorities in London and other areas of high land values have complained that the prospective burden of compensation deters them from refusing permission for extensions to blocks of flats.[7] This problem has now been dealt with in 1985 by an amendment of the law which is now embodied in section 114(b) of the Act of 1990; this excludes the enlargement of a block of flats which would result in either an increase in the number of dwellings in the block or an increase of more than one-tenth in the cubic content of any dwelling contained in the block.

This paragraph, it is thought, applies only to physical alterations and not to a change of use. Moreover, improvements or other alterations which do not materially affect the external appearance of the building are not development at all except for war damage repairs and the provision (after 5 December 1968) of underground rooms.[8]

(4) The carrying out on land used at a material date for agriculture or forestry of any building or other operations required for that use; the erection, enlargement or improvement of the following is excluded, however:

(a) dwellinghouses;
(b) buildings used for the purposes of market gardens;
(c) buildings used for other purposes not connected with general farming operations or with the cultivation or felling of trees.

(5) The winning and working, on land held or occupied with land used for agricultural purposes, of any minerals reasonably required for that use.

(6) Any change of use from one purpose to another within any use-class specified in the Use-Classes for Third Schedule Purposes Order.

This Order and the original Use Classes Order made in 1948 for the purposes of section 12(2) of the Act of 1947 were in identical terms. However, the original order made under what is now section 22(2) has been amended on a number of occasions[9] with the result that the two orders are no longer identical; some of the use-classes and some of the definitions are now different. Where, however, the

7 See [1985] JPL 1.
8 1990 Act, s. 55(2)(a).
9 See now the Use Classes Order 1987.

two orders are in identical terms, the Third Schedule Order need not be considered because the change of use in question will not be development at all.

(7) Where part only of a building erected before 1 July 1948, or other land is used for a particular purpose, the use for that purpose of an additional part not exceeding one-tenth[10] of the part used for that purpose on 1 July 1948, or on the day thereafter when the building or land first began to be so used.

(8) The deposit of waste materials or refuse in connection with mineral working on a site used for that purpose at a material date.

Compensation in respect of Schedule 3 development

Compensation is payable in respect of restrictions on Schedule 3 development under section 114 of the Act of 1990. The conditions are as follows:

(a) the development must fall within Part II of the Schedule;

(b) planning permission must have been refused, or granted subject to conditions, by the Secretary of State either on appeal or under section 77 of the Act of 1990;

(c) it must be shown that the value of the interest in respect of which the claim is made is less than it would have been but for the Secretary of State's decision;

(d) the claim must be submitted to the local planning authority within six months of the Secretary of State's decision unless he agrees to an extension of time.[11]

VALUE OF INTEREST

There is no definition of the words 'interest in land' in this Part of the Act of 1990 but it would appear from the rules for assessing compensation in section 117 that the interest must be either the freehold or a tenancy, or at least an option to purchase;[12] a claim may be made by a mortgagee but not in respect of his interest as such, and he must account to the mortgagor for any compensation he receives.

The amount of the compensation will be the difference between:[13]

---

10 Measured in the case of buildings by cubic content, and in the case of other land by area; 1990 Act, Sch 3, para 7.

11 General Regs, reg 14.

12 *Oppenheimer v Minister of Transport* [1942] 1 KB 242, [1941] 3 All ER 485.

13 1990 Act, s. 114(2).

(a) the value of the interest as affected by the Secretary of State's decision; and

(b) the value it would have had if the Secretary of State had granted the permission or had granted it unconditionally, as the case may be. If, in refusing permission the Secretary of State undertakes to give permission for any other development, regard must be had to that undertaking in assessing compensation.[14]

It appears from the very recent decision of the Court of Appeal in *Richmond Gateways Ltd v Richmond upon Thames London Borough Council*[15] that the value of the interest under paragraph (b) above is to be taken as the value which the property would have if sold on the open market with the relevant planning permission.

> Permission had been refused for a penthouse flat on top of an existing block of flats. It had been agreed that the way of deciding whether the permission would have increased the claimant's interest was to value the penthouse had it been erected and to deduct the costs of construction and sale: if the total cost was less than the notional sale price, the difference would indicate the amount which the land would realise on an open market sale.
>
> It was held that there was no requirement that the profits of a notional property developer should be deducted.

A refusal of planning permission will not necessarily reduce the value of the claimant's interest in the land even though it deprives him of a potential profit. This is illustrated by *A L Salisbury Ltd v York Corpn.*[16]

> In 1953 the planning officer wrote to the owners of shops in a certain street asking them to consider, in the event of their rebuilding, or altering the front elevations, setting the ground floor back by five feet to create an arcade. All the shopkeepers agreed except the claimants who in 1958 applied for permission to rebuild the front without setting back the ground floor. Permission was refused by the Minister on appeal.
>
> A claim for compensation was then made under paragraph 3 of the Third Schedule, was disputed by the Corporation and was accordingly referred to the Lands Tribunal.
>
> Held: the loss of display space entailed in setting back the ground floor would not reduce the rental value of the shop since an arcaded front would in the narrow streets of York greatly improve the flow of pedestrians and lead to more custom. Accordingly no compensation was payable.

Disputes as to the payment of compensation are dealt with by the

14 1990 Act, s. 114(3)(b).
15 [1989] 39 EG 171, CA.
16 (1960) 11 P & CR 421.

Lands Tribunal[17] subject to right of appeal by way of case stated to the Court of Appeal on points of law. The liability for compensation falls on the local planning authority not the Secretary of State.[18]

17 1990 Act, s. 118.
18 Ibid, s. 114(2).

Chapter 21

Compensation for restrictions on new development

Compensation is payable under Part V of the Act of 1990 for restrictions on new development – that is development other than Schedule 3 development – provided the following conditions are satisfied:

(1) A planning decision must have been made on or after 1 January 1955, whereby permission for new development was refused or granted subject to conditions.

(2) The land in question must have an unexpended balance of established development value at the time of the decision.

(3) The claimant's interest in the land must have been depreciated in value as a result of the decision.

(4) Compensation must not be excluded under section 121, 122 or 123.

These conditions must now be considered in detail.

The planning decision

The words 'planning decision' mean a 'decision made on an application under Part III'.[1] Applications under Part III of the Act include applications for planning permission and for any detailed consents required as a result of a grant of permission on an outline application. A decision on either type of application may therefore give rise to a claim for compensation.

The decision may be that of the local planning authority or the Secretary of State on appeal or under section 77 of the Act of 1990. It is not necessary that the decision should have been the subject of an appeal to the Secretary of State.

If the local planning authority fail to give a decision within the proper time, the applicant may appeal to the Secretary of State as if

---

1 1990 Act, s. 336.

permission had been refused.[2] It is submitted that this does not operate as a deemed refusal for the purpose of claiming compensation.

The unexpended balance

The origin of the unexpended balance has been explained in chapter 19 but certain points require further explanation.

Although a claim under section 58 of the Act of 1947 could be made in respect of each separate interest in the land, there can be only one unexpended balance for any piece of land. Where more than one claim was established the unexpended balance is the aggregate of the established claims as subsisting on 1 January 1955.[3]

In converting one or more established claims into an unexpended balance, an addition of one-seventh is made.[4] This is intended to be in lieu of interest from 1 July 1948 to 1 January 1955, but no further additions can be made.

The unexpended balance attaches to the land: that is, upon a sale or gift of the land, the benefit of the unexpended balance passes automatically to the new owner.

The conversion of the established claims as subsisting on 1 January 1955, gives the amount of the *original* unexpended balance. This amount can be ascertained by applying to the Secretary of State for a certificate.[5] The original balance may be reduced or extinguished in certain cases and may be increased in others.

REDUCTION OR EXTINGUISHMENT OF ORIGINAL UNEXPENDED BALANCE

Where compensation is paid under Part V of the Act of 1990 in respect of the depreciation of one or more interests in land, the amount of the compensation is to be deducted from the unexpended balance which will be reduced or extinguished accordingly.[6] If the planning decision extended to part only of the land, the unexpended balance will be apportioned, and it will be the balance attaching to the part affected by the planning permission which will be reduced or extinguished.

Where land is compulsorily acquired by or sold to an authority possessing compulsory powers, the unexpended balance will be

2 See ch 7, p. 149, above.
3 I e after deducting any payment made under Part I or V of the 1954 Act.
4 1990 Act, Sch 12, para 2(3).
5 Ibid, Sch 12, para 20.
6 Ibid, Sch 12, para 13.

extinguished. If the compulsory acquisition or sale extends to part only of the land, the unexpended balance will be apportioned. The situation is further complicated where there are separate interests in the land. Thus, where there is a leasehold as well as the freehold interest, the authority may acquire both or they may acquire the freehold and wait for the lease to expire in the ordinary way. In the latter event (provided the lease has more than a year to run) the unexpended balance will be reduced by the amount attributable to the freehold. Similar principles apply where (as may occasionally happen) the authority acquire the leasehold but not the freehold.

Where land has been compulsorily purchased, compensation will be payable for damage sustained in consequence of the severance of the land from other land held therewith. Compensation will also be payable in respect of injurious affection to any land whether or not it was held with the acquired land. It would be outside the scope of this book to go into details of a subject which is in effect part of the law of compensation for compulsory purchase. It should be noted, however, that any unexpended balance attaching to the severed or injuriously affected land may be reduced or extinguished in consequence of the compensation paid for the severance or injurious affection.[7]

Where compensation is paid by the local planning authority for the revocation or modification of planning permission, the Secretary of State may make a contribution to the expense incurred by the authority and that will reduce any unexpended balance attaching to the land.[8]

In the four cases described above the unexpended balance has been reduced or extinguished because a payment has been made out of it the basis of such payment being that the owner of the land has been prevented from realising the development value of the land. The government considered it equally logical that the unexpended balance should be reduced or extinguished where the owner is allowed to realise the development value. Speaking on the Second Reading of the Bill in the House of Lords, the Lord Chancellor said.[9]

> That balance, *of course*, is progressively reduced to take account of payments and of the realisation of development value by building or other development.

The unexpended balance is reduced by the value of any new development (that is, development other than Schedule 3

7 1990 Act, Sch 12, paras 16, 17, 18.
8 See ch 22, below.
9 HL Official Report (5th series) col 444. Author's italics.

development) initiated at any time on or after 1 July 1948.[10] The value of the development will broadly speaking be the amount by which the value of the land with planning permission for the development in question exceeds the value which the land would have if permission for that or any other new development were refused. The valuation is to be made by reference to the prices prevailing at the time the valuation is made;[11] this will not be the time when the new development was carried out but the next occasion on which the unexpended balance has to be ascertained.[12]

These provisions do not apply to (i) land in respect of which compensation has become payable under section 59 of the Act of 1947; (ii) any development initiated before 1 July 1955, in respect of which a development charge has been incurred or would have been incurred but for one of the statutory exemptions.[13]

INCREASE IN UNEXPENDED BALANCE

The unexpended balance will be increased where any compensation is repaid as explained in chapter 23. It may also be increased in a few exceptional cases where compensation has been paid for severance or injurious affection under section 36 of the Act of 1954.[14]

Depreciation of the claimant's interest

The claimant must be able to show that the value of his interest in the land has been depreciated in consequence of the planning decision in question.[15] The only interests which qualify for this purpose are a fee simple and a tenancy.[16] No claim can be made in respect of other interests in the land such as a mortgage or a rent charge. In certain circumstances a mortgagee can require the Secretary of State to pay any compensation money direct to him, and should the mortgagor fail to make a claim the mortgagee may do so instead. Similar provisions are made in respect of rent charge owners.[17]

It may happen that the claimant's interest extends to land which

---

10 1990 Act, Sch 12, para 14.
11 Ibid, Sch 12, para 15.
12 Ibid, Sch 12, para 14(1).
13 Ibid, Sch 12, para 14(2), (3).
14 This would only happen in a few cases between 1 January 1955 and October 1958.
15 1990 Act, s. 120.
16 Ibid, s. 119(4).
17 See the Compensation Regs, regs 9, 10, 12.

has not been affected by the planning decision, if so, the claimant is entitled to compensation only in respect of the land actually affected. Similarly his interest may extend to land, which, although affected by the planning decision, has no unexpended balance; in that case, he can claim only in respect of so much of the land as has an unexpended balance.

Exclusion of compensation

Even if all other necessary conditions have been fulfilled, no compensation can be claimed in the following cases:

(1) Change of use   No compensation is payable for a refusal of permission for any development which consists of or includes the making of a material change in the use of any building or other land.[18] The drafting of this particular provision has been the subject of much criticism. It clearly excludes compensation in such cases as the change of use of existing premises from, say, a house to offices; and it is equally clear that no compensation is payable for refusal of permission to change the use of land where no building or other operations are involved. The difficulty arises over such cases as refusal of permission to build, say, houses on agricultural land. This is not development *consisting* of a change of use because building operations are excluded from the word 'use',[19] but it might be argued that it *includes* a change of use in that where planning permission is given for the erection of a building, the permission is to be construed as including permission to use the building for the purpose for which it is designed.[20] The government emphasised that it was not intended to exclude compensation in such cases, but it must always be remembered that statements in Parliament are not authority for the construction of a statute.

(2) Advertisements   No compensation is payable for a refusal of consent for the display of advertisements.[1]

(3) Conditions   No compensation is payable in respect of the following conditions:[2]

18 1990 Act, s. 121(1).
19 Ibid, s. 336.
20 Ibid, s. 75.
 1 Ibid, s. 121(1).
 2 Ibid, s. 121(2).

(a) a condition as to the number or disposition of buildings on land – but for this purpose a condition prohibiting development of a specified part of the land is to be treated as a refusal of permission as respects that part of the land and so may attract compensation;[3]
(b) as to the dimensions, design, structure or external appearance of any building or the materials to be used in its construction;
(c) as to the manner in which the land is to be laid out, including the provision of facilities for parking, loading or fuelling vehicles;
(d) as to use of buildings or other land;
(e) as to the location, design or construction of any means of access to a highway, other than a service road;
(f) any condition imposed on permission for mineral working.

(4) Statutory conditions No compensation will be paid in respect of conditions requiring the development to be begun within a specified period.[4]

(5) Premature development No compensation is payable for a refusal of permission if the reason (or one of the reasons) given for the refusal is that the development would be premature having regard to either:
(a) the order or priority, if any, indicated, in the development plan (for example, in the programme map) for the development of that area; or
(b) any existing deficiency in the provision of water supplies and sewerage services, and the period within which any such deficiency may be expected to be made good.

If, however, fresh application is made after a lapse of seven years, and permission is again refused on ground (a) compensation will be payable.[5]

(6) Unsuitability of land No compensation will be paid for a refusal of permission if the reason (or one of the reasons) given is that the land is unsuitable for development on account of liability to flooding or subsidence.[6]

(7) Land acquired by public authorities Land may have been compulsorily acquired by or sold to an authority possessing compulsory purchase powers (other than statutory undertakers or the British Coal Corporation), and a planning decision made after the date of notice

3 1990 Act, s. 121(8).
4 Ibid, s. 121(4). For such conditions see ch 8, pp. 174–5, above.
5 Ibid, s. 121(5), (6).
6 Ibid, s. 121(7).

to treat or the contract of sale. In that case, the authority is not entitled to compensation for that planning decision, nor is any person who derives title to the land from that authority after 1 July 1948.[7]

(8) Land belonging to statutory undertakers or the British Coal Corporation No compensation is payable for a planning decision affecting operational land of a statutory undertaker or the British Coal Corporation.[8]

(9) Other planning permission available No compensation is payable if permission is available for some other development of a residential, commercial or industrial character; that is, development consisting wholly or mainly of houses, flats, shops, offices, industrial buildings (including warehouses) or any combination of these.[9]

PROCEDURE FOR MAKING AND DETERMINING CLAIMS

A claim for compensation must be sent to the local planning authority for transmission to the Secretary of State within six months of the date of the decision or such extended period as he may allow.[10] On receiving the claim the Secretary of State must first consider whether the conditions for payment of compensation are satisfied. If they are not satisfied, the Secretary of State will invite the claimant to withdraw his claim.[11] If the claim is not withdrawn, the Secretary of State must give a decision and the claimant can appeal to the Lands Tribunal.[12]

REVIEW OF PLANNING DECISION

At this stage, the Secretary of State may decide to review the decision which has given rise to the claim for compensation. In this connection, he may do one of two things. First, he may decide to substitute a decision more favourable to the applicant, but he can only do this where the decision was that of the local planning authority and there was no appeal. A decision more favourable to the applicant means:
(a) in relation to a refusal of permission, a grant of permission either unconditionally or subject to conditions, either for the whole or part of the land concerned; or

7 1990 Act, s. 123(1).
8 Ibid, s. 123(3).
9 Ibid, s. 122.
10 Ibid, s. 127(1), (2), (3).
11 Ibid, s. 127(7).
12 Ibid, s. 127(8); Compensation Regs, reg 7.

(b) in relation to a grant of permission subject to conditions, either an unconditional grant or a grant subject to less stringent conditions.

Secondly, the Secretary of State may decide to grant permission for some other form of development. This he can do, even if there has been an appeal or if he himself gave the decision on a reference under section 77 of the Act of 1990.

Before giving a formal direction for either of these purposes, the Secretary of State must give notice of the proposed direction to the local planning authority and to any person who has claimed compensation and has not withdrawn his claim. The authority or the claimant may then make objections and ask to be heard by a person appointed by the Secretary of State for the purpose.

If the Secretary of State decides to go ahead with the proposals, he will embody them in a formal direction; notice of this direction must be given to the local planning authority and the persons claiming compensation. The latter may wish at this stage to modify the claim for compensation because the effect of the direction will almost certainly be to reduce the amount of the claim if not to extinguish it altogether.[13]

DETERMINATION OF COMPENSATION: AMOUNT

In order to determine the amount of compensation, it is necessary first to consider whether the whole of the land in question is 'qualified land', that is, any part of the land affected by the planning decision which at the time of the decision has an unexpended balance.[14]

The following situations may then arise:[15]

(1) Where there is only one claim, and the whole of the land affected by the planning decision is qualified land, then the amount of compensation will be the lesser of the following amounts:

(a) the amount by which the value of the claimant's interest, or so much of it is as subsists in the qualified land, is depreciated in value by the planning decision;

(b) the amount of the unexpended balance attaching to the qualified land.

(2) Where the whole of the land is qualified land, but there is more than one claim in respect of the same area of qualified land, then it is necessary to consider whether the aggregate amount of compensation payable in respect of all the claims would exceed the amount of the unexpended balance. If the aggregate would exceed the amount of

13 1990 Act, ss. 80, 81.
14 Ibid, s. 125(2).
15 Ibid, s. 125(3)–(5).

the unexpended balance – but not otherwise – the unexpended balance must be allocated between the interests concerned. The amount so allocated to each interest will then be the maximum amount payable in respect of that interest.

It may happen that no claim has been made in respect of one or more of the interests in the qualified land. It is clear that any such interest is to be ignored; it is not to be brought into the allocation so as to reduce the amount of the unexpended balance available for those who have made claims.

(3) In the preceding two paragraphs, it has been assumed that the whole of the land is qualified land and that (if there is more than one claim) the separate claims relate to the same area. Where these conditions are not satisfied, the amount of compensation payable in respect of any interest is to be determined as follows:

(i)   first, there must be ascertained the amount by which any interest in the whole or part of the land affected by the decision has been depreciated in value;

(ii) secondly, the land concerned must be divided into as many separate parts as are necessary to ensure that each part either (a) consists of qualified land with one or more interests relating to the whole of it; or (b) is not qualified land;

(iii) the depreciation in the value of the interest (as ascertained in paragraph (i)) is then to be apportioned between the separate parts mentioned in paragraph (ii); this apportionment is to be made according to the nature of the separate parts and the effect of the planning decision in relation to each of them.

The amount of compensation payable in respect of each interest will be the aggregate of the amounts payable in respect of each part, subject, of course, to the amount of the unexpended balance available in respect of those parts; this will involve apportionment of the unexpended balance.

DETERMINATION OF COMPENSATION: PROCEDURE

In determining the amount of compensation, the Secretary of State is to 'cause such investigations to be made and such steps to be taken as he may deem requisite'. Having taken such steps as he deems requisite, the Secretary of State must prepare a statement of his findings, notice of which is given to the claimant, and (if the findings involve an apportionment of the unexpended balance) to any other person interested in the land.[16]

16 Compensation Regs, reg 6.

Any person who has received notice of the Secretary of State's findings may then appeal to the Lands Tribunal.[17]

REGISTRATION OF COMPENSATION

Where the amount of compensation exceeds £20, the Secretary of State must notify the district council (in London, the London borough council) and, if that council is not the local planning authority, that authority; the council with whom the notice is deposited is to register it in the register of the local land charges.[18]

Minerals

Claims for compensation in respect of minerals will be affected by the Minerals Regulations made under the Act of 1962 and kept in force under the Act of 1971 and now by the Act of 1990. The Regulations modify the financial provisions of the Act in its application to minerals.

Some of these modifications result from the fact that minerals may be held separately from the land in which they lie. Where ownership of surface and minerals was severed before 1 July 1948, a claim for loss of development value is treated as a separate unexpended balance.[19] Where the freehold is severed after that date, the unexpended balance (if any) is also to be apportioned between the minerals and the remainder of the land.[20]

---

17 Compensation Regs, reg 7.
18 1990 Act, s. 132.
19 Mineral Regs, reg 9(2).
20 Ibid, reg 9(1).

Chapter 22

Compensation for revocation or modification of existing rights

Where planning permission has been granted on an application, that permission may be revoked or modified by an order under section 97 of the Act of 1990.[1] Where such an order is made, compensation will be payable under section 107 of the Act.

There is also in effect a revocation or modification of planning permission if permitted development rights granted by development order[2] are withdrawn by the revocation or amendment of the order or if a direction[3] is issued requiring an application to be made for express permission. If such permission is refused or is granted subject to any conditions other than those prescribed by the development order, compensation can be claimed under section 107.[4]

The Act of 1947 had provided that compensation should be paid for:

(a) any expenditure rendered abortive by the revocation or modification;

(b) loss or damage directly attributable to the revocation or modification, but only exceptionally would this include compensation for the depreciation in the value of the land.

These provisions gave effect to the principle of the Act of 1947 that, in the absence of special circumstances, compensation should not be paid for loss of development value. With the partial restoration of development values to private ownership under the Act of 1954 that basis was obviously no longer applicable. The Act of 1954 accordingly provided that in cases arising on or after 1 January 1955, the compensation payable for revocation or modification should include loss of development value, whether or not the land has an unexpended balance of established development value; these provisions are now contained in the Act of 1990.

---

1 See ch 9, above.
2 Eg the rights granted by the GDO: see ch 6, pp. 116 ff, above.
3 Eg a direction under the GDO, art 4: see ch 6, pp. 125 ff, above.
4 1990 Act, s. 108.

Claims for compensation

Compensation under section 107 may be claimed by any person interested in the land who can show that:
(a) he has incurred expenditure in carrying out work which has been rendered abortive by the revocation or modification; or
(b) he has otherwise sustained loss or damage which is directly attributable to the revocation or modification.

The words 'a person interested in the land' may include contractual licensees as well as those having a legal or equitable interest such as the freehold or tenancy.

In *Pennine Raceway Ltd v Kirklees Metropolitan Council*[5] the claimants were promoters of motor car and motor cycle racing and had entered into an agreement with the owner of an airfield to equip the airfield with pits, car park, safety fencing; after a trial year the consideration payable to the owner was to be £500 per meeting and this sum was to be reviewed every five years.

The local authority directed under article 4 of the General Development Order that the use of the airfield for motor car or motor cycle racing should no longer be permitted. The company lodged a claim for compensation for abortive expenditure but the local authority denied liability on the ground that the company was not 'a person interested in the land.'

The Court of Appeal held that a person who like the appellants had an enforceable right against the owner of the land to use the land in the way which had now been prohibited was a person interested in the land within what is now section 107 of the Act of 1990.

HEADS OF CLAIM

Abortive expenditure This head includes expenditure on plans and other preparatory matters whether or not any physical work has actually been done.[6] With the exception of expenditure on plans etc, the expenditure must have been incurred *after* the grant of the permission which has been revoked or modified.

Other loss or damage This head may include such items as expenses incurred in securing release from a building contract entered into after the grant of the permission which has been revoked or modified

5 [1983] QB 382, [1982] 3 All ER 628.
6 1971 Act, s. 164(2). *Holmes v Bradfield RDC* [1949] 2 KB 1, [1949] 1 All ER 381.

and may even include loss of profit on contracts which would almost certainly have been obtained but for the revocation of the permission.[7]

Depreciation in the value of the land   Loss or damage directly attributable to the revocation or modification may include depreciation in the value of an interest in the land, and in many cases this will be the most important item of claim. The amount of compensation for depreciation will be the difference between (a) the value of the interest with the benefit of the permission prior to its revocation or modification; and (b) the value of the land subject to the revocation or modification assuming that permission would be given for appropriate Schedule 3 development.[8]

The assumption that permission would be available for Schedule 3 development is reasonable where the permission which has been revoked or modified related to 'new development'. But it creates a problem where the permission which has been revoked or modified was for Schedule 3 development. Where the permission was for development falling within Part II of Schedule 3, the practical solution would be to apply for compensation under section 114 as if permission had been refused or granted subject to conditions;[9] if the liability to compensation is disputed, it may be necessary to apply again for the permission which has been revoked or modified with a view to obtaining a decision which would form the basis of a claim under section 114.

PROCEDURE

Claims for compensation under section 107 of the Act of 1990 must be made to the local planning authority within certain limits of time:

(a) where the claim results from an order revoking or modifying planning permission, the claim must be made within six months of the date of the order unless the Secretary of State agrees to an extension of time;[10]

(b) where the claim results from a refusal or conditional grant of planning permission following the issue of a direction[11] withdrawing permitted development rights, the claim must be made

---

7 *Hobbs Quarries Ltd v Somerset County Council* (1975) 30 P & CR 286.
8 1990 Act, s. 107(3), (4).
9 See ch 20, above.
10 General Regs, reg 14.
11 See fn 3, above.

within six months of the refusal or conditional grant of permission, unless the Secretary of State agrees to an extension of time;[12]

(c) where the claim results from a refusal or conditional grant of planning permission following the revocation or amendment of a development order the application must have been made within 12 months of the date on which the revocation or amendment came into effect.[13]

The compensation is payable by the local planning authority.[14] Any dispute as to the payment of compensation may be referred to the Lands Tribunal.[15]

The Secretary of State is authorised by Schedule 11 of the Act of 1990 to make regulations modifying the basis of compensation in respect of orders revoking or modifying planning permissions for mineral workings.[16]

Contribution by the Secretary of State

Compensation under section 107 of the Act of 1990 is payable by the local planning authority and is not dependent upon an unexpended balance. But instead of first granting permission and later revoking or modifying it, the authority might well have refused permission or granted it subject to conditions at the outset. Had that been done, compensation would not have been payable under section 107 but it might have been payable under Part V by the Secretary of State.

The Act of 1990 contains provisions under which the Secretary of State may contribute towards the compensation actually paid by the local planning authority. Where compensation for depreciation exceeds £20, the local planning authority are to give notice thereof to the Secretary of State together with particulars of any apportionment.[17] He may come to the conclusion that, had permission been refused or granted as modified, in the first place, compensation would have been payable by him under Part V of the Act; in that case he may[18] pay to the local planning authority an amount not exceeding the *lesser* of the following:[19]

12 General Regs, reg 14.
13 1990 Act, s. 108.
14 Ibid, s. 107(1).
15 Ibid, s. 118.
16 See ch 24, pp. 365 ff, below.
17 1990 Act, s. 113.
18 The use of the word 'may' suggests that the Secretary of State has a discretion, but when the Bill for the 1954 Act was in Standing Committee of the House of Commons, the Minister said that the intention was that the contribution should be paid. H of C Official Report (5th series) cols 618–621 (Standing Committee C, 16 June 1954).
19 1990 Act, s. 113.

(a)   the amount of the compensation for depreciation paid by the authority;
(b)   the unexpended balance at the date of the making of the order in respect of which the compensation was paid.

Where such a contribution has been paid it is logical that the amount of the unexpended balance should be reduced accordingly and provision for this purpose is made by the Compensation Regulations. On the other hand, it would be unreasonable that the unexpended balance should be reduced as a result of a transaction between the Secretary of State and the local planning authority without the owner of the land having the opportunity of presenting objections.

The Compensation Regulations require the Secretary of State to give notice of his intentions to any person having an interest in the land or who is likely to be affected by the reduction of the unexpended balance;[20] these persons then have the right to object on certain specified grounds[1] and, if these objections are not accepted by the Secretary of State to appeal to the Lands Tribunal.[2]

Discontinuance orders

Where a discontinuance order is made under section 102 of the Act of 1990,[3] the local planning authority will be liable to pay compensation (1) to any person who has suffered damage by the depreciation in the value of an interest in land to which he is entitled; (2) to any person who is disturbed in his enjoyment of the land.[4] Furthermore, any person who carries out work in compliance with the order, such as the removal of buildings or plant and machinery, is entitled to recover his expenses;[5] compensation may be reduced by the value to the claimant of any timber, apparatus or other materials which he has removed.[6]

As regards (1) above, it would seem that the interest must be the freehold or a lease, including the equitable interest created by a binding contract for sale; a claim may be made by a mortgagee but not in respect of that interest as such, and he must account to the mortgagor.[7] A claimant under (1) must be able to show that he has

20 Eg a mortgagee.
 1 Reg 14.
 2 Reg 15.
 3 See ch 9, pp. 180 ff, above.
 4 1990 Act, s. 115(2).
 5 Ibid, s. 115(3).
 6 Ibid, s. 115(4).
 7 1990 Act, s. 117(3).

suffered damage by reason of the depreciation in the value of the land; so, where the discontinuance order contains a grant of planning permission for some other purpose,[8] that must be taken into account.

(2) above presumably extends to persons occupying the land under a licence, and the reference to 'enjoyment' includes commercial as well as personal enjoyment.

Claims for compensation must be made within six months of the date of the order unless the Secretary of State agrees to an extension of time.[9] Disputes as to compensation will be referred to the Lands Tribunal.[10]

The Secretary of State is authorised by Schedule 11 of the Act of 1990 to make regulations modifying the basis of compensation for discontinuance orders in respect of mineral workings.[11]

8 See ch 9, p. 181, above.
9 General Regs, reg 14.
10 1990 Act, s. 118.
11 See ch 24, p. 367, below.

Chapter 23

Repayment of compensation

Where compensation has been paid for loss of development value, and permission is subsequently granted for some profitable form of development, it is only reasonable that the compensation should be repaid. The Act of 1990 contains provisions for the repayment of the following classes of compensation:

(1) compensation under either Part II of the Act of 1954, Part VI of the Act of 1962, Part VII of the Act of 1971 or Part V of the Act of 1990 in respect of planning restrictions on new development imposed after 1 January 1955;[1]

(2) compensation under either Part IV of the Act of 1954, Part VII of the Act of 1962, Part VIII of the Act of 1971 or section 107 of the Act of 1990 in respect of orders revoking or modifying planning permission after 1 January 1955;[2]

(3) compensation under Part V of the Act of 1954 in respect of planning restrictions or the revocation or modification of planning permission between 1 July 1948 and 1 January 1955;[3]

(4) payments under section 59 of the Act of 1947 for loss of development value in connection with certain classes of war damaged land.[4]

Types of repayment

No provision is made for the repayment of compensation under section 114 of the Act of 1990 for restrictions on Schedule 3 development[5] or of payments under Part I of the Act of 1954.[6] Where compensation for revocation or modification of planning permission is concerned, it is only the compensation for depreciation in the value of the land (as

1 See ch 21, above.
2 See ch 22, above.
3 See ch 19, p. 335 above.
4 See ch 19, p. 333, above.
5 See ch 20, above.
6 See ch 19, p. 305, above.

distinct from compensation for abortive expenditure, etc) that is to be repaid.

The provisions as to the repayment of compensation should be clearly understood by solicitors and surveyors; failure to advise the client properly may render the solicitor or surveyor liable for professional negligence.

The compensation will not necessarily be repaid by the person who received it. The compensation will have been paid to the owners of the freehold or leasehold interests in the land at the time. Repayment must be made by the person who subsequently carries out certain types of development, who may be a successor in title to the person receiving the compensation. This liability to repay must therefore be taken into account in considering terms of sale or lease.

It is no doubt for this reason that successive Acts make careful provision for entering compensation payments in the register of local land charges. In the case of compensation under paragraphs (1) and (2) above, the Secretary of State is to serve a 'compensation notice', notifying the local authority of any payment exceeding £20, who are then to enter the details in the register of local land charges. The compensation notice may apportion the payment as between different parts of the land; and if it does so, the details of the apportionment will also be entered in the register of local land charges. If there is no apportionment, it is to be assumed that the compensation is distributed rateably over the land.[7] Similar provisions as to apportionment and registration applied to compensation under Part IV of the Act of 1954 and payments under section 59 of the Act of 1947.[8]

If, for any reason, the details of a compensation payment are not entered in the register of local land charges, the provisions as to repayment do not apply as against a purchaser of the land.[9]

Where a compensation notice has been registered, certain types of new development must not be carried out until a specified sum has been paid or received.[10] Where the compensation arises under paragraphs (1), (2) or (3) above, the repayment provisions apply to:

(a) development of a residential, commercial or industrial character, being development which consists wholly or mainly of houses, flats, shops, offices or industrial buildings (including warehouses);

(b) mineral development;

(c) any development which having regard to its probable value, the

7 1990 Act, ss. 111, 132.

8 1954 Act, ss. 39, 57.

9 *Stock v Wanstead and Woodford Borough Council* [1962] 2 QB 479, [1961] 2 All ER 433; *Ministry of Housing and Local Government v Sharp* [1970] 2 QB 223, [1970] 1 All ER 1009.

10 1990 Act, ss. 111, 133.

Secretary of State considers should be subject to the provisions for repayment of compensation.

Paragraph (c), however, does not apply if the owner of the land has obtained from the Secretary of State a certificate that it is not reasonable that the compensation shall be repaid.

The amount of the compensation to be repaid is determined by reference to a 'development area', that is, the land on which the proposed development is to be carried out. If the development area is identical with or includes the whole of the land mentioned in the compensation notice, the amount to be repaid will be the amount specified in the compensation notice; in other cases it will be an appropriate proportion of the amount shown in the compensation notice. The Secretary of State may remit the whole or any part of the repayment if he thinks it necessary to encourage the development to take place, but this is entirely within his discretion.[11]

11 1990 Act, ss. 112, 134.

Chapter 24

Special provisions as to minerals

As we have seen in an earlier chapter,[1] planning authorities have extensive powers of control over the winning and working of minerals. The mineral planning authority can make orders revoking or modifying planning permission, discontinuance orders, prohibition orders, suspension orders and supplementary suspension orders.[2]

In some cases these powers will be used so as to require the mineral operator to take steps to prevent or remedy damage to the environment. The minerals extraction industries have accepted that, in some circumstances, it would be reasonable that part of the cost of such preventive or remedial action should be borne by the mineral operator and that the planning authority should pay a reduced rate of compensation. To give effect to these principles the law was amended in 1981 to permit the payment of compensation on a reduced basis where mineral compensation requirements are satisfied; these provisions are now contained in Schedule 11 of the Act of 1990.

The phrase 'where mineral compensation requirements are satisfied' is an unfortunate piece of shorthand. These requirements are the conditions which must be satisfied to enable the local planning authority to pay reduced compensation; where these conditions are not satisfied full compensation must be paid on the normal basis.

We will now consider each type of order in turn:

(1) Orders revoking planning permission Compensation is payable on the normal basis;[3] mineral compensation requirements cannot apply.[4]

(2) Orders modifying planning permission Mineral compensation requirements will be satisfied if (a) the order does not impose restric-

---

1 See ch 15, p. 280, above.
2 See ch 15, pp. 282, 283, above.
3 See ch 22, p. 360, above.
4 The special rules, Sch 11, apply only to orders modifying a previous planning provision: see Sch 11, paras 2, 3.

366 Special provisions as to minerals

tions on mineral working; (b) the planning authority carried out 'special consultations' before making the order;[5] and (c) broadly speaking, the steps required by the order are limited to those required for the protection of the environment.[6] Where these requirements are not satisfied, full compensation is payable.[7]

(3) Discontinuance orders Compensation for a discontinuance order in respect of mineral workings is to be assessed on the normal basis set out in an earlier chapter,[8] but the compensation may be reduced where mineral compensation requirements are satisfied. The minimum compensation requirements for this type of order are (a) that the order imposes restrictions on the continuance of mineral working[9] or requires the removal of buildings plant or machinery; (b) that the mineral working began at least five years previously; (c) that there were special consultations.[10]

(4) Prohibition orders Compensation for a prohibition order will be assessed on the same basis as for a discontinuance order, but may be reduced where mineral compensation requirements are satisfied. The minimum compensation requirements for this type of order are (a) that the mineral working began not less than five years previously; and (b) that there were special consultations.[11]

(5) Suspension and supplementary suspension orders Compensation for orders is to be assessed on the same basis as for a discontinuance order, but may be reduced where mineral compensation requirements are satisfied; for these orders, the only mineral compensation requirement is that there have been special consultations.[12]

5 'Special consultations' mean consultations by the mineral planning authority with (a) all persons with an interest in the land or the minerals in it; and (b) where the land is in a non-metropolitan county, the district council: 1990 Act, Sch 11, para 12.
6 1990 Act, Sch 11, para 4.
7 See above.
8 See ch 22, pp. 360, 361, above.
9 Minimum compensation requirements cannot be satisfied if the order requires mineral working to be discontinued.
10 1990 Act, Sch 11, para 5. As to special consultations see fn 5, above.
11 Ibid, Sch 11, para 6. As to special consultations see fn 5, above.
12 Ibid, Sch 11, para 7. As to special consultations see fn 5, above.

Mineral compensation modifications

The amount by which compensation is to be reduced where mineral compensation requirements are satisfied is prescribed by the T & CP (Compensation for Restriction on Mineral Workings) Regulations,[13] and may be summarised as follows.

Prohibition orders, suspension orders, supplementary suspension orders Where the claimant is the only person interested in the site, the compensation is reduced by a prescribed sum of £5000.[14] If more than one person is interested in the site,[15] the prescribed sum must be apportioned between the different interests and compensation payable in respect of each interest is reduced by the appropriate portion of the prescribed sum.[16]

Orders modifying planning permission: discontinuance orders Where the claimant is the only person interested in the site, the compensation is reduced by (a) the sum of £2,500 or (b) ten per cent of the sum which is to be calculated by multiplying the annual value of the right to work minerals at the site by a specified multiplier whichever is the greater (but subject to a maximum deduction of £100,000).[17] The multiplier varies according to the estimated life of the site (or, where more than one mineral is being worked, of each mineral).[18] If more than one person is interested in the site, the sums referred to in (a) and (b) must be apportioned. There must also be an apportionment if more than one mineral is being worked.

---

13 1985 (SI 1985 no 698).
14 Claims may be made by a person interested in the land and also by a person who is without an interest in the land but has an interest in the minerals: reg 4(2).
15 Reg 5.
16 Reg 7.
17 Reg 6, sch 1.
18 1985 Regs, sch 2.

Index

Action area
identification of, 13–15
Administration
central, 31–40
Commissioner for Local Administration, 320–322
Local Commissioner for, 320–322
local, 40–46
local planning authority's responsibility for, 40
Parliamentary Commissioner for, 319–320
Advertisement
censorship, ban on, 237
conservation area, in, 265, 270
control of, 15
display –
building –
change of use of land, as, 85–86
erected on, whether, 77
consent, without, an offence, 183*n*
development, not in itself, 129–130
enclosed land, on, 238
examples of, 237
external part of building, on, as change of use, 129–130
hoarding, erection of, as development, 129
inside buildings, 236
incorporated in fabric of building, 238
meaning, 237
outdoor –
amenity, considerations of, 237
'challenge' by local planning authority, 236–237
consent –
deemed, 239–240
express –
application for, 240–241
development, where involving, 241

Advertisement – *continued*
outdoor – *continued*
consent – *continued*
express – *continued*
refusal of, 241
required though development not involved, 236
revocation or modification of, 241
display involving development, 241
election notices, 238
enforcement of control, 241
'existing', challenge to, 236–237
generally, 129–130, 236 *et seq.*
principles of control, 237–238
public safety, considerations of, 237
Regulations –
advertisements to which not applicable, 237
generally, 237
special control, areas of, 241–242
specified classes deemed to have consent, 239–240
traffic signs, 239
statutory, 238–239
Aerodrome
agricultural buildings near, 122
Agreement
development, to restrict or regulate –
enforcement, 213–215
generally, 208–213
Secretary of State's guidance on policy, 208
Agriculture
agricultural –
land –
planning permission affecting, 13
safeguarding of, 26–27
unit, form of purchase notice, 228
uses, building, etc., operations for, 121–123